Modern Elementary
Education

(*In alphabetical order*)

CALHOUN C. COLLIER   MICHIGAN STATE UNIVERSITY

W. ROBERT HOUSTON   UNIVERSITY OF HOUSTON

ROBERT R. SCHMATZ   WISCONSIN STATE UNIVERSITY, STEVENS POINT

WILLIAM J. WALSH   MICHIGAN STATE UNIVERSITY

Modern Elementary Education
Teaching and Learning

Macmillan Publishing Co., Inc.
NEW YORK
Collier Macmillan Publishers
LONDON

Copyright © 1976, Macmillan Publishing Co., Inc.
Printed in the United States of America

A portion of this material has been adapted from
the authors' *Teaching in the Modern Elementary School,*
copyright © 1967 by Macmillan Publishing Co., Inc.

Macmillan Publishing Co., Inc.
866 Third Avenue, New York, New York 10022

Collier Macmillan Canada, Ltd.

Library of Congress Cataloging in Publication Data
Main entry under title:

Modern elementary education.

Includes bibliographies and index.
1. Elementary school teaching.   2. Education,
Elementary—Curricula.   I. Collier, Calhoun Crofford,
(date)
LB1555.M59   372.1'1'02   75–9706
ISBN 0–02–323770–8

Printing: 1 2 3 4 5 6 7 8   Year: 6 7 8 9 0 1

Preface

Teaching in the elementary school is a personal challenge. To a prospective teacher or an experienced professional the daily opportunity to interact with pupils is a rare, treasured opening into the intricacies of human thought and action. To be successful, these interactions must be intimate to the learning and growth potentials of the individual child. Every strategy and response relate directly to the interpersonal relationship that develops between the child and the teacher.

As teachers who have worked in classrooms in many countries of the world and who are continually involved in the improvement of the process of teaching, we are keenly interested in your growth and development as an elementary teacher. We intend to share with you the experiences of classroom teaching as well as the implications of recent theory and research in the field of education to provide a base for the ultimate decisions you will make when working with children.

Our approach to the challenge of teaching in the classroom is divided into pertinent chapters and sections of emphasis in the pages that follow. At the beginning of each chapter is a set of cognitive-based objectives that will help you focus your experience and interests as well as to guide your reading. At the end of most chapters is a summary of the ideas and problems presented followed by a unique section of activities that should help you translate the chapter objectives into viable performances with children.

We have drawn upon portions of an earlier work, *Teaching in the Modern Elementary School,* for patterns of emphasis and support that have proven to be successful for professional work with children in the classroom. Although there are selected bibliographies for additional reader interest at the close of each chapter, extensive citations to research and experimental theory have been purposefully modified to encourage continuous reader interest and comprehension. In short, this is a created design for you to sense and react to the challenge of teaching in the elementary school. The design will not only test your understanding of basic principles, theories, and classroom applications but will probe your ability to translate these objectives into demonstrable activities. We assume that you will have an opportunity to demonstrate your comprehension of elementary school objectives in some capacity in the classroom before and after those classroom experiences commonly identified with student or intern teaching. These alternative activities are frequently available as "participant options" in elementary schools. Your instructor will be able to provide more information on the availability of such options in the local area.

Finally, the authors reflect a feeling of optimism about the opportunities for you to realize individual challenge and success in the elementary classroom, but self-realization of the intrinsic pupil-to-teacher relationship depends heavily upon your insight into the total learning process. This confidence in your success justifies our commitment to this work and the field of professional education.

C. C. C.
W. R. H.
R. R. S.
W. J. W.

Contents

Modern Elementary Education

Chapter 1

Society in Transition: The Elementary School

The elementary school in which you will teach or may now be teaching is likely to be quite different from the school of a decade or so ago. Society has changed, schools have changed, you have changed, and pupils have changed. If you are boxed in by traditional thinking and experiences of previous years, you will be condemned to remain confined by yesterday's realities.

In one of his delightful detective stories, Sir Arthur Conan Doyle describes an exchange between Sherlock Holmes and his trusted assistant, Watson. As the two men were approaching their second-floor apartment, Holmes asked Watson this question, "How many steps lead up to our flat?" When Watson responded that he did not know, Holmes said brusquely, "There are seventeen. Both of us have climbed those same steps for years, but the difference is that you only *saw* the steps while I *observed* them." The parallel of the Holmes and Watson conversation with that of the insight of a professional educator and the layman or elementary school pupil is quite striking. The latter two groups only *see* the schools whereas the professional educator is trained to *observe* schools. As an elementary school pupil, you may have felt you knew all about schools because you were spending five or six hours each day in one. However, you never directly experienced many of the vital aspects of the school—teacher-planning periods, faculty meetings, curriculum-development conferences, record keeping, and professional activities. You were a student *in* the school, but now, as a professional educator, you must become a student *of* the elementary school. This book is dedicated to facilitating your development of this skill.

In each chapter, a set of specific objectives will guide your reading and activities. After reading this introductory chapter, you should be able to do the following:

1. Describe some of the social and technological changes occurring today and relate them to teaching in the elementary school.
2. Distinguish between melting pot and cultural pluralism as social concepts.
3. Assess the role of schools as educational institutions with that of other institutions that educate children and youth.   .
4. Describe some changes in elementary schools today.
5. Discuss some of the competing values for the school's attention.
6. Discuss different styles of teachers.

A Changing Society

Although change has always been a part of the lives of men and society, never before has it been so incredibly rapid or exhilarating. The forces accelerating change have never been greater. Twenty-five per cent of all the peoples who ever lived are alive today; 90 per cent of all the scientists who ever lived are alive today. By the year 2000, 75 per cent of the American population will be concentrated in urban areas, and their median life span will approach eighty years or more. As Margaret Mead once wrote, "No man will ever again die in the same world in which he was born." Thus, this section briefly documents some of the changes that have occurred and are likely to happen in the coming years that affect elementary education.[1]

Only a few hundred years ago, change occurred very slowly. Man was born, lived, and died in an environment that differed little from that in which his father and grandfather had lived. For most people, living was at the sustenance level. Famine or a great sickness could strike at any time, and man's life expectancy was less than half of what it is today. Most people were engaged in the production of food. Education was primarily a function of the home; mothers taught daughters and fathers taught sons. Although a few of the boys might be apprenticed to a trade outside of the immediate family, even this was usually with close relatives.

[1] For an interesting description of the changes occurring in the early seventies, see Theodore H. White, Ch. 7, "The Web of Numbers: A Message from the Census to Politics," *The Making of a President, 1972* (New York; Bantam, 1973), pp. 177–208.

Changes so readily apparent today have occurred as the result of two revolutions. The first was mechanical and took place about a hundred years ago. *Mechanical energy* replaced *muscular energy* through the successive uses of steam power, the gasoline engine, and electricity. No longer did man and the domesticated animal provide the only power source available. Inventions such as the cotton gin, the railroad, and the thresher freed man from arduous tasks to which he had previously been chained.

About thirty years ago, the second revolution fueled the fire storm of change. This revolution was chemical, electronic, and nuclear. Through chemistry, man reconstituted natural elements to form useful man-made products—new fabrics such as dacron and nylon, new paint, new cosmetics, new plastics. Many of the items on store shelves today and generally taken for granted would not have been available thirty years ago. Electronic developments have made color television commonplace in the United States and the radio a constant companion of people all over the world. In rural Guatemala or Southeast Asia, a man carrying a heavy burden to market listens to an inexpensive, portable transistor radio. Miniaturization has made possible communication and other electronic marvels during the past decade. Events occurring anywhere on the globe can be viewed almost anywhere else via television in just four tenths of a second. This marvel is made possible by communications satellites poised in orbit above the earth, which relay pictures and sound beamed to them from one point on the surface of the planet back to another point on earth.

Medical techniques, drugs, and medicines that were developed in the last three decades have extended man's life expectancy. With these new benefits have come challenges, such as moral questions of abortion, birth control, cell manipulation, and death (Should life be maintained through expensive treatment even though the patient is in pain with an incurable disease? When is a person dead?).

Elementary school children today take for granted many of the changes brought about by these revolutions. Television, plastics, and polio vaccine are old hat in the United States. Although we as adults may marvel at such things as television, rockets, or astronauts walking on the moon, children have grown up with them. Most elementary students were born after those first tenuous, limited, but magnificent orbits of the earth by John Glenn.

Each of us has a mental picture of the exterior world, our vision of reality. Some notions closely approximate reality; others are completely incorrect. In a rapidly changing society, these images must keep pace with reality. As new knowledge extends or outdates the old, people must relearn today what they thought they knew yesterday.

At the beginning of this century the world population was 1.6 billion; today it exceeds 3.5 billion, and by the year 2000 it is expected to reach 7 billion. This escalation of growth, illustrated in Figure 1–1, apparently will continue until there are not enough resources to feed people ade-

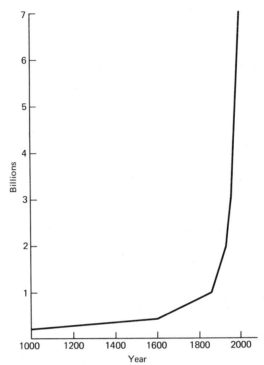

FIGURE 1–1. *World Population Growth.*

quately, unless devastation depletes the population drastically or man finds a successful and moral means of population control. Other changes described in this chapter could be shown as a similar curve on a graph as in Figure 1–1.

Within the United States, population patterns have shifted. A hundred years ago we were basically a rural nation. The move has been toward an urban way of life. First, towns became cities, then metropolitan regions. Now these are expanding into gigantic megalopolitan complexes with millions of people concentrated in a highly industrialized area crisscrossed by superhighway networks, marked by slums and slum clearance projects, characterized by fewer personal contacts between neighbors, and regulated by greater and centralized governmental control.

We are also a mobile nation—every year approximately one family in four changes its residence. This, in turn, produces a temporary living style with a greater number of apartment dwellers and shallower community roots. Although a few people may never travel more than a few miles from where they were born, the vast majority is exploring every segment of the country. Highways clogged with campers, converted buses, and automobiles during summer vacation time attest to this. Mobility of people is but one indication of the increased transience of our country. Few things are permanent. Kleenex, paper napkins, and the cost of repairs make us the "throw-away generation." People more readily change jobs, few people actually own their homes, clothing styles and automobiles change regularly, and schools are built with temporary portable classrooms. Changed orientation toward material goods affects personal relations. People are more concerned with the present than with the future. A feeling of temporariness pervades most human relations. Many social activities today can be described as search behavior, where new friends are sought to replace those who have moved or who no longer share common interests.

As man has extended his resources through mechanical and electronic energy, he has been able to devote a greater proportion of his own time to leisure. Although the five-day week is standard, many companies are converting to thirty-five hour or four-day work weeks. This new pattern of living has resulted in a boon in vacation cottages, boats, and hobbies. Attendance at spectator sports such as football and baseball as well as the number of television hours devoted to them continues to increase. Bowling, tennis, golf, and neighborhood craft groups have become popular. Disneyland competes with Disneyworld in Florida, Astroworld in Houston, and Six-Flags-Over-Texas in Dallas. Most workers today are engaged in the production of *services* rather than *goods*, just the reverse of employment practices a hundred years ago. Only 6 per cent of the economically active population is engaged in agriculture.[2]

Alvin Toffler, in his challenging book, *Future Shock*, points out another characteristic of today and tomorrow—overchoice. The number and variety of soaps on the grocery store shelf, entertainment modes, life-styles, magazines, automobiles—everything that we contact—increase rapidly. There comes a time when choice, instead of freeing the individual, becomes so complex and costly that it strangles him.

Whereas knowledge is still considered important, processes utilized in solving problems, thinking creatively about new situations and interactions, and ways to search out new data sources are increasingly vital. In education alone, thousands of textbooks and hundreds of professional and popular journals spew forth so many new findings, ideas, and theories that the average professional person cannot even read them. As a teacher, you must handle efficiently an increasing professional knowledge base and stimulate your pupils to explore and employ problem-solving strategies.

Melting Pot or Cultural Pluralism

Glowing generalities about life in America tend to obscure the vast differences among life-styles of people; one only has to observe people

_____

[2] Alvin Toffler, *Future Shock* (New York: Bantam, 1970), p. 14.

around him to note the differences. Differences in environment create varied needs for school programs. The child living on a Kansas farm is not likely to be educated in the same way as his cousin in suburban Los Angeles or the child in a New York ghetto. The experiential background of these children is different. The teacher and a class in rural Kansas might study about cattle and milk in quite a different way from that used by the teacher and a class in New York. To document these differences, trail three children during a rather typical week: a boy on a Texas farm, a girl living in a suburb of Lansing, Michigan, and a boy living in a South Side slum area of Chicago.

Bill lives in northeast Texas on a farm; his family owns fifteen milk cows. Whereas his father uses an automatic milking machine, Bill is responsible for feeding the cows hay from the loft in the barn. Bill catches the school bus a quarter of a mile down the road, and it takes him twelve miles to a consolidated school. A hot lunch, financed through government grants and subsidized with surplus food, is served each noon. Some of the children in the school live in the community whereas others, like Bill, are the children of farm families. Children living in town seem continually to be elected to every office and honor in the school, whereas those riding the bus are seldom even nominated.

After returning home from school, Bill sometimes watches his favorite television programs before bedtime. Saturday afternoon and evening always include a trip to town, a movie, and shopping for the entire family. Bill's family attends the small community church every Sunday; most other activities are farm-related—Home Demonstration Club, annual stock show, and Future Farmers of America.

Ann lives in a new subdivision just outside Lansing, Michigan. In December a new school was opened just three blocks from her home. It is modern in every detail—large open spaces, a learning resources center, team teaching, carpeting, and an experimental curriculum. During the fall, Ann attended Central School each morning while waiting for her school to be completed. Half-day sessions are relatively common in the school district, which has difficulty keeping up with rapidly increasing enrollments. Most residents of the district work in professional or managerial jobs. School officials proudly point out that the achievement level for the school is well above the national average. These children are pressed by parents and peers to *compete* in order to *succeed*. It is interesting to note that the local child guidance clinic has a large proportion of its cases from this area. Pressures on children build up and sometimes explode.

As an active, bright, and interested ten-year-old, Ann models her lifestyle on that of her parents. She is involved in many activities. She is an active Girl Scout, meeting with her troop on Mondays after school. On Tuesdays and Thursdays she takes skiing lessons at the nearby ski resort.

Next spring she plans to enroll in ice-skating lessons at the local rink. Saturday mornings she is scheduled for piano lessons, and each evening she practices at least thirty minutes in addition to doing heavy homework assignments from school. The telephone is in almost constant use as Ann and her friends discuss the day's happenings even though they are less than a block apart. Her life is a busy one; and that of her parents, even busier. They are involved in many community activities, enjoy cultural and athletic events in the area, and entertain friends and business associates regularly.

Although Sam's life in South Chicago is quite different from Ann's and Bill's, he too is exploring a life-style. His father builds bridges for the highway department, building forms and pouring concrete. During the winter months, he is often out of work because of cold weather. Despite the fact that Sam lives less than five miles from Lake Michigan or downtown Chicago, he has seen neither. The brownstone house in which he lives was designed for one family seventy years ago; now six families and fourteen children are cramped in every nook and corner. One bathroom services them all. The oppression resulting from many families living together produces feelings of personal and social claustrophobia, and the ever-present insecurity caused by being out of work and out of money burdens an already tense household.

The boys on Sam's block have formed a gang called the Blue Buzzards. They spend many daylight hours together plotting ways they can defend their block from the Panthers, who live on the next block. Stores of rocks, sticks, and links of chain are strategically cached in case of attack. Forays into Panther country occasionally occur to test their strength and to provide excitement.

School is a bore; it does not prepare Sam for his afternoon activities. Discussions of faraway places are meaningless, and he sees no reason for learning science. He plans to quit school as soon as he is sixteen; after all, his father never attended school, yet the family status is equal to that of any of his friends.

The environment, needs, and educational program of the three children sketched herein dramatize the vast differences among children in our country. In the typical classroom, one finds differences as great as these. There are no pat lesson plans, no standard textbooks, no universal formulas for a successful elementary school experience. Teachers must consider the needs of the individual children in their room and tailor the curriculum to meet those needs.

The America of the nineteenth century was thought of as a great "melting pot" in which the vast multitudes of immigrants were readily assimilated. This was not so, for each new group was forced to cling together for mutual support in an alien land. At the turn of the century, signs in Boston proclaimed, "Help Wanted, Irish Need Not Apply." This same discrimination was logged against the Polish, Italians, Puerto Ricans, and Germans at other times and places. For the blacks who came in slavery, the Chinese who were brought to build the railroads, the Mexicans who moved north in search of a better life, and the American Indians who were segregated on reservations, assimilation was far more difficult and still remains a problem today. As we approach the close of the twentieth century, these peoples often are told through actions and words that they are inferior to other Americans.

With high hopes a new concept sweeps America today—cultural pluralism. Through this concept, the contributions of various races, ethnic groups, and religious groups are cultivated and cherished. Minority groups can be proud of their unique backgrounds and contributions. School curricula, too, are beginning to reflect this change in emphasis, and teachers are expected to consider the specific backgrounds of children in their classes.

Education Is Changing

The role of education is more complex than in the days of agrarian America. In the past the basic purpose of education was to *transmit* the culture to succeeding generations. With the rapid changes currently occurring, culture must not only be transmitted, but also *translated* to succeeding generations. The ideals, values, and morals of the past must be converted into language and operations that are important in today's and tomorrow's worlds.

Schools are the basic educational institution in our society, but not the only one. The church, home, governmental and nongovernmental agencies (Boy Scouts, community recreation department, YMCA), and communication media (newspaper, television, magazines) all are *educational* agencies. They are designed to communicate knowledge, change opinions, broaden perspectives, transmit current events, teach new skills, and improve human interaction. While some are multipurpose in scope, many are designed to work specifically with children. Each was organized and structured to meet particular needs (recreation, maintenance of interest in the cultural heritage of the past, motivation of people to purchase a certain brand of toothpaste). They are, in effect, *limited* educational agencies. Each is designed to impact the education of children and youth in a limited domain, and often it represents the views of one segment of society. The school, on the other hand, is broader in its support, its purpose, and its audience. Furthermore, the school and its educational employees are *accountable* to society (as well as subgroups of society such as parents, voters, and boards of education) for the quality of learning by youth. As societal needs evolve, schools must keep pace.

Elementary Schools Are Changing

To meet the needs of changing society, the elementary school is in flux today as never before. In the paragraphs that follow, an attempt is made to document some of the current changes and trends.

The length of the school year has increased steadily from an average of 132.3 days in 1870, to 144.3 days in 1900, and 179.1 days in 1962. Several school districts are experimenting with year-round or extended-year schools, in which some pupils are on vacation during any part of the year. In this way a greater utilization of school buildings is afforded; however, at this time there does not appear to be a significant trend in this direction.

While the total number of pupils in elementary and secondary schools continues to increase, the number of school districts decreases. In 1931, 127,500 school districts were organized in the United States; in 1941, 115,500; in 1951, 71,000; by 1961, 35,500 and by 1966, the number of districts had dropped to 24,464.[3] Centralization of population and consolidation of many small independent school districts into larger units seems to account for the trend. Many one room schools disappeared during this time.

BUILDINGS AND FACILITIES.   Even the architecture of elementary schools reflects change. Gone are the days of the rectangular two- or three-floor elementary school with its central staircase, T-shaped hallway, wooden floors, and classrooms of uniform size. Typical elementary schools built in the last few years have been limited to one floor, numerous wings, considerable glass surface, tile and carpeted flooring, and perhaps a graceful, free-flowing roof line. The interior is likely to contain an office area with facilities for special consultant assistance (for example, nurses and speech correctionists), a teacher's lounge and workroom, and a health room.

A learning resources center may open directly onto several classrooms adjoining it. In fact, large open spaces rather than classroom boxes are the trend in schools today. Patterson Elementary School in Jefferson County, Colorado, for example, was built with one large instructional space for almost five hundred boys and girls and twenty teachers and teacher aids working together. With supervised study spaces located in the center of the room, teachers work with small groups of boys and girls around the exterior walls. A few miles away, at Walnut Hill Elementary School in the Cherry Creek School District, groups of teachers and paraprofessionals work under the direction of a master teacher with some hundred students in each of three instructional centers. Gone are the traditional desks and

[3] Abstracted from Kenneth A. Simon and W. V. Grant, *Digest of Educational Statistics* (Washington, D.C.: U.S. Department of Health, Education and Welfare, 1964), p. 44, and from Alvin Renelzky, *Standard Education Almanac* (Los Angeles, Calif.: Academic Media, 1968), p. 142.

other furniture often found in elementary school classrooms; these are replaced with functional furniture modules (foot-square boxes, round table-tops, shelving), which may be put together to fashion tables, writing surfaces, or individual seating arrangements. Each child has a tray to hold books and instructional materials. Although the elementary schools you teach in may not be like these two, a growing number of open-concept schools are being built in the United States.

Architects, in cooperation with teachers and consultants, now develop plans that are designed to house and serve educational programs. Larger cities increasingly employ specialists to insure the development of functional educational facilities. For the first time, schools are being built for learning!

Utilization of technology plays a greater part in improving the education of today's children. Rarely was a 16-mm. movie projector to be found in an elementary school thirty years ago; today it is common. Teachers employ overhead projectors with the same facility their predecessor once used with the chalk and chalk board. Learning resources centers contain not only books, reference materials, and journals, but also audio listening posts for foreign language instruction or mathematics drills, a science experimental corner, displays of social studies projects, and an educational television receiver. Increasingly, portable television cameras and screens are used by teachers. Children making talks before the class may be televised and recorded or video taped, so that they can later see and hear themselves and improve their performance; athletic performances may be televised for the same reason; creative drama by students (such as a fictitious trip to Mars) may be televised and later shown as a program to other students; teachers use portable television to record their own teaching and to replay it later so that they may analyze their performance and improve their style. Many school districts purchase and maintain extensive film and slide collections today; and projectors, tape recorders, 8-mm. cameras and other audio-visual equipment are common classroom equipment. In years to come, this equipment will probably be supplemented by more elaborate and perhaps more effective instructional tools.

PROGRAMS.   Major reform in elementary school curriculum was initiated about fifteen years ago, when various subject areas became the focus for concerted revision by curriculum theorists, specialists in the various subjects, and school personnel. Reform efforts have generally developed in three areas. First, the content is organized in relation to the structure of the discipline itself. Broad principles and generalizations are stressed and applied in many different contexts. Second, an increasing emphasis is placed on problem-solving procedures. With the pupil slated to live in a world yet undreamed of, it is imperative that he be equipped with appropriate tools of analysis to help him make decisions in that future world. Third, an emphasis is placed on the objectives the student is to attain, not simply the activities that he will participate in. This emphasis provides a viable direction for the school program and leads to a means for evaluating student achievement. Because of its crucial role in the continuing development of society, the elementary school has become the battleground for special interest groups. These groups recognize the importance of schools and their educational programs in shaping the thinking of America's children and therefore strive to mold and control them.

Patriotic and veterans groups often press for their own particular brand of "nationalism," charging that the schools are not adequately teaching the precepts on which this nation was founded. Commercial firms and philanthropic foundations publish educational materials and develop school programs designed to emphasize their particular products or ideas. Sometimes large grants of money or materials are made to those schools or teachers who will stress a particular point of view. Toothpaste companies furnish classrooms with quantities of their products (toothbrushes, comic books, charts, and detailed lesson plans) for teaching health. Automobile manufacturers distribute booklets on measurement theory and application and their use in the automobile industry. A foundation spends millions of dollars developing a new organizational plan for individualizing instruction and makes it available at a nominal cost to any school willing to undertake the project. A traveling cowboy demonstrates bicycle safety (noting the particular features of the company employing him); an Indian describes the plight of his people on modern reservations. Each has his own message, sales appeal, and eye on the school for a captive and often receptive audience.

For some people science is the final source of power between world ideologies. They press for greater expenditures on scientific endeavors and educational programs leading to scientific expertise. The merits of democracy, for them, depend on being the first to land on the moon, to explore far-off planets, to fly jet planes at twice the speed of sound, and to explore the depths of the earth's oceans. They believe the school curriculum should emphasize these subjects in the elementary school so that trained scientists and mathematicians might evolve at the college level.

Other groups advocate the teaching of humanities to solve social problems, and some suggest a greater role for religious and moral training. They feel that the overpowering stress on science and technology, coupled with tremendous population concentrations, is causing man to be insensitive to the needs of the individual. Their school program focuses on personalizing instruction, even at the expense of employing modern technological media.

Schools are constantly pressured to return to the program of yesteryear —to the good old days. Those supporting this position believe that the curriculum of the elementary school should emphasize the three Rs to the exclusion of other subjects. Some parents, not understanding the new mathematics, linguistics, or science, would prefer that their children learn content similar to that which they were taught. Other traditionalists suggest that buildings constructed today contain too many frills, too much glass, expensive carpeting, and nonconforming building shapes, whereas only a few years ago a school "looked like a school."

All of these factors, recognizing the pivotal position of the elementary school, would like to mold it to their image. Clearly noting the basic objectives of the school and developing effective programs within this complex situation are an ever-present necessity for an effective system of public elementary schools.

Teacher Expectation Is Changing

The preparation of teachers has greatly changed in the past few years. In one of her fascinating books for children, Laura Ingles Wilder describes her preparation and experiences as a teacher in the Midwest just prior to the turn of the century.[4] With an eighth-grade education and passing marks on a county examination, she was ready at sixteen to teach school. She lived with a school board member during the three-month term and walked across the prairie to her one-room school with its potbellied stove and multiaged pupils, one of whom was older than the teacher. The supplies, books, and equipment in the school were meager, but her preparation for teaching was even more inadequate.

Educational requirements have increased during the past few years. In 1920 not a single state required a baccalaureate degree for its lowest regular teaching certificate. Two states had initiated such a requirement by 1930; eleven, by 1940; twenty-one, by 1950; thirty-nine, by 1960; and forty-seven, by 1970. Despite this apparent lack of aggression on the part of legislators, the preparation level has increased dramatically in the past few years. In 1972–73, 97.8 per cent of the elementary school teachers in the United States had at least a baccalaureate degree, and 25.4 per cent had a master's degree or higher.[5]

A recent movement in teacher education emphasizes competencies that prospective teachers are to demonstrate rather than activities in which they participate. This movement, called competency-based teacher education, has captured the imagination of many educators during the past few years. Competency requirements to be demonstrated by prospective or in-service teachers are defined as explicit objectives, with activities that facilitate the student's achievement of these stipulated competencies. Re-

---

[4] Laura Ingles Wilder, *These Happy Golden Years* (New York: Harper, 1953).

[5] *Teacher Supply and Demand in Public Schools, 1973* (Washington, D.C.: National Education Association, 1974), p. 38.

sponsibility for achieving and demonstrating these objectives is placed on the student, and he is held accountable for them. During the past few years, a number of states have instituted certification requirements based on competencies rather than on courses. This trend has pressed teacher education institutions to reexamine their curriculum and to make it relevant to the real needs of teachers. No longer can esoteric subjects be taught simply because they are of interest to the instructor. Each objective and each experience is tested in the crucible of experience with live children in actual classrooms.

Preparation programs also recognize that master teachers perform in a wide variety of styles. Recent research indicates that some teaching virtuosos are child-focusers, some task-focusers, some pragmatists; yet all three groups are professional educators.[6] One is concerned primarily with how children feel; the second emphasizes completion of tasks and projects; while the third considers situational variables in making decisions.

Not all teachers, however, exhibit professional behavior. A large segment of the population in the study was referred to as contented conformists. We are certain that you at one time or another have encountered these teachers, who are contented with the way schools are operated and the way the curriculum is currently being taught. They consider themselves only a medium for transmitting the dictates of others to the younger children.

A fifth teaching style identified in the study was that of so-called timeservers. They complete the required hours at school, but their real interests lie outside their work. Any attempt by the administration to hold in-service programs or to stipulate activities outside school hours is met by strenuous cries of anguish and anger. In the classroom their discipline is rigid, not because they want their children to be well disciplined or to achieve certain tasks, but because a highly disciplined class is easier to manage.

Ambivalents, a sixth group, waiver between rigid discipline and permissiveness, between highly structured lessons and pupil choice of activities, between love and hate for their children. The fluctuation cycle may be as short as minutes or hours or as long as weeks, but these teachers continually resolve inner conflicts between an idealist concept of teaching and the realism of actual classroom experiences.

The last group, the alienated, probably should never be admitted to teaching and are never happy with it or its rewards. They composed a very small percentage of the population and usually dropped out after a short time.

---

[6] Ann G. Olmstead, Frank Blackington III, and W. Robert Houston, "Stances Teachers Take," *Phi Delta Kappan*, **4**, No. 5:330–334 (Jan. 1974).

Commensurate with increased professional preparation and degrees have come higher salaries for teachers. Figure 1–3 summarizes the average salaries of instructional staff in the United States from 1946–1947 to 1969–1970. Both the actual average salary and a base line (buying power) for the salary are shown in the graph. During this twenty-three-year period the actual salaries of teachers have almost quadrupled, from $2,254 to $8,840. Because of inflation, actual gains have not been so great. If we use 1969–1970 as a base, the average teacher's salary in 1946 would have purchased goods and services equivalent to $3,943; in 1969–1970 this same figure is $8,840, over twice the actual buying power. Similar gains in salary and buying power no doubt may be expected in the future.

WILL I GET A JOB?   For those entering a preparatory program of any type, this is a crucial question. For many years anyone who graduated with a bachelor's degree in elementary education was virtually assured of a job. The number of students was expanding rapidly, and salaries were relatively low when compared with those of other professions.

Today there is a surplus of people trained to be teachers. Figure 1–2 provides an estimate of trends in elementary teacher surplus and demand conditions. The figure shows that over the past few years a general teacher shortage has changed to a general teacher surplus.

This general surplus obscures several variables. First, in some local areas there is a shortage despite the national picture. These are typically in the southern part of the country, in faster growing areas, in large cities, and, interestingly enough, in the more isolated rural areas. You may wish to investigate conditions in your locality.

Second, in some specialized areas of elementary education, there ap-

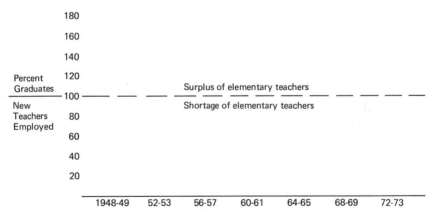

FIGURE 1–2. *Elementary Education Graduates as Per Cent New Teachers Employed.* (Teacher Supply and Demand in Public Schools, 1973 [*Washington, D.C.: National Education Association, 1974*], *pp. 28, 34.*)

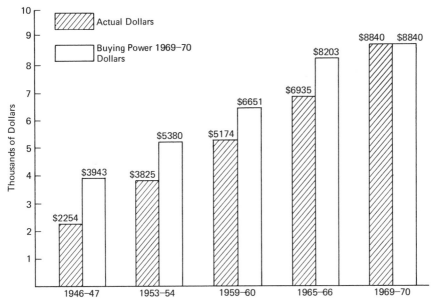

FIGURE 1–3. *Average Salary of Instructional Staff and Buying Power.* (*U.S. Department of Health, Education, and Welfare,* Projections of Educational Statistics to 1969–70 [*Washington, D.C.: U.S. Government Printing Office, 1971*], *p. 95; and National Commission Teacher Education and Professional Standards,* Milestones [*Washington, D.C.: NEA, 1964*], *p. 25.*)

pears to be greater demand. These include special education, remedial reading, early childhood education, middle school education, and bilingual programs. These areas are constantly shifting and thus should be investigated. Teachers who have developed a particular area of expertise often find it easier to find employment.

One last comment: there are elementary teaching jobs available each year; the competition today for them simply is greater than previously.

The Responsibility for Change

The rapid changes that have occurred in our society and in education within the past few years are readily documented. In this chapter the changing cultural milieu, with its many divergent needs, interests, and purposes, has been briefly described. It is within this arena that we must strive to educate children. The teacher of the future must be prepared not only for *what is,* but also for *what is to be.* The changes that have occurred are but a prologue to even greater changes in the future. It is indeed a challenging time, but a promising one for the elementary school and for those professionals who choose to devote their life to it.

SUGGESTED ACTIVITIES

1. Changes in the world in which we live are occurring so rapidly as to be unbelievable. In your library find an article or book that speculates on the future and react to it. To what extent do you agree or disagree with its prognostications for the future? You might read the following: *Science and Technology in the World of the Future,* ed. by Arthur B. Bronwell (New York: Wiley-Interscience, 1970); Isaac Asimov, "The Next Hundred Years: Science-Based Estimates of What the Century Ahead May Bring," *The World Almanac and Book of Facts,* 1968 centennial edition (New York: Newspaper Enterprises, Inc., 1968), pp. 39–41; R. Buckminster Fuller, "The Prospect for Humanity," *Saturday Review,* Aug. 29, 1964, pp. 33–44; *Learning for Tomorrow,* ed. by Alvin Toffler (New York: Vintage, 1974).
2. Two contrasting papers on the role of the teacher are presented in the book *Curriculum Crossroads,* ed. by A. Harry Passow (New York: Bureau of Publications, Teachers College, Columbia University, 1962). Margaret Lindsey, in "Decision-Making and the Teacher," pp. 27–40, urges clarification of the teacher's role in decision-making, whereas Sloan R. Wayland, in the section entitled "The Teacher as Decision-Maker," p. 41–52, views the teacher as a functionary in a bureaucratic system. Read and react to these two positions.
3. Why have you decided to become an elementary school teacher? What do you know about teaching? List the relevant conditions that you considered in making this decision about a life vocation. What other factors could or should be considered?
4. Outline what you think might be an ideal elementary school ten years from now. What might be the responsibilities of the teacher in such a situation? Do not be afraid to dream a little on this activity.
5. Each member of a panel of college students is to decide upon his future vocation, enumerate its potential and disadvantages, and tell why he chose this particular field. You represent the elementary school teacher. What would you tell the audience, who are also college students?

SELECTED BIBLIOGRAPHY

Block, James. *Mastery Learning in Classroom Instruction.* New York: Macmillan Publishing Co., Inc., 1975.
Counts, G. S. "Dare the Schools Build a Great Society?" *Phi Delta Kappan,* 47 (Sept., 1965), pp. 27–30.
Forrester, J. W. *World Dynamics.* Cambridge, Mass.: Wright-Allen Press, 1971.

Hicks, William V., W. Robert Houston, Bruce D. Cheney, and R. L. Marquard. *The New Elementary School Curriculum*. New York: Van Nostrand Reinhold Company, 1970.

Houston, W. Robert and Robert B. Howsam, *Competency-based Teacher Education: Progress, Problems, and Prospects*. Palo Alto, Calif.: Science Research Associates, 1972.

Hyman, Ronald T. *Ways of Teaching*. Philadelphia: J. B. Lippincott Co., 1974.

Illich, Ivan. *Deschooling Society*. New York: Harper & Row, Publishers, 1970.

Learning for Tomorrow. Ed. by Alvin Toffler. New York: Vintage, 1974.

Metropolitanism: Its Challenge to Education. Ed. by Robert J. Havighurst. Sixty-seventh Yearbook, NSSE. Chicago: University of Chicago Press, 1968.

Palardy, J. Michael. *Teaching Today: Tasks and Challenges*. New York: Macmillan Publishing Co., Inc., 1975.

Ryan, Kevin and James M. Cooper. *Those Who Can, Teach*. Boston: Houghton Mifflin Company, 1972.

Science and Technology in the World of the Future. Ed. by Arthur B. Bronwell. New York: Wiley-Interscience, 1970.

Toffler, Alvin. *Future Shock*. New York: Bantam Books, 1970.

Chapter 2

Behavioral Sciences in the Teaching Process

An axiom often verbalized in teacher education programs is that the instructor "teaches the whole child." In practice, however, teachers often consider only the actions of the child in their classroom. The child's stance in the class, achievement on academic maneuvers, and behavioral patterns are thought of as indicative of the *individual*. Teachers often forget that school comprises only one aspect of a child's total life. What he does during the other sixteen hours or more of the day, on weekends and during the first five years of his life influences his value system, what he does or does not do in school, his understanding of academic and school related activities, and his success. In many respects school is an artificial environment and thus alien to many children.

Understanding the confluence of factors that influence a child's lifestyle, actions, and value orientation is an important prerequisite to teaching him. It requires that the teacher develop in-depth understanding of the various behavioral sciences—anthropology, sociology, psychology, cultural geography, urban sociology, cultural economics, and linguistics. Understanding human behavior and acting on that understanding are a vital aspect of teacher preparation. This aspect includes not only understanding, *concepts* of the behavioral sciences, but also developing *skills for analyzing and interpreting* human behavior. Sometimes the teacher must view an event from the perspective of the pupil—to "walk in his moccasins," if decisions are to result in effective instruction.

Although considerable rhetoric and numerous studies have highlighted the plight of the minority group child in the traditional classroom, teaching the minority group child for the first time is a shattering experience for many teachers. The black child in the newly integrated school system is often confronted with a totally new environment and meets social, cultural, and academic expectations far beyond his experience or knowledge. The white child, too, experiences confusion; he becomes aware of differences in speech patterns, vocabulary, and study habits. He may hear one thing at home about the other races and experience another at school. The Mexican-American and the Puerto Rican have been told in many different ways that they are inferior and unacceptable at school. Why? Because they speak with an accent. And yet, they may speak and understand two languages better than those who look down on them.

Teachers often find themselves confronting children of different races with little preparation in understanding cultural and social differences. Stereotypes create erroneous first impressions and misunderstandings on the part of different races, ethnic groups, and members of religious affiliations. Teachers are faced with a wide range of academic abilities and an even wider range of social differences. Although most schools have now accomplished physical desegregation, actual integration in terms of understanding, respect, and equal educational opportunities for all children has not yet been reached.

The following excerpt from an interview with a white teacher in a new environment facing racially different students poignantly describes the plight of many beginning teachers:

> My first few weeks in the classroom were appalling. The majority of my students did not see teachers as guides in the growth of their mental abilities, nor was there the awe that I had as a child for teachers. The children who taxed my endurance were those who demanded my reaction to their personalities every minute. If their names were not on the weekly list of helpers, then they accused me of playing favorites; if they couldn't answer every question I posed, they refused to do anything. My principal finally impressed upon me that many of these children, because of their background, could see no point in school, no goals for the future, and no hope for success. He kept trying to make me understand that *survival*, not *approval*, is the one thing they could understand. It is easy for me to understand these things mentally; accepting them emotionally is another matter.
>
> What worries me most is the quality of my instruction. It is difficult to develop a practical program that will work with thirty pupils. Too many of them need constant attention. The well-adjusted, capable child is being

penalized because presenting him with challenging ideas loses out to chaos in the corner.

This chapter provides an overview of several salient aspects of the behavioral sciences and thus provides a basis for other parts of the volume. To be an effective teacher, however, your preparation program should include more extensive study than is provided herein. Such study certainly would focus on psychology—child growth and development, learning theory, motivation, and measurement—but also on social forces impacting children.

Objectives for this chapter follow shortly. They will guide your reading and provide a basis for assessment. You may add other objectives that you wish to pursue relative to this aspect of teaching. Remember that in teaching it is not adequate simply to know about something; it is your use of that knowledge in your instruction, interpersonal relations, and professional activities that is important.

Cognitive objectives for this chapter include the following:

1. The reader will be able to describe nonschool variables affecting children's behavior, including family, economic influences, power, and values.
2. The reader will be stimulated to explore one behavioral science in greater depth and relate his knowledge to teaching.
3. The reader will be able to describe the basic stages of children's growth and development.
4. The reader will be able to describe and contrast the theories of Piaget, Gagné, and Bruner, and note differences in instruction resulting from each theory.

Family Life Influences Children's Actions

Not only is family life in America changing today, but it is far more divergent than many believed. Many prospective teachers come from homes where the nuclear family consists of a mother, father, and children living in a single dwelling; parents accept responsibility for the growth, development, and education of their children. Each individual in the family plays a role—the father as provider, the mother as householder, and the child as learner-developer. Arensberg has provided a distinct and penetrating analysis of this small family type.[1]

[1] Conrad M. Arensberg, "The Family and Other Cultures," *The Nation's Children* (New York: Columbia U. P., 1960), pp. 60–61.

The imperative of our family system, basing the small household on the conjugal pair, isolating that pair to free them to command their own destinies and satisfactions and to confer on them nearly complete and untrammeled authority over minor children (except where the state and community limit them), are not easy ones. Nor is the task our educational ideal assumes a simple one: to prepare each and every man and woman to be in adulthood spouse, parent, householder, and family head all at once. These imperatives of our present small, conjugal type of family, with its minimum kinship entanglement and support, ideally require each person to find a mate for himself, to love the spouse, to share the upbringing of children with him or her, to maintain a household with him, to find chief emotional identification in the little family growing up around this spouse and partner freely chosen and freely retained.

The influence of living in a heavily populated urban area has changed traditional family roles. No longer are children and their parents mutually dependent upon one another for emotional support and companionship. Children tend to spend more time with their peers. During the upper elementary and secondary school years, boys particularly begin to build small, well-developed gangs (in some parts of the country the athletic team has tended to become the youth's gang). In both white and black urban ghettos, boys bunch together for survival. Boys of Spring Branch, Texas, classify themselves as jocks (athletes), freaks (longhairs), kickers (cowboys) and straights. Each has his own culture, mores, dress, habits, values, and friends. Often fights break out between groups. In more recent years, groups of young girls (flocks) seemingly are imitating the gang philosophy of the boys.

Recently an adult described his boyhood:

We lived in south Chicago on the same block all my life. It was a long block with lots of kids, and we had a gang, the Panthers, who protected our block against gangs from other blocks. You see, each block had its own gang. Whenever we went anywhere, we went together. One year I delivered newspapers on three of these blocks, and sometimes I had to ride my bike like the wind through the other two for protection; I never really felt safe, but was never harmed throwing papers. We did have caches of rocks and sticks stashed at both ends of the block in case we were attacked. We spent hours deciding how we would defend ourselves, but occasionally we would invade the Bears' territory to exercise our muscle. Most people today can't seem to understand that this block was my life; this was our turf, our honor, and defending it was everything.

Emotional trials of loved ones or problems resulting from a move to a new location place additional tension on the nuclear family. Think what this means to children. Their friendship patterns are destroyed; they must reorient themselves in a new community, with new acquaintances, new teachers, new rules. With one family in four moving each year, you can expect considerable turnover in the most stable classes. For many families, a move ties them together more closely; for others, the trauma is so great as to disintegrate family cohesiveness. Think back to the varied life-style described in Chapter 1, and consider how difficult it might be for those elementary school students to exchange places.

During the past hundred years, the nature of the father's job and its relation to the family have changed. Children rarely know very much about what their father does to earn a living. They do not see him at work; and even if they did, they probably would not understand the job's intricacies, traumas, and successes because that job is so wrapped up in technology and specialization. Thus, children are denied participation in a major part of their father's life. In a recent meeting of Boy Scouts and their parents, both groups identified this as a major topic they wanted to discuss in their family, but did not. One of the basic educational modes of the past, emulating one's parents, is thus denied most children today.

Changing roles of men and women also are affecting family life. According to recent figures, one mother out of every three works. When a company moves its offices to another city, mothers may transfer to the new location, taking along their husbands and families. Only a few years ago, it was unthinkable that the woman's vocation would determine where the family would live. The search for equal opportunities for all mankind (regardless of race, religion, or sex) has influenced the status of females. Women's Lib is more than a term, more than a phrase. It is a concept that has grown out of our evolving culture. Male stereotypes, particularly among middle-class Americans, also are changing. Men may show emotion in time of grief, joy, or triumph. We are still more reserved than many Europeans, however, where two men may greet each other with a hug and kiss.

One out of every five families represents a broken home. *Broken* in this context, implies that one of the parents is dead or institutionalized, or that the parents are divorced or separated. As is the case with working mothers, the result is usually a decrease in the amount of contact a child has with either parent.

Perhaps, as Alvin Toffler suggests, the population press and increasing governmental control over every aspect of life will become the death knell of the small family unit. In modern Israel, for example, many children are raised in community-operated, full-time nurseries on *kibbutzim* or communal farms. Both China and the Soviet Union have experimented with communal state nurseries, in which all children were raised together, apart from their parents. Aristotle, over 2,500 years ago, recommended this as the ideal procedure for raising children who could contribute to the state most effectively.

In California, a number of communes have grown up with fifteen to twenty-five adults and a dozen children living together with everyone, not just the natural parents, responsible for the education and discipline of the children. In the Oneida community, all property is held in common, and children are considered the responsibility of the entire community.

With both divorce and children born out of wedlock becoming more prevalent, a greater proportion of children in elementary schools are being raised by a single parent. This is particularly true in black urban ghettos. There is no stigma attached by the community either to the mother who raises children by more than one father or to her frequent trips to the Welfare Office for food stamps, food stuffs, or welfare checks. Yet these conditions often horrify the middle-class teacher with different value orientations. It is not adequate for the teacher simply to know *of* the family relations of the children he is teaching; he must understand the child's perspective in relation to them. Furthermore, many stories found in primary grade reading books, which depict traditional middle-class family units, have little meaning for many of these children.

POWER

The concept of power is just beginning to be understood by people in all walks of life. Leaders of minority groups and labor unions influence action in every walk of life through governmental acts and court decisions. They have learned that power can be a positive force.

For years people considered power to be evil. Lord Acton, an eighteenth-century English historian, wrote that "power tends to corrupt, and absolute power corrupts absolutely." The American historian Henry Adams was more blunt when he wrote that "power is poison." Their comments oversimplify the subject of power. They fail to recognize that power is an element in all of life. Virtually every decision a person makes that affects another person includes some aspect of power. Power, then, is the ability to influence the actions and decisions of others.

Children exercise power over each other in their daily actions. When a five-year-old says to another five-year-old, "You'd better like me or I won't play with you," he is threatening use of the power of affection. Selecting teammates for a ball game on the playground, choosing another student to go to the library with him, or sharing an apple are all forms of power displays by children. Teachers who understand the nature of power and the processes involved therein organize their instruction to accommodate children's power needs through structured classroom interaction and management procedures; and in the process they wield considerable power themselves over children, their parents, and their peers.

To understand power better and also the way to exercise it effectively, consider the conclusions of Harold Lasswell, a political scientist, and Abraham Kaplan, a philosopher, who studied power and its uses in several societies. They identified forms of power common to everyone. From their list, Paul M. Dietterich listed eight sources of power representing widely held values. His list, reproduced herein in Table 2–1, may provide data for discussion and for decision-making as a teacher.[2]

Many people today are beginning to recognize the ways in which others have used power to oppress and are finding new muscle in their own power maneuvers. This expansion of the power base has been termed a "power explosion." Exploited people want not to be *dependent on,* but *interdependent with* all other people. Black power, brown power, poor people's power, youth power, woman power, and power to the people are but a few of the manifestations of this movement. The cries are strong and persistent that injustice occurs whenever a person is not permitted to participate in the decision-making processes that affect his life. This makes him powerless, and the resulting injustice causes him to become alienated.

Who are some of these people just now beginning to discover their power potential? What is their life? How does it compare with what you have enjoyed? Consider first this account of the life of migrant workers in the United States as reported in *The New York Times.*[3] The story was based on testimony given on July 20, 1970, to the U.S. Senate Subcommittee on Migrating Labor by several physicians.

Table 2–1   Sources of Power

To live a minimally human life, a person needs the following kinds of power:	
Affection:	Love and friendship.
Enlightenment:	Knowledge, insight, and information concerning personal and cultural relations.
Power:	The capacity for affecting policies of others with the help of actual or threatened sanctions.
Rectitude:	The moral values of virtue, goodness, righteousness.
Respect:	Status, honor, recognition, prestige, reputation.
Skill:	Proficiency in arts, crafts, trade, or profession.
Wealth:	Money, goods, and services that accrue to the person in any way.
Well-being:	Health and safety to the person.

[2] Paul M. Dietterich, *The Pattern of Power* (Nashville, Tenn.: The Graded Press, 1971), p. 41.

[3] *The New York Times,* July 26, 1970. © 1970 by The New York Times Company. Reprinted by permission.

For a child born with brown skin in one of the southern tier of states, of farm-migrant parents who speak a different language from most Americans, the future is already charted.

The young Chicano—or Mexican-American—migrant will move with his parents through the citrus groves of Florida or California, stoop over the beans and tomatoes in Texas, hoe sugarbeets in western Kansas, crawl through the potato fields of Idaho or Maine, and pick cherries in Michigan, moving with the season and the harvests.

He will sleep, crowded with his family, in shells of migrant housing without heat, refrigeration, or sanitary facilities. He will splash barefoot through garbage-strewn mud infested with internal parasites and drink polluted water provided in old oil drums.

By the age of 12 he will have the face of an adult and his shoulders will form in a permanent stoop. He will acquire the rough dry skin and the pipestem arms and legs that indicate a lack of vitamins and proteins. He will be surrounded by children infected with diseases of the intestines, blood, mouth, eyes, and ears and thus condemned to poor learning records at school—when they are able to attend school at all . . .

The minimum wage law has been applied by Congress only to the largest farms and the minimum for farm workers has been set at 30 cents an hour below that for other workers. Employers of migrants who pay by piecework avoid even this minimum.

Migrants and other farm workers . . . are excluded from coverage by the National Labor Relations Act, which protects the rights of other workers to organize in an effort to improve their lot. And the child labor law does not prevent migrant families from taking their children into the fields to help. When no one is able to work, the family rarely qualifies for welfare aid.

The physicians' testimony was based on study of conditions among migrants in counties in Florida, Texas, and Michigan. Dr. Gordon Harper who visited camps in Michigan, concluded his testimony with an impassioned indictment: "If the only way to insure simple dignity, self-respect and health for our brothers, is to wait until they can buy their way into a place in our national sun, that is terribly sad commentary on the moral economy of our country.

The migrant laborers' life expectancy is 49. Their infant and maternal mortality is 125 per cent of the national average. Their death rates from influenza and pneumonia are 200 per cent—and from tuberculosis 250 per cent—of the national rate. Their wages are too low to cover medical care.

Migrants have suffered because they have lacked power. The more than a quarter of a million migrants are scattered throughout the country, do not vote in elections because of their frequent moves, and contact power sources only when in trouble.

The valiant red man met Columbus in his voyages to the New World, lived with "made and broken treaties" for over four hundred years, was massacred and herded like cattle onto reservations, subjugated to the white man's will and law, and even today is at the bottom of the list of American poor. The average family living on an Indian reservation earns no more than $1,500 in cash each year. Three fourths earn less than $1,330 per year, the poverty index level set by the Office of Economic Opportunity. Unemployment rates for Indians often exceed 50 per cent.[4] For more than a hundred years the Bureau of Indian Affairs has subjugated Indians, making decisions not for their good, but for the welfare of the bureaucracy or private enterprise that worked with them. In his poignant book *Bury My Heart at Wounded Knee*, Brown describes the plight and despair of the American Indian during the past century. Although a few Indians have managed to leave the reservation and enter into American life, the vast majority are still powerless in almost every way.

Blacks are by far the largest of the deprived groups, accounting for one out of every ten Americans. But income for blacks remains at only slightly more than half of the median income for whites. Because of governmental and court pressures, a growing number of blacks are being placed in managerial or professional positions; as a race, however, they are still concentrated in the least-skilled and lowest-paying occupations. Blacks suffer more from crime, infant mortality, lower health services, and poor educational systems than whites.[5] The report mentioned in note 5 also relates the place of whites in the ghettos. Its insight helps one to understand the perspective of blacks who feel powerless in a white-dominated world.[6]

> What white Americans have never fully understood—but the Negro can never forget is that white society is deeply implicated in the ghetto. White institutions created it, white institutions maintain it, and white society condones it.

Power, then, is exercised in every aspect of American life and has deep implications for the teacher. What he perceives to be possible in the classroom; how he thinks of himself in relation to administrators, parents, and children; and how he acts are all colored by his perception of power and its relation to him. Children, too, are encouraged or inhibited by their concept of power, and the teacher who understands and acts on this will be more effective than one who does not.

[4] Robert L. Bennett, "Toward a New Era for American Indians," *The American Federationist* 71:14 (Dec. 1966).

[5] *National Advisory Commission on Civil Disorders* (Washington, D.C.: U.S. Government Printing Office, 1968), pp. 251–252.

[6] Ibid., p. 1.

Cultural Economic Influences

An economic elite controls wealth in the United States. In 1965 the New York Stock Exchange advertised that stock was widely held in the United States; twenty million persons owned shares of stock. A person was defined as a shareholder if he owned one share of stock. Actually, only 1.6 per cent of Americans as a group owned 32 per cent of publicly owned assets, 92.2 per cent of all stock, *all* state and local tax-exempt bonds, 38.2 per cent of federal bonds, 36.2 per cent of mortgages and notes, and 16.1 per cent of real estate. The wealth of this nation tends to be concentrated in the hands of a small group of people.

To a great extent the distribution of wealth influences the behavior of pupils. Some ways are obvious, whereas others can only be inferred from more subtle evidence. In many ways this section is an extension of the previous one on power—for economics has become a major source of power as well as a tool of those wielding power. Three ideas are particularly important for the prospective teacher.

First, income is directly related to the health and environmental stimulation of the child. When resources are limited, families spend less for fruits and other foods that provide a well-balanced diet. This directly affects children's health and physical development. Furthermore, they are more reluctant to go to a doctor when ill; and yet because of diet, they are more likely to be ill.

The intellectual stimulation of the home is also directly related to income. The extensiveness of travel; the number of objects and games in the house for the child to look at, play with, and learn from; and the opportunities to play the violin, ride horses, attend a football game or opera are all related to the resources available in the family. The richness of the child's environment as a source of stimulation facilitates the ease and adequacy with which he develops learning concepts.

The second economic factor concerns the function of education in equipping children to use the tools of society. As society becomes more complex, the repertoire of tools available becomes more extensive and diverse. Although the stone ax may have been the major tool ten thousand years ago, today tools range from manipulation of abstract ideas to handling concrete objects. School custodians handle a hand broom, but also a complex heating and ventilation unit. Teachers employ intellectual skills, operate 16-mm. movie projectors, and deal with attendance records.

Learning to work with these tools is a function of the educational system. People in different work roles perceive and employ tools at varying levels. A gas station attendant may know how to check the oil and battery water in a car without knowing exactly how they contribute to the automobile's operation or the laws and principles of physics and chemistry undergirding their action. An auto mechanic, on the other hand, must understand the basic components of the engine, recognize normal working conditions, and diagnose difficulties. An accountant may make judgments about the automobile on the basis of written information. He may not actually have seen the mechanic, the automobile, or the driver; but on the basis of records such as mileage, gasoline consumption, and repair bills, he can make recommendations relative to the future status of the car. The gasoline attendant, the mechanic, and the accountant may know very little of each other's job and even less about the tools of their respective trades; yet all are interrelated and interactive, using different tools and methods to deal with the same subject.

Pupils from families of a higher socioeconomic status tend to have higher school achievement than those from families of a lower socioeconomic status even when both groups may be equal in intelligence. We know that parental encouragement may account for much of the measured achievement differences between pupils of different socioeconomic levels.

Among a large segment of the population, the manipulation of abstractions is not considered a productive activity. Only about 20 per cent of working adults perform professional and managerial tasks for a living, where the tools are predominately conceptual and abstract. Another 20 per cent or more engage primarily in fairly routine clerical activities, which, although requiring relatively simple operations, involve manipulation of words and numbers rather than concrete physical objects. For many of these people, accomplishment and self-esteem are linked to the manipulation of abstractions; this value orientation reinforces the behavior of their children toward academic achievement. For the remaining 60 per cent of the population, however, such parental reinforcement of school activities is nonexistent or minimal.

The perspective of the lower socioeconomic child may be understood through a football analogy. Consider a stranger who had never before witnessed or heard of a football game. He witnesses a well-padded individual running with a small object while pursued by men with different colored clothing. People watching the game become excited, especially when the player crosses a particular white stripe. The player, who is a successful hurler of the object, is idealized and made a folk hero. Why would anyone want to fight so hard to carry a small object on a field? Why would people want to engage in such a bruising exercise? Think about the tools and skills of football, the values our society has placed upon skillful use of them, and the difficulty a stranger to our country might have in understanding their significance. The parallel of that stranger to the conceptual stance of the child viewing intellectual skills and tools may be very close.

The third aspect related to economics concerns the degree to which an individual feels he has some control over his life; what he does voluntarily will systematically determine what happens to him. The Coleman Study reported that pupils who express a feeling of being able to control their fate and those who perceive themselves as right tend to have higher achievement levels than those who feel less in control or less talented. When related to blacks and whites, both children and adults, results indicate that blacks are more likely to attribute success to luck. Whites are more likely to attribute it to hard work. Coleman found, however, that when black children felt that success was likely to result from hard work, then their achievement was higher than that of whites who considered luck as the controlling factor.

A number of studies have shown that children do better on subsequent tests when teachers write encouraging remarks on their original test papers. This practice by teachers may be effective, in part, because the pupil is reinforced by a feeling of success through his own efforts. From learning theory we know that positively reinforcing a particular action will increase the probability of that action's recurring, whereas negatively reinforcing a response will reduce its probability of recurrence.

Reinforcement of success or failure seems to be related to feelings of external control. But how does this specifically affect a school child through economic variables? We have already noted the influence mothers have on the intellectual development of their children. Children reflect their parents' expectations for success or failure in them.

Differences in economic power enjoyed by different persons result in differences in status and feelings of self-esteem engendered by this power. A family with high income may own two automobiles. This provides the wife with a greater range of stores from which to buy food, clothing, and household items. She can select the lowest prices or drive to several stores to purchase a particular item that is attractive. If she lives in a high income neighborhood, the stores within her area are more likely to carry a wider range of goods. The mother in a low income family may have to walk to the grocery store, limiting her selection to nearby stores. Those with irregular incomes are more likely to buy on credit, which means not only interest payments, but also the necessity for shopping where credit is available (which is likely to be at a store with higher prices).

Lower income families not only pay higher prices for goods out of their lower incomes, but also receive inferior public services. They receive less police protection, attend generally poorer schools, and have poorer streets. Suburbanites not only avoid paying for some services they receive while working in the city, but also receive the benefit of subsidized roads in leaving the city after work. When applying for bank loans or credit, lower income families are likely to pay higher rates of interest. Favorable markets, interest rates, life-styles, schools, governmental services, and housing accrue to those who are most able to pay for them. Their range of choice is greater, and they have greater control over their destiny. This feeling of worth and control is reflected in school achievement by their children.

CULTURAL VALUES AND INDIVIDUAL ACTION

In preceding sections of this chapter, we have explored several factors that influence children's actions. Undergirding all those factors are the values they hold. These values determine their actions and provide direction for the choices they make. This value system is shaped and molded by the subculture to which they owe allegiances.

A value is an arbitrary conception by an individual or a group of what is *desirable* in human experience. As children grow up, they are besieged by a constant barrage of evaluations by their culture. They learn to cope with reality, and for them reality is interpreted by those with whom they associate. Each expects to go or not to go to college. Each cherishes or does not cherish intellectual pursuits. Each person's code of ethics relative to stealing, telling the truth, or confronting others is shaped by his perception of what others tell him is "right."

Children learn to value as a result of looks of disapproval, smiles, rewards, verbal instructions, and the actions of those they respect. Their community shapes them just as they, in turn, will shape others.

All concepts of what is desirable combine both cognitive and affective meanings. Individuals internalize their ideas of right and wrong, good and bad, and invest them with strong feelings.

Values are not readily changed. Although they may appear outmoded and ridiculous to others, they provide continuity ·and security to those holding them. A value system undergirds the various rules, behavioral patterns, and norms of each subculture. They are so imbedded in that subculture that they are invisible to its members.

But that perspective, accepted and seldom challenged, becomes the basis for viewing other persons or groups. Each believes his values and lifestyle to be better than those of others. Indeed, if one accepts the environmental circumstances and basic assumptions of a subculture, its value system usually becomes reasonable and rational.[7] When one reads *The Godfather*, a story about the leader of a Mafia family, it is easy to be persuaded that the code of the underworld family is consistent and just

[7] Several anthropological studies provide perspective in understanding value systems. For example, read Margaret Mead, *Growing Up in New Guinea* (New York: Mentor Books, 1930); idem, *Continuities in Cultural Evolution* (New Haven, Conn.: Yale U.P., 1964); Melford Spiro, *Children of the Kibbutz* (Cambridge, Mass.: Harvard U.P., 1958); or Beatrice Whiting, *Child Rearing in Six Cultures* (New York: Wiley, 1963).

and that those who break the code by going to the police could justifiably be killed. So it is, too, with a motorcycle gang, a baseball team, a sorority, the Lions Club, or a very fundamentalist religious church—consider the circumstances, accept their underlying assumptions about the world, and you will be pressed to accept the values they hold.

Unfortunately, most people are so imbued with their own cultural bias that they cannot perceive that of others. They screen all actions through their own set of values. Several years ago, a French priest, Abbé Dubois, set out in India to show Hindu men of learning how irrational their religion and values were. At the end of the journey, frustrated and irritated, he wrote, "Being fully persuaded of the superlative merits of their own manners and customs, they think those of other people barbarous and detestable, and quite incompatible with real civilization."[8] The good abbé, however, failed to recognize his own biases as he interacted with the Indians.

This tendency to place one's own group at the center is referred to by sociologists as *ethnocentrism*. Whereas the United States provides an underlying value framework, the various subcultures play variations on this theme.

Subcultural groups often shout their identities to the world. Shriners wear red fezzes; band members, their uniforms; Rotarians, a pin; and convention participants, a ribbon. In Guatemala, both native men and women wear clothing distinctive of their village, just as Scottish plaids distinguish the various clans. Blacks use a distinctive handclasp and call each other "brother." Motorcycle gangs wear black leather jackets. Hippies and flower children, rebelling against war, wealth, and their elders, wear their hair long and their clothing plain and generally ragged. Each group has evolved a set of values; these outward manifestations merely symbolize to the world their sect. From actions of these groups have grown stereotypes for them, expectations of the rest of society for their action and values.

Often, too, the actions of a few impact the thinking and mores of many. Most men wear their hair longer today than a decade ago, even though they at one time may have disapproved of boys with shoulder-length hair. The handclasp of the blacks is used by many professing brotherhood with all mankind.

Teachers who work with children from the various subcultures in the United States may tend to respond to students' actions through their own value orientations. Consider your values, for example. What is important to you? What do you hold dear? *Who* is important? When you have achieved something, *whom* do you want to know about it—and *what* is

[8] Abbé J. A. Dubois, in Henry K. Beauchamp's *Hindu Manners, Customs and Ceremonies*, 3rd ed. (Oxford: Clarendon Press, 1947).

the nature of that achievement? In ten years, what would you like to be doing? If you could describe an ideal life at that time, what might it be? How have you spent your *free* time during the past month? Answering these questions can begin to help you assess your own value system; comparing that with value systems of others will make it more explicit. Knowing yourself is a prerequisite to knowing others; knowing children is a prerequisite to teaching them.

As a teacher, you will have some impact on the values of children, particularly if they envision you as a "significant other"—a person whose approval they seek. Remember, however, that children are constantly bombarded with value-laden stimuli. There is constant pressure to conform to social values and roles. Often adults who impose these standards regard them as natural and desirable, not even being aware of the constant pressure they are putting on children. Such social influence is often so subtle as to be hidden from casual observation.

Initiation into society occurs in steps and stages. In Africa, the Bambara regard life as a progression from an animal-like state through a series of initiations and graduations to a state of union with the divine. In the first initiation, a child is inducted into the order of lions, which permits him to run errands and perform other tasks for his elders. He then progresses through five other stages as he struggles through life for self-perfection and self-realization.[9]

The American child, at the bottom rung of *his* ladder as he goes to kindergarten, may be as frightened as the Bambara child on the bottom rung of his ladder. The first grader looks up to the fifth grader, the tenderfoot Boy Scout up to the Eagle, and the freshman up to the senior. The ladder itself is a manifestation of a set of values inherent in a cultural system.

Becoming enculturated may be more complex for the child of today than it was a hundred years ago. At that time, all messages for his conduct were consistent; he understood what society expected of him and would later expect of him as an adult. The church formed a prominent part in his life, the community in which he lived was typically small and isolated, and all those he contacted knew him and his family personally.

Mass communication has expanded his world, but it brings mixed messages to him. He hears his teachers, political leaders, and others espouse their dedication to peace; but all around are signs of war. He is told that cooperation and group actions are important, but he receives praise and awards only when he individually outperforms others. He is told that education is important because it will enrich his life; but he soon learns that certificates, diplomas, and degrees are really important. Not educa-

[9] Alan R. Beals, *Culture in Process* (New York: Holt, 1967) pp. 16–17.

tion, but the symbols of education are what are required to get a job and advance.

Schools once stood for a single value system, local and based on Christian ethics. The teachers were usually from the local area; they knew the children and the mores of the community.

The practice of celebrating Christmas and Easter and having a daily prayer has been questioned by non-Christian groups and ruled unconstitutional by the Supreme Court. Controversy has led schools to abandon moral, ethical, and aesthetic values as integral parts of the curriculum. For any proposition, someone is for it and someone else equally against it. Thus, the gap has widened between the values schools were to teach and represent and the values actually taught.

With schools neutral toward value positions and a growing cadre of subcultures demanding their own values as important—children contacting personally or through television contradictory value orientations, teachers who are professionally competent but who do not know the community or parents and thus tend not to reflect community-established values—with all these contradictory messages, children find it increasingly difficult to develop a consistent value system. Schools and teachers can help in this process. In an excellent book on teaching values, Raths, Harmin, and Simon suggest eight steps for getting started in such a program:[10]

1. Work toward a psychologically safe classroom climate. Student growth tends to flourish when they feel accepted, supported, relaxed, and generally unthreatened.
2. Work at eliminating tendencies to moralize. Values that are thoughtfully chosen, prized, and acted upon do not come from a process of adult manipulation. You may argue for a particular value, but insure that alternative arguments are presented, and respect students' rights to adopt an alternative view.
3. Start slowly, but not too slowly. Begin with strategies you feel comfortable with. Sets of materials and ideas are included in the Raths book.
4. Keep administrators and other teachers informed.
5. Talk about value—clarifying process in tentative terms. Until you have worked with value theory long enough to obtain the kind of results desired, talk in tentative terms.
6. Prepare for some conflict. Any new venture will antagonize someone, particularly if it deals with a sensitive area like values.
7. Make ideas fit you. Revise ideas from others to fit your situation; adapt; don't simply adopt.

[10] Louis E. Raths, Merrill Harmin, and Sidney Simon, *Values and Teaching* (Columubs, Ohio: Merrill, 1966), pp. 168–174.

8. Encourage several colleagues to join you. When teaching values, seek support by asking other teachers to try out ideas and procedures.

To their list we would add a ninth item—constantly evaluate the objectives you are seeking and the activities used to achieve them. For this, some teachers find it valuable and imperative to use a few parents as a "sounding board." Although absolutely vital to a generic educational program, teaching values is fraught with many potential problems.

LEARNING AND TEACHING

What is learning and how is it related to teaching? This question has absorbed psychologists and educators for many years, and yet the answer is still not clear. Despite thousands of research studies and hundreds of interlocking and often conflicting theories, we still know very little about how man learns. We know even less about the relationship between instruction and learning. But there are some clues, some guidelines to aid us in our search.

Learning is defined by De Cecco as "a relatively permanent change in a behavioral tendency and is the result of reinforced practice."[11] He employs the term *behavioral tendency* to distinguish *learning* from *performance*. We can observe performance, but not learning. Performance is the outward manifestation of learning, but not everything learned is immediately translated into changed performance. From your reading of this chapter, you should have learned something, but this may not have been exhibited through behavior. At some future time you may react to an individual, teach a child, or hypothesize the reason for a pupil's behavior based on learning that has just occurred. But learning will not have occurred then; it is happening now. Thus, De Cecco refers to a "behavioral tendency" rather than a "behavior" when defining learning.

Reinforced practice is readily demonstrated in some learning situations, such as memorizing the multiplication facts, swimming, or typing. The concept also functions in less obvious situations. We learn our prejudices, attitudes, and social skills; they are not innate. As we practice them, they are reinforced by external forces and become more consistent, more resolved, more integrative of our personal style.

Just as some learning is not immediately and readily translated into observable behavior, some behaviors are not indicative of learning. De Cecco suggests three behavior areas not indicative of learning: instincts,

[11] John P. De Cecco, *The Psychology of Learning and Instruction: Educational Psychology* (Englewood Cliffs, N.J.: Prentice-Hall, 1968), p. 243.

maturation, and temporary states of the organism.[12] *Instincts* or reflexes such as breathing or blinking one's eyes are not learned; we are born with them. *Maturation* includes growth tendencies such as bone structure, height, and weight, which are relatively independent of specific learning conditions. Man does not walk until his legs are strong enough to support his weight. The third area includes *temporary conditions* due to factors such as fatigue, habituation, or drugs. Mental or physical fatigue can result in unresponsiveness to stimuli. A person who is tired may not be able to employ his knowledge or even recall necessary details of the situation. The same is true for drugs. Some drugs produce or inhibit behavior changes, although they are temporary. Excessive alcohol may blot out the name of a person or many of the events of an evening. Finally, habituation dulls man's responsiveness to those stimuli that continually confront him. The noise of a busy street will keep one awake, but after a period of time, one becomes oblivious to it. In fact, should traffic cease, that silence might awaken the person from a sound sleep. Then, too, odors from a paper mill are not so obvious after a few hours. In each of these three areas, where learning may not be inferred, however, the case is not clear. Maturation is clearly linked to learning as Piaget reminds us, the line between instincts and learned behaviors is not clear, and some drugs can permanently influence learning and memory.

Teaching, on the other hand, implies *intent*: the intention of someone to bring about specified changes in the learning and behavior of others. The classroom instructor is the classic example of a teacher, but our culture is virtually filled with teachers. The advertisement in the newspaper that describes a new substance and its pleasant effects on a person intends to bring about change in your behavior—to cause you to purchase that product. The TV weatherman, describing "highs" and "fronts" obviously is attempting to teach us about weather conditions and patterns, not merely forecasting tomorrow's rainstorm.

Consider, however, the case of the child who touches the hot stove, burns himself, and never does it again. He may have *learned* about hot stoves, but the *stove* did not *teach* him. The stove did not intend to teach; thus there are cases of learning without teaching. In a classroom, the instructor may teach the mathematics concept $(a + b)\ (a - b) = (a - b)^2$ in such a way that half the class learned the principle and could describe and use it, whereas the other half did not. Did the teacher "half teach"? Certainly not; his intention was clear, but he was *successful* with only half of his students. Although our goal is *successful teaching* in schools, rationally we must recognize that not all teaching is equally successful and that teaching and learning are not two sides of the same coin.

[12] Ibid., pp. 245–246.

Several basic conditions are important to learning—contiguity, practice, reinforcement, generalization, and discrimination.[13] Recognizing their relevance is important for the successful teacher. *Contiguity* is the almost simultaneous occurrence of stimuli and responses. In one of Pavlov's experiments, the dog salivated at the sound of a bell because he had been fed previously when the bell tolled. The stimulus (bell) was contiguous with the response (salivation). A flash card with *dog* written on it is shown to a child; he verbalizes "dog." The card is the stimulus; the spoken word, the response. Teaching includes many such instances where the stimulus object is presented at the same time the child is expected to respond. In many disadvantaged homes, children do not associate words and objects because the word is not uttered by the child or adult when the object is identified.

In the definition of learning, *reinforced practice* was included. Practice is the repetition of a response in the presence of the stimulus. Typically, few things are retained over a period of time unless they are practiced. Practice is of diminishing importance in more complex learning. In learning to solve problems, for example, one finds it of less importance if other conditions are properly attended to.

Reinforcement is a major condition in most learning. "Overwhelming evidence supports this generalization: Rewarded responses tend to be repeated in given situations; unrewarded responses tend to be discontinued. This statement, known as the law of *effect*, was first enunciated by the great American educational psychologist, Thorndike"[14] in 1911. Verplanck[15] conducted a study in which subjects were reinforced when they expressed an opinion. Opinion statements began with phrases such as "I think . . . ," "I believe . . . ," or "It seems to me." Although the subjects were unaware of the influence being used, experimenters nodded their heads, smiled, listened more attentively, and readily agreed whenever an opinion was expressed. The number of opinion statements increased with such reinforcement; and when it was withdrawn, the number of such statements sharply decreased.

Van Wagenen and Travers[16] studied the effects of overt response and being reinforced for it. They tried to determine whether nonparticipating students learned as much as participating students, those who made overt responses and obtained direct feedback. Working with pupils who were

[13] This section has heavily drawn from De Cecco, op. cit., pp. 248–263.

[14] De Cecco, op. cit., p. 250.

[15] William Verplanck, "The Control of the Content of Conversation: Reinforcement of Statements of Opinions," *Journal of Abnormal and Social Psychology*, 51:668–676 (1955).

[16] R. Keith Van Wagenen and Robert M. W. Travers, "Learning Under Conditions of Director and Vicarious Reinforcement" *Journal of Educational Psychology*, 54:356–362 (1963).

learning the correct English term for a written German word, they found that children in the direct learning group learned and retained more than those who did not interact with the teacher.

Extinction occurs when a reinforcer is withheld to weaken a response. With animals, the relationship between extinction procedures, such as nonfeeding (stimulus) and response, is clearly evident. With human beings, it is far more complex. We do not know how the individual will interpret negative reward or lack of reinforcement. The pupil whose classroom behavior is negatively reinforced may consider the *attention* he is receiving from the teacher to be positive reinforcement. Thus, punishing him may actually be encouraging him to continue the behavior for which he is being punished.

The fourth condition related to learning is *generalization*. Learning that is limited to a series of discrete incidents would be extremely limiting. The human capacity to generalize from one situation to another permits a multiplier effect in learning. The person who learns the color blue learns to respond "blue" to various hues of blue while ignoring red or yellow as potential blues. After studying several number sentences, such as $4 + 2 = 2 + 4$, $18 + 9 = 9 + 18$, $4\frac{1}{2} + \frac{1}{3} = \frac{1}{3} + 4\frac{1}{2}$, the child generalizes that the sum remains the same when the order of addends is changed (commutative property). This generalization can then be applied in numerous other situations. Some generalizations in social contexts lead to stereotyping ethnic or religious groups and can become a negative rather than positive factor.

Discrimination, the fifth and last condition, occurs when the individual makes different responses to two or more stimuli. A child chooses red and ignores pink, adds when he sees the $+$ sign and multiplies when the $\times$ is included in the number sentence, distinguishes between a collie and a shepherd, and plays soccer with a ball different from the one used when he plays basketball or baseball. In each case, he has learned to discriminate.

The tendency for most teachers is to emphasize discrimination over generalization. Travers[17] writes that "many teachers will mark unusual metaphors and figures of speech as 'unclear' and will suppress generalization in the literary field. Despite the efforts to the contrary on the part of many school officials, the prosaic development of precise discriminations generally takes precedence as an objective over free, creative, and often undisciplined expression."

In this section we have explored some basic notions of learning and teaching. As we define them, they are separate but interrelated phenomena. During the past six decades, a number of educators have attempted to draw specific instructional strategies from theories of learning. For the

[17] Robert W. Travers, *Essentials of Learning* (New York: Macmillan, 1963), p. 123.

most part, the relation remains shrouded in mystery with conflicting research findings and theories. Human behavior is too complex and the factors that impinge on it too numerous and unrecognized for it to be readily changed. Teaching, too, is a complex of teacher and environmental variables, which interrelate with learning in so many imperceived ways that if a direct relation does exist, it is obscured.

CHILD GROWTH AND DEVELOPMENT

During the 1930s Olson and others explored the developmental patterns of children. They examined teeth, measured bones, weighed children, tested them, and projected a norm and deviation pattern for children that for the first time provided a data base line. These studies and others that have been conducted during the past thirty years lead to several generalizations that are appropriate for teachers who are designing instructional programs.

During the preschool years, the emotional development of the child is all-important. The way he interrelates with his nuclear family and the ways others react to him make an imprint, which he never loses. The neighborhood group provides feedback to him on his own worth, and as he grows older, he spends successively more time with them. The child's intellectual development changes more during this time than at any other point in his life. He learns hundreds of words of vocabulary and concepts and learns to speak in sentences. In many families, where intellectual endeavors are not cherished, he is not positively rewarded or encouraged to explore the intellectual; what is learned is happenstance, whereas other families rejoice over the child's every accomplishment, new idea, new word, new mathematical achievement.

The five- to eight-year-old experiences two changes as he enters school: a social change as he leaves the home and a mental change as he begins formal educational studies. These two changes press him to accept a new life-style, a new value system, and heavy new concepts and relationships (both human and intellectual). By five his handedness is usually well established and should not be changed. His permanent teeth begin to appear, with the two upper front teeth coming in about age six, looking like "two giant tombstones" as one teacher described them. During this time, many children dislike experiencing new situations alone; they prefer group explorations, for in the group they find some security. They are continually active and need constant change of pace in the classroom.

From ages nine to twelve, the so-called preadolescent stage, the child experiences slow steady physical growth, preparing for the extremely rapid adolescent spurt. Girls' growth precedes that of boys by several months, and in later preadolescence, girls may tower above boys—physically, emotionally, and mentally. Boys develop gangs; indeed, many specialists refer to this as the "gang age." Sports are important to them, providing competitive games and group activities. The cleavage between the sexes is never greater than at this period. Intellectually, children tend to search for more data in matters they are interested in, to explore, and to publicize their exploration. They have, for the most part, learned the basic information securing skills of reading and basic arithmetic and can apply them to social and scientific situations.

Developmental Theories of Jean Piaget

While American psychologists were studying the growth and development of children, a Swiss learning theorist, Jean Piaget, was conducting monumental research and building a pervasive theory of learning and development. Although he began his studies in 1919, his work was not recognized in the United States until the early 1960s.

During that time Piaget had interviewed thousands of children, asking them to attempt to perform a series of structured tasks and recording their responses. From these studies he concluded that all children pass through a set sequence of developmental stages.

An important concept for Piaget is conservation. In a classic conservation experiment, he pours liquid into two containers of equal size and shape. The child examines them and affirms that the quantity in each is the same (Figure 2–1 A). The liquid in one container is then poured into a wide flat dish (Figure 2–1 B), and the child asked to decide whether the containers still have equal quantities of liquid. Before conservation, the child will assert that one or the other of the containers now has more liquid (as though the shape of the containers determined the amount). After the child is able to "conserve" quantity, he recognizes that container shape does not affect the amount of the liquid.

Clay is used in a second experiment. The child examines two balls of clay (Figure 2–2 A) and removes bits and remolds them until he believes they contain the same amount of material. One ball is then reshaped as a long thin cylinder (Figure 2–2 B) and a flat patty (Figure 2–2 C) and also broken into several pieces (Figure 2–2 D).

After each operation, the child is asked to compare the mass of the

A   B

Figure 2–1. *Piagetian Conservation of Volume Experiment.*

A   B   C   D

FIGURE 2–2. *Piagetian Conservation Experiment with Clay.*

two materials. After conservation, the child recognizes that shape has no effect on the mass of the clay.

Such experiments may be used by teachers as indicators of the child's intellectual development. Piaget has described hundreds of such experiments in his many books. Reading those books and trying some of his experiments provide an excellent aid to understanding children. Care should be exercised, however, in the way questions are asked (so as not to reveal bias or correct answer), in the procedures used in the study, and in the conclusions drawn from them. Interviewers for Piaget train for months before their protocols are used in research findings.

Children develop through a series of continuous transformations of thought processes. According to Piaget, a developmental stage is a period of months or years that are somewhat homogeneous in thought processes, yet each stage is evolutionary as the child evolves into more mature concept achievement. Because of this continuous change process, specific stages are often difficult to delineate. Piaget has specified four primary stages of development: sensorimotor, preoperational thought, concrete operations, and formal operations. Although the *sequence* in which children pass through these stages remains constant, the *ages* at which each completes the various stages vary.

Sensorimotor intelligence develops from birth to the appearance of language, that is, until about two years of age. This stage is characterized by the progressive acquisition of the permanence of an object. By the end of this period, the child has acquired what Piaget calls "object permanency"; he no longer acts as if objects disappear completely once they are out of his sight.

By the end of the first month of life, not only can the child perceive relatively minor differences in the object he views, but he shows a preference for complex patterns over simple stimuli. For example, when shown two rectangular frames of equivalent size, but one with a crosshatch design on its interior, the young child will make definite movements toward the more complex rectangle. During the latter part of the sensorimotor intelligence stage, the child becomes aware of "self-other," and language begins to appear.

The second stage, *preoperational thought*, extends from approximately two years of age to six or seven years. Thought at this stage is based largely on perception; but only one aspect, dimension, or relation usually is considered in making judgments. In the experiment with liquids in containers of various shapes, the child at this stage will consider only height, for example, in making his decision—thus neglecting other dimensions and drawing an incorrect conclusion.

Mental manipulation at this stage merely represents what the child would actually be doing physically with objects. As he progresses through this stage, he is increasingly able to internalize symbols and to discriminate between words and the concrete objects they represent.

In the third stage, *concrete operations*, the child considers two or three dimensions simultaneously instead of successively. This stage lasts from six or seven to eleven or twelve years of age. The child no longer centers his attention on a particular aspect of an action and is able to mentally reverse his action. Piaget defines operation as an action of the child that (1) can be internalized symbolically, (2) is reversible, and (3) is never isolated. During the concrete-operations stage, the child develops conservation of concepts in this order—substance, weight, and volume. No longer would he be confused by the change in container size or by the different shapes of clay.

About the age of seven the concrete-operations child develops an interest in playing games involving rules and is capable of cooperative endeavor with others. Committees, task forces, and projects are interesting and stimulating for him; puzzles and complex competitive games may be used effectively by the teacher.

Beginning at about eleven or twelve years of age, the child develops abstract thought patterns and enters the fourth stage, *formal operations*. In contrast to the child whose thought still depends upon manipulation of concrete objects, the adolescent is capable of forming hypotheses and deducing all the possible consequences from them. These new operational abilities open unlimited possibilities for him to participate in the development of abstract thought.

The most important general property of formal operational thought, the one from which Piaget derives all others, concerns the *real* versus the *possible*. When approaching a new problem, the child begins by formulating all the possibilities and then determining which ones are substantiated through experimentation and logical analysis.

Many educators have turned to Piaget's theory to seek help for new pedagogical approaches. His theories and experiments, however, are not directly convertible into teaching strategies and materials. Whereas a child's reaction to a Piagetian task will enable a well-trained researcher to determine the child's intellectual level, these same tasks or experiments cannot be directly taught to the child and thus improve his competencies. Although Piaget's experiments should not be taught in the elementary school, the results of his experimentation provide viable and important new insights for teachers.

LEARNING BY REINFORCEMENT

A contemporary psychologist, B. F. Skinner, believes that behavior can be controlled by outside forces, thus basically disregarding maturation and growth theories. Skinner controls behavior by reinforcement, which is immediately applied. The reinforcement or reward may take the form of praise, food, prizes, or attention. For example, Bill's teacher cheers and praises him each time he plays baseball, for he knows Bill is not good, but will improve with practice.

The theories of behavior modification of Skinner have influenced all aspects of our society. Nursery school teachers dispense chocolates for right answers or approved behavior. Football coaches give players a decal to paste on their helmet as a reward for outstanding play. Tokens are provided patients in mental institutions for maintaining personal cleanliness; tokens, in turn, can be exchanged for things the patient wants.

Skinner criticizes traditional teaching methods, pointing out three major shortcomings:

1. The lapse of time between action and reinforcement. Some exam papers are not handed back until days after they are written.
2. Lack of a well-organized presentation of stages in teaching complex skills.
3. The relative infrequency of reinforcement. With large classes and split sessions, the amount of reinforcement a teacher can supply to individual students is severely limited.[18]

As an alternative to traditional instruction, Skinner proposes programmed instruction. In this application of his learning theories, the ultimate goal is formulated in terms of student behavior. Working backward, the designer of instruction sets up a series of small steps, which lead to the desired behavior. Each step is such that students are successful in completing it, and step by step they are "programmed" toward the objective. Each step, referred to as a frame, includes a statement, question, or stimulator, to which the learner makes a response and gets immediate feedback.

Skinner claims programmed instruction has these advantages:

1. The learner is actively responding, practicing, and testing each step of what he has learned. Each succeeding frame adds to the learning foundation of the preceding frames.
2. The learner gets immediate knowledge of results.

[18] Richard L. Morgan, "Theories of Learning," *Psychology: An Individualized Course* (New York: Westinghouse Learning Corp., 1972), p. 9.

3. The learner moves at his own pace.
4. The method is obviously one-to-one instruction, not mass education.[19]

If you examine a programmed textbook or the frames in a teaching machine, the first few frames would seem clear, simple, and self-evident. Indeed, if you work sequentially through all steps, they appear to progress slowly and are easily mastered. But try skipping ahead several dozen frames. They appear much more difficult without the intermediate steps.

CONTENT ANALYSIS AND ROBERT GAGNÉ

Robert Gagné is concerned with the content of the disciplines being learned. For him, observable changes in human behavior comprise the only criteria for inferring that learning has occurred. He would expect teachers to state their objectives specifically and behaviorally. Each of these objectives could then be classified as to its complexity and level, with supporting or prerequisites identified through objective-analysis. When a person can perform a certain function under specified conditions, Gagné concludes that he has demonstrated that he has learned something; he has demonstrated a "capability." Figure 2–3 illustrates a capability with its prerequisite capabilities. The individual who has demonstrated Capability A, for example, is assured of also possessing capabilities B, C, D, E, and F. Furthermore, if he were unable to demonstrate Capability A, the teacher could simply test him on prerequisites to determine possible problem areas.

Gagné identified eight types of learning: *problem-solving, rule-learning, concept-learning, discrimination-learning, verbal association, chaining, stimulus-response learning, and signal-learning.*[20] If a capability, for ex-

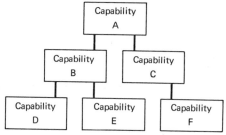

FIGURE 2–3. *Gagnéan Pyramid of Competencies.*

[19] Ibid.
[20] Robert M. Gagné, *The Conditions of Learning,* 2nd ed. (New York: Holt, 1970).

ample is *problem-solving*, then the learner must first develop lower-order capabilities such as *rule-learning* and *concept-learning*. These, in turn, require *discrimination-learning* and *signal-learning*. Thus, it is possible to take a specified behavior that the student is to learn and through analysis complete a map of the prerequisites necessary. The resulting pattern identifies what is to be taught and in what order.

The eight types of learning identified by Gagné are described in the following paragraphs, beginning with the most elemental and progressing to the most complex.

In *signal-learning*, the individual acquires a conditioned response to a given signal. Signal-learning responses are diffuse and emotional, and the learning is involuntary. Pavlov's studies of conditioned responses in animals illustrate signal learning. Salivation of a dog upon hearing food poured into his feeding dish or the withdrawal of a hand upon sight of a hot object are two examples of conditioned responses.

Whereas the responses from signal-learning are diffuse and emotional, the responses in *stimulus-response learning* (often called operant conditioning) are fairly precise physical movements. Training a dog to sit, stay, or lie down are examples of stimulus-response learning. At first the trainer may use a leash, but later the verbal commands suffice to achieve a response.

In *chaining*, frequently called skill learning, the person links together two or more units of stimulus-response learning. Limited to nonverbal sequences, chaining requires proper sequence of stimulus-response units. The elementary school child acquires many such chains: running, writing, catching, or throwing, each of which requires a set of sequenced muscular responses.

Verbal association is a form of chaining, but the links are verbal units. The simplest verbal association is that of naming an object, which involves a chain with two links—observing an object and identifying it.

With *multiple discrimination*, the student learns different responses to stimuli that identify something, but that might be confused with other similar things or phenomena. Identifying the make and model of automobiles or the names of children in a classroom are examples of multiple discrimination learning. In each case, the learner associates each automobile model or individual person with its or his distinctive appearance and correct name, and with no other name.

Concept-learning involves responding to stimuli in terms of their *abstract* characteristics, such as position, shape, color, and number, as opposed to concrete physical properties. The concept of *chair* may be expanded by the learner to refer to chairs that are padded, straight-backed, rocking chairs, of various colors, of various sizes, with or without arms.

Principle-learning requires the person to relate two or more concepts. Principles are, in effect, chains of concepts. One example of principle-learning is found in the relation of a circle's circumference to its diameter ($C = \pi d$). Several separate concepts (circumferences, pi, and diameter) are linked together.

In the set of events called *problem-solving*, an individual uses principles to achieve a goal. In the process of achieving this goal, however, he becomes capable of new performances, using his new knowledge. What is learned, according to Gagné, is a higher-order principle, which is the combined product of two or more lower-order principles.

PROCESS LEARNING AND JEROME BRUNER

Whereas Robert Gagné's emphasis is primarily on the *product* of learning, Jerome Bruner emphasizes the *process* of learning.[21] Bruner summarizes his psychology of learning in these words:

> to instruct someone in these disciplines is not a matter of getting them to commit the results in mind; rather, it is to teach him to participate in the process that makes possible the establishment of knowledge. We teach a subject, not to produce little living libraries from the subject, but rather to get a student to think mathematically for himself, to consider matters as a historian does, to take part in the process, not a product.[22]

For Gagné, the crucial question is, "*What* do you want the child to know?" For Bruner, it seems to be, "*How* do you want the child to know?" Gagné emphasizes *learning*, whether it is by *discovery*, by review, or by practice. For Bruner, the emphasis is on learning by discovery. It is the *method* of learning that is significant.

Bruner, like Piaget, emphasizes the child as a developing organism. Each child passes through stages that are biologically determined and age-related. Instruction is dependent primarily upon the developmental level that the student has attained.

The curriculum that is derived from the learning theories of Gagné and Bruner leads to programs that are quite different. Gagné emphasizes problem-solving as the highest level of learning, with lower levels prerequisite to it. For him, the appropriate sequence in learning (and thus teaching) is from these lower levels toward problem-solving. The teacher begins with simple ideas, relates them, builds on them, and works toward the more complex capabilities sought.

[21] Adapted from Lee S. Shulman, "Perspectives on the Psychology of Learning and the Teaching of Mathematics," in *Improving Mathematics Education for Elementary School Teachers*, ed. by W. Robert Houston (East Lansing, Mich.: Michigan State U., 1968), pp. 23–37.

[22] Jerome S. Bruner, *Toward A Theory of Instruction* (Cambridge, Mass.: Harvard U.P., 1966).

Bruner, on the other hand, *begins* with problem-solving, which, in turn, leads to the development of necessary skills. He poses a problem to be solved and uses it as the catalyst to motivate learners to develop the necessary prerequisite skills.

Program concepts and sequences included in the elementary school curriculum generally have been based on the theory espoused by Robert Gagné. Simple concepts are introduced early, then built on in a spiraling curriculum, which begins with kindergarten and continues throughout formal schooling. Textbooks and curriculum guides reflect this logical analysis and instructional sequence. Programmed text follow these same procedures, but are typically more explicit and include a greater number of finely defined prerequisites, make fewer assumptions about exterior learning experiences, and exert greater control in the mode of presentation.

Several instructional programs based on the theories of Bruner have been introduced in recent years. In mathematics, the mathematics lab has permitted pupils to explore and discover concepts and relations as they manipulated materials and solved problems. "Man, A Course of Study," was designed by Bruner to introduce children to social studies concepts through problem-solving, whereas the American Association for the Advancement of Sciences (AAAS) has written and tested "Science, A Process Approach." In practice, divergent learning theories contribute to each of these programs, for even as they emphasize process, the content is sequenced, and the selected problems are made relevant for children of particular ages.

These various programs reflect the varied concepts of Bruner, Piaget, and Gagné on *readiness*. Over a decade has passed since Jerome Bruner wrote ". . . any subject can be taught effectively in some intellectually honest form to any child at any stage of development."[23] Bruner supported this famous statement by noting that the basic ideas of science and mathematics and the basic themes that give form to life and literature are very simple. Only when these ideas are formalized in terms of equations and complex verbal statements do they become incomprehensible to the young child. Inhelder, who worked closely with Piaget for many years, feels that instruction should accommodate the natural thought processes. Basic ideas of geometry, for example, are appropriate for children in the elementary school provided they are intuitively pursued through material that the child can handle himself rather than through formal mathematical postulates and theorems.

Piaget's experiments led him to relate readiness to the child's maturation and development. Bruner's famous pronouncement, on the other hand, captures his attitude relative to readiness; he feels that the child is always ready for a concept in some manner. Gagné, however, relates readi-

---

[23] Jerome S. Bruner, *The Process of Education* (Cambridge, Mass.: Harvard U.P., 1962), p. 33.

ness to the development of subskills and subconcepts rather than to the child.

SUMMARY

In this chapter, we have explored several basic concepts of human nature and behavior related to teaching. These have been drawn from several of the behavioral sciences and suggest some aspects for continued study. Each child's social and cultural perspective provides a screen through which he views the world. Teachers who attend only to his school-related behavior neglect a vital part of his life and an opportunity to influence him. Time spent studying and exploring basic concepts of the behavioral sciences is time well spent, for it provides not only a deeper understanding of human interaction, but provides a rationale for making educational decisions as well.

SUGGESTED ACTIVITIES

A. In addition to reading about community influence, engage in activities that will give you firsthand experience with communities. The following list was devised for teachers by staff at the University of Toledo.[24] Engaging in *some* of them will be a real learning experience. However, choose from the list, carefully keeping in mind the community, the school, and the staff.

1. Spend a few hours in a prowl car traveling with a team of policemen in the inner city. Listen to the squad car radio. Ask questions. If the policemen park and walk the beat, walk with them.

2. Sit in the waiting room of the maternity ward of a county or city hospital whose patients are mostly charity cases. Strike up a conversation with other people in the waiting room.

3. Go to a magistrate's court, and keep a list of the kinds of cases brought before the magistrate. Who are the people? How are they handled? Write how you would feel if in their position.

4. Hand out birth control or other health department pamphlets on a ghetto street or, with permission, in a store. Strike up conversations with the recipients.

5. Go to an inner city elementary school, and read a story to a child in kindergarten or first grade. The child must be held on your lap.

[24] "Individually Guided Education," *Principals' Handbook*, (Melbourne, Fla.: Institute for Development of Educational Activities, 1971), pp. 61–63.

6. Wear old clothes and sit in the waiting room of a state employment office. Listen, observe, and talk to some of the people sitting next to you. Read the announcements on the bulletin board.
7. Attend church services some Sunday in a storefront church.
8. Compare prices and quality of a list of grocery staples at the chain store supermarket in your own neighborhood with one of the same chain in the inner city. Also check the weights on about five or six prepackaged meat or produce items.
9. Borrow a portable tape recorder and interview an elderly citizen who has lived in an inner-city neighborhood for ten or more years.
10. Live for three days on the amount of money a typical welfare recipient receives.
11. Spend a morning making the rounds with a visiting public health nurse.
12. Go to a community health center, and take a seat in line. Observe attitudes of personnel who work there. Talk to some of the patients coming for help.
13. Read at least two issues of black newspapers published in your own city or in New York, Los Angeles, or Chicago.
14. Compare the prices on the same brands and models of record players, TV sets, and transistor radios at your local appliance or department store with those on display in a credit store in the inner city.
15. Find someone with a real complaint about a landlord who does not give him heat or has not repaired a leaking roof or broken toilet, and offer to help him get it fixed. Call city hall for help.
16. Attend a meeting of a civic group.
17. Go to a local food store at the time that an inner-city school is dismissed. Buy something the kids buy, and drink or eat it slowly while listening and observing.
18. Get on a suburban-bound bus some morning and ride with black domestics going out to clean houses in the suburbs.
19. Spend a morning with a visiting teacher in making visits to inner-city school neighborhood homes.
20. Go to a Goodwill Industries store, and see how many school clothes you could buy for a family of four children if you had $15 to spend.
21. Turn off the heat two nights in December or February, and spend the night in a cold house. Reflect on feelings about this experience.
22. Read *Manchild in the Promised Land*, or *Go Tell It on the Mountain*, or some other book that tells what it is like to grow up black in America.
23. Stop into a neighborhood bar in the inner city for a drink. Anticipate the reaction a black person might get if he came into a bar in your own neighborhood.

24. Help chaperon a dance at a community center, central city YMCA, or neighborhood center.
25. Do a survey on the manner in which garbage is collected on various streets in the inner city. Compare with the garbage pickup service in your own neighborhood.
26. Go to the local campaign headquarters for the Democratic and Republican parties, and work a couple of hours with local people, either canvassing, distributing leaflets, or making phone calls.
27. Buy lunch in a black restaurant during the noontime rush, when you will be the only white person there.
28. Go to an area into which black families are beginning to move. Survey the names of the real estate companies who have signs up. Try to find out if they have been involved in blockbusting in other areas of the city.
29. Interview a deputy from the sheriff's department or representative of the board of health on some recent evictions or repossessions he has handled.
30. Talk to school dropouts, and find out what they think needs to be changed to keep kids in school.
31. Make up a large poster on rat control, and ask an inner-city apartment house superintendent if you can tack it up in the hallway of his building.
32. Take a batch of dirty clothes, and wash it in the Laundromat in the ghetto area. Talk to any of the other mothers waiting for their wash.
33. Send a letter to the editor of a daily newspaper on any discovery you made during your exposure to these activities.
34. Ask a middle-class black or Spanish-American (possibly a student in one of your classes) where he or she lives. Find out, also, about any experience the child's parents have had with real estate agents.
35. Join with three other teachers, and do a survey of people who were relocated owing to urban renewal.
36. Go to a small, independent food store in the neighborhood a week before welfare checks come out, and note the prices on various staples. Go back on the day the checks come out, and see if there are any price changes.
37. If you are male, get a haircut from a black barber.
38. Answer an advertisement in the newspaper for a common laborer's job or for assembly work in a factory. Fill out the application blank. Go for the interview if one is called for.
B. Read from one of Piaget's books, select two experiments, and test at least ten children. Then write a report of your experience, describing how the children responded and what you concluded, but also what *you* learned about interviewing children.

C. Using the learning ladder of Gagné, classify concepts in a mathematics, science, or social studies textbook. Relate your classification to passages in the textbook, and report on developmental sequences. To what extent are they interrelated and cyclical? Do they progress from simple to more complex?

D. Observe children during school hours; what do they do and how do they relate with other persons? One example of such an observation schedule would observe Child A during the first five minutes of each hour, Child B during the next five minutes, and Child C during the third five-minute period. Continuing these observations during an entire day promotes varied settings for data collection.

SELECTED BIBLIOGRAPHY

Bany, Mary A., and Lois V. Johnson. *Educational Social Psychology.* New York: Macmillan Publishing Co., Inc., 1975.

Beals, Alan R. *Culture in Process.* New York: Holt, Rinehart & Winston, Inc., 1967.

Bernard, Harold W. *Human Development in Western Culture.* Boston: Allyn & Bacon, Inc., 1966.

Bruner, Jerome S., et al. *Studies in Cognitive Growth.* New York: John Wiley & Sons, Inc., 1968.

De Cecco, John P. *The Psychology of Learning and Instruction.* Englewood Cliffs, N.J.: Prentice-Hall, Inc., 1968.

Dietterich, Paul M. *The Pattern of Power.* Nashville, Tenn.: The Graded Press, 1971.

Gagné, Robert M. *The Conditions of Learning.* New York: Holt, Rinehart & Winston, Inc., 1965.

Hamacheck, Don E. *Human Dynamics in Psychology and Education.* Boston: Allyn & Bacon, Inc., 1968.

Illich, Ivan. *Deschooling Society.* New York: Harper and Row, Publishers, 1970.

Köhler, Wolfgang. *Gestalt Psychology.* New York: Mentor Books, 1947.

Lovell, K. *The Growth of Basic Mathematical and Scientific Concepts in Children.* New York: Philosophical Library, 1961.

Lugo, James O., and Gerald L. Hershey. *Human Development: Mutidisciplinary Approaches to the Psychology of Individual Growth.* New York: Macmillan Publishing Co., Inc., 1974.

Margolin, Edythe. *Sociocultural Elements in Early Childhood Education.* New York: Macmillan Publishing Co., Inc., 1974.

Piaget, Jean. *The Child's Concept of Number.* New York: W. W. Norton & Company, Inc., 1965.

——— *The Language and Thought of the Child.* Cleveland: Meridian, 1955.

——— *Science of Education and the Psychology of the Child.* New York: Orion, 1970.

Raths, Louis, et al. *Values and Teaching.* Columbus, Ohio: Charles E. Merrill Publishers, 1966.

Chapter 3

Developing Instructional Objectives

In preceding chapters, the changing nature of society and current concepts of the behavioral sciences and their relevance to teaching have been discussed. This background should be of assistance in looking at contemporary elementary schools in a more realistic perspective.

The elementary school program is a mixture of *what has been, what is,* and *what is to be.* Since the beginning of American public education, change has been a continuing characteristic of the elementary school. This changing nature of elementary education undoubtedly has not been as rapid as some wished, but perhaps it has been more rapid than others desired. The program of school experiences for a particular group of youngsters at any given period of time has been, and still is, primarily dependent upon the goals or objectives we hold important for elementary education.

A review of the history of our schools indicates that they have deep roots in American culture and are products of the times. If goals are to be significant, schools must change with the times. In recent years, alterations and innovations in elementary schools have been introduced at an increasingly rapid rate. A few of these may have been the result of some teacher's whim, dream, hunch, or vivid imagination. For the most part, however, current theories and practices in elementary education are goal-oriented. If objectives are to result in appropriate pupil experiences and effective educational programs, teachers must be sensitive to cultural and societal changes, such as economic, social, political, and technological, and must be able to apply current knowledge and concepts from the behavioral science field. The preceding chapter was devoted to the behavioral sciences, particularly sociology, philosophy, and psychology, and to the way concepts from these areas relate to the learning-teaching process.

The following cognitive objectives should guide your reading of this chapter:

1. The reader will be able to trace the evaluation of elementary school objectives.
2. The reader will be familiar with various sources that affect the formulation of objectives.
3. The reader will be able to describe the need for writing objectives.
4. The reader will be able to state objectives clearly and precisely.
5. The reader will be able to formulate cognitive and also affective and psychomotor objectives.

Evolution of Objectives

Education has evolved in focus with American society beginning with the inevitable changes in the objectives of education that the immigrants brought to America from Europe. Likewise, the transition from a wilderness existence through a largely rural, agrarian society to an increasingly urban, technological, space-age society has produced changes in educational objectives.

Regardless of the number of years or the level of the elementary school in which a person teaches, the primary instructional objective undoubtedly has been to provide the best possible educational experiences for boys and girls. The teacher has selected content, chosen learning-teaching materials, and pursued teaching strategies in an effort to achieve one or more objectives. In the future, as in the past, we must be willing to change elementary school objectives in terms of changing needs. This is as it should be because schools are societal institutions; and the more dynamic a society, the greater the need for change will be in its schools.

The objectives in the early years of the American elementary schools were primarily concerned with mental growth and were generally stated in terms of knowledge and skills. Educational experiences in the schools of colonial America were limited primarily to instruction in reading and religion to fulfill the colonists' objective of propagating their religious teachings. For many years school experiences continued to be rather limited—generally to the three Rs and for a select group of pupils, many of whom never completed an elementary school program. Of course, the need for a comprehensive formal education by all people was not as great in colonial days as it is today. However, an enlightened and responsible citizenry as a requisite for active participation in a democratic society was encouraged by many of our early leaders.

Even though the importance of educating the masses was recognized early, there were few people properly trained to offer anything more than a rudimentary education. Some arithmetic—mainly ciphering—and some writing, in addition to reading and speaking, were introduced into the early schools; but generally these areas were not thought to be very important. These subjects were also considered difficult, and most of the teaching done in them was by roving teachers called arithmetickers and scriveners. In discussing fundamental concepts of education, Crow and Crow remind us ". . . that the essentials of a rudimentary education for the masses, even through the eighteenth century, were considered to be spelling, reading, and religion; therefore these usually were the only subjects taught in the fixed, free school."[1]

The objectives and scope of elementary education have seen many changes since the dame schools and the Latin grammar school. Beginning about the latter part of the eighteenth century, the value of education seemed to become more evident to people of all socioeconomic levels. Since that time greater efforts have been made to broaden and refine educational objectives, expand school offerings, and improve instructional methods. The educational philosophy that contributed much to this progress was influenced greatly by early educational reforms and by writers such as Johann Pestalozzi, Johann Herbart, Friedrich Froebel, William James, Horace Mann, and Henry Barnard.

Consistently, as American societal life has become more complex, increasing opportunities have been made available for people to continue their education by extending public educational institutions through the university level; and more people from all strata of society are seeking extended education. Perhaps more than ever before, there exists a critical need to help youngsters to gain a better education than in any prior generation, to live personally satisfying lives, and to make wise decisions competently and confidently in an increasingly complex world.

True, the elementary school no longer has the major responsibility for providing almost entirely the formal education for the United States populace.[2] Yet, today, the elementary school has perhaps an even more difficult task of providing the *foundation for continuing education.* An important objective of elementary education, then, is to help people learn *how to learn* and *how to experience personal enjoyment in learning.* We should

[1] Lester D. Crow and Alice Crow, *Introduction To Education* (New York: Am. Bk. Co., 1966), p. 14.

[2] An extended discussion of this responsibility will be found in Ch. 4.

strive for an elementary school that is more concerned with developing in each pupil a real *zest* for learning than for a specific quantity of learning or for what is learned. In an era when those on the accountability bandwagon are pushing for minimum performance in the various subject areas, teachers also need to be concerned with promoting continuing development of the enthusiastic, exploratory nature children generally have when they first enter school.

Since the school is continuing to enroll more children representing a wider strata of socioeconomic backgrounds, an important objective must be to provide educational experiences that meet a diversity of pupil and societal needs and interests. Within this context, teachers in the elementary school have the responsibility of helping pupils grow and develop in many areas. Mental growth or intellectual development is still an important objective; but the child's physical, social, emotional, aesthetic, and character growth and development are also concerns of the contemporary school. In discussing educational objectives, Foshay states, "In pursuing high intellectual goals, it is not necessary for a moment that we overlook the fact that man, in addition to being an intellectual creature, is also an emotional, a social, an aesthetic, a biological, a creative and a spiritual creature."[3]

If our school objectives are going to square with our democratic society ideal of helping each individual realize his true potential, the elementary school has a much more diverse role now than it did in the early part of this century.

NEED FOR OBJECTIVES

Teachers are being asked to become involved in updating, redefining, revising, or perhaps constructing for the first time a set of objectives for the school in which they are employed. Lest the task of formulating a set of objectives be considered "just another chore," teachers should understand the need for, or the functions of, objectives.

Because teaching is basically a decision-making process, a teacher has to make many decisions every day regarding the learner and some aspect of his program of experiences. These decisions, for the most part, are made in terms of values and outcomes we hold important for elementary school children.

Well-defined objectives offer the teacher a sound basis for making valid decisions relative to desired changes in the learner. An objective as

[3] Arthur W. Foshay, "A Modest Proposal for the Improvement of Education," *What are the Sources of Curriculum? A Symposium* (Washington, D.C.: Association for Supervision and Curriculum Development, 1962), p. 13.

defined by Robert Mager is "an *intent* communicated by a statement describing a proposed change in a learner—a statement of what the learner is to be like when he has successfully completed a learning experience."[4]

Teachers are well aware that the main intent of instruction is to help children learn—to effect a change in the learner's behavior. When requested to write objectives, however, many teachers ask such questions as: "Why do we need to do that when we already know what we want children to learn?" "Would we not accomplish more if we spent the time with the youngsters?" "Won't a set of objectives hamper my freedom in doing what I want with pupils?" For the most part, questions similar to the above are raised by teachers who do not understand the functions of objectives. When there is an understanding of the functions of objectives, generally the need becomes apparent. We need objectives because of the functions they perform.

Objectives Give Direction

Objectives serve as sign posts or direction signals, so that both the teacher and the learner know where they are headed. Learning can be educative or miseducative. Objectives direct our educational efforts toward the development of learning behavior that is desirable for the individual and for the society in which the school exists. The process of arriving at objectives can point the direction toward providing better continuity of educational experiences through elementary, middle, and high school.

Objectives Guide the Selection of Experiences

Possible learning activities that can become a part of the school program are infinite; therefore, choices must be made. The chance of selecting an activity that is the most appropriate and most satisfying for the learner is much greater if it is chosen in terms of the purpose or purposes it is supposed to achieve. Checking activities against objectives helps to assure the teacher that the experience fits the maturity level of the pupil. When the learner recognizes the experience will move him toward achieving the objective, he is more likely to view the activity "as worth doing." Objectives help us determine priorities, so that the experiences we provide are those that are most valuable.

Objectives Help to Provide Balance

Educational programs are made up of many components. Owing to teacher interest or pressures from some source, one or more of these components may be emphasized to the almost complete neglect of others. For instance, in the past, many children have been shortchanged in science

---

[4] Robert F. Mager, *Preparing Instructional Objectives* (Palo Alto, Calif.: Fearon, 1962), p. 3.

experiences because teachers did not feel well prepared in, or did not enjoy teaching in, that area.

Pressure groups can easily influence some educators to overemphasize one area, for example, the academic or intellectual development to the neglect of other important developmental areas. A teacher may unconsciously give undue emphasis to certain experiences. For instance, in mathematics, children may be spending much of their time on abstract drill and neglecting the development of interest, understanding, ability to attack problems, and the recognition of important relationships.

A comprehensive set of objectives does not insure a balanced program, but it provides the teacher and the learner a means of regularly and quickly checking to determine if one or more desirable learning objectives are being neglected.

Objectives Provide a Foundation for Evaluation

Around the nation the public is demanding more accountability in our schools. As educators continue to find ways to increase monetary support for schools, the citizenry will increasingly want better answers to the question, "What are we getting for our money?"

Without clearly formulated objectives, there is no sound basis for evaluating instructional programs and pupil progress. Educational objectives represent what the school is trying to accomplish—the learning behaviors held important for children. Evaluation consists of determining the progress made toward a previously set objective or objectives. Without well-defined objectives the school does not know where it is headed. If you do not know where you are headed, how can you make a valid evaluation to determine if the goal has been reached, or how far you have moved toward the goal, or whether the most effective means of reaching the goal have been utilized?

Objectives are needed as the foundation for building a comprehensive program for evaluating pupil progress. The program of learning experiences and instructional methods should be evaluated in terms of their contribution to the attainment of the school objectives.

Objectives Provide a Basis for Change

Change simply for change's sake should not be equated with progress. Change in schools should be made in terms of whether the change contributes to a better education for boys and girls. Viewed in this context, the relationship of change and school objectives needs to be considered.

If school objectives are still held to be important after careful examination, but are not being realized, then changes that are needed to make the objectives attainable must be considered. This may call for a change in the kinds of learning experiences selected, in learning materials, or in teaching strategies.

School organizational structure and classroom grouping practices need to be examined frequently to determine if they facilitate to the fullest extent the achievement of professed objectives; if not, change is in order.

Objectives can become static and outmoded unless they are continually reviewed and revised in terms of new experiences and current knowledge relative to children and how they learn and the effect of dynamic societal forces.

Sources of Objectives

In a democratic society where the goal of universal education is to meet a diversity of needs and interests, school personnel should consider as many sources as possible in determining educational objectives. For instance, more realistic statements of objectives might emerge if we rely on ideas from (1) teachers' and school administrators' preparation background and experience, (2) the nature of the learner, (3) the learning process, (4) needs of society, (5) national professional groups and associations, (6) local and state curriculum groups, and (7) subject matter specialists.

Educators' Preparation and Experience

What teachers and administrators have learned through formal professional preparation and actual contact with children rightfully becomes an important factor in determining objectives. Because of their specific preparation and direct experience with children in learning situations, teachers are in a more favorable position than any other segment of our society to crystallize beliefs into sound educational philosophies. Because objectives are really reflections of philosophies, there need to be teacher philosophy inputs into statements of objectives. For this to happen, teachers must actively participate in the formulation of statements of objectives for elementary education.

Nature of the Learner

The first concern in the formulation of objectives is consideration of the child. Understanding the nature of learners at various stages of maturation is needed to determine objectives that are appropriate. Objectives ought to reflect pupils interest, needs, and abilities. Studies in child growth and development provide a source of objectives adaptable to a particular group of learners.

Learning Process

Because objectives function to provide direction in selecting learning experiences and teaching techniques, it is essential that the way in which learning takes place be given serious consideration. Learning occurs when a change of behavior takes place in an individual as a result of an interaction experience with some aspect of his environment. Judicious selection of objectives and related learning experiences are more likely to occur if the teacher understands factors or conditions that affect learning. Some of these are breaking tasks into small steps and providing cues, rewards, reinforcement, and feedback. Writings dealing with the learning process such as those by Piaget, Bruner, Skinner and Gagné are sources of information to be considered when formulating objectives.

Needs of Society

One source of objectives that warrants serious consideration is the society that supports the school. Attitudes, beliefs, and desires, both of American society in general and of the local community, affect the school's objectives. Implications for educational objectives should be ascertained by analyzing such societal factors as population growth; mobility of population; technological developments; social, economic, and political developments; family living patterns; hours in the work week; per capita income; standard of living; use of leisure time; and communication media.

Local and State Groups

Sources of objectives are to be found in many current statements and curriculum guides that have been developed by state departments of education and intermediate and local school districts. This is not to say that these can be transplanted as appropriate for your group of youngsters. The specific needs of each community or specific school must be analyzed. However, objectives developed by other educators can be used as sources of ideas and representations of other people's thinking on similar problems.

National Groups and Associations

During the past five decades several national committees and commissions have developed major statements on educational objectives. These reports have received wide circulation and have served as important sources in the formulation of objectives for many schools and school systems.

OBJECTIVES IN PERSPECTIVE

To understand the contemporary elementary school, teachers must realize that the present program is neither something that just happened nor the result of a wild dream. Education and American society have developed in a close relationship. Growing out of this relationship is the modern elementary school with deep roots in our democratic culture.

Since education throughout the history of our country has been deeply rooted in the ideals, hopes, and aspirations of people, many individuals and groups have, from time to time, formulated educational objectives. Many of these sets of objectives have played an important part in guiding the direction of elementary education and should be studied to understand the evolution of the American elementary school.

For lack of space, one cannot attempt to discuss in detail the many formulated statements of objectives that have appeared in print. However, because of the frequent reference and wide acceptance that have been and continue to be given by public schools to two particular sets of objectives, it is pertinent that they be considered.

The Educational Policies Commission

The Educational Policies Commission of the National Education Association, in 1938, identified four major objectives that they believed public schools ought to accomplish. The essential components of each of these objectives are discussed in detail in separate chapters of *The Purposes of Education in American Democracy*.[5]

The commission recognized that some of the objectives should receive more emphasis at one educational level than another, but it was their clear intent that each of the objectives receive attention at all levels, kindergarten through senior high school. The objectives listed in the commission's report are as follows:

1. The Objectives of Self-realization. The specific objectives were concerned with the inquiring mind, speech, reading, writing, number, sight and hearing, health knowledge, health habits, public health, recreation, intellectual interests, esthetic interests, and character.
2. The Objectives of Human Relationships. The more specific objectives were concerned with respect for humanity, friendship, cooperation, courtesy, appreciation of the home, conservation of the home, homemaking, democracy in the home.
3. The Objectives of Economic Efficiency. The more specific objectives were concerned with work, occupational information, occupational choice, occupational efficiency, occupational adjustment, occupational appreciation, personal economics, consumer judgment, efficiency in buying, and consumer protection.
4. The Objectives of Civic Responsibility. The more specific objectives were concerned with social justice, social activity, social understanding, critical judgment, tolerance, conservation, social applications of science, world citizenship, observance of the law, economic literacy, political citizenship and devotion to democracy.

[5] Educational Policies Commission, *The Purposes of Education in American Democracy* (Washington, D.C.: National Education Association of the United States, 1938).

Mid-century Committee on Outcomes in Elementary Education

The report of the Mid-century Committee on Outcomes in Elementary Education, prepared by Nolan C. Kearney, was published in 1953.[6] It describes what the committee of outstanding educators recommended as obtainable and measurable objectives of elementary education. The nine objectives listed are concerned with the broad areas of (1) physical development, health, and body care; (2) individual, social, and emotional development; (3) ethical behavior, standards, values; (4) social relations; (5) the social world; (6) the physical world; (7) esthetic development; (8) communication; and (9) quantitative relationships. Within each of the above listed areas, the report examines five types of behavioral changes at three age-grade levels. Kearney's grid (Figure 3–1) helps to visualize the intersection of the behavioral continuum.

Even though Kearney's report states that the objectives listed should be integral aspects of an elementary school program, it was recognized that children are complicated creatures and should not necessarily be expected to progress consistently or uniformly toward all objectives.

A recent document entitled *The Common Goals of Michigan Education* stated that ". . . education must help each individual acquire a positive

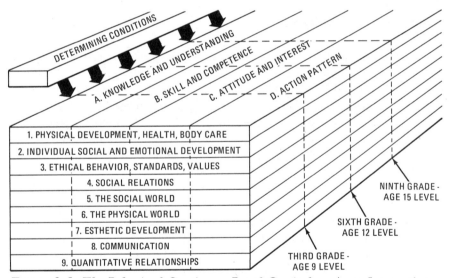

FIGURE 3–1. *The Behavioral Continuum-Broad Curriculum Areas Intersecting Major Behavior Categories. (Chart 2 from* Elementary School Objectives: A Report Prepared for The Mid-Century Committee on Outcomes in Elementary Education, *by Nolan C. Kearney, © 1953 by Russell Sage Foundation.)*

[6] Nolan C. Kearney, *Elementary School Objective* (New York: Russell Sage Foundation, 1953).

attitude toward schools and the learning process so that, as a result of his educational experience, he is able to achieve optimum personal growth, to progress in a worthwhile and rewarding manner in the career of his choice, and to render valuable service to society."[7] In the area of student learning, thirteen specific goals were identified to which the school must relate:[8]

Goal 1. *Basic Skills.* The four basic skills are: (1) the ability to comprehend ideas through reading and listening; (2) the ability to communicate ideas through writing and speaking; (3) the ability to handle mathematical operations and concepts; and (4) the ability to apply rational intellectual processes to the identification, consideration and solution of problems.

Goal 2. *Preparation for a Changing Society.* Education must encourage and prepare the individual to become responsive to the needs created and opportunities afforded by an ever-changing social, economic, and political environment both here and throughout the world.

Goal 3. *Career Preparation.* Education must provide each individual the opportunity to select and prepare for a career of his choice consistent to the optimum degree with his capabilities, aptitudes, and desires, and needs of society.

Goal 4. *Creative, Constructive, and Critical Thinking.* Education must . . . enable the individual to deal effectively with situations and problems which are new to his experience in ways which encourage him to think and act in an independent, self-fulfilling, and responsible manner.

Goal 5. *Sciences, Arts, and Humanities.* . . . to gain knowledge and experience in the area of the natural sciences, the social sciences, the humanities, and the creative and fine arts so that his personal values and approach to living may be enriched by these experiences.

Goal 6. *Physical and Mental Well-Being.* Education must promote the acquisition of good health and safety habits and an understanding of the conditions necessary for physical and mental well-being.

Goal 7. *Self-Worth.* Education must respond to each person's need to develop a positive self-image within the context of his own heritage and within the larger context of the total society.

[7] Michigan Department of Education, *The Common Goals of Michigan Education* (Lansing, Mich.: 1971), p. 5.

[8] Ibid., pp. 5–7.

Goal 8. *Social Skills and Understanding.* Education must provide for each individual an understanding of the value systems, cultures, customs, and histories of his own heritage as well as of others.

Goal 9. *Occupational Skills.* Education must provide for the development of the individual's marketable skills so that a student is assisted in the achievement of his career goals . . .

Goal 10. *Preparation for Family Life.* Education must provide an atmosphere in which each individual will grow in his understanding of and responsiveness to the needs and responsibilities inherent in family life.

Goal 11. *Environmental Quality.* Education must develop within each individual the knowledge and respect necessary for the appreciation, maintenance, protection, and improvement of the physical environment.

Goal 12. *Economic Understanding.* Education must provide that every student will gain a critical understanding of his role as a producer and consumer of goods and services, and of the principles involved in the production of goods and services.

Goal 13. *Continuing Education.* Education must promote an eagerness for learning . . .

These selected sets of objectives have been listed here with exiguous comments, but it is hoped that they will be helpful to the teacher as he plans educational objectives. In considering objectives for the contemporary school, we need to maintain and support existing objectives that are still appropriate, to revise or drop those no longer compatible, and to develop new ones to meet our needs.

There should be and always will be changes in educational objectives to meet the ever-changing needs of the learner and of society. We also know that schools differ from community to community, and what may be considered a high priority objective in one school may not, and perhaps should not, receive a high degree of emphasis in another school. The important thing is that a teacher have clearly in mind carefully determined and significant objectives toward which to work, though realizing that no set of objectives should be considered a panacea.

Writing Objectives

Throughout the years, teachers have talked about educational objectives, goals, or aims. There is little doubt that teachers have formulated many important objectives that they hoped children would achieve. In the past, however, educational objectives have been stated in such vague or general terms that it has been difficult to determine the desired intent of the goals or the degree to which they were attained.

Recently much has been spoken and written about accountability in education and the importance of stating our objectives clearly and more precisely, so that the effectiveness of instructional programs can be evaluated. If we assume that teaching-learning experiences should result in a change in pupil behavior, then instructional objectives need to be stated in specific enough terms to describe the behavior a pupil is expected to exhibit. In other words, when objectives are stated, the present emphasis is to write them in terms of what the pupil should be able to do at the end of the instruction rather than what content is to be covered or what the teacher will do during the instructional period.

The intended learning outcomes of an instructional situation should be clearly communicated to those directly related to the situation—school personnel, pupils, and parents. This is the primary purpose of writing objectives. Too often, when objectives are written, verbs that are open to many interpretations are used to describe expected pupil behavior. Such statements are so meaningless that the intent of the objective is not communicated effectively to others. For instance, using words to describe pupil behavior, such as *knows, comprehends, understands, enjoys, appreciates,* and *believes,* fails to communicate what performance is expected unless the behaviors that show the learner has these qualities are also specified. When you use action verbs such as *write, list, state, make, solve, construct, draw, identify, describe, compare, assemble,* and *differentiate,* your chances are much greater of specifying behavior that can be communicated and evaluated consistently.

Even though we have been careful to select action verbs to describe the behavior expected, it is sometimes necessary to clarify further the behavior by stating the conditions under which the pupil will perform and the criterion of acceptable performance.[9] For example, consider the following three objectives:

1. Understands computation.
2. Can do computation, using subtraction.
3. Given ten examples in subtraction, he can solve eight correctly.

Which of the above objectives communicates what the learner will be *doing* to show that he has achieved the objective? Certainly the first statement, "understands computation," fails to define any behavior that

[9] Robert F. Mager, op. cit., Ch. 5 and 6.

could be accepted as evidence of understanding. The statement is too vague to communicate the intent.

The second objective states clearly what the pupil will be doing. He will be doing computation. The condition under which the behavior will occur is also stated. He will be using subtraction when computing.

The third statement not only identifies the behavioral act and the conditions under which the behavior is to occur, it also defines how well the learner is to perform (criterion of success) when demonstrating he has met the objective.

From the three statements of objectives just considered, do you not agree that the third statement communicates a much clearer picture of what is expected in achieving the objective?

Let us examine another set of objectives:

1. Knows how to punctuate correctly.
2. Given ten sentences containing a variety of punctuation errors, the pupil can, with at least 90 per cent accuracy, correct the punctuation errors.
3. Can write a story with very few punctuation errors.

Which of the statements tell what the pupil will *do,* under what *conditions* the behavior will take place, and the *minimum level* of expected performance? If you chose the second statement, you are correct.

We have illustrated one approach to stating learning outcomes by writing a separate statement for each objective that identifies the specific behavior pupils are to exhibit as evidence of attaining the objective. Another approach to writing objectives, which Gronlund believes holds some advantages over single statements of objectives, is to ". . . state first the general instructional objectives and then to clarify each objective by listing a *sample* of the specific behavior we are willing to accept as evidence of the attainment of that objective."[10] When objectives are written, the emphasis is on forming statements that describe *learning outcomes* (end products) instead of *learning processes*. These learning outcomes would include knowledge, understanding, skills, attitudes, interests, and appreciation.

Gronlund offers the following procedure for defining instructional objectives in behavioral terms:

1. State the general instructional objectives as expected learning outcomes.

[10] Norman E. Gronlund, *Stating Behavioral Objectives for Classroom Instruction* (New York: Macmillan, 1970), p. 4.

2. Place under each general instructional objective a list of specific learning outcomes that describes the terminal behavior students are to demonstrate when they have achieved the objective.
   (a) Begin each specific learning outcome with a verb that specifies definite, observable behavior.
   (b) List a sufficient number of specific learning outcomes under each objective to describe adequately the behavior of students who have achieved the objective.
   (c) Be certain that the behavior in each specific learning outcome is relevant to the objective it describes.
3. When defining the general instructional objectives in terms of specific learning outcomes, revise and refine the original list of objectives as needed.
4. Be careful not to omit complex objectives (e.g., critical thinking, appreciation) simply because they are difficult to define in specific behavioral terms.
5. Consult reference materials for help in identifying the specific types of behavior that are most appropriate for defining the complex objectives.[11]

An example of a general instructional objective followed by a sample of specific behaviors that describe the learning goal is the following:

Understands meaning of sets.
1. Can separate a group of objects into sets.
2. Given several sets, can state a characteristic that describes each set.
3. Distinguishes between equivalent and nonequivalent sets.
4. Distinguishes between equivalent and equal sets.
5. Given two or more sets, can form intersection set.
6. Given two or more sets, can form union set.

The six specific learning outcomes represent a sample of the kinds of behavior a pupil would be expected to demonstrate when he has satisfactorily achieved the general instructional objective "understands meaning of sets." The list of specific learning outcomes also illustrates what is meant by the general or complex objective.

Writing statements with clarity is not an easy task, especially in the affective and the psychomotor domains. Anytime one attempts to describe behavior in terms that communicate, one is faced with the problem of semantics. One means of increasing the probability of stating objectives clearly and precisely is to develop a taxonomy of objectives—a classification

[11] Ibid., p. 17.

of learner behavior directly related to expected outcomes. You will find the handbooks on taxonomies of educational objectives by Bloom (1956) and Krathwohl (1964) *helpful guides* in classifying objectives and in selecting terms that convey the intent of a particular objective. Developing a taxonomy of educational objectives ". . . requires the selection of an appropriate list of symbols to represent all the major types of education outcomes. Next, there is the task of defining these symbols with sufficient precision to permit and facilitate communication about these phenomena among teachers, administrators, curriculum workers, testers, educational research workers, and others who are likely to use the taxonomy. Finally, there is the task of trying the classification and securing the consensus of the educational workers who wish to use the taxonomy.[12]

Innumerable objectives could be written in terms of the variety of educational outcomes. In order to restrict the number of objectives sufficiently so that there is a chance to achieve them, but at the same time make sure we are not neglecting important outcomes of education, we need some type of classification system. Bloom, Krathwohl, and their associates have classified objectives into three major domains: *cognitive domain, affective domain,* and *psychomotor domain.* Although pupil behaviors in each of these domains probably is not mutually exclusive, it would seem helpful to consider those behaviors that are more closely associate, at least by definition, to one domain than another.

The intended behaviors in the *cognitive domain* (emphasizing mental acts such as recall or recognition of knowledge, understanding, and thinking skills) were organized into six major classes and arranged into a hierarchial order of behavior from knowledge, the simplest level, to evaluation, the most complex level. The six major categories of objectives were divided into subclasses from the simplest level of behavior to the most complex. *The cognitive domain objectives* in outline form are[13]

1. Knowledge—involves the recognition and recall of facts, processes, patterns, or specific settings.
   Knowledge of Specifics
   Knowledge of Terminology
   Knowledge of Specific Facts
   Knowledge of Ways and Means of Dealing with Specifics
   Knowledge of Conventions
   Knowledge of Trends and Sequences
   Knowledge of Classifications and Categories
   Knowledge of Criteria

---

[12] *Taxonomy of Educational Objectives,* ed. by Benjamin S. Bloom (New York: McKay, 1956), p. 11.
[13] *Taxonomy of Educational Objectives* (op. cit.), pp. 201–207.

Knowledge of Methodology
Knowledge of the Universals and Abstractions in a Field
Knowledge of Principles and Generalizations
Knowledge of Theories and Structures

Examples of objectives in the area of knowledge:

Is able to say the letters of the alphabet in order.
Can name the three most densely populated states in the United States.
Is able to recall all the basic facts of addition.

2. Comprehension—represents lowest level of understanding. Involves translating, interpreting, summarizing, and recognizing consequences of what is being communicated without necessarily seeing its full implications.
   Translation
   Interpretation
   Extrapolation

Examples of objectives in the area of comprehension:

Given pairs of sets, the learner can identify which pairs are equivalent; can interpret social data.
Given a paragraph, the learner can pick out words beginning with the same consonant.

3. Application—involves abstracting ideas, theories, principles, methods, and so forth, and using these in a different situation.

Examples of objectives in the area of application:

Uses a calibrated ruler to make precise measurements.
The learner can read correctly from a paragraph, eight out of ten words with the *tion* ending.

4. Analysis—involves dividing a whole into its constituent parts to clarify the relationships between the ideas.
   Analysis of Elements
   Analysis of Relationships
   Analysis of Organizational Principles

Examples of objectives in the area of analysis:

Shows interest in mathematics by using free time at the math table.
Demonstrates positive attitude toward reading by the quantity and variety of books read voluntarily.
After reading a section of a book, is able to state relationships among ideas.

5. Synthesis—involves arranging parts into a whole constituting a pattern or structure not clearly in the original entity.
   Production of Unique Communication

Production of a Plan, or Proposed Set of Operations
Derivation of a Set of Abstract Relations
Examples of objectives in the area of synthesis:
Can write a mathematical generalization, for example, describing the commutative property.
After studying pertinent data on community X, the learner can state proposals for reducing juvenile delinquency in the community.

6. Evaluation—involves using a set of criteria to assess and make decisions about material and methods for specific purposes.
Judgments in Terms of Internal Evidence
Judgments in Terms of External Criteria
Examples of objectives in the area of evaluation:
Is able to identify logical fallacies in arguments.
Can apply a given set of criteria to judge a completed art project.
Assesses the consequences of alternative actions.

The *affective domain* behaviors (emphasizing the emotional processes such as attitudes, interests, values, appreciations, and personal adjustments) were organized into five major categories and arranged into a hierarchial order from the simplest behavior, receiving, to the most complex behavior, characterization. These five categories were further divided into subcategories from the simplest to the most complex. The *affective domain objectives* in outline form are[14]

1. Receiving—involves an awareness and willingness to receive and attend to certain phenomena and stimuli.
Awareness
Willingness to Receive
Controlled or Selected Attention
Examples of objectives in the area of receiving:
When presented with several different sounds, is able to differentiate the sounds.
Shows an awareness of the interdependence of classroom members.
Listens attentively to and respects the viewpoints of others.

2. Responding—involves actively attending to and a low-level-commitment reaction to certain stimuli or phenomena.
Acquiescence in Responding
Willingness to Respond
Satisfaction in Response

[14] For a condensed version of the taxonomy, see David R. Krathwohl et al., *Taxonomy of Educational Objectives* (New York: McKay, 1964), pp. 176–185.

Examples of objectives in the area of responding:
Accepts responsibility for personal safety and the safety of others.
Takes pleasure in conversing with many different kinds of people.
Enjoys writing poetry and reading it to others.

   3. Valuing—involves consistency or response that a phenomenon has worth and the learner's behavior can be associated with a belief or attitude.
   Acceptance of a Value
   Preference for a Value
   Commitment

Examples of objectives in the area of valuing:
Deliberately examines a variety of viewpoints on controversial issues before forming an opinion on them.
Writes letters to the editor on issues he feels strongly about.

   4. Organization—involves consistency, stability, and internalization of the belief or value.
   Conceptualization of a Value
   Organization of a Value System

Examples of objectives in the area of organization:
Attempts to determine the characteristics of a tree leaf.
Forms judgments about the general public's responsibility to conserve energy.
Tries to regulate eating habits in accordance with sound health principles.

   5. Characterization by a value or value complex—involves persistent behavior that is consistent with a set of internalized values to which the individual is committed.
   Generalized Set
   Characterization

Examples of objectives in the area of characterization by a value or value complex:
Readily revises opinions and judgments in light of new evidence.
Shows consideration of, and respect for, others.
Accepts logically drawn conclusions.

The *psychomotor domain* behaviors emphasize physical responses or motor skills involving neuromuscular coordination such as manipulation of objects, athletic accomplishments, writing, speaking, singing, playing musical instrument, and art endeavors. At the present time a taxonomy of psychomotor objectives has not been completed. However, the area is receiving increasing attention. "The following variables can be used to classify those behaviors which can be included in the psychomotor domain."[15]

1. Frequency—rate or number of times an individual performs a psychomotor skill.

Examples of objectives:

Can bounce and catch a rubber ball fifty times in one minute.

Is able to walk a balance beam (walking board) carrying a glass full of water without spilling the water three times out of four tries.

From a reclining position on back, pupil can do twenty sit-ups in thirty seconds.

2. Energy—amount of strength or power an individual needs to perform a psychomotor skill.

Examples of objectives:

Can hold a regular-sized crayon and color an area inside a closed curve without coloring outside the line.

Is able to extend right arm and left leg at the same time and hold the position for fifteen seconds.

Can jump a rope for two minutes in a rhythmic motion, alternating legs.

3. Duration—length of time an individual persists in performing a psychomotor skill.

Examples of objectives:

Given a list of words on cards, the learner will sit at a table for a prolonged period arranging the cards into categories, e.g., fruits, toys, animals, and so forth.

Using modeling clay, the learner spends a great part of his free time making letters and arranging the letters into words.

The learner voluntarily sits at math table and arranges colored blocks into various patterns.

In discussing the *psychomotor domain,* Hoover and Hollingsworth offer the following four levels in ordered sequence from the simple to the complex.[16]

1. Observing—observing an experienced person perform with particular attention to the sequence and end product.

[15] *Developing and Writing Behavioral Objectives* ed. by Robert J. Armstrong, Terry D. Cornell, Robert E. Kraner, and E. Wayne Robertson (Tucson, Ariz.: Educational Innovators Press, 1968), p.33.

[16] Kenneth H. Hoover and Paul Hollingsworth, *Learning and Teaching in the Elementary School* (Boston: Allyn, 1970), pp. 57–58.

Examples of objectives:

Watches the teacher's aide place six colored cards in a pattern of red, white, blue, red, white, blue.

Observes attentively as the teacher uses a pencil to draw a ring, then uses a crayon to color area inside the ring.

2. Imitating—makes deliberate effort to follow directions and sequence.

Examples of objectives:

Given six colored cards, the learner attempts to place them in a pattern of red, white, blue, red, white, blue.

The learner tries using a pencil to make a ring and to color the inside of the ring, using a crayon.

3. Practicing—can perform entire sequence more or less habitually.

Examples of objectives:

The learner can arrange six cards into a pattern of red, white, blue, red, white, blue more or less habitually.

Using a pencil, the learner makes a ring and colors the inside without much effort.

4. Adapting—continues to improve by adapting minor details that influence his total performance.

Examples of objectives:

Given four cards, one each of a different color, the learner can arrange the cards in a given pattern.

The learner uses a pencil to make an enclosed figure and colors the inside using a crayon.

Much disagreement exists as to the best way of stating educational objectives. In fact, there probably is no one best way to state all objectives.[17] The emphasis in this section is on encouraging you to use all available sources to formulate statements of objectives as clearly as possible. "It is quite possible that the use of behavioral referents is not the only way or the best way of achieving meaningfulness. It appears, however, that it is the best method now available."[18] Whether objectives are behavioral or nonbehavioral, specific or general, and whether the outcomes can be or should be formally measured, the objectives still need to be stated clearly, so that there is no question on the part of either the teacher or the learner as to the intent and the kinds of evidence that indicate fulfillment.

[17] Selected references designed to assist you to write specific objectives are included in the bibliography. You are encouraged to select one or more of these instructional guides and develop expertise in writing objectives.

[18] Ralph H. Ojemann, "Should Educational Objectives Be Stated in Behavioral Terms?" *Elementary School Journal*, 69, No. 5:234 (Feb. 1969).

IMPLEMENTING OBJECTIVES

We have stressed the importance of writing objectives in clear terms. But unless objectives can be implemented, the best-written set of objectives will have little effect upon the education of children. For objectives to have operative significance, they must become the *guiding* forces behind a teacher's thinking and action as he plans and organizes learning experiences to achieve hoped-for educational outcomes. What are these hoped-for outcomes? There are all sorts of learner behaviors. Shall we attempt to implement objectives that describe the widest possible range of behaviors, or shall we set priorities? Shall most of our objectives be at the lower level, or shall they range from the simple to the complex? Shall objectives be geared to a group of pupils or to the individual learner? Shall objectives be stated in general terms or in specific terms? Shall most of the objectives be in the cognitive domain, or should there be a balance among the three domain classifications? Are the objectives in harmony with current educational philosophy and basic principles of learning? Once you have answers to questions such as the above, the chances are good for arriving at a set of efficacious objectives and of translating them into a program of experiences where the desired outcomes are reasonably attainable.

In arriving at a set of objectives toward which to strive for implementation, we favor first formulating a rather comprehensive list of outcomes. Modify and revise this list until the objectives are stated operationally. Identify and discard those that are relatively unimportant. Carefully analyze the remaining list and select a set of operational objectives that

1. Represent long, medium, and short range goals.
2. Present a reasonable balance among cognitive, affective, and psychomotor outcomes.
3. Have a good chance of being attained.
4. Are relevant in terms of the general society, the school setting, and the particular learners.
5. Contain some outcomes and standards of performance deemed essential for the total group and some concerned primarily with individual development.

Teachers are under much criticism presently for promoting the trivial, for stressing cognitive learnings while devoting little attention to the affective and psychomotor areas of development, and for not maintaining relevant instructional programs. The process we have outlined for arriving at a set of operational objectives will lead to effective instructional results and the removal of much of the criticism just mentioned.

In implementing objectives, we must carefully consider the divergent differences of learners. The question is often asked, "How can I write objectives that have any appropriateness until I am working with a group of children?" Any set of objectives should be considered tentative. However, a well-thought-through set of objectives formulated prior to working with a classroom of youngsters provides guidelines within which to make adjustments to meet group and individual needs in the important areas of learning. You may well find that a general behavioral goal is applicable to all pupils, but alternatives can be provided through the specified levels of behavior and the criterion levels of expected performance. Just as one objective may be applicable to several pupils, analysis of an objective may reveal that it can contribute to more than one desirable outcome. For objectives to be appropriate and capable of being implemented, you, at all times, must be ready to modify them in terms of the particular group of youngsters and in light of new experiences and knowledge.

SUMMARY

In attempting to provide educational experiences that meet a diversity of pupil and societal needs and interests, an elementary school teacher has to make many decisions regarding the learner and aspects of his learning experiences. A set of carefully defined objectives stated in terms that clearly and concisely communicate the desired changes in the learner offers the teacher a sound basis for making valid decisions.

Clearly stated objectives that have a good chance of being realized are needed as direction signals, so that both the teacher and the learner know that their efforts are leading toward the development of learning behavior that is desirable for the individual and for the society in which the school exists.

What may be a realistic objective for one group of youngsters may not be for another, or what may be a valid educational objective today may become quickly outmoded. Objectives need to be continually reviewed and revised or changed in terms of current knowledge relative to children and how they learn, and the effect of societal changes.

SUGGESTED ACTIVITIES

1. Choose a concept usually taught in one of the subject matter areas (mathematics, social studies, language arts), and write a single statement objective that describes the specific behavior pupils are to exhibit as evidence of achieving the objective. Include in the statement the criterion of acceptable performance.

2. Using Gronlund's procedure, write two general instructional objectives appropriate for pupils at your teaching interest level. Follow each objective with a sample of specific pupil behaviors that you would accept as evidence the learning outcome has been attained.

3. Bloom and his associates have classified educational objectives into three domains—cognitive, affective, and psychomotor. Choose a particular area of the elementary school—lower, middle or upper—and write two objectives for each of the domains, with one of the objectives illustrating the simplest level of behavior and the other the most complex level.

4. Much disagreement exist as to whether all objectives should be expressed in specific behavioral terms. Many people argue that the outcomes of some objectives we hold important are so unpredictable that they can not be expressed in behavioral terms. Either defend or refute this statement with supporting evidence.

5. José has been added to your fourth grade today. His parents are migrant workers and will probably move to another seasonal job in a few weeks —and another school for José. You have temporarily seated him with your slowest group pending more evaluation data. Pat joined your class yesterday, having returned from a three-year stay in Switzerland. She has presented the room with a homecoming gift of a portable digital calculator designed and manufactured by her father's company. With her knowledge of four languages, she has been temporarily assigned to the advanced group of the class. If you were developing objectives that would include individual interests, needs, and abilities, how would you determine those for José and Pat? How would the objectives differ? How would they be similar? Could you accommodate the other class members with those objectives developed for the two new class members? Explain.

SELECTED BIBLIOGRAPHY

Dickens, M. E. "Values, Schools, and Human Development." *Clearing House* (Apr. 1974), 473–77.

Eisner, E. W. "Educational Objectives: Help or Hindrance?" *Educational Review*, 75 (Autumn 1967), 250–260.

Foshay, Arthur W. "A Modest Proposal for the Improvement of Education." *What Are the Sources of Curriculum?* A Symposium. Washington, D.C.: Association for Supervision and Curriculum Development, 1962.

Gagné, Robert M. *The Conditions of Learning.* New York: Holt, Rinehart & Winston, Inc., 1965.

Gronlund, Norman E. *Stating Behavioral Objectives for Classroom Instruction.* New York: Macmillan Publishing Co., Inc., 1970.

Hoover, Kenneth H., and Paul M. Hollingsworth. *Learning and Teaching in the Elementary School*. Boston: Allyn & Bacon, Inc., 1970.

Howe, H. "Start With The Schools: Developing a More Humane Society." *Saturday Review of Education* (March 1973).

Krathwohl, David R., Benjamin S. Bloom, and Bethram B. Masia. *Taxonomy of Educational Objectives. Handbook II: Affective Domain*. New York: David McKay Co., Inc., 1964.

Mager, Robert F. *Preparing Instructional Objectives*. Palo Alto, Calif.: Fearon Publishers, Inc., 1962.

Margolin, Edythe. *Sociocultural Elements in Early Childhood Education*. New York: Macmillan Publishing Co., Inc., 1974.

McAshan, H. H. *Writing Behavioral Objectives*. New York: Harper and Row, Publishers, 1970.

Ojemann, Ralph H. "Should Educational Objectives Be Stated in Behavioral Terms?" *Elementary School Journal*, **68**, No. 5 (Feb. 1968), 223–31, and **69**, No. 5 (Feb. 1969), 229–35.

Scrivens, G. H., and E. G. Scrivens. "Behavioral Objectives and the Learning Psyche." *Clearing House* (May 1973), 529–31.

Tanner, Daniel. *Using Behavioral Objectives in the Classroom*. New York: Macmillan Publishing Co., Inc., 1972.

Taxonomy of Educational Objectives. Handbook I: Cognitive Domain. Ed. by Benjamin S. Bloom. New York: David McKay Co., Inc., 1956.

Chapter 4

The Evolving Curriculum

Past and present historians have identified specific technological developments as influential in accelerating the development of mankind and his
societies. Breakthroughs in man's "discovery" include fire, the wheel, the
architectural arch, gunpowder, barbed wire, fossil fuels in locomotion, and,
more recently, nuclear energy. Yet it is quite probable that seers of the
twenty-first and following centuries will consider the inclusion of *formal
education* as the development of this century that has had the most decided impact upon mankind and the evolutionary products that will mark
the success of its efforts.

As an instrument of society, the school centers upon curriculum as
the organization of its total efforts to further the pattern of its continuous
development. Flexible if not fragile in its fluctuation between societal expectation and evaluated outcomes, the curriculum provides the support
for the cumulative efforts of a society bent upon improving its position in
the struggle for success in an environment that now realistically includes
other members of the solar system. To encompass the extent of these
developments is a formidable task. To sample or test the contribution of
integrated segments poses questions of selection, integral cooperation, and
evaluation to mention a few qualifiers. One senses the frustration of the
Far Eastern fable participants who in their limited sensory exploration
attempt to describe an elephant solely on the physical properties of the

trunk, the tail, or a solitary leg. For the curriculum *is* a total effort of mankind to survive and as such presents an everchanging, multidimensional approach to all members of society. Admittedly, the beginning portion of this organizational pattern represented by the elementary school conveniently provides a limitation for study; but with some Asian populations now growing in numbers by an excess of two children per minute, the problems of society are developing at a heretofore unbelievable rate.

Alvin Toffler challenges us with one of the problems of our success, namely, the members of our population who "live faster" than those who live around them. This segment of 2 to 3 per cent of the world population (future group) must somehow be accommodated with the 25 per cent who are found in today's urban areas (present group) as well as the remaining 70 per cent of the population who are primarily agricultural (past group).[1] Obviously, the curriculum developments of education must promote a multiheaded salvo to realize contact with an *ever-expanding* spectrum of needs. Truthfully, the success of curricular effort spawns increasing problems; and as elementary education is an integral portion of the success, it also must respond to the problems of the society it serves.

We, by necessity, will be somewhat selective in our examination; but as a result of our study, you should be able to do the following:

1. Sense and appreciate the emphasis placed upon a child-centered curriculum.
2. Recognize the intricate interrelationship between the needs and problems of society and the objectives of elementary curriculum.
3. Appreciate the contributions of past curricular efforts to the evolving pattern now developing in the schools.
4. Identify and differentiate between various grouping plans prevalent in school organizations.
5. Grasp the significance of change in the increased responsibility of the teacher in initiating and responding to contemporary challenges.

THE DEVELOPING ELEMENTARY SCHOOL CURRICULUM

Traditionally, the expectations of the school community centered upon pupil development of communication arts and manipulative skills. Formal education had been seen as a somewhat demanding process of transmitting skills and knowledge from one successful generation to another. But in the process of extending a minimum level of civilization from the east to

[1] Alvin Toffler, *Future Shock* (New York: Random, 1970), pp. 37–39.

the western shorelines of the United States in the late nineteenth century, it was recognized that the school could also serve as a means of initiating desired changes in the society itself. In more recent years, massive private, state, and federal funds have been expended for education practices and procedures in the schools so as to influence change in selected segments of society.

As could be expected, opposition has developed to the use of tax-supported schools specifically to influence designated segments of society toward preconceived social goals. There are those who profess that the curriculum of a school encompasses all activities of youth designed to aid them in adapting to the political, social, and economic demands of their environments. Singular efforts to overemphasize portions of this curriculum for social remediation attempts at the expense of others tend to distort an optimal school program. Conversely, those supporting the school's endorsement of a strong social mission in its curriculum point to excesses in specialized fields of academic skills and disciplines.

If we accept the predication that the nation's schools will continue to be in the focus of both local and federal agencies, it would seem obvious that the elementary and middle school curricula will increasingly seek a developmental pattern of activities for a widely divergent group of educational and societal needs.

The Challenge of the Present

Earlier discussion has documented the necessity for assuming a degree of unpredictability in the evolving tax-supported elementary school as it and its staff move continually to adapt to the changes in society and its expectations. The early 1970s, for example, witnesses an unprecedented increase in demands by the schools upon their local and state tax supports, the former triggering renewed protests against the property tax as the basis for local school revenues. With the ratio of urban to rural school youth increasing from two to one to three to one in a twenty-year period, the distribution of the tax moneys in state support systems was also challenged. With support ingredients such as these joining with the other urban-nonurban societal issues of school bussing, racial and ethnic pupil-population mix, sex education programs, and the evolution-nonevolution philosophical controversies, the school curriculum could be considered anything but static.

Teachers and their impact upon curriculum practices are also involved in the contemporary scene, especially as related to those possessing advanced-degree, work and teaching experiences. The late 1920s and early 1930s frequently recorded school boards bargaining with individual prospective teachers for services at the lowest possible annual salary. With teaching positions scarce, it was not uncommon for two or more teachers seeking a professional vacancy continually to lower their minimum salary expectations as the other proposed a lower minimum. With the development of professional salary schedules based heavily upon teacher preparation, experience, and merit performance in the classroom, school boards are now somewhat more curtailed in individual bargaining efforts. Too often, a retiring teacher's position is now filled with a professional replacement at the bottom of the salary position. The replacement's low salary position conserves tax dollars when compared to the higher position of his predecessor—but valuable curriculum support is lost with the experience, advanced degree work, and system knowledgeableness departing with the retiring teacher. With the continuation of restricted tax support and the present professional salary system, school curricula will suffer as the better prepared, experienced staff are replaced by those who must assume a trial-and-error approach to reach the status of professional confidence so necessary to adjusting to individual and group curricular needs. A compounding factor of particular importance to the beginning teacher is the now diminishing mobility of teachers, who formerly experienced successful teaching in various school systems and challenging locales as a desirable outcome of mastering differing curricular philosophies or accommodating changing personal and family obligations. Unless some drastic change develops in school funding or in teacher supply, few school systems will be able to maintain a teacher personnel policy that will provide somewhat equal qualifications for the replacement of teachers who are leaving the system. Success in encouraging graduate level teacher experiences in curricula design and innovation seemingly will be limited mainly to tenured staff already in service. Recruitment of advanced-degree, experienced, and meritorious teachers for specific curriculum improvement will be denied both to the schools and the teaching profession unless some modification of financial supports system or professional salary schedules is forthcoming.

In short, teachers and their role have changed as has society. At present a wide spectrum of innovations and sometimes conflicting practices are proposed for the improvement of the school curriculum. In the process, completely new systems and strategies are evolving, with flexibility and evaluation a minimum expectancy of the individual teacher. The hand of past teaching experiences is there to be held—but only for encouragement and support as the elementary teacher reaches forward for a better understanding of tomorrow's elementary child.

Growth and Development

Both the culture and the elementary curriculum of the United States possess qualities of uniqueness. The early elementary schools of this country, however, were often crude transplants from prevailing school systems of Europe. Although the American southern colonies favored the English system and retained its philosophy in their respective schools, educational historians give more consideration to the northern colonies and their Reformation-type schooling. As products of the European religious Reformation, adults of the early colonies of the North emphasized the religious motive as a basic philosophy of colony life. Their schools, in turn, reflected community values and expectations. It is interesting to consider that without such an emphasis upon religion, the character of the early American and European schools might have been somewhat different. Consider the educational scene without the action of Luther and the Reformation, without the emphasis upon each individual's own Bible material, without Gutenberg and the printing press, without conflict in religious practices. Consider education without the intangibles of sympathy and firmness of religious convictions—all relate to a sequence of events quite basic to the emergence of a formal elementary school.

There is some disagreement about the effects of the so-called Deluder Satan Act of 1647, which is credited by some historians with establishing the public elementary school. Although many of its implications are debatable, it is obvious that the Massachusetts action did establish the responsibility of government for education.[2] From the beginnings of mass-produced reading materials in 1500 to governmental, tax-supported responsibility for education in 1647 is a chronological bridge of less than 150 years. Yet the implications and growth of the period are notable. Ragan has set forth the transitional stages in Table 4-1.

Significant Change

No longer was the elementary school curriculum primarily for mastery of the process for reading the Bible. The narrowness of teaching and the fragmentation of the curriculum in 1600 were now in 1976 altered by constitutional responsibility to all of the people represented in the governmental structure. Outmoded was the feeling that elementary education was primarily a family decision and that the quality, if not the quantity, was determined by the family's social position and income. Public schools were *not* to be populated primarily by paupers, by immigrant workers, or by boys. It would require many years for a majority of schools to move to this position of philosophy and practice in the United States. Once achieved, however, frequent backward steps will continue to occur. There exists considerable professional concern that the present plight of many urban schools represents a regressive development. Nevertheless, the curriculum was roughly shaped for use in the crucial years of growth and development with national and community change.

[2] For an interesting viewpoint see Henry S. Commager's introduction to William H. McGuffey, *McGuffey's Fifth Eclectic Reader—1879 Edition* (New York: New American Library, 1962).

TABLE 4-1
Developmental Pattern of American Education*

	Colonial: 1647–1776	National: 1777–1876	Regrouping and Growth: 1877–1929	Contemporary Role: 1930—
DOMINANT MOTIVE	RELIGIOUS	POLITICAL	ECONOMIC	SOCIAL-INTELLECTUAL
Content	Reading, writing, spelling, arithmetic, prayers, hymns, catechism	Reading, writing, spelling, arithmetic, physiology, hygiene, grammar, history, geography, drawing, music, agriculture, good behavior	Reading, writing, spelling, arithmetic, physiology, hygiene, English, grammar, language, history, Constitution of U.S., geography, music art and handiwork, citizenship, manual training, homemaking, civics, physical education, nature study, literature, good behavior	Language arts, social studies, arithmetic, science, arts and crafts, health and physical education
Administrative organization	Nongraded	Nongraded	Graded Departmental Platoon	Grade divisions disappearing
Typical schools	Dame schools Apprentice schools Reading and writing schools Ciphering schools	Kindergartens Eight-year elementary schools	Nursery schools Kindergartens Six-year elementary schools	Early childhood Later childhood

Methods	Individual memoriza-tion	Monitorial Group instruction	Recitation Supervised study Units (individual) Project method	Recitation Experience units Committees
Curriculum organization	Separate subjects	Separate subjects	Separate subjects Correlation Fusion	Separate subjects Correlation Integration
Professional education of teachers	None	Normal schools	Teachers colleges Schools of education In-service education	Experiments in functional types of teacher-education
Control of curriculum making	Local	Local and state	State departments of education National committees	National committees State committees Local committees
Materials of instruction	Hornbook New England Primer	Nongraded textbooks	State-adopted texts for each subject	Textbooks, libraries, excursions, audio-visual materials

* From *Modern Elementary Curriculum*, Fourth Edition, by William B. Ragan and Gene D. Shepherd. Copyright 1953, © 1960, 1966, 1971 by Holt, Rinehart and Winston, Publishers. Reprinted by permission of Holt, Rinehart and Winston, Publishers.

Herbert von Borch, born in China and educated in Germany, identifies the responsibility of education in America as the product of both political and social development:

> millions of children of barely assimilated parents had to be brought up to be American citizens, and the public and parochial schools became an agency for eliminating the distinctions between minorities. This they could hardly do by sticking to a classical curriculum confined to literature and the sciences. So it came about that the American school child was expected to learn social relations, good manners, the rules of the democratic game and civic-mindedness along with the mastering of Shakespeare and algebra. The needs of society came first, and the child was not so much educated as socially "adjusted."[3]

CURRICULUM DEVELOPMENT AND CONTRAST

It is presumptuous to assume that one living in the present era of civilization can in a given moment return mentally to an age of the past and comprehend the contribution of the elementary school curriculum to the intricate developments of an adventurous society and nation. Adding to the difficulty were the conflicting societal expectations. The role of the school varied widely. Teachers and materials used in the schools of Virginia were quite different from those of the Connecticut schools. Both areas influenced the early teaching of the Western schools, but the amalgamation of the latter eventually produced a school-community relationship that personified a model or example of a close, integrated school community. Yet this high-water level was not achieved quickly.

Because of its recency, the curriculum of the rural "little red schoolhouse" has been frequently examined. These small, one-room (and not always red) schools were, in fact, a sophisticated form of school and curriculum that evolved with the westward movement. Their heritage was rich with potential. First, the teacher was frequently hired for the position as a full-time employee, although in some instances he was a part-time minister or a student preparing for another profession. Second, the school population represented the adult inhabitants of a given section of land. By law, the school land was reserved for this purpose and served to attract land buyers with families, just as modern suburban housing developers include nearby school facilities as a selling feature. Third, the school and the teacher were accountable to the school board and the community. As a product of rural elementary schools, they had rather firm convictions about

[3] Patrick O'Donovan et al., *The United States* (New York: Time-Life Books, 1965), p. 154.

the normal procedure for an elementary school and its occupants. Fourth, the pupils' ages were somewhat similar. In the early years of the public elementary school, the school population would run chronologically from five to fifty years. In the 150 years starting with 1700, the "backlog" of potential pupils often brought together child and adult working to achieve common goals. Learning to "cipher" (arithmetic) with an extreme range of chronological and intellectual ages frequently was more than the inept teacher could accommodate. The harsh discipline and the rigor of assignments were not necessarily points of development, but of survival. Fifth, the curriculum made some valid assumptions that skills would be emphasized, but that other pupil and community values would be included. Webster's *Elementary Spelling Book,*[4] better known as the *Blue Backed Speller,* indicates a partial concern for appropriate materials and by doing so provides insight into the occupation and interests of the pupil. The revised edition of the speller appeared in 1880 and indicated as a major change the "substitution of living words in the place of those words which have become obsolete."[5]

In the early pages of the speller, the illustrative sentences pointed to the prevailing age and environment.

> She fed the old hen.
> The hen was fed by her.
> See how the hen can run.
> I met him in the lot.
> The cow was in the lot.
> See how hot the sun is.
> It is hot today.
> See the dog run to me.
> She has a new hat.
> She put the hat on the bed.
> Did you get my hat?
> I did not get the hat.
> My hat is on the peg.
> She may go and get my hat.
> I will go and see the man.
> He sits on a tin box.[6]

Later portions of the book involve illustrated sections for the more sophisticated speller-reader, but frequently utilized material foreign to the community:

[4] Noah Webster, *The Elementary Spelling Book,* rev. (New York: American Book Co., 1880), p. 7.
[5] Ibid., p. 7.
[6] Ibid., p. 19.

The stag is the male of the red deer. He is a mild and harmless animal, bearing a noble attire of horns, which are shed and renewed every year. His form is light and elegant, and he runs with great rapidity. The female is called a hind; and the fawn or young deer, when his horns appear, is called a pricket or brocket.[7]

Few if any pupils saw a red deer, which is indigenous to Scotland, in their lifetime. The only generic term applicable to the deer of the West was *fawn*, yet Webster, in attempting to break a prevailing pattern of memorization, introduced identification and descriptions of animals generally foreign to the interests or community-experience patterns of rural youth.

Other examples used in early school materials are common to our national history, but many attest to the development of a curriculum with at least a rudimentary awareness of community growth and expectation. Spell downs, school Christmas programs, spelling bees, cakewalks, boarding teachers, teacherages—all these and others centered on school-community actions that made what occurred in school more than a predicated series of events carried on in a somewhat sterile environment. With this evolvement came a growing concern for identifying the role of the school in terms of activities moving beyond a transmission of academic information. Charles sees this in a societal development:

> Human beings are bundles of potential when they are born. These potentials can become realized through educative processes. Informally, a child learns much, mainly about the way of life of the group into which he is born. If the group is very simple, he may receive no other sort of education at all. Many societies, civilized and primitive alike, do not like to leave education to the random chance processes of informal education. Thus, they institute special, formal educative organizations, or schools, to insure that the young will be exposed systematically to those subjects that are basic both to their own welfare and to that of the society. So it has been with the Manos, with the Athenians and with the Chinese. And so it is . . . with the Americans.[8]

An educational wag once compared the elementary school curriculum to alcoholic inebriation—something to be *experienced* individually, not to be defined by an authority. As a matter of record, authorities have attempted to contain the description of school activities historically, psychologically, philosophically, and in some instances, economically. Delineating an action is difficult, especially so in the absence of a "typical"

---

[7] Ibid., p. 139. Another example of this was Mrs. Trimmer's *Story of the Robin* (New York: Heath, 1908). The robin described and pictured was the English bird, foreign to the United States. The book enjoyed a good sale.

[8] M. R. Charles, *A Preface to Education* (New York: Macmillan, 1965), p. 67.

situation. Our discussion has attempted to point to the human-historical base for present curriculum. Hahn has defended a theory of curriculum based upon personality.[9] He centers the theory upon stages of development, learning, socialization of the individual, free society, and the role of the adult. In a discussion of some fifty-five aspects of this approach to curriculum, six features apply directly to the work of the school:

1. The major task of the school is the personality growth of the child.
2. Children will learn better in schools where curriculum experiences are provided to aid the child in solutions to his major internal conflicts.
3. School education involves as a major goal the freeing of the child from impending, distorting inner conflict. The success of the school as a mediator between the culture and the individual depends upon this being accomplished.
4. Subject matter in the curriculum has two broad functions in individual growth: (1) at different stages of development particular subject matter has symbolic meaning related to the individual's growth problem; and (2) it constitutes, when adequately selected, the reality of society's expectations as to what must be known if the individual is to participate in his culture.
5. The organization of subject matter scope and object matter sequence is most effective when related to the stages of personality development and the problems characteristic of them.
6. Schools organized so that neurotic and undemocratic solutions are not perpetuated are more effective in fostering child growth than schools that do not consider this in curriculum making.[10]

More traditionally, curriculum was reserved for those subjects included in the school course of study, that is, the subjects taught day by day in the classroom. This "narrow-field" approach has been broadened through the influence of many educators (not to mention the classroom teacher). The wide-field approach attempted to include not only the inculcation of knowledge adjusted to individual abilities, but also to identify the role or responsibilities of each individual in a growing society. These concepts of expansion are summed up neatly by Ragan as follows:

1. The curriculum exists only in the experiences of children; it does not exist in textbooks, in the course of study, or in the plans and intentions of teachers. The course of study has the same relation-

[9] Aubrey Hahn, *Elementary School Curriculum: Theory and Research* (Boston: Allyn, 1961), p. 7.
[10] Ibid., pp. 8–9.

ship to the curriculum that a road map has to the actual experiences involved in taking a trip. In order to evaluate the curriculum of the school, it is necessary to observe carefully the quality of living that goes on in it.

2. The curriculum includes more than content to be learned. The selection of useful, accurate content is a very important responsibility of teachers, but content does not constitute the curriculum until it becomes a part of the experience of the child. The amount of content that becomes curriculum for one child may differ from that which becomes curriculum for another. The human relations in the classroom, the methods of teaching, and the evaluation procedures used are as much a part of the curriculum as the content to be learned.

3. The school curriculum is an enterprise in guided living. Instead of being as broad as life itself, the school curriculum represents a special environment that has been systematized, edited, and simplified for a special purpose.

4. The curriculum is a specialized learning environment deliberately arranged for directing the interests and abilities of children toward effective participation in the life of the community and nation. It is concerned with helping children enrich their own lives and contribute to the improvement of society through the acquisition of useful information, skills, and attitudes.

5. The problem with which the curriculum worker is concerned is not merely that of deciding what subjects should be taught, of improving the mind, or of increasing knowledge; it is also a problem of improving individual and community living.[11]

As we delve into comparative specifics of wide-ranging philosophies of curriculum, complex inner-philosophical conflicts emerge. Many observers choose identifiable groupings around which clusters of associated viewpoints can be accumulated for subsequent generic contrast. Ronald Doll, for example, feels that all seeking curricula improvement aspire for citizenship development and improvement of the thinking process as well as customary goals of health and self-insight. Traditional educators would approach the common goals by filling the mind of the pupil with a wealth of information gained from the past, emphasize a liberal arts study to cultivate an intellectual elite, accept the world as it develops, and make positive adjustments to it in a conformist approach. In contrast, liberal or progressive leaders would utilize only the knowledge of the past that would serve their personal needs, accept practical and liberal arts programs equally

[11] Ragan, op. cit., p. 4.

in the sense of servicing personal application, emphasize the individual pupil and a range of programs to meet his immediate needs, and stoutly maintain that the world can be converted into an ideal environment.[12]

Obviously, the curriculum of a school must be flexible, continually evaluated, and adaptable to meet rapidly changing expectations of society. So important is this process that the rigidly bound covers of an elementary school's curriculum "guide or outline" become passé. The circulation of such monuments of inflexibility in itself is somewhat indicative of educational stagnation.[13]

One should also recognize that apart from the stimulation of curricula controversy, conflict, experimentation, and evaluation, the contributions of allied research in the fields of sociology, physiology, and psychology have been noteworthy, particularly in the present decade. Recent social and legal challenges to the previously accepted programs of the schools attest to impacts of these studies. The basic practices of a child's physical maturity for beginning schools, groupings determined by standardized testing, and promotions geared to established norms exemplify the kind of procedures now open to question as a result of parallel fields research.

Coupled with these challenges is the inherent inertia within schools and personnel, which resists rapid change, even when documented and seemingly worthy of study and consideration. At the present time, for example, there is mounting evidence that there are "considerable numbers" of children entering kindergarten or early primary grade levels who already have reading competencies or are obviously ready for beginning reading skills. Yet there remains a recognizable reluctance in many teachers, regardless of age or experience, to accommodate this potential before the traditional first-grade, textbook-oriented strategies are initiated. Conversely, the need of some pupils to delay the process of initial reading skills for an extended period of time is a difficult position to accept by otherwise progressive teachers of reading (see Chapter 12 for greater detail on readiness).

Curriculum philosophy, then, represents an intangible factor of pragmatic implementation of past and current knowledge of how children learn and develop. As with a playground teeter-totter, the position of the child at a given moment, whether up or down, depends upon the action of the other person, regardless of the role of the pivot or fulcrum. Comprehensive, continuous cooperation of all participants in the school and community certainly underlies all efforts to improve curriculum. This effort must accommodate the extremes of thought and implementation as well as the common, safer middle ground of compromise effort and action.

[12] Ronald C. Doll, *Curriculum Improvement: Decision-Making and Process* (Boston: Allyn, 1970), pp. 15–19.

[13] The following sections, particularly Ch. 14, will treat this tendency in greater detail.

Achieving Curriculum Goals

If an elementary school recognizes its many responsibilities to pupil and community, how does it go about achieving the goals and objectives challenging it for successful operation? Here lies the keystone of the educational structure, the classroom and the teacher.

> The school staff examines research dealing with factors that influence learning, experiments with techniques for gaining a better understanding of children, analyzes recent social trends and makes surveys of the local community. It formulates tests of educational objectives, evaluates instructional materials, prepares curriculum guides, and develops the overall design of the curriculum. These activities are, however, means to an end—the improvement of living and learning in the classroom. It is in the individual classroom that the actual improvement of the curriculum takes place.[14]

Frequently, resource units, guides to subject-matter approaches, courses of study, and textbook series are available for study, reflection, modification, and utilization. Pupil records, resource files, teaching units, and daily lesson plans also are sources of information for the teaching approach. Add the friendly counsel of teachers and administrators, and the individual teacher moves into the major focus of the curriculum spotlight.

> Furthermore, if pupils' experiences are to improve, teachers must likewise have new and improved experiences since is is axiomatic that the blind cannot be expected to lead the blind. Curriculum improvement is, according to the broadened view, more than alteration or re-arrangement of pupil experiences according to a simple, preconceived plan: it involves the reeducation of teachers through individualized in-service education and constructive supervision.[15]

Responsibilites of Staff in Curriculum

In truth, the broad-fields approach to curriculum goals demands more from a teacher than the narrow, traditional program. It requires a better-prepared teacher, integrative planning, and skilled methodology.

> The teacher who views curriculum as an emerging educational experience will, of necessity, see her role as being much more vital, much more involved, and certainly, more demanding of her creativity and perception than if she were to view the curriculum as a "fixed" plan for education of children.[16]

[14] Ragan, op. cit., p. 182.
[15] Doll, op. cit., p. 21.
[16] Albert Shuster and Milton Ploghoft, *The Emerging Elementary Curriculum* (Columbus, Ohio: Merrill, 1963), p. 27.

It is the superintendent of schools or a designated administrator of the schools who is most frequently responsible to the board of education for the curriculum of the schools. In many instances, it is the elementary school principal who is delegated the responsibility for implementing changes for progress and for working with the staff of the school to determine which activities or responsibilities are most effective for the school and the community. It is common for a given school to be involved in a new testing program, to be a test section or control for an experimental program in science, to be studying the feasibility of a remedial reading program involving programmed teaching materials, and to be discussing whether the newly formed nongraded school organization pattern is fitting into a "middle-school" concept as suggested by a standing curriculum committee. Decisions can be democratic or autocratic, but the demands of curriculum become all-inclusive and, as such, constantly confront teachers and administrators with new potential and direction. The school itself, then, must be an integral unit for curriculum, with its actions connected and pointing to specific pupil behavioral goals. Whether the activity involves decorating a Maypole or marking an achievement record—the long-range goal is pupil- and community-centered.

Including the needs of the community within the responsibilities of the teaching staff is often easier to accept in philosophy than in practice. A report of a recent parent-teacher conference involving a classroom practice identified a source of parental and community concern.

> *Teacher:* Mrs. Tamnek, why do you object to our unit on the use of the home telephone? We have featured this unit for many years at this school and have many fine comments from parents on its positive assistance in improving telephone manners for our children.
>
> *Parent:* I have no objection to the school teaching children some basic rules about using the phone. My husband and I do protest teaching our daughter to answer the phone by saying, "Hello, this is the Tamnek residence, Mary Lou speaking." In our neighborhood we want our children to answer "Hello"—and that's all. No name, no number, no information at all unless they're sure who is on the other end of the call. You're teaching them to encourage the stranger, the kooks or the salesman who use the phone only for their own personal need. I want the kids to say "Hello" only—and if they don't know who's calling, hang up!
>
> *Teacher:* I sense your concern and I can see how a young child could be placed in a rather compromising position if the caller was unscrupulous in his questions. But, I trust you can appreciate the need to orient the child to the use of the phone and the responsibility that goes with it.

Parent: Well, it might have made sense years ago, but today we've got to teach kids how to protect themselves first. What you teach Mary Lou about answering the phone we have to un-teach when she comes home. You know what I mean?

Does the teacher know what the parent has in mind, or, in a larger sense, is the school aware of a change in social mores? It is probable that the easiest solution to the problem is most commonly followed—drop the unit from the curriculum. However, servicing the needs of the community is not always realized by this action. The question remains whether the present underlying concern of the parent remains a responsibility of the teacher and the school. What action would seem feasible for a teacher in these circumstances?

Curriculum—Heritage of the Past

Most elementary schools continue the early established, plant-and-harvest cycle—commencing classes in the fall and dismissing them in the spring, leaving the summer months and pupils educationally idle, but available for field work in agriculture. The release of two week days, Saturday and Sunday, is deeply rooted in religious and early colonial practices. Those who travel abroad today are conditioned in advance for foreign time utilization, such as siestas, but are a bit bewildered at school children attending classes on Saturdays and in some instances evenings.

The teacher today was the "master" yesterday, and the slow learner formerly occupied the accepted dunce's chair and high stool. Obviously, a study attempting to link present and past practices would probably be a multivolume series and representative of a relatively small section of activities. Nevertheless, the presence of these influences of the past affect more than school practices, and the resulting diversity of organizational patterns as well as the methods for teaching children reflect development, evolution, and belated accommodation.

The following morning plan for a school day framed by a teacher is in terms of the tasks represented by his daily schedule and lesson plans.

8:30 Attendance, lunch count, pledge of allegiance, recording duties.
8:40 Social studies projects, bulletin-board committee, proofing class newspaper, order next month's film.
9:15 Reading groups. Use film readers with Meadowlarks.
9:40 Physical education in multipurpose room. Team planning.
10:10 Science activities, assignments, and reports.
10:30 Discussion and plans for next week's field excursion to newspaper plant. Check on math module file.
11:00 Visit from the student antipollution committee. Plans for individual assistance.
11:10 Music.
11:40 Rest rooms and lunch lines.

One might question whether this would be a typical plan or if it was designed for a teacher in a self-contained classroom. Are the children grouped by intelligence or by other abilities? Frankly, this schedule segment is similar to a school's curriculum inasmuch as the intent (and effectiveness) depends upon other factors that are not generally apparent in planning briefs or published monographs. In this instance, we might briefly examine the teacher's plan and draw some representative possibilities for differing curricular approaches.

Either a graded or a nongraded *school organization* could accommodate our sample schedule. The *graded plan* is probably the more traditional and common of the two. In its simplest form, children are advanced from one level or grade to the next each academic year. Our high schools and universities follow the same patterns although there are exceptions in which a student can complete a high school program in less than four years. Universities have added flexibilities to their programs to permit various degree plans to be completed on the basis of realizing minimum competencies, experience equivalencies, and accelerated course sequences. A *nongraded* arrangement is considered a prerequisite before genuine grouping or individualization can be accomplished. Since such groupings are in our teacher's plan, a nongraded form cannot be ruled out. On the other hand, a conservative grade plan would not be as fitting in an atmosphere where an obvious variety of people and activities seemingly are operating. We should recall that no single organizational plan will meet the curricular needs of a wide variety of school-communities.

A degree of *pupil grouping* is suggested by our teacher's plans with reading groups and with activity and research committees as well as with some grouping in physical education and music. Individual attention is noted in social science, mathematics, and antipollution. We are at a loss to interpret the basis of the grouping. The Meadowlarks reading group could be formed on the likeness of reading levels in the group. It is not apparent whether the Meadowlarks remain as a homogeneous group in, say, the bulletin board committee or whether intraclass groups are multidimensional and heterogeneous without recourse to intelligence, academic performance, or basic skill performance. One senses that reading is not the basic for all grouping in this class, although too often this skill and intelligence scores tend to weigh heavily when elementary groups are created, especially in the early school years.

If we attempt to match the abilities of the teaching staff, the resources of the school and the needs of the students, some *schoolwide teaching procedure* must evolve. The one-teacher-one-room assignment was an early form of the *self-contained classroom*, which made the teacher the master of all skills and knowledge for one determined group of students. Although modifications of this form are probably predominating at this time, our schedule would suggest an existing modification, if not a contrasting combination. Some *departmentalization* of teaching could be in operation, especially in physical education, where another room is in use. Possibly our teacher is responsible for some teaching in mathematics, reading, music, and social studies. It is also probable that some shared responsibility is in operation with another teacher or student groups in *team teaching*. Note that the team planning is scheduled while at least some of the students are in physical education. Conceivably our teacher involved here has responsibility with teaching science for a number of groups of students in addition to those who meet at the 8:30 A.M. session. In turn, other teachers are assuming teaching leadership roles in areas such as language arts, yet planning all actions in teamwork. *Individualized* teaching shows strongly in the plans with provision for varying interests and levels of participation. Certain degrees of encouraging individual *competencies* are being attempted in the use of modular teaching in mathematics. We could assume the latter is self-pacing and also involves self-evaluation as a teacher's check often focuses on the progress of the individual students as they move through modular sequences of tasks, experiences, and problem-solving. But now we are moving to a point of assuming a teacher's role in developing a phase of curricular implementation from a simple morning's planning schedule. At most, it represents some possible interlocking implementation of a school's philosophy, employing representative and current procedures, each of which is unique to itself; but when linked and operating in cooperative response to a given need, it represents curriculum in action.

Our schedule and its inherent potentials are but one-dimensional approaches without the philosophy and ideas inherent in the students, staff, and community.

> Classroom and school organization merely facilitate the transmission of culture—the set of experiences that adults provide for their young. Organizational patterns do not and cannot transform a mediocre school into a superior school. A superior school gets that way primarily through curriculum considerations, firmly rooted in philosophical frameworks, not necessarily from organizational modifications.[17]

If the past experiences of schools and societies have a common expectation, it would be the continuous change in philosophical expectations. The assumption of this tenet strongly points to the conclusion that a school curriculum that is not responding to the needs of a community is itself insensitive to an enlarging gap between the heritage of the past and the life-style of its present youth.

[17] Joe L. Frost and G. Thomas Rowland, *Curricula for the Seventies: Early Childhood Through Early Adolescence* (Boston: Houghton, 1969), pp. 225–226.

Responsibilities of Communities in Curriculum

Pupil and community expectations vary by school, by system, by region, and by state. It is not possible to gear a comprehensive elementary school program to a large school population without attention to variations in the needs and expectations of different schools and communities. Although this is quite obvious in comparing the community needs of a rural consolidated school of two hundred students in a desolate region of the western Plains with a congested school serving thousands in a deprived city area, it is more difficult to sense the diverse needs *within* school systems. Because of its complexity, however, a comparison will serve to illustrate the differences within an elementary school in three representative, but fictitious school settings.

1. Marystown, New York—Flagel Elementary School. Constructed in 1897, with additions in 1922 and 1955; grades 1–6, four sections per grade. Class size averages thirty-six pupils; total school enrollment approximately 900 students, twenty-four teachers. Average teacher age, forty-eight years. No cafeteria. Average family income approximately $4,150. Children are Caucasian, Puerto Rican, black, and Cuban.
2. Antilla, South Dakota—Byron Community School. Constructed 1964; grades K–6, two sections per grade. Class size averages twenty-three per room. Total school enrollment approximately 325 students, fifteen teachers. Average teacher age, thirty-seven years. Cafeteria, gymnasium, swimming pool. Average family income approximately $12,000. Children are Caucasian.
3. Short Peak, Colorado—Glory Consolidated School. Constructed 1940; grades 1–8, one or two sections per grade. Class size averages eighteen per room. Total school population approximately 150 students, eleven teachers. Average teacher age, forty-five years. Restricted hot-lunch program. Average family income approximately $5,000. Children are Caucasian.

Would a common elementary curriculum fit the needs of pupil and community in these representative areas? What portions would be common to the three? Would a teacher in Marystown succeed equally well in Antilla? Antilla in Short Peak? Short Peak in Marystown? Have the requirements of these schools in terms of curriculum changed in the past? Will they possibly change in the future?

The elementary schools supported by tax moneys have moved toward an inflexible "common" curriculum of *sameness*. Community expectations encourage the identifiable features of individual classrooms, textbooks, sanitary facilities, and parent-pupil conferences. Other state and regional organizations have made the school responsible for pupil attendance records, teacher certification, and safety precautions. Yet as the trend toward urbanization continues, the need for more separation, or *differentiation*, of curriculum implementation has occurred.

In most cities today, a few minutes' drive will identify good schools from others—all within the same geographical, if not organizational, unit. Suburban schools are in the main quite different from "downtown" city schools. They differ in both subtle and obvious ways. Some schools pay additional stipends for teachers working in impoverished neighborhood schools or "initiate" the novice or transfer teacher for the first few years of teaching or until resignations renew the search for teaching candidates. In short, the pupil and localized community differ greatly so as to prohibit the typical middle-class curriculum's being utilized in elementary schools at the two socioeconomic extremes.

Three reactions to the suburban-urban problem merit the attention of the profession: specialized teacher preparation, specialized materials, and private contracting. All three in main form or individual school variation from the original models attempt to provide material and instruction tailor-made to the needs of urban and inner-city schools. They espouse a belief that teaching the child in the inner-city requires methods and materials different from those commonly used in suburban or rural schools. Many feel that *all* instruction should be changed drastically to meet the needs of youth today, but for the moment the thrust in these three areas pinpoints those needs of the urban child.

Specialized teacher preparation assumes dimensions of both pre- and in-service variations. At the undergraduate university level, programs are emerging that select promising young teacher candidates at the freshman or sophomore levels and fit them to a broad-based preparation program that endorses a heavy experience pattern of observation, participation, and teaching the youth of the inner-city. Much of the academic course work of those preparing for teaching in these areas is specifically designed for this challenge, and the classes themselves are frequently conducted in the inner-city elementary school buildings. Experienced elementary teachers who are especially competent in working with urban youth are recruited to supplement the selected university instructional staff. In many instances, these programs are encouraged financially by foundation or governmental moneys to both participating schools and universities as well as to the prospective teachers themselves. Because the inception of these programs is relatively recent, potential success is still somewhat hypothetical, although the unusual interest in the graduates displayed by inner-city school systems could be interpreted as the type of success that is indeed realistic if not also philosophical.

Graduate-school interest in in-service education for urban education is somewhat restricted, in the main emphasizing individual teacher needs within advanced-degree program offerings, although some experimental, advanced-degree programs themselves are slanted to urban centers or schools where sufficient revenues are available to support staff and materials. Both professional teacher organizations and urban school districts endorse in-service education for experienced teachers as a major ingredient in attempting to improve educational opportunities for city youth. Unfortunately, little financial support has been forthcoming to the graduate-level programs from state or federal services.

Specialized materials for use in the urban schools, especially where minority groups predominate, have been slow in developing. It has been difficult for even the best-prepared teachers to succeed in overcoming the handicaps inherent in using supplementary teaching materials in inner-city classrooms, where a high percentage of the examples, illustrations, and activities are geared to suburban lifestyles. This has been particularly noted in textbook series where the inherent planning of the scope and sequence of the materials is based upon individual and group progress that is frequently excessive for those in the urban environment. In states where standardized testing and comparative assessment scores are employed to determine indirectly pupil growth and development, the inability of urban schools to compare favorably is often attributable to inappropriate as well as inadequate teaching materials. Encouraging progress has been noted whereby schools themselves develop materials that approach a more meaningful means of communicating with these youngsters. The inclusion of appropriate and timely free-reading materials for children's literature and areas of social studies at the national level is particularly encouraging. It is also likely that the success of national television programs designed for urban children has espoused a number of school projects to produce local film and video tape segments as an aid to the teacher in the classroom.

Current efforts to convert or adapt contemporary materials for use with behavioral goal programs has been proposed as one of the more promising means of individualizing needed areas of emphasis for children in schools with limited materials of any type. In addition to the collection of materials of specific use for the individual or group, the development of self-pacing curricular components parallels the interest of schools in eliminating many of the detrimental side effects of the traditional graded plan structure discussed earlier in this chapter.

Private contracting or *performance contracting* is a contemporary phenomenon with an unknown future based upon available evaluation. With programs involving an extreme use of methods and materials, it was typically an offer of a private corporation to realize a minimum growth rate in a given group of school age children within a predetermined period of time for a specific compensation sum. Although means of selecting the children and measures of determining the rate of educational development were established in contract agreements with the individual board of education, the majority of details as to *how* the rate was to be achieved was left to the contracting corporation. In most instances, the children covered by the contract were urban children in public schools. The areas to be emphasized were primarily skill development, although this factor was often the dictate of the board rather than of the contracting agency.

The materials employed ranged from complex computers to extrinsic reward materials, such as personal radios for students. Teachers involved were frequently recruited from the schools, although management personnel were often selected from other fields and occupations. In-service programs were pragmatic in direction, and the expectations of the contract preselected the curricular emphasis with those that were not an expectation of performance generally relegated to lower priorities.

The early financial support for this curricular approach by the federal agencies encouraged many schools to participate, especially those discouraged by the results of more conventional teaching strategies. In other instances, financially pressed systems were entranced by the contract assurance of growth or forfeiture of corporation compensation. The hopes that a sophisticated computer programmed to work patiently with an educationally handicapped child of the ghetto was in itself a challenge that caught the fancy of the population.

Evaluation of these programs to date has been conflicting and incomplete with extremes in the scale of success. Some programs, or modifications of originals, are still operative, and a more valid evaluation will probably rest with continuing efforts. As to curriculum reform, limited developments have continued as direct results of these efforts. Apparently, some use of programmed computer materials is continuing; and specialized materials and methods remain, such as films, audio and visual tapes, skill-development library selections, and remedial methods involving extrinsic reward systems. Possibly more important to curricular development are the secondary observations and experiences gained from these ventures. It was common, for example, that children "under contract" enjoyed brightly painted rooms, which were carpeted and air-conditioned. The contrast in the same inner-city school with the stark, wooden-floored, open-windowed classroom was not lost on the school student body, teaching staff, and school district, especially if a degree of improvement was enjoyed. In addition, the use of favorable teacher-pupil ratios, abundant teacher supply, and variable program scheduling was demonstrated as a feasible entity. Lastly, the recognition that the nation's largest corporations were developing contracting divisions to implement contract agreements added a value to the process of preparing children of all abilities who heretofore had been overlooked—even though the possible profit motive could be recognized in partial justification of the corporate interest.

These and related problems exemplify the crucial position of the present-day curriculum efforts and foretell, in part, some ventures of the future. Is it not possible that there eventually should be more curriculum flexibility between elementary schools within a metropolitan district than exists between school districts outside urban areas?

It is possible to discern patterns of curriculum change by noting changes in the community and its expectations. A similar concern exists with the pupils. Of course, intelligence scores or achievement gains are one index, but there are also others. One of the authors was connected with an elementary school involved in an experimental music program. Over a period of years this program concentrated on a sequential development of composition and performance with string instruments. At the time the experimental program was completed, the elementary school stringed-instrument graduates received first-chair honors in the junior and senior high school ensembles and orchestras and monopolized the various community musical groups. Because of the concentrated efforts of a school program, the social and aesthetic life of a community were influenced. Such influences are more intrinsic than collecting funds for band uniforms or cheerleader costumes. Yet all are involved in the total school curriculum, willingly or unwillingly.

FINANCING THE PROGRAM

A pressing concern of the elementary school is the financial support needed to implement its curriculum. Cutting corners has been a practice in school operations, and in many schools such actions have curtailed program development. Room and school budgets have been traditionally modest. Only in comparatively recent years have teachers in the elementary school been able to match the salary scale of high school teachers.

State support for education has enabled the elementary school to move more rapidly toward realizing goals, but the support has not kept up with the rising costs of school operation. At the federal levels of government, few funds have been allocated to the elementary schools until recent years. With the advent of matching-funds provisions, the areas of science, mathematics, and foreign languages were temporarily able to gain funds to provide needed supplements to their program activities, equipment, materials, and evaluation. Special education, guidance, and evaluation areas have been added to the funded areas.

In recent years, the various pressures on the local, state, and national economics have pushed the property tax percentages devoted to education to record high levels. Locally, the communities have increasingly protested the tax burden. Although this school support in many states is more than matched by state funds, the frequent requests from school boards for higher millage levels are meeting negative response. Considerable attention is being afforded plans for school support that shift the tax from the local property holdings to other sources ranging from income to conglomerate contribution plans, including sales and gambling revenues. At stake are the inequalities existing between school districts having equal millage rates, but with wide variation in taxable property, so that some children are theoreticaly supported by thousands of dollars of tax revenue whereas others have expectations of less than a hundred. States hesitate to support some school districts from general revenue funds at the exclusion of other districts that are somewhat better supported financially. In the plans that will eventually be initiated, the possible role of the federal government cannot be logically overlooked. In the arrangements employed, the need for the school child for increased educational opportunities remains paramount.

In spite of these breakthroughs, many schools are still sparsely supplied with funds to implement locally oriented curriculum activities. Schools are continually faced with the enigma of diverting programs to the direction where outside support can be secured or to maintain skeleton-type efforts within the local source of financial support. One school system, for example, had eighteen pilot or experimental programs in operation within two academic areas in one school year. These operations were defended as contributing to the future direction of subsequent locally centered curriculum activities. A comparable school system in the same region at the same time had one and was not dissatisfied. Perhaps the contrast is extreme, but the principle is not, namely, to what extent the *desire* for curriculum experimentation and development should be influenced by the *availability* of state, federal, or foundation funds. There is no quick, valid answer to such current conditions. In most instances, the decision will be made in the light of "best fit" to the school and community expectations.

Some Problems Involved in Current Curriculum Change

One key to determining the involvement of the elementary school and community in contemporary curriculum study is the abundance of problems such studies produce. It is a healthy outcome, a strong indication that teachers and the school are looking beyond success to those issues and problems that are particularly relative.

By deft maneuvering perhaps some rather elusive or nebulous concerns can be identified, with the stated intention not to be inclusive, but rather to display for consideration.

1. *How to maintain contact with the rapid changes in society.* The school curriculum is lagging owing to the rush of society to ur-

banize and the resulting frustrations that beset society. Are citizens' committees the answer?

2. *Should the neighborhood school concept be maintained?* Current problems of housing, district organization, and mobility of school population provide some valid reasons for examining the common base of school organization. Decentralization of large urban districts is involved as is the issue of metropolitan bussing.

3. *Can our nation maintain a free public education for all elementary youth?* Once a proud realization of our forefathers, the actual implementation of a comprehensive curriculum places many financial burdens upon communities and government. It is suggested that we cannot survive without such provisions, but dropout rates are visible weaknesses.

4. *To what extent does the local school curriculum depend upon the direction of subject matter specialists?* Some critics of our curriculum say that school programs are "too important" to be left to the direction of professional educators, parents, and children. Some current experimental programs and materials reflect a move toward expertness in academics.

5. *Should teacher preparation be geared to elementary schools of departmentalized nature rather than self-contained classrooms?* Costs of elementary school instruction and the pressures for more subject-matter depth in given areas of teacher preparation have promoted this question.

6. *Are parents and communities to be expected to exercise more or less influence on school curricula as technological changes increase?* As the demands of curriculum change increase, are parents and pupils qualified to make decisions involving basic school operations?

7. *Do elementary schools sacrifice control of curricula as state and federal funds increasingly support local school operations?* This problem will increasingly test local school philosophy in terms of long- and short-term involvement.

8. *What is a minimum responsibility of curriculum implementation to the preparation, recruitment, and retention of qualified teachers and administrators?* At present, there is relatively little community action to prepare and retain competent teachers. What factors are paramount?

9. *How can an active curriculum in the elementary school be accurately and continuously monitored to provide day-by-day improvement?* Curriculum change is often more difficult than curriculum insertion. To add to and prune on a continuum is vital to the success of a cooperative approach.

10. *How can problems basic to the process of continual curriculum*

improvement be identified, isolated, and solved? Schools and communities have been primarily concerned with solving problems as they occur rather than systematically anticipating the solution of a problem affecting future curricula.

11. *Should split sessions or half-day schools be maintained when results of student growth condemn their aborted curriculum?* Many of these temporary arrangements have remained for more than a decade. School patrons refuse financial support to eliminate them although students are suffering educationally.

12. *Is the teaching profession moving toward specialization of teaching environment—rural-suburban-urban?* Some suggest certification of these specializations is more pressing than grade level or academic minimums.

13. *Are the proponents of teacher accountability seeking to influence the long-range curricular goals?* To many teachers the means of determining success and failure relate directly to teacher implementation of curriculum and performance of students in academic disciplines. Teachers continue to maintain that student development of desirable attitudes, appreciations, and understandings are also their responsibility and that these cannot be accurately measured.

CURRICULUM, THE TEACHER, AND THE FUTURE

As in the classroom, the emerging development in the elementary curriculum will be heavily influenced by the teacher. The degree of responsiveness, innovation, and tenacity exhibited by groups and individuals within the school staff will determine the future success of the school itself. The promise suggested by technological advances in supplementing the instructional process can only be guided and utilized by the teacher who is willing to try new ideas and to think in the process. Obviously, a teacher can instill a working vocabulary of two thousand words in the future adult citizen regardless of the condition of the school building, the ethnic background of the pupil's home, or the temperature of the classroom. What is important is whether a mastery of eight thousand or ten thousand words *has meaning* to the future of the individual and to the society that requires an educated citizen to help decide the future of the group.

Whether measured in terms of words, muscle coordination, or music appreciation, the role of the teacher in initiating and implementing a dynamic curriculum implies a role of creativeness, sensitivity, and leadership that does not enjoy a parallel elsewhere in our society. The emerging curriculum cannot ignore the problems of society or the increasing needs of the individual for intelligent survival. The teacher and the curriculum are bonded by the problems as well as the pressures of the developmental environment.

SUGGESTED ACTIVITIES

1. Mr. Aubrey, the principal, has called the staff together for the last of a series of four meetings. The last meeting will close with a formal staff vote upon a question that has been the topic of discussion for the preceding three sessions. The issue is deceptively simple—shall the Irving School offer a foreign language as an integral part of the curriculum? Five mothers have made the request, representing a minority of the school parents—but an extremely influential one. All the parents who signed the petition for the language inclusion come from the "better" side of the school district and rightfully expect their children to enter college eventually. The major opposition has been from a vocal number of the staff and a few parents who prefer experimentation in vocational areas, such as typewriting, home economics, and hobby crafts. It is probable that the final vote will be split in half. If this prediction occurs, what direction should future discussion and work follow? Should the teachers' vote decide such proposals? What action is available to parents if the proposal is eventually shelved? Are such proposed curriculum inclusions valid? What factors of curriculum construction are involved in such questions?

2. If a curriculum pattern is developed for a neighborhood school, what relationships should exist between this development and the curricula that exist for other elementary and middle schools? For the total school system?

3. A new experimental program in physical education has been offered to the Adams Elementary School. Nationwide in character, it provides for a two-year test period at the third-grade level. Among other features it would require the third-grade teachers to provide a minimum of two hours per week from the present curricula for the experiment. Should the request be accepted? Upon what factors should the decision be made? How can the factors be justified?

4. Classroom teachers are often encouraged to enrich the curriculum beyond minimum expectancies. If we assume that this practice is educationally valid, how does the teacher determine the extent of the enrichment activity? How can such extension of class activities avoid duplication with work in following years? To what extent are records and evaluations used to determine the degree of enrichment? Should it be provided for all pupils? Why?

5. Considerable attention has been given to the establishment of a regional or national set of minimum "standards" for school curriculum. With the increased mobility of families, for example, such minimums would assure some degree of "sameness" of education throughout the country. Consider the advantages and disadvantages of such a proposal. What major questions are raised by such possibilities? Implications?

6. Examine the curriculum of the elementary school as you saw it as a pupil and as you see it now. Identify five changes that have occurred. Likewise, identify five practices or areas of effort that have not changed. Attempt to identify a rationale or reasons why practices of curricular approach have evolved or changed. What are the justifications cited for lack of change?

7. Try to isolate or locate two or three specific curricular practices that are included in the school's operational procedures that are local in nature or are found operating only in a single school system. Discuss the implications of these practices. Weakness? Strength?

SELECTED BIBLIOGRAPHY

Anderson, Vernon E. *Principles and Procedures of Curriculum Improvement,* 2nd ed. New York: The Ronald Press Company, 1965.

Atkinson, Carroll, and Eugene Maleska. *The Story of Education.* New York: Bantam-Matrix, 1964.

Charles, M. R. *A Preface to Education.* New York: Macmillan Publishing Co., Inc., 1965.

Cook, Ruth C., and Ronald C. Doll. *The Elementary School Curriculum.* Boston: Allyn & Bacon, Inc., 1973.

Doll, Ronald C. *Curriculum Improvement: Decision-Making and Process,* 3rd ed. Boston: Allyn & Bacon, Inc., 1974.

Frost, Joe L., and G. Thomas Rowland. *Curricula for the Seventies: Early Childhood Through Early Adolescence.* Boston: Houghton Mifflin Company, 1969.

Hass, Glen, Joseph Bondi, and Jon Wiles. *Curriculum Planning.* Boston: Allyn & Bacon, Inc., 1974.

Hertling, James E., and Howard G. Getz. *Education for the Middle School Years:* Readings. Glenview, Ill.: Scott, Foresman and Company, 1971.

Kozol, Jonathan. *Free Schools.* Boston: Houghton Mifflin Company, 1972.

Lavatelli, Celia, Walter Moore, and Theodore Kaltsounis. *Elementary School Curriculum.* New York: Holt, Rinehart & Winston, Inc., 1972.

Manning, Duane. *Toward a Humanistic Curriculum.* New York: Harper and Row, Publishers, 1971.

McGuffey, William H. *McGuffey's Fifth Eclectic Reader—1879 Edition.* New York: New American Library, 1962.

Nerbovig, Marcella, and Herbert Klausmeier. *Teaching in the Elementary School,* 4th ed. New York: Harper and Row, Publishers, 1974.

O'Donovan, Patrick, et al. *The United States.* New York: Time-Life Books, Inc., 1965.

Ragan, William, and Gene Shepherd. *Modern Elementary Curriculum.* 4th ed. New York: Holt, Rinehart & Winston, Inc., 1971.

Rogers, Vincent. *Teaching in the British Primary School.* London: Macmillan & Company, Ltd., 1970.

Sowards, G. Wesley, and M. M. Scobey. *The Changing Curriculum and the Elementary Teacher.* San Francisco: Wadsworth Publishing Co., Inc., 1961.

Taylor, Joy. *Organizing the Open Classroom.* New York: Schocken Books, Inc., 1972.

Webster, Noah. *The Elementary Spelling Book,* rev. New York: American Book Company, 1880.

Chapter 5

Organizational Patterns: Vertical and Horizontal

There are many facets to the problem of organizing the elementary school to provide the best educational program possible. Since colonial days, people have grappled with the problem of assigning pupils and facilitating their involvement with curricular experiences and teachers.

In the attempt to solve the problem of elementary school organization, consideration may be given to such factors as (1) world, national, state and local concerns; (2) the number of pupils and the number of teachers; (3) the relationship of the school to other schools in the district—elementary, middle, and secondary; (4) form of administration, for instance centralized or decentralized; (5) the extent and quality of physical facilities; (6) the amount of money available for instructional purposes; and (7) the physical geography, community demographic patterns, and population shifts. To a large degree, organizational patterns reflect the beliefs and philosophies of school administrators, teachers, and the community or school district in which the school is located.

A quick review of the history of education reveals that school systems have utilized a variety of organizational patterns for instructional purposes. These include such plans as graded, nongraded, multigraded, multiage, homogeneous, heterogeneous, departmentalized, self-contained, open classroom, individualized, dual progress, and team teaching. Patterns of organization that have existed or those currently in use generally are classified into two major types, vertical and horizontal. Thus, we speak of children progressing through the school on both a vertical and a horizontal axis, or in two directions. Vertical organization is the plan employed by the school for classifying and moving learners through the elementary school from point of entry to a point of completion. Horizontal organization is the school's operating procedure of providing for pupil-teacher interaction during the school year, in other words, the school's means for dividing the pupil population into instructional groups and the allocation of teachers to work with these groups at various points on the vertical axis.

Some of the more common patterns within each of the two major types of school organization will be discussed in this chapter. As you examine these patterns, keep in mind that patterns of organization are only frameworks within which teaching-learning occurs or fails to occur. A particular organizational pattern can promote or hinder learning; but, in the final analysis, it is how the knowledgeable, skillful, creative, and sensitive teacher works with learners within an organizational pattern or combination of patterns that makes the teaching-learning experience fruitful for both teacher and pupils.

The following cognitive objectives should guide your study of this chapter:

1. The reader will be able to distinguish between vertical and horizontal school organization.
2. The reader will be familiar with several factors that influence school organizational patterns.
3. The reader will be able to state several advantages and disadvantages of the nongraded and of the graded organizational pattern.
4. The reader will be able to describe the essential elements of four or five different horizontal patterns.

VERTICAL ORGANIZATION

Although schools have experienced many reform movements, vertical organization has remained rather rigid through the years. For the most part, only two basic plans have been used to move pupils from point of entry to point of departure or completion. These two plans are called the graded school and the nongraded school.

The Graded School

The graded school is the oldest and most common vertical pattern of school organization used in our country today. Though the graded school concept dates back to the establishment of the Boston Quincy Grammar

School in 1848, elementary schools were not always organized in this manner. Early schools in America drew from sparsely populated areas, which dictated that schools were organized and conducted for small groups of children encompassing an age range of many years.

Not until the latter half of the nineteenth century did the graded school become the established pattern. Several conditions of this period contributed to the widespread acceptance and approval by local school districts of the graded school plan of organization. Among these factors were a rather rapidly increasing population; recognition of the need for a universally educated public, which necessitated the need to deal efficiently and economically with large groups; poorly prepared teachers; and the lack of varied teaching-learning materials.

The graded school pattern of organization may be viewed as simply assembling children into grades in accordance with their chronological age. This concept of grouping for education was founded on the premise that accomplishments were primarily the result of differences in willingness to work. A certain package of knowledge and skills was deemed appropriate for mastery at each graded level. If a student applied himself, he would be successful in school and move on to the next grade. Anyone who did not perform as prescribed could try to do so the following year.

The graded school operates on the assumption that a child progresses at a fixed and prescribed rate of subject-matter accomplishment or achievement each year in school and that comparable progress should be made in each subject area. There is much evidence that many children are unable to meet the "standard" set for the grade and therefore are forced to repeat the year's work. Most children not promoted in our present graded system do just that—they repeat last year's work, with little that is new or different. Educators can rightly be criticized for contributing to a serious human waste in inflicting early failure on a slow first grader or in regulating the progress of a highly motivated or gifted child merely because schools are shackled to the restrictive lockstep grade level concept.

Like all good school administrators, James Philbrick, who is credited with establishing the graded Quincy Grammar School more than 125 years ago, was striving to improve the operational structure of his school, as well as to facilitate instruction. The graded school concept, which Mr. Philbrick started, may have served well, at least at the time, as an administrative procedure for operational purposes—at least, for handling relatively large numbers of children and staff. But his policy of classifying children primarily on the number of years in school never really served adequately the instructional program.

Through legislation, states have prescribed the point (age) at which a child may enter school, but state laws do not set the completion point for the elementary school. Admission to school is usually on the basis of chronological age. The exact date will vary from state to state. Where kindergartens are a part of the normal elementary school sequence, a child generally must have reached his fifth birthday on a prescribed date to be able to enroll in school. Dates sometimes used are December 1 or September 1. This means that a child born on the second of December would not be permitted to enter school until the following September. At such time he would then be almost a full year older than a classmate whose birthday was in November. In most classrooms there are children almost a year apart in age. The oldest child in a first grade might be just one day younger than the youngest child in the second grade.

Recent findings in educational psychology, sociology, and human learning have resulted in many questions being raised about the graded school. Older children from middle or upper socioeconomic homes are at a decided advantage in their early experience, whereas younger children and those coming from deprived neighborhoods are placed at a disadvantage. Many children experience difficulty with graded materials in the primary grades and soon learn to associate their academic failures with themselves. This negative self-image causes pupils to accept failure and reject the notion of success. Although the older and socially advantaged pupil usually has a positive experience in the graded structure, the upper limits of grade expectations contribute to poor work and study habits. The child who can complete an assignment faster than the majority of the class and who has no motivation to go beyond this assignment soon learns to slow down and pace himself to the average pupils. If he does not slow down, he may use the extra time to get into trouble.

One of the most distressing problems of the graded school is the requirement that a decision be made on passing or failing at the close of the academic year, regardless of the individual's rate of learning. When rigid grade standards are adhered to in a school system, a large number of pupils fail in the primary grades and again in junior high school. This results in a high rate of dropouts in high school, as it is a rare individual who will fail twice and still complete his secondary education. The boy or girl who reaches age sixteen in the eighth or ninth grade can seldom be induced to believe that school has more to offer him than the adult world.

Discontent with the graded organizational plan arose soon after its inauguration. The history of education reveals many modifications of the graded plan designed to remove some of the limitations and weaknesses in the rigid organizational pattern. Beginning in 1869 with the St. Louis Plan, we have witnessed such attempts as the Elizabeth Plan, Cambridge Plan, Dalton Plan, Pueblo Plan, Gary Plan, Winnetka Plan, Portland Plan, and the Santa Barbara Plan. Much dissatisfaction exists because these and other plans have not solved school organizational problems. We, therefore, find ourselves in an era of extensive innovation and experimentation with school organization.

The Nongraded School

A relatively recent approach to school organization—nongradedness—can be found in one form or another in every section of our country. All indications lead one to believe that the present trend toward a nongraded organizational plan for the elementary school is deeper rooted, more seriously considered, and more widespread than previous efforts for improvement, at least within the last century.

Identifying the reasons for the emergence of the modern nongraded school is rather difficult. Certainly, the old one-room school offered some of the possibilities and opportunities implied in the present-day nongraded concept. The famous Winnetka and Dalton plans attempted to break down the existing uniform graded structure expectations in that the pupils had individual "tasks," which they could complete over varying periods of time. Several places claim they were first to start a nongraded program. Western Springs, Illinois, started a nongraded program in 1934, but it died before reaching adulthood. Milwaukee is generally conceded to have the oldest program, which has been in continuous operation since 1942. No doubt, a few scattered communities had nongraded programs more than thirty years ago, but only since the late 1950s has the plan enjoyed rapid growth. School systems probably have a variety of reasons for changing their organizational patterns, but two primary reasons for moving to a nongraded structure seem to be (1) dissatisfaction with promotional policies inherent in the graded plan and (2) the desire to provide for a fuller realization of the development and learning of all children.

In recent years, there appears to be a new awakening to human variabilities. It has been said that children are like fingerprints—all are different. Youngsters in school represent a wide range of human variability. Children progress at different rates, and the measurable achievement of an individual child varies among the curricular areas. If one studies the results on a standardized test by a group of youngsters, it is rather evident that the scores show few children on grade level. The nature of learning is continuous, but even within an individual the rate of learning varies from time to time and from area to area. The problem is how to provide a learning situation that most nearly fits individual needs.

Nongradedness is a movement in this direction. Basically, nongraded means an organizational structure in which grade names and grade divisions are eliminated. Nongradedness is an arrangement that permits a flexible grouping and organization of curriculum content that enables children of varying abilities and rates of maturity to experience continuous progress of learning. A break is implied from focusing attention on arbitrary amounts of material to be learned by all children in a class each year (grade level standards) to a newer concept of how well a child is independently achieving in terms of his or her ability and overall development.

The nongraded school is a concept of school organization that eliminates annual grade barriers to pupil progress. Each pupil is encouraged and assisted to progress at his own rate, which is determined by his academic aptitude, socioeconomic standard, and emotional-physical capacities. In this way, the above-average pupil is not restrained from progressing beyond the expectations of his age group, as there is no upper limit established. Below-average or less mature pupils are not required to undertake impossible tasks merely because of a predetermined standard of expectation based on chronological age. Curriculum adjustments are made without the necessity of passing or failing pupils at the end of every year on the basis of achievement measured over a short period of time.

The nongraded concept had its start in the primary grades and has found by far its greatest growth at that level. In most of primary nongraded plans, the traditional first three grades, one, two, and three, are organized as one unit, encompassing a three-year span of time. Most of these plans are built upon a strong kindergarten experience. The child enters the nongraded unit from his kindergarten experience and progresses at his own rate for the next three years. This three-year unit span may consist of several levels, and the child is placed on a level, or moved from level to level, that best serves the individual's total needs.

In attempting to understand the nongraded unit span, one needs to compare it with the usual span of having children divided into grades, largely on the basis of age. Let us trace the possible progress of three children if they were in each of the two plans by examining Figure 5–1.

In the graded structure, certain materials and instructional content are arbitrarily assigned to each grade level, and children typically are expected to take one year to complete the segment. Grouping within a classroom helps teachers vary instruction, but there remains the basic question of promotion or retention at the end of the year.

Mary obviously had completed only about one fourth of what was expected at the end of the year as represented by the line separating

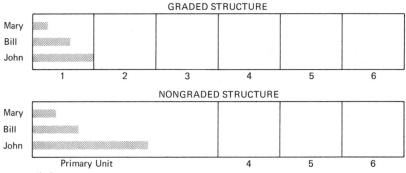

FIGURE 5–1.

grades one and two. In terms of the graded philosophy and expectations, a decision to retain Mary (by her it may be interpreted as failure) would not be very difficult to make. Certainly her progress indicates strongly she could not expect to find success in grade two.

Bill's case is much different. Determining whether he should be promoted or retained would be a very difficult decision. He is almost exactly half way between where he started the year and where he is expected to be at the end of the year, by grade standards. Would it be better for Bill if promoted or retained? On the basis of what is expected in the second grade, can he "make it" if promoted? The decision, at best, is probably a guess. Cases such as Bill's probably contribute to many conscientious teachers' becoming "prematurely gray."

John's case is the delight of graded teachers. He fits the concept beautifully. He was supposed to be at the demarcation line between grades one and two at the end of the year. His indicated progress has him at that point. Without question, he is promoted to second grade with confidence that he will be able successfully to complete that segment next year.

Now, let us consider these same three children if they were in a nongraded structure. The nongraded program, like the graded program, has materials, content, and expectations that are thought appropriate for the primary unit or to its "levels," but these are not assigned on a narrow specific length of time for each child to complete. Rather, teachers examine each child's progress and rate of progression through the instructional levels. Moving from one level to another would occur when teachers have social, emotional, and achievement evidence that indicate it is most feasible and appropriate for the child to change levels. In a nongraded program, it is unlikely that Mary and Bill would make significantly more progress than they would in a graded structure. John might well have advanced beyond the first grade's expectations if motivated and encouraged to do so. More importantly, in neither case do decisions have to be made at the end of the first formal year of schooling relative to promotion and retention. If Mary continues at the present pace, she may take four years instead of the usual three to complete the primary unit; however, she continues the next year from where she was at the end of this year, working on a continuum. The chances are good that Bill will be able to complete the work of the three-year span in the normal time. John may well complete the primary unit in two years instead of three. Neither child will repeat unnecessary work or skip important aspects of the program as he progresses from one year to the next.

Figure 5–2 attempts to portray the progression during the first three years of school beyond the kindergarten in a graded structure and a nongraded structure. As a child progresses through school in a graded structure, he moves, for instance, from the first-grade level to the second-grade level to the third-grade level and similarly through the other grade levels. Notice that the steps from one level to the next are big steps, in fact, too big for many young children to manage or handle satisfactorily. The nongraded structure overlaid in the figure on the graded structure breaks down the first three years of school beyond kindergarten from three big steps to twelve relatively small steps or levels. These smaller, shorter steps enhance easier mobility for youngsters from one level to another. Some school systems designate some of the levels as enrichment levels, thus not expecting all youngsters to accomplish all twelve levels. For example levels five and nine might be considered enrichment levels.

Implementation of a program of nongrading may radically reduce "failure" from the school lives of elementary age children. Unfortunately, when teachers in nongraded schools are not in complete agreement with the concept of nongrading, they may continue to teach as they did in a graded school. They use the same books, materials of instruction, and measures of pupil performance as are found in graded schools, and expect

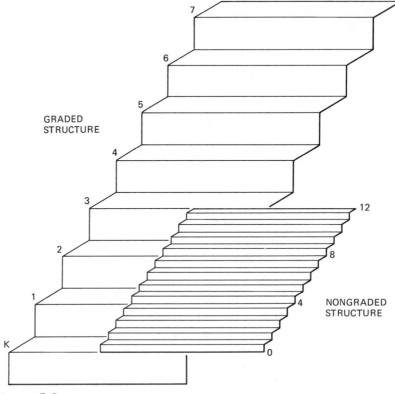

FIGURE 5–2.

grade-type results from pupils. This problem suggests that the change from a graded organization to a nongraded one requires far more than an administrative decision. Both teachers and parents need to understand and be committed to the nongraded program and maintain continuous communication on pupil progress within this framework. A nongraded program depends upon a broad reeducation for the entire school community if it is to be successful.

It has been suggested by some that all grade-level bench marks be removed from a school when a nongraded program is adopted. However, this is easier said than accomplished. Textbooks, workbooks, and tests have a deep-rooted, grade-level orientation as a basic organizational framework. Teachers, administrators, and parents have long had personal association with the identity of grade levels. It is not possible to move rapidly away from a program that has become so deeply a part of the school lives of several generations of adults without involvement of all who are connected with children and education.

Some schools utilize the same teacher for two or three years of work with the same group of children, or for the entire duration of either the primary or intermediate block. This permits the teacher to work with children in the fall at the approximate level reached the previous spring without an unnecessary time lag. It does, however, expose a child to the unique strengths and weaknesses of that particular teacher for a long period of time.

The primary or intermediate block plans generally are flexible enough to permit some children to progress through a block in less than three years or to extend the time in the block to more than three years. Ideally, all children would be provided for in a manner that would permit adjustments within the classroom to take into account their individual needs. In general, the primary-intermediate blocks would have the effect of drastically reducing pupil failure. The majority of schools using the nongraded approach have developed only the nongraded primary block and have continued with a graded program in the intermediate grades. The nongraded primary plan appears to pupils, especially first-graders, where the failure rate is somewhat higher, a real advantage. The same advantage could be afforded intermediate-grade pupils if grade-level barriers were removed from grades four through six. Results of current programs show promise of providing a sound educational basis for freeing pupils from the lock-step pattern of the graded school. In a survey of 550 nongraded schools, Anderson and Goodlad[1] found that when studies using statistical measures of achievement were made, differences in favor of the graded plan were

[1] Robert H. Anderson and John I. Goodlad, "Self-Appraisal in Nongraded Schools: A Survey of Findings and Perceptions," *Elementary School Journal*, 62:261–269 (Feb. 1962).

rare. Responses to questions relating to social, emotional, and personal adjustment of children were overwhelmingly positive in favor of non-graded plans.

A report by DiPasquale[2] on an ungraded plan indicated that a marked decline in truancy occurred when grade levels were eliminated in the elementary school of one community. The children were reported to be better adjusted to school both socially and emotionally. They had greater pride in their school than had ever been true in the years when the graded plan was in operation. Although skeptical at the beginning of the nongraded programs, many teachers soon became strong supporters because of the differences noted in pupil performance.

Disadvantages or Problems Associated with the Nongraded Plan
    1. Getting people to change their thinking from graded concepts.
    2. Inadequate teacher preparation in nongradedness.
    3. Grouping and classifying children.
    4. Evaluating and reporting pupil progress.
    5. Maintaining curriculum balance.
    6. Preventing "levels" from becoming rigid.

Advantages Associated with the Nongraded Plan
    1. Provides span of time adaptable to lags and spurts in development and growth of children.
    2. Reduces failure or pupil retention rate.
    3. Markedly reduces pressures for both pupils and teachers.
    4. Alleviates artificial barriers associated with promotion in graded system.
    5. Increases teacher awareness of pupil individuality.
    6. Encourages teachers to use a wider variety of teacher-learning materials.
    7. Provides more flexibility.
    8. Is more compatible with what is known about child development.
    9. Pupil progress is more continuous.
    10. Leads to improvement in total school program.

Horizontal Organization

Horizontal organization refers to the way schools arrange curricular experiences, pupils, and teachers for interaction purposes. Although schools use two vertical organizational patterns, numerous horizontal patterns also

[2] Vincent C. DiPasquale, "The Relation Between Dropouts and The Graded School," *Phi Delta Kappan*, 46:132–133 (Nov. 1964).

are utilized. For purposes of discussion, horizontal organizational patterns are usually classified into three categories: those pertaining primarily to children, those pertaining primarily to teachers, and those pertaining primarily to curriculum. Some of the more commonly found patterns in each category are briefly discussed.

Organizational Patterns and Children

In any school situation there are more pupils than teachers; therefore, some means must be used in assigning children to respective teachers. To ask the question, "Should we group?" begs the issue, for some kind of grouping is necessary for X number of pupils and X number of teachers to work together for an X period of time within an X amount of space.

Throughout the history of American schools, educators have attempted to group children for effective instruction. During the past 125 years or so countless grouping plans have been tried, modified, abandoned, or adopted. History of education records many well-known plans, such as the Platoon Plan, the Dalton Plan, the Winnetka Plan, and the XYZ Plan. But space does not permit an historical review of grouping. Instead, let us rather briefly consider some of the more commonly practiced grouping procedures in today's elementary schools.

Homogeneous Grouping

This is a widely used means of grouping and has received much attention in the literature. In homogeneous grouping a deliberate attempt is made to place children together in terms of likeness on one or more criteria. The grouping of pupils homogeneously for instruction stems from the desire to reduce the wide range of human differences in a given classroom, thereby improving the teaching-learning situation. Homogeneously, pupils may be grouped in terms of criteria such as chronological age, ability, or achievement.

Reading test scores are used frequently as the basis for grouping children homogeneously in terms of achievement. Children reading above the norm may be placed in one classroom, children reading at or near the norm are placed in a second classroom, and those reading below the norm are placed in a third classroom. When reading scores are used as the basis for grouping, there is little assurance that these same children are also similar in arithmetic, spelling, handwriting, language skills, or any other area. In fact, the range of achievement in other subjects is likely to be as great as if the groups represented a random sample.

At times I.Q. scores have been used as a basis for grouping pupils, but a multitude of problems are encountered when this is undertaken. Some pupils with high intelligence scores do not perform academic skills compatible with those scores. Parents frequently object to their children being assigned to a classroom on the basis of an I.Q. test. One might also question the ethics of such a procedure in a democratic society. In addition, teachers who are assigned to teach only low-achieving pupils resent the assignment and may perform at a rather low level themselves. It is because of reasons such as these that the majority of elementary school classrooms are organized on a heterogeneous basis. When homogeneous grouping is used in the elementary school, it is found more frequently in the upper elementary level than in the primary level. This is because of the need to look beyond one academic area as a basis for homogeneous grouping. Many schools using homogeneous grouping in the upper elementary grades do so in conjunction with a program of departmentalization with pupils grouped homogeneously within each of the subjects. The grade level is completely reshuffled for each class, so that one subject area does not become the basis for assigning an individual to a group. When this type of grouping does occur, it requires considerable responsibility on the part of each individual pupil in getting to his assigned class, a task that is easier for upper elementary children.

Undoubtedly, homogeneous grouping offers some advantages, but the disadvantages seem to outweigh the advantages of the belief that children can actually be homogeneously grouped. Though the range of differences may be reduced in terms of any one variable, many individual differences, such as pupil's tastes, temperments, interests, aims, aptitudes, and attitudes, still exist within any group. If teachers are to meet individual needs, they still find it necessary to adapt standards and to use a variety of materials and methods. Teachers and pupils both find it difficult to offset the label or stigma attached to the "fast" or "high ability" group and to the "slow" or "low ability" group.

Heterogeneous Grouping

In this plan a deliberate attempt is made to group together a cross section of youngsters. Every teacher at each teaching level can expect to have a classroom of children representing a general cross section of the pupil population. Whereas in homogeneous grouping likeness was the key word, diversity is the guiding principle in heterogeneous grouping. Some children will have unique and obvious problems, whereas others will be well adjusted and stable; some will possess great potential, others little; some will be high achievers and some low achievers; and some will have a positive attitude and others a negative attitude toward school.

Teachers tend to favor working with heterogeneously grouped children, pointing out that homogeneous grouping often concentrates problem, low-motivated, or slow-learning children, thus increasing the burden on the teacher of these groups. Some schools reduce the size of classes taught by teachers assigned to "slow" groups. However, this practice places excessive and sometimes unreasonable numbers in the classrooms of other teachers, who soon raise objections about their poor teaching situation. Heterogeneous grouping, at least, tends to equalize the classroom challenge and responsibility of all teachers. Supporters of this organization claim that regardless of the criteria used for grouping, every classroom of youngsters soon becomes heterogeneous with the growth patterns and rates of learning among individuals soon destroying group homogeneity.

If differences in a group are recognized, understood, valued, and utilized by both teachers and pupils, learning as represented by democratic competencies should be enhanced. A group needs a range of abilities suited to a range of jobs. Many tasks can best be accomplished by pooling the diversified strengths of pupils. It certainly would seem that the more diverse the group, the more opportunities we have for helping children develop the competencies, skills, and attitudes necessary for living in a democratic society. It is likely that heterogeneity will always have a valid role in education because a teacher who seeks to meet individual needs will make any group more heterogeneous rather than less.

Multiage Grouping

One of the more modern grouping practices is multiage or interage grouping, according to which children are grouped on the basis of planned heterogeneity to increase individual differences. The groupings usually consists of children spanning a three-year age period, such as five through seven, six through eight, or nine through eleven. The exact age levels that are combined are not as significant as is the fact that the group is a planned mixture on the basis of such factors as age, sex, ability, achievement, emotional or social maturity, learning styles, and interests.

Advocates claim that multiage grouping (1) enhances individualization of instruction because the teacher better conceptualizes the diversity in the group or class; (2) provides children opportunities to interact with a group that is similar to the group they socialize with outside of school; (3) offers opportunity for pupils to have experience in playing all the leadership roles—dependence, independence, interdependence; (4) provides opportunities for children to learn from each other (Younger children may model themselves after older children; and the older children, in turn, may find themselves in some aspect being challenged, equalled, or surpassed by younger children.); and (5) offers more flexibility in placing a child in a class—with a teacher and other children—where the chances for continuing growth and development are best.

Multiage grouping with it's planned wide mix of differences offers the possibility of rich learning experiences. Dealing effectively with such a wide range of differences, however, may be either too much of a challenge or actually a more complex task than some teachers can handle.

Research offers few if any conclusive answers to questions regarding the relative values of different grouping patterns. Regardless of how children are grouped to place them with a teacher in a class, much within-class grouping will be necessary to meet changing circumstances. Decisions as to the form or forms of grouping to be used should be based on knowledge of goals or purposes, pupils, faculty, teaching methods, materials, and size and arrangement of school plant. There probably should be no established grouping pattern; rather, ample opportunity for flexibility should be maintained. Finally, grouping may enhance or inhibit certain kinds of learning, but answers to the knotty questions inherent in providing adequately for the uniqueness of individuals lie more in—the *way we teach—what happens with the class—the healthy human relations and interactions—and the variety and quality of experiences*—rather than in some mechanical means of grouping.

HORIZONTAL PATTERNS AND TEACHER UTILIZATION

Each school system—and sometimes each school—has adopted some horizontal organizational framework within which the teaching staff works to plan and implement effective curricular experiences with children. Some of the most accepted and widely used plans are discussed in this section.

Self-contained Classroom

In the self-contained classroom one teacher is responsible for all the school experiences of a group of pupils for a school year. The school day would be devoted to working together as a unit from the time of arrival until dismissal. This permits flexible use of time to meet the needs of a particular situation. In other words, a highly interesting and successful learning experience does not have to be suddenly interrupted because the ringing of a bell signifies the ending of a school day period or because it is "time" for the pupils to work with another teacher. Among other advantages of the self-contained classroom claimed by its proponents are the following: (1) it facilitates the teacher's becoming acquainted with each pupil assigned to the class; (2) it offers many opportunities to help pupils integrate learning in various curricular areas into a meaningful whole; (3) group interaction and interpersonal relationships are fostered; and (4) better evaluation can be made of the pupil's overall progress.

Some of the more frequently mentioned disadvantages by critics of the self-contained classroom follow: (1) it places unrealistic demand upon the teacher (For instance, many teachers do not possess a high degree of interest and competence in all curricular fields; therefore, some areas may be overemphasized and others slighted.); (2) growing, developing youngsters need association and interaction with more than one teacher during the school year; and (3) teachers and pupils in a self-contained classroom tend to become isolated from other teachers and children in the school.

Recognizing the unique challenge facing the self-contained classroom teacher of approximately thirty pupils, many school systems provide supporting assistance. In addition to the principal, supporting personnel might include the school secretary, nurse, psychologist, social worker, librarian, and possibly consultants in selected curricular areas, such as reading, mathematics, music, art, and physical education.

Not all self-contained classrooms are "pure" in the sense that the teacher is responsible for 100 per cent of the activities in his room. Many schools use some modification of the self-contained concept and employ specialists to teach some subjects. In the past, music, art, and physical education were the three areas most often assigned to teaching staff as special areas. At present, there is a trend toward employment of special teachers in other areas, including speech, science, and mathematics. Generally, schedules are arranged so that the special teachers come to the various classrooms and teach for a period of time several days a week. It is also possible that special facilities, such as art and music rooms, may be available for the special area teachers to use. Planning and correlating all the school experiences of children assigned to his classroom is still the self-contained classroom teacher's responsibility.

Even though the self-contained classroom is one of the earlier forms of school organization, it continues as the prevailing practice, especially in the primary grades. A survey of 2,318 elementary principals conducted in 1968 revealed that, in kindergarten through third grade, better than 95 per cent of the schools surveyed used the self-contained plan. Although it was less widely used in upper elementary grades, approximately 70 per cent of the sixth grades were reported using the self-contained approach.[3]

Departmentalized Classroom

Departmentalization has the elementary school organized into academic subject matter areas much as most high schools are organized. Whereas the self-contained classroom teacher typically teaches all the academic subjects, in the departmentalization pattern a teacher teaches only one or two subjects to all pupils at the level or levels to which the teacher is assigned. Typically, the school day is organized into periods, perhaps of varying length. In some elementary schools children may change classes throughout the day, receiving reading instruction from one teacher in one classroom and then moving to another teacher in another classroom for the next subject. Another innovation of the departmentalized

[3] Department of Elementary School Principals, *The Elementary School Principalship in 1968* (Washington, D.C.: National Education Association, 1968), p. 66.

plan is to have the children remain in the same classroom with the teachers changing rooms each period. Schools that utilize departmentalization consider the teacher to be a subject-matter specialist as contrasted with the self-contained classroom teacher considered to be a generalist. The curriculum of elementary schools has become increasingly complex as the needs of our society have dictated a more complex way of living. During the past several years there have been constant additions to subject-matter expectations for elementary school children. In recent years, this pressure has led to increasing forms of departmentalization in the elementary school, particularly in grades four, five, and six.

Those who favor departmentalization claim several advantages. Among these are the following: (1) teachers can concentrate on building a depth of competence in one or two curricular or subject-matter areas; (2) special materials and equipment needed for an academic area can be provided more easily; (3) departmentalization provides pupils both contacts and experiences with several teachers; (4) it makes it possible for pupils to progress through school by academic subjects rather than by grades; (5) it offers greater opportunity for helping pupils to understand a subject area in terms of its structure; and (6) it provides better articulation with the middle school program.

Some of the disadvantages of departmentalization follow: (1) a pupil needs to remain under the supervision of one teacher, who can gain a more complete understanding of the child's needs; (2) fewer opportunities for children to recognize and understand the interrelatedness of the various subjects studied exist; (3) teachers may become more concerned with developing academic competence in a particular subject than in working with children relative to their individual differences; (4) many interruptions of learning occur because of scheduled time to work with another teacher in a different subject; and (5) it is more difficult for pupils to establish a good working relationship with several teachers than with one.

Semidepartmental or Dual-Progress

The semidepartmentalized or dual-progress plan of organization attempts to combine the advantages of the self-contained and the departmental classroom approaches and also the strengths of the graded and nongraded patterns. Since the turn of the century, various plans have been developed wherein a pupil would spend part of the day in a self-contained classroom and the other part of the day with departmentalized teachers, who are specialists in a subject. One of the more recent organizational patterns, and one that has received considerable attention, is the *Dual-Progress Plan* developed by George D. Stoddard.

Except for one period of physical education taught by a specialist in that area, a child in the dual-progress plan spends a half day, either morning or afternoon, receiving counseling and instruction from one teacher in what Stoddard calls the "cultural imperatives"—language arts and social studies. This segment of the program basically employs the self-contained approach and the grade-level system for assigning and promoting children. During the other half of the school day, the pupil moves from room to room receiving instruction from a subject-matter specialist in what Stoddard refers to as the "cultural electives"—mathematics, science, music, and art. This segment of the program employs the departmental approach and the nongraded system for assigning and promoting pupils.

Some advantages claimed for semidepartmentalization or the dual-progress plan are as follows: (1) pupils work in each curricular area with a teacher who is well prepared in the subject and enjoys teaching it; (2) the self-contained classroom or homeroom teacher has an opportunity to get to know each child well; (3) each classroom can be supplied with special materials and equipment to serve as a "learning laboratory" in a subject area; (4) the plan offers the possibility for a child to work and progress in some curricular area on the basis of interest, ability, and achievement; (5) a feeling of belonging is facilitated owing to the fact that a pupil spends a half day in one room with the same group; (6) pupils can benefit from experiencing several teachers instead of one; and (7) there is good utilization of the school plant.

Some of the disadvantages associated with semidepartmentalization or the dual-progress plan are the following: (1) definite scheduled periods of time to work with departmentalized teachers may interrupt learning when a child is most interested or involved; (2) it is difficult to justify in the dual-progress plan which areas are to be "imperatives" and which are to be "electives"; (3) working with so many children each day, teachers find it difficult to understand and plan for individual needs; (4) record keeping on a large number of pupils can become a burden; (5) teachers experience difficulty in finding enough time for cooperative planning to foster interrelationship between the different subjects; and (6) difficulties may stem from having some aspects of the program operating on the grade-level system and others on nongradedness.

Team Teaching

One of the relatively new innovations in school organization is team teaching. The team teaching plan of organization appears to have originated in 1957 with the program initiated in the Franklin School, Lexington, Massachusetts, in conjunction with the Harvard Graduate School of Education. The idea apparently met with rather popular acceptance. Since 1957 programs of team teaching, although varying widely, have been adopted by many schools at all levels—elementary, middle, and secondary —throughout the country.

Some people may perceive team teaching to be only an adaptation of departmentalization or nongrading, but actually it goes beyond these changes. Team teaching has been defined as "a type of instructional organization, involving teaching personnel and the students assigned to them, in which two or more teachers are given responsibility, working together, for all or a significant part of the instruction of the same group of students."[4] This means that team teaching is not only concerned with the relationship of the teachers, but also with the pupils and the learning environment. Indeed, many of the underlying principles of nongrading and multigrading are also found in the notion of team teaching. All of these ideas are concerned with individual progress and an arrangement of instruction that permits flexibility and efficiency for teachers and pupils. A team approach makes it possible for a variety of interests to be pursued within a given classroom both by the teacher and the learner. Regardless of the size of the basic group, a team of teachers is able to divide the group into segments suited to need and interest and thereby take into account needs that are neglected in more structured environments.

Whereas most teams have three or more faculty members, some have only two. More important than the size of the team is the degree to which team members feel a "joint responsibility" for planning, instructing, and evaluating. In schools where the means for sharing these responsibilities have not been mutually determined, team teaching is likely a misnomer. Generally, the teacher-pupil ratio is about one to twenty-five or thirty. If there are three teachers on the team, you might expect seventy-five to ninety pupils to be assigned to the team.

Some teams are organized very informally with each member assuming similar roles and having equal team status. The group may elect its leader or coordinator, if there is one, with the position rotating. Other teams are hierarchical in design with every team member's role and function rather carefully and precisely defined. There seems to be no established pattern for selecting and rewarding the team leader. Some continue full-time teaching duties, some are relieved of part of the normal teaching load, and others are given a supplemental salary increase. The leader is expected to assume the responsibility of coordinating the team's planning and instructional, counseling, and evaluating functions as well as serving a liaison role with the administration and other teams. Therefore, the team leader should be an outstanding teacher with a wide background of experience and possessing the personal characteristics of initiative, stability, diplomacy, patience, and organizational skills.

In forming teams, one should consider such factors as the willingness to serve as a team member, compatability of personalities and philosophies, differing academic competencies and interests, experience, and ability to respect and communicate with others.

[4] Judson T. Shaplin and Henry F. Olds, *Team Teaching* (New York: Harper, 1964), p. 15.

In addition to offering a better utilization of each teacher's strengths, team teaching was conceived as a means of providing greater flexibility in grouping, scheduling, and the use of school plant facilities. The pupil would spend part of his time in large groups, mainly receiving information; part in small groups or individual pursuits, interacting with others in reconstructing and refining information, developing skills, and applying learnings. Schools that are to incorporate the philosophy of team teaching must provide the flexible physical environment in which these ideas can become operational. Team members also need blocks of time and physical space conducive to working together in planning procedures and activities that enable pupils to profit from the flexible possibilities.

In addition to matters related to the organization, staffing, planning, and evaluation of programs involving a team approach, it is also necessary that there be general understanding within the community. The team approach requires that parents understand the benefits that can be derived if they are asked to support such changes. Therefore, involvement of the community in such changes is a must. However, such change does not occur by itself; leadership and direction by the profession are required if tomorrow is to be better than today.

Some advantages claimed for team teaching are the following: (1) it facilitates flexible grouping on the basis of need; (2) teachers can concentrate more time and effort in building a particular academic strength, talent, or interest into a specialty; (3) it is a way to encourage outstanding teachers to remain in the classroom; (4) more efficient and effective use of school facilities and instructional materials result; (5) there is a better chance for a pupil to have readily available a teacher who can help with a specific problem; (6) a more extensive set of learning experiences can be offered than by an individual teacher; and (7) better understanding of each child can be obtained by pooling the viewpoints of team members, all of whom work with the child.

Some disadvantages associated with team teaching are as follows: (1) staffing a team with members committed to the flexibility idea associated with team teaching is a problem; (2) there is difficulty in selecting a team who can work together harmoniously; (3) many elementary school buildings are not conducive to team teaching; (4) it is difficult to locate or select enough well-qualified and effective team leaders; (5) some teachers do not like to work under conditions where peers can continually evaluate their performance; and (6) young or inexperienced teachers may be overwhelmed and simply tend to go along with ideas of experienced teachers.

Differentiated Staffing

Differentiated staffing is a relatively new, flexible, instructional organizational pattern for deploying teachers and paraprofessionals at various responsibility levels so as to make optimum use of their training, talents, interests, and commitments. Chapter 6 of this book is devoted to differentiated staffing.

Open Education

Open education, sometimes referred to as open schools or open classrooms, is one of the more recent trends in American education. This informal organizational approach to education has gained momentum rapidly since the Plowden Report on English infant and junior schools published in 1967. In addition to the English primary school influence, the open education concept is supported in the philosophical and psychological writings of John Dewey, Jacques Rousseau, Friedrich Froebel, Johann Pestalozzi, Jean Piaget, Maria Montessori, and Joseph Featherstone.

Open education is concerned with a flexible organization of space and program, but even more important are the structure and organization of the learning climate. Open education is characterized by such factors as (1) a stimulating, relaxed environment rich with easily accessible learning resources, both human and material; (2) the encouragement of self-reliance and responsibility by permitting pupils freedom to move about freely and to make choices from many alternatives as to what they will do and the learning resources they will use; and (3) the importance of learning basic skills and a structure that provides a sense of order and direction, both of which are considered important to effective open education. In this respect, Roland Barth maintains, "A well-organized, consistent, teacher-directed classroom probably has a far less harmful influence upon children than a well-intentioned but sloppy, permissive, and chaotic attempt at an open classroom in which teacher and child must live with contradiction and conflict."[5]

In discussing the structure and organization of open education, Vito Perrone describes a typical day in one teacher's open classroom as follows:

> The first hour of the day is devoted generally to "free activities." Children pick up where they left off the previous day or begin something else. After approximately an hour, the class gathers for a planning session. . . . In the planning session everyone draws up a personal plan for the day. The teacher generally uses this occasion to call attention to new additions to the learning centers and new possibilities for using outside resources. She also takes this opportunity to organize a specific time to meet with particular groups of children (she names them) to work on a specific skill. . . . After the planning session, the children go into the various learning centers. The teacher then moves about the room, working with individual children and small groups. She asks questions, suggests other resources for extension of a particular activity, encourages, listens, and learns. At the

[5] Roland S. Barth, "So You Want to Change to An Open Classroom," *Phi Delta Kappan*, 53:99 (Oct. 1971).

end of the day, the children come together again to evaluate and share what they have learned or found particularly interesting.[6]

Open education offers an alternative to our traditional school organizational patterns. However, if we believe that individuals are unique and that learning patterns differ and if we wish to make the best use of available space and the fullest use possible of community learning resources, there can never be an open classroom or open school model up for widespread adoption.

SCHOOL ORGANIZATION AND DECISION-MAKING

Teachers and administrators in school districts throughout the country are caught in the "Let's change school organization" syndrome. Many changes in school or classroom organization are made simply in terms of what is popular at a given time—join the bandwagon group. Some plans are adopted primarily because of the strong persuasive powers of an individual advocating a particular method of organization.

Selecting the most appropriate organizational pattern is admittedly a difficult task. Better decisions could be made, however, if the school staff became knowledgeable about a variety of organizational patterns and evaluated these against an agreed-upon set of criteria. Figure 5–3 shows "an

Key	Self-contained Classroom	Team Teaching	Departmentali-zation	Modular Scheduling	Differentiated Staffing	Nongraded School	Graded School	Multi age Grouping
N.A. Not applicable + Meets criteria − Does not meet criteria ///// Partly applicable								
1. Continuous Progress								
2. Differentiated Rates and Means								
3. Student Objectives								
4. Assignment to Instructional Groups								
5. Flexibility in Group Size								
6. Close Relationship								
7. Sense of Identity								
8. Security and Structure								
9. Teacher Competence and Interest								
10. Formulation of Objectives								
11. Planning and Decision Making								
12. Colleague Evaluation								
13. Career Ladder								

(left margin label: Criteria of School Organization)

FIGURE 5–3. *Organizational Grid.*

[6] Vito Perrone, *Open Education: Promise and Problems* (Bloomington, Ind.: The Phi Delta Kappa Foundation, 1972), pp. 18–19.

organizational grid designed to improve decision making in school organization and thus reduce the likelihood of inappropriate decisions. A staff can fill in the various categories by using the key at the bottom of the grid."[7] A staff using this grid idea might wish to formulate their own sets of criteria and organization patterns.

School District Organization

The overall local school administrative organizational unit is the school district. Each state is composed of several school districts of varying size. The trend in recent years has been to consolidate smaller independent school districts into larger units enrolling children from kindergarten through grade twelve.

The boundaries of a school district are usually a combination of natural and man-made division lines. A boundary might be a river, lake, or stream, or a railroad track, street, or freeway. The resulting school district tends to be uneven and, when viewed on a map, may appear to be quite illogical and haphazard. This is because any typical, planned school district soon becomes pressured out of shape as population shifts occur or political or financial pressures weld the unusual district shapes. Teachers new to a district, student teachers, or first-year teachers unfamiliar with the district may find no reason for the district lines. A simple demarcation would be a city, town, or county forming the district. In some more rural areas this is frequently the situation. In urban or suburban areas, one may find children with the same city address, but have the possibility of enrolling in any one of at least five different districts. These districts can assume rather unusual shapes; some in at least one state resemble an elongated T or $\perp$ with the vertical line as long as twelve or fifteen miles, but only a few blocks wide.

Annexation of smaller school districts to the larger neighbors, housing developments, and deterioration of inner-city areas result in a metamorphic condition for a onetime stable school district. Figure 5–4 portrays a hypothetical city school district.

Decisions must be made as to how the school population will be divided into division levels, because the typical school district enrolls students from elementary through high school. Distinctions between elementary and postelementary schools have never developed into a clear-cut pattern. Grades that constitute part of the elementary school in one district may be included in the middle school or junior high school in another

[7] Donald A. Myers and Robert Sinclair, "Improved Decision Making For School Organization: What and What For," *The National Elementary Principal*, **52**:44 (Jan. 1973).

FIGURE 5–4. *A Hypothetical City School District.*

district. The adaption of school organization to meet the needs of the local school district has been the usual practice. Local boards of education designate which grades will be considered as elementary and which grades will be considered as secondary. State boards or state departments of education, in many cases, grant teaching certificates that overlap some elementary and secondary grades.

The five basic patterns of school organization shown in Figure 5–5 are representative of schools in America today. These are the 6–3–3, the 6–6, the 6–2–4, the 8–4, and the 5–3–4 organizational plans.

Contained in a local school district, generally, will be one or more senior high schools, two or more middle schools or junior high schools, and several elementary schools. Around each of these buildings is formulated a school boundary district within the overall local school district. If there are two high schools, each will serve approximately one half of the present or projected high school student population. However, if the local school district is a city district, one school may be located nearer to the center or downtown than the other. Generally, this is because it probably once was the only high school for the entire city. Finding a suitable loca-

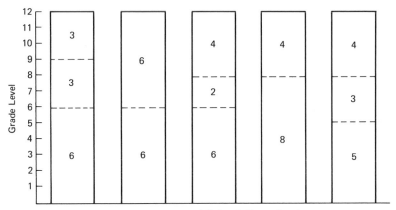

Figure 5–5. *Representative Patterns of School Organization.*

tion for the second high school has plagued many a school board and superintendent.

Each senior high school enrolls pupils who have completed middle schools within their boundaries. Therefore, more than one middle school district may be located in a single high school district. Figure 5–6 shows the location of senior high and middle schools in a hypothetical city school district.

The elementary schools located throughout the city are the school unit most closely aligned with the neighborhood served. Generally, several elementary schools serve as feeder schools for each middle school. Figure 5–7 illustrates the location of elementary school districts within our hypothetical city complex.

For many years, the most widely used plan of organization in the United States has been the 6–3–3. This provides an elementary school program of six years exclusive of kindergarten. Inclusion of kindergarten as a part of the elementary school program traditionally has been a local decision that is encouraged more in some states than in others. Recently, most states have been attempting to promote kindergarten programs as a regular part of the public schools through legislative appropriation funds. In addition to establishing kindergarten as a part of the regular school program, many school systems throughout the country have developed prekindergarten programs. Generally, these programs are not paid for out of regular school funds; instead, parents who wish to enroll their child in the preschool program pay the school a nominal fee to defray operating expenses.

A promising organizational pattern is the middle school, which began to develop rapidly in the 1960s. With this emphasis on developing a truly "bridging school" between the elementary and high school and the grow-

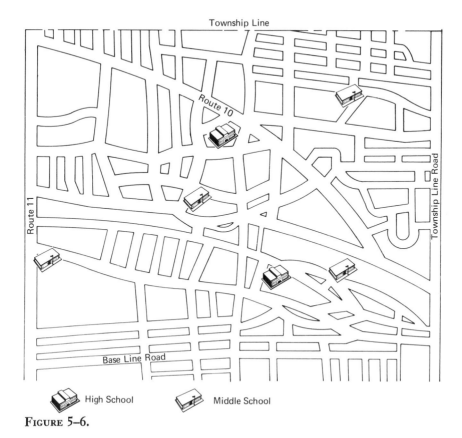

Township Line

Route 10

Route 11

Township Line Road

Base Line Road

High School   Middle School

FIGURE 5–6.

ing concern for extending school to include younger children (ages three to five), the currently fastest growing school districtwide pattern of organization seems to be K–5, elementary; 6–8, middle school; and 9–12, high school. This pattern of organization offers a promising structure within which to develop three distinct, although interrelated, programs of schooling that closely parallel periods of human growth and development. The *elementary school* would focus on childhood—the *middle school* would focus on the period between childhood and adolescence—the *high school* would focus on adolescence. Certainly, the *middle school* serves as a "bridge" between the elementary school and the high school. This has also been a goal of the junior high school. If the *middle school*, however, is to be a more successful program than the junior high school, it must "bridge" the educational needs of the learner between childhood and adolescence. William Alexander, a *middle school* proponent, believes the program should not be patterned after either the elementary or secondary models. He says, "The concept that must direct the development of middle

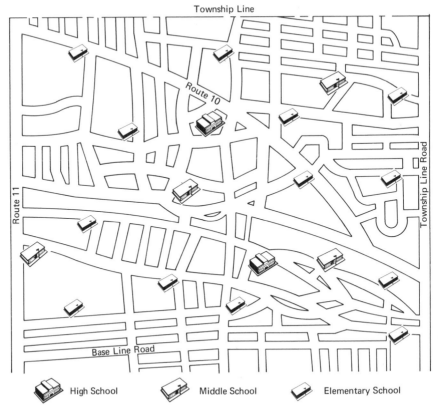

Township Line

Route 10

Route 11

Township Line Road

Base Line Road

| High School | Middle School | Elementary School |

FIGURE 5–7. *Location of Elementary Schools in Relation to Secondary Schools.*

schools is squarely focused on the period of human growth and development occurring between childhood and adolescence and embracing as its
central influence the onset of puberty."[8]

The middle school usually includes children in grades 6–8 or 5–8.
Simply grouping these grades together will make little or no difference.
The middle school concept does offer a challenging alternative within a
school system to improve the middle years of the K–12 educational span.
One thing that is certain is that the number of middle schools continues
to increase rapidly. In a survey conducted in the 1969–70 school year,
Kealy reported there were a total of 2,298 middle schools in the United
States. This was twice the number reported in 1967–68. He also stated,
"As in the 1965–66 and the 1967–68 surveys, the 6–8 grade organization is

[8] William M. Alexander, "Introduction: How Fares the Middle School?" *The
National Elementary Principal*, 51:9 (Nov. 1971).

most common, accounting for 58.2 per cent, followed by the 5–8 pattern at 25.4 per cent."[9]

What does this rapidly developing trend toward middle schools mean for the K–5 or K–4 elementary school? Elementary educators *must* be concerned! Should they continue existing programs with the older children gone? What desirable changes should and can be made? What changes in teacher preparation does the trend imply?

SOME FORCES AFFECTING SCHOOL ORGANIZATION

Many contemporary sociopolitical forces affect change in school organization. Among these forces are (1) decentralization and community control, (2) desegregation and integration, and (3) alternative schools.

Decentralization and Community Control

In recent years several large city school systems have implemented some form of decentralization as a response to pressures to reorder the power and authority structure. The argument has been that the central board of education and central staff are too far removed from the local school and that those more directly concerned, local school staff and representatives of the community served by the school, should have more decision-making power and responsibility for the day-to-day operation of the school.

Decentralization takes many forms as city school systems attempt to implement the concept. Some cities still retain central office administration of instruction and support services, but have developed a systematic means of getting local school staff and community reaction and advice in the decision-making process. Some large school districts have been divided into subgeographical areas, each area headed by an administrator. Other districts are divided into a number of community school districts, each controlled by a locally elected board representation of the community served by the school. In most decentralized areas, there appears to be more community participation than community control. Among the cities experimenting with some form of decentralization are Detroit, Washington, New York, Philadelphia, Los Angeles, and St. Louis.

Desegregation and Integration

Most of the efforts toward desegregation and integration in the public schools have been in response to pressures to eliminate racial disparities

---

[9] Ronald P. Kealy, "The Middle School Movement, 1960–1970," *The National Elementary Principal*, 51:23–24 (Nov. 1971).

and to provide equal education opportunities. Strong pleas have been made for implementing multiethnic or multiracial schools as a means for educating for living effectively in a democracy. Alvin Loving, in making a case for multiethnic schools, expresses the belief that ". . . all children should learn the contributions of the many subcultures of America to our total society. I think they ought to learn it together in a face-to-face situation of blacks, whites, browns, yellows, and reds. It then becomes meaningful and they see each other as human beings each with his own rich contribution to the totality that is America."[10]

Intradistrict or interdistrict bussing has been a hotly debated issue in recent years as a means of achieving better racial or ethnic balance in our schools. Bussing children to achieve racial balance has raised anew many questions as to the validity of the "neighborhood school" and "freedom of choice" concepts. Some recent writings indicate that desegregation and cultural integration may have to be accomplished on a broader basis than school busing. Bane and Jencks advocate school busing be justified in political and moral terms rather than on effects of children in school:

> busing ought to be justified in political and moral terms rather than in terms of presumed long-term effects on the children who are bused. If we want an integrated society, we ought to have integrated schools, which make people feel they have a stake in the well-being of other races. If we want a society in which people are free to segregate themselves, then we should apply that principle to our schools. There is, however, no compelling reason to treat schools differently from other social arrangements, including neighborhoods. Personally, we believe in both open housing and open schools. If parents or students want to take buses to schools in other neighborhoods, school boards ought to provide the buses, expand the relevant schools, and ensure that the students are welcome in the schools they want to attend.[11]

ALTERNATIVE SCHOOLS.   Disappointment and dissatisfaction with presently organized schools has led to a plethora of newly founded private alternative schools. Most of these schools employ a flexible organizational structure and emphasize a high degree of community participation and also a positive and humane learning environment. Anderson[12] suggests that

[10] Alvin D. Loving, "A Case For Multi-Ethnic Schools," *Phi Delta Kappan*, 53: 280 (Jan. 1972).

[11] Mary Jo Bane and Christopher Jencks, "The Schools and Equal Opportunity," *Saturday Review of Education*, 55:41 (Sept. 16, 1972).

[12] Robert H. Anderson, "Organizing and Staffing the School," *The Elementary School in the United States*, seventy-second Yearbook of the National Society for the Study of Education (Chicago: U. of Chicago Press, 1973), pp. 221–242.

within public education, a single school system could provide many different kinds of schools and offer parents the option of sending their children to the school of their choice. Within a school system there might be such choices as a school or schools that are open, highly structured, nongraded, graded, integrated, segregated, team teaching, self-contained, and departmentalized.

Some people argue that the traditional school model has been too isolated from the actual life of the surrounding community. Some districts are establishing "educational parks" as a means of bringing school and community activities into a closer relationship. The increasing concern over the high cost of constructing school buildings and the increasing desire to help children perceive better the larger society has resulted in using "community space" for educational purposes other than the traditional schoolhouse. Children in communities throughout the country "are spending much of their school time in the community itself, studying and learning in places that don't look at all like schools—local museums, stores, business and industrial facilities, art centers, music and theater groups, or the local courthouse."[13]

As a professional person, you will have the responsibility of being knowledgeable as to the various school and classroom organization plans, of being flexible in adapting to change if change is desired in the school community, and of continually evaluating school practices in your classroom and community. Types of school organization must be developed that will enhance the attainment of changing educational goals.

SUMMARY

Patterns of school organization fall into two major types—vertical and horizontal. Within each of the types a variety of practices are employed in various school systems throughout the country. The most common patterns within both types of organization have been discussed in this chapter. No one pattern will serve all purposes well. Each school system needs to develop continually and employ patterns that best meet the particular needs of its pupils, teachers, and community. In the final analysis, it is not the organizational pattern itself, but the creative teacher working within the framework of perhaps a combination of patterns that makes the teaching-learning experience worthwhile or not worthwhile for both teacher and pupils.

[13] Clinchy Evans, "The Vanishing Schoolhouse," *The National Elementary Principal*, **52**:24 (Sept. 1972).

1. The principal has mentioned several times the need to change from the graded school organization to something more appropriate. What patterns would you suggest for consideration? If asked to make a presentation on the pattern you prefer, what would you say?
2. If you had a choice of working with pupils grouped homogeneously, heterogeneously, or by a multiage plan, which form of grouping would you prefer? Why?
3. Several teachers in your building have been discussing the possibility of trying team teaching next year. They ask what you think of team teaching. What can you tell them about its advantages and disadvantages?
4. Plans are being made for a new elementary building because of current overcrowding and continuing housing expansion in and around your community. Pressure is being exerted to make this new building an "open school." Take a stand on "open education" and defend your position.
5. You have been chosen as the "chairperson" of a group charged with making a recommendation for changing the vertical organization of your school. Your group is charged with submitting a recommendation three months from today. Identify several factors to consider in evaluating various organizational patterns.

SELECTED BIBLIOGRAPHY

Alexander, William M. "Introduction: How Fares The Middle School?" *The National Elementary Principal* (Nov. 1971), 8–11.

Bane, Mary Jo, and Christopher Jencks. "The Schools and Equal Opportunity." *Saturday Review of Education* 55 (Sept. 16, 1972), 37–42.

Barth, Roland S. "So You Want To Change To An Open Classroom." *Phi Delta Kappan*, 53:99 (Oct. 1971).

Blitz, Barbara. *The Open Classroom: Making It Work.* Boston: Allyn & Bacon, Inc., 1973.

Department of Elementary School Principals. *The Elementary School Principalship in 1968.* Washington, D.C.: National Education Association, 1968.

The Elementary School in The United States. Ed. by John I. Goodlad and Harold G. Shane. Seventy-second Yearbook of the National Society for the Study of Education, Part II. Chicago: University of Chicago Press, 1973.

Evans, Clinchy. "The Vanishing Schoolhouse." *The National Elementary Principal* 52 (Sept. 1972), 23–26.

Garvelink, Roger H. "Anatomy of a Good Middle School." *The Education Digest* (Feb. 1974), 14–16.

Loving, Alvin D., Sr. "A Case For Multi-Ethnic Schools." *Phi Delta Kappan* 53 (Jan. 1972), 279–80.

Myers, Donald A., and Robert Sinclair. "Improved Decision Making For School Organization: What and What For." *The National Elementary Principal,* 52:44 (Jan. 1973).

Osmon, Howard, and Sam Craver. *Busing: A Moral Issue.* Bloomington, Ind.: The Phi Delta Kappa Foundation, 1972.

Perrone, Vito. *Open Education: Promise and Problems.* Bloomington, Ind.: The Phi Delta Kappa Foundation, 1972.

Chapter 6

Differentiated Staffing
in the School

We are in the midst of a movement in school and society to individualize, and we are not sure in many instances how best to accomplish those portions of the movement that fall within our responsibility. In some instances, reactions have changed the posture of society immediately whereas in others, noticeable experimentation has occurred, but significant change in education, for example, has not been realized. Specifically, dancing forms have moved couples apart to perform individually; established religious groups have been forced to embrace guitars as well as electric organs; politicians have catered to pizza, bagels, and soul food campaign dinners rather than fried chicken; and automobile manufacturers offer hundreds of accessories, models, and colors—not just a black four door with or without bumpers. Even the traditional attire of the American male has been challenged.

> Men's suits really *are* uniform; they look the same on a man as they do on the rack in the clothing store; they hide the fact that one man may be muscular, another flabby, one soft, one bony, one hairy, another smooth. The pants give no hint of a man's legs, and when they wrinkle along body lines, they are quickly taken to the dry cleaners to be pressed back into straight lines. [In contrast] Jeans express the shape of legs, heavy or thin, straight or bowed. As jeans become more wrinkled, they adapt even more to the particular legs that are wearing them. Sitting across from a man in a business suit, it is as if he did not have a body at

all, just a face and a voice. Jeans make one conscious of the body, not as something separate from the face but as part of the whole individual.[1]

Educationally we have moved away from the Parents-Teachers Association in favor of local or school groups for communicating between teacher and parents. Girls now are afforded more participation in school and community sports, and elementary teachers can be a gender other than *she* without being denied admission to the weekly meeting of the town's stomach club. But in individualizing pupils in terms of challenging their abilities to the fullest, we have little more to offer than to assign Charles to section two of grade four in the Pleasantville Elementary School—that will be Mrs. Trilpit's room. Sound familiar? It has been since the late 1800s. Malvina Reynolds and Pete Seeger even put the problem into musical form:

> Little boxes on the hillside
> Little boxes made of ticky-tacky
> Little boxes on the hillside
> Little boxes all the same
> There's a green one and a blue one and a yellow one
> And they're all made out of ticky-tacky
> And they all look just the same.
>
> Little people in the houses
> All go to the university
> And they all get put in boxes
> Little boxes all the same
> And there's doctors and there's lawyers and business executives
> And they're all made out of ticky-tacky and they come out all the same.
>
> All play on the golf course
> All drink their martinis dry
> And they all have pretty children and the children go to school
> And the children go to summer camp
> And then to the university
> And they all get put in boxes and they come out just the same.[2]

One recognizes that the teacher of an elementary school child has much greater responsibility today than at the turn of the century. The range of abilities of a class group as well as the span of their individual development has increased. The teacher fully realizes that the amount of knowledge is expanding at a mind-boggling rate, children are gaining a

---

[1] Charles A. Reich, *The Greening of America* (New York: Random, 1970), p. 236.
[2] Malvina Reynolds, "Little Boxes," from Pete Seeger's Columbia Records album *We Shall Overcome*. Words and music by Malvina Reynolds © Copyright Schroder Music Co. (ASCAP) 1962. Used by permission.

bewildering amount of experience enhanced by mass media, and the expectation of parents for the growth and development of the child has never been higher. Multiply this situation by the movement of formal education to provide satisfactory experiences for the child in both academic and social environments. Can an elementary teacher realize all these expectancies in a self-contained classroom? If not, how?

Of the many alternatives available if the teacher and the school say that they cannot succeed in the present situation, one organized proposal suggests, in simple terms, that the teacher concentrate professional efforts in those fields and activities that demand her expertise and delegate other classroom responsibilities to nonprofessionals. With proper preparation and skilled coordination from an administration-teacher team, the teacher should be able to teach in her chosen field and place responsibility on different individuals when nonspecialist or community resource personnel can perform as well, if not advantageously, with the pupil. The theory of *differentiated staffing* matches the expanded needs of youth in our schools with a structured approach involving a range of adult (and sometimes student) talents to enhance and focus multiresources upon the teaching effort.

The differentiated staffing concept is relatively new and not without reservation and conflict from within and without the profession. Some disciples of the idea claim it as the first movement to liberate the teacher "really" to teach the individual child whereas opponents claim it attempts to apply business management procedure to reduce the prestige and power of the professional teacher. In the following sections of this chapter cognitive objectives have been developed for the reader so that he or she should be able to

1. Describe the basic tenets of the differentiated staffing organizational movement in terms of individualizing instruction.
2. Contrast the developing models of organization for differentiating the staffing of elementary schools.
3. Describe and compare components of the rationale for adapting differentiated staffing modules.
4. Describe and explore the problems of implementing differentiated staffing in the schools.
5. Describe and relate the conflicts of differential staffing to future growth in elementary education.

THE PROBLEM OF BEING DIFFERENT

Since the early days of formal education mankind has tended to view the process of education as possessing a hig degree of similarity or likeness.

Intracultural ambitions tend to develop a uniformity of procedure for both the schools and the instruction that is encouraged.

Adventurers, explorers, and religious missions often acknowledge that the life-styles of peoples in separate parts of the world differ widely, but at the same time record degrees of amazement that the approach to formal education also *differs* from that form and style enjoyed by the traveler in his own country. In some way, anything in education that differs from one's own personal experience generally receives sympathy or criticism in that it is *different* from rather than like other programs. Too often, both professional and lay observers of the school scene assume that educational agencies should be more alike than they are different whether relating to method, materials, or structure. Early one-room schools of the West, for example, were identical in size, shape, and fixtures. Even the teachers were stereotyped. Until recent years, films and television portrayed the one-room school and its occupants in terms of similarity rather than unique differences. Some variation of this typecasting was practiced in the disposition of the teacher—sweet or sour—and the color of the wood school siding—red or white. Even today it would be difficult to break the stereotype of sameness with the image of an even-tempered middle-aged man teaching in a two-room Western school—painted green.

If we can accept the premise that a modern elementary school in a given community differs in its purposes and procedures from schools located in other counties, states, and nations, then it would follow that in identifiable ways the method of teaching could vary—be different from approaches utilized in other learning centers. In short terms, teaching must be *differentiated* to realize the expectancies of differing community expectations. In determining *how* it is to be different, *what* resources will be used, *who* will be responsible in the total combination of teaching effort, and *when* all will be combined in a preplanned program —we have in purpose and practice the philosophy of differentiated staffing.

> Differentiated staffing begins when different teachers do differing things. Another way . . . the thousands of tasks (jobs) little and large, are grouped into areas of commonalities. This "task grouping" then becomes the job assignment of some member of the differentiated staff.[3]

In the age of specialization, proponents for school improvement feel that a more efficient utilization of school and community resources can be realized and that differentiated staffing holds such promise.

[3] Richard A. Dempsey and Rodney P. Smith, *Differentiated Staffing* (Englewood Cliffs, N.J.: Prentice-Hall, 1972), p. 202.

DEVELOPMENTAL BACKGROUND

At the turn of the present century the move from a rural to an urban society was discernible in the increased responsibilities placed upon the school. As discussed in earlier chapters, teaching the basic skills alone was not sufficient for an education-hungry taxpayer and an evolving society. With these new demands for a broadened curriculum, a larger concentration of children in the urban areas encouraged beginning attempts at specialization and the shifting of total teaching responsibility to more than one teacher. In rural areas the move to consolidate isolated, low pupil population schools into multiroomed physical plants upset the traditional pattern of one teacher teaching six to eight grade levels. In some instances, two or more rural one-room schools were physically dragged together and, with a minimum of expense, joined into a multiroomed elementary school. Teaching "load" and responsibility evolved into varying degrees of specialization and, as in urban schools, the "lower or upper" grade teacher emerged.

In an interview with a gallant, classroom-scarred veteran of the early consolidation movement, one of the authors raised the problem of specialized versus nonspecialized teaching and solicited her viewpoint on the current conflicts of approach. Perhaps surprisingly, she favored even more differentiation of responsibilities and marked her release or freedom to teach more effectively with the day the school board hired a school janitor to start the room stoves and carry out the ashes! In a similar vein, many self-contained elementary teachers today voice the feeling that they can more fully realize child and parental expectations when they can be freed of some of the tasks that are not within their fields of expertise or that require professional time. These teachers of the twentieth century feel that a review and reassignment of the "duties" of a self-contained classroom teacher to a school staff with a wide range of interests and capabilities would provide each teacher with an opportunity to challenge the child with confidence and educational efficiency. If we enjoyed professional improvement in the teaching process in the nineteenth century by differentiating between the role of a teacher and a janitor, it would indeed be fitting in the twentieth century to see if additional divisions of the teaching role could be identified and implemented in better realizing the role of the school and the education staff.

There is some agreement in the profession that we should explore the advantages of initiating a change in school policy in this direction. Fortunately or unfortunately, few clear-cut models for change have developed across the nation. Because the structure, staffing, and responsibilities of each school vary, so does the procedure for redesigning the new alignment of responsibility. Realistically, the entire movement has shallow roots in history and even now suffers from lack of communication between practicing districts and with other professional models or similar movements of change.

Historically, it is difficult, if not impossible, to credit a single person or group with the creation of the concept of differentiated staffing as it is known and practiced today. Partial credit at least should be shared by a group concerned with a completely new approach to secondary school instruction. Directed by J. Lloyd Trump, the Commission on the Experimental Study of the Utilization of the Staff in the Secondary School was charged in 1956 by the National Association of Secondary School Principals to propose a plan for stimulating "imaginative research and developments aimed at improving organization and staffing in secondary schools."[4] With an emphasis upon quality instruction the commission envisioned a future school staffed by differing types of people and concentrating upon their specialized skills to work collectively with students in groups ranging from an individual to more than one hundred students. Personnel types included (1) *professional teachers* of both generalized and specialist teaching abilities; (2) *instructional assistants*, who were assigned to work directly with the professional teachers and pupils; (3) *clerks*, who were responsible for keeping records, typewriting, and so forth; (4) *general aids*, who were adults who would assist and supervise students in large meeting rooms, cafeteria, library, and so forth; (5) *staff specialists*, who would include professionals in specialized service fields of health, guidance, remedial reading, and so forth; (6) *community consultants*, who would be drawn primarily from the local community when their qualifications and resources exceeded those of other staff in areas of social problems, specialized knowledge, travel experience, and so forth. The commission sought to use teachers exclusively in the teaching role with other school expectations to be assumed by staff prepared and generally paid for those differing responsibilities. (See Table 6-1.) The teachers were urged to teach in large group settings those concepts that could be treated successfully for one hundred students as well as with fifty. Likewise, small group or individual teaching approaches were to be utilized by teachers when their instructional goals would best be realized in these settings.

Although this report was designed for secondary schools almost two decades ago, the concept of school differentiation was firmly established . . . teachers were hired to teach, clerks to type, aids to run errands, and professional specialists to service those areas where particular talents (physical and mental) were needed. In the process, the commission rec-

[4] J. Lloyd Trump, *Images of the Future—a New Approach to the Secondary School.* Commission on the Experimental Study of the Utilization of the Staff in the Secondary School—Summary Report, Urbana, Ill., 1959.

TABLE 6–1
Trump Secondary School Staffing Plan for Unit of 400 Students*

Staff Classi-fication	Preparation	Number or Assigned Time in hrs/wk
teacher specialist general teachers	masters plus	10
instructional assistants	bachelors plus specific training	200 hours
clerks	high school grad in business	100 hours
general aids	high school	50 hours
community consultants	unusual competence	variable
staff specialists	training in area of specialty	variable

* Adapted from J. Lloyd Trump (director), *Images of the Future*, Commission on the Experimental Study of the Utilization of the Staff in the Secondary School—Summary Report (Urbana, Ill.: 1959), pp. 20–21.

ognized that children would benefit if assignments were not tied to specific degrees of "sameness" in age, training, professional preparation, specialization, and compensation. Thus high school graduate typists could work with professional educators as well as with retired adults or school dropouts. This basic premise was to later cause concern in many professional groups and possibly to restrain the development of differential staffing in its multi-faceted forms.

A teacher in New York borrowed staffing practices from the medical profession in the 1960s to propose alternatives to the traditional school pattern; and although his model was not so identified, it contributed significantly to differentiated staffing as it is known today. Myron Liberman of the American Federation of Teachers proposed a plan to combat some of the problems confronting teachers and schools in the 1960s with a concern for recruiting and retaining good teachers as well as revitalizing the image of the profession in the eyes of the public—and the taxpayer.[5] While Trump built a minimum unit of ten professional teachers plus auxiliary staff for secondary schools, Liberman envisioned an elementary school grouping of twenty with three "specialized" and seventeen "general" teachers. The three were patterned after physician leaders and would have

[5] Fenwick English, "The Differentiated Staff: Education's Technostructure," *Educational Technology*, 10, No. 2:25 (Feb. 1970).

their doctoral degrees whereas the seventeen teachers would be comparable to nurses and would certify with bachelor's degrees. Liberman felt that superior salaries paid to the three leaders could be used to recruit teachers and to retain the desirable, successful members of the team. By differentiating role and responsibility, the program espoused would also reduce overall school costs and place a heavy share of teacher preparation on classroom contact with overall supervision by the doctoral degree staff leaders.

Somewhat parallel to the financial support given to Trump by the Ford Foundation was the aid given to Dwight Allen in his development of a differentiated staffing model commonly called the Temple City (California) plan. This plan with subsequent modifications is most often cited as a base prototype for most of the differentiated staffing plans that have developed. (See Figure 6–1.) When this plan is compared with the staffing model of Trump, the similarities overwhelm differences and to a certain extent differ in detail because of fundamental differences in teaching secondary rather than elementary students. As for the Trump suggestion of utilizing large class groups in excess of one hundred wherever efficient and feasible, few elementary models include that feature. (One of the authors, however, has observed an elementary classroom television reception involving an excess of one hundred students in one group monitered by five to seven general-type classroom teachers.) For detailed specifics on concurrent models see Fenwick English, who identifies and compares their functions in detail.[6]

Non-tenure			
master teacher (doctoral or equivalent)	Non-tenure		
	senior teacher (masters or equivalent)	Tenure	
		staff teacher (bachelors and certified)	Tenure
			associate teacher (bachelors or intern)
2/5's teaching responsibility	3/5's teaching responsibility	100% teaching	100% teaching
12 months assignment	10-11 months assignment	10 months assignment	variable
← teacher assistants →			
← educational technicians →			
← clerks →			

FIGURE 6–1. *Temple City Differentiated Staffing Plan.* (*Adapted from Dempsey and Smith, op. cit., p. 20.*)

[6] Ibid., pp. 24–27.

RATIONALE FOR DIFFERENTIATED STAFFING

In political circles, candidates traditionally maneuver to avoid being the first speaker where more than one individual speaks on any common topic. Speaking from the second position gives one the advantage of agreeing with favorable comments of the first speaker as well as disagreeing and/or counterpointing original slips of the tongue. In educational circles, the traditional self-contained elementary classroom unit has been in the limelight of public attention for many decades and its shortcomings as well as strength can be rather easily analyzed. A well-polished common model has been developed—one that appears mentally at the mention of the term self-contained classroom—almost a Pavlovian conditioning reaction in spite of the fact that relatively few schools actually adhere strictly to the design today. However, as a unit of operation, it connotes *sameness* in school organization, staffing, teacher preparation, and so forth. It also provides a theoretical base for identifying weaknesses in current educational approach and outcomes. Proponents of differentiated staffing identify the weaknesses of the self-contained classroom staffing plan and, once it is dissected, apply new staffing approaches to implement their curricular goals. It should be noted that proven elements of the curricular goals developed under self-contained plans have as yet to be achieved in competing plans of organization—in fact, are retained in schools that have moved to team teaching, departmentalization, and other variations. Differentiated staffing to date has not consistently demonstrated a degree of competency sufficient to discharge totally strong elements of the self-contained classroom—but has moved strongly in attempting to improve those areas of obvious weakness by suggesting that differentiated staffing will provide needed strength, as the discussion that follows indicates.

Teacher Preparation

Differentiated staffing realizes that few elementary teachers receive sufficient preparation for teaching all the subjects to all ranges of children at all levels of ability—from a typical four-year university program. Teacher certification is moving to the equivalent of a five-year cumulative course sum for minimal continued certification.

In-service Preparation

Most in-service programs are geared either to broad-ranging professional interest topics or to singular items of aid to a small segment of teacher need. Differentiated staffing points to the common school or district practice of training most of the teachers to do the same thing with little variation or preparation for "decoding" the specific needs of the variations within each group of pupils.

Individual Teacher Competency

Past challenges in the curriculum seldom encompassed the ranges of teacher ability, competency, and interest. Most school programs expected teacher performance levels commensurate with "average" teacher expectancies. This leveling of the "highs" of teacher interest or "lows" of understanding in certain disciplines tended to focus upon a middle ground of activity for all teachers and classrooms rather than provide encouragement in those areas where superior interest and/or competencies existed. Differentiated staffing movements contend that teachers are *not* homogeneous and equal assignments and authority are not valid.[7] Team teaching, departmentalization, and organizational breakdown of self-contained classroom teaching assignments are encouraging but in themselves can become oppressive in arbitrary restriction of areas of concentration, that is, content center versus concept development. Differentiated staffing assumes that elementary teachers cannot be all things to all pupils—thus the necessity of concentrating on those interests and competencies that a teacher can discharge most successfully.

Teacher Assistance in the Classroom

Teacher assistance in the classroom has remained as a formal if not unwieldy activity. Allen and Kline summed it accurately:

> Help for the teacher remains the same—supervisors and consultants and curriculum coordinators and administrators—always within the context that inservice education will somehow overcome incompetence and inadequacy, never in the equally plausible and increasingly important context of legitimate obsolescence or expected, systematic growth.[8]

Differentiated staffing feels that in many instances critical examination of a problem area might suggest dropping the concept or activity. If it is to be retained, find a person or procedure that will encourage a more successful result for children. It has been suggested that the more formal assistance to the teacher encourages a false sense of challenge to succeed by retention and coordinated diligence rather than recognizing that the problem cannot or should not be resolved in the context of today's education. The elementary curriculum has been bloated too frequently by retention of concepts where interested, intelligent, and qualified teacher action would be to modify or delete the idea completely. Differentiated staffing is frequently designed to provide this opportunity and decision for

[7] William B. Hedges, "Differentiated Teaching Responsibilities in the Elementary School," *National Elementary Principal*, 47:48–54 (Sept. 1967).

[8] Dwight W. Allen and L. W. Kline, "Differentiated Teaching Staff," *National Business Education Quarterly*, 37:13 (May 1969).

the school by meshing the responsibility for qualified teachers to analyze the problem and to consider alternatives at the pupil level.

Educational Cost Factors

Educational cost factors are increasingly influential in maintaining or improving school programs. New influences upon the schools today demand analysis and accounting that are often impossible to retrieve in our more conventional approaches to learning. The long-range effects of assessment programs, measured accountability, changing financial support systems, and the knowledge explosion itself demand flexible and changing approaches. With lower teacher turnover rates and higher levels of academic achievement a factor of school budgets, differentiated staffing suggests one means of utilizing the specialized skills and interests of certified teachers within a working system, including temporary and part-time personnel—and with a funding support that rewards the vertical and horizontal differentiation of function and time. In some elementary school districts serious discussion has been given to the undesirable decision to close down the facilities because they cannot continue to operate under the limited financial support available. With 75 per cent to 80 per cent of the school dollar pegged to staff salary systems, it is apparent that improving the use of the staff funds available is a major consideration. In one midwestern state, only a last minute temporary loan to a city school system from the legislative bodies averted the closing of facilities serving over a million and a half school patrons.

Considerations for Adopting Principles of Differentiated Staffing

Any major change in school operations typically produces a variety of personal and professional reactions from the staff and the community. Often the response to change is unpredictable and can trigger unrelated, if not remote, issues. The state and federal movement to daylight saving time in the early months of 1974 produced little reaction in some communities, but in other areas, particularly the more heavily populated school districts, social protests developed quickly. Political figures in the latter areas voiced similar concerns and in resulting debates and elections the spreading influence of a single act magnified actions far beyond the possible expectations of the time change proponents.

When differentiated staffing appears as a possibility for school consideration, preplanning must include the possible reactions to the innovation by groups in the school and community. For years public and private fund-raising campaigns have plotted their efforts against a continuum of group rejection. Political campaigns of recent years have geared their organizations to the segments of the electorate that have been identified in advance as having degrees of acceptance or rejection to particular portions of a candidate's position on established issues. As schools are an integral agency of society, their movement toward any type of change will also solicit reactions from community patrons. Even today, state and regional movements to reconsolidate small school districts to serve better their school populations (as well as to economize in operation expenses) produces deep and heartfelt feelings on the part of the parents —and voters. Few efforts of the school today, therefore, are undertaken without attempting to explain the philosophy, plans of implementation, costs, and anticipated results of the action. In spite of sincere efforts on the part of the school, proposed issues are frequently rejected or voted down or serve to anchor movements to change school or board memberships in the future.

Exemplary of a move to gain staff acceptance of a proposed implementation of differentiated staffing in a school system is the following overview or pattern of justification[9] given to a staff-administrative council to accomplish six major school concerns:

1. Minimize the increase in school budgets.
2. Maximize the use of staff strengths.
3. Evaluate the needs of the community and clientele.
4. Define job positions for delineation of responsibility and use of paraprofessionals, volunteers, aids, clerical help, and supplies.
5. Evaluate the availability of resources, materials, space, time, and equipment.
6. Increase the effective translation of research findings into effective teaching practices.

Once the *concept* of improvement of the school through delineated and identified areas (as just shown) is accepted, more specific problems and singular definition of points in the philosophical or pragmatic outcome of the school can be developed. Examples of these that could develop from an overview (such as the one shown earlier) could be

[9] (a) Sequences adapted from research model designed by Bernard Curtis and author in conjunction with the Mott Foundation research group, "A Differentiated Staff Proposal for Averill School," presented by Clyde Campbell to the Lansing (Mich.) School's Instructional Council, Spring 1970; (b) *A Selected Annotated Bibliography on Differentiated Staffing,* compiled by Bernard McKenna (Washington, D.C.: National Commission on Teacher Education and Professional Standards, National Education Association and ERIC Clearing House, Oct. 1969); (c) National Education Association, National Commission on Teacher Education and Professional Standards, "The Teacher and His Staff: Differentiated Roles for School Personnel" (Miami Beach, Fla.: NCTEPS, State Chairman and Consultants Conference, June 1968).

1. To capitalize on the talents, skills, experience, and interests of school personnel, so that each child will receive optimum instruction.
2. To individualize instruction.
3. To use staff effectively with many different levels of preparation and competency.
4. To increase precision of learning, diagnosis, prescription, and treatment.
5. To implement appropriate instructional procedure.
6. To narrow the gap between the discovery and the implementation of new knowledge.
7. To provide accountability for curriculum development, process, and evaluation.
8. To give staff financial rewards commensurate with the ranges of their responsibility.
9. To foster flexible organizational structure that increases the use of resources.
10. To create an administrative organization that facilitates continuity and coordination among all levels.
11. To define and redefine personnel by function administratively.

Often a proposed project is accepted for study and implementation with the understanding that additional inclusions will become a logical outgrowth of actions motivated by the study. These could include evaluation of existing programs, facilities, cost analysis and strategies for in-process evaluation.

It is obvious that detailed, conscientious, and cooperative planning is dictated by procedures proposed in conjunction with the implementation of differentiated staffing. Time, individual effort, and patient research are vital to successful program development. An interesting insight into the degree of research and preplanning that can be developed is the identification of a continuum of staff characteristics or behaviors that can be expected in a group considering the adoption of organizational change such as differentiated staffing (see Table 6–2). Although categories are made of individual groups, it is probable that most staff would have difficulty placing themselves completely within one category . . . preferring to establish their true position between, or extending to, two postitions on the behavioral scale. It must also be assumed that change for the sake of change is not in itself a justifiable claim. In fact, it is possible that the cumulative resistance to a proposed innovation that has been drawn from a wide range of staff personnel can be interpreted as change that is *not* needed or required. Again, this comparison of need against a differentiated staffing model or plan reflects awareness of current change regardless of outcomes.

TABLE 6–2
Summary of Characteristics and Communication Behavior of Adopter Categories*

Characteristic or Behavior	Innovators	Early adopters	Majority Early	Majority Late	Laggards
1. Time of adoption	First 2.5 per cent to adopt new ideas	Next 13.5 per cent to adopt	Next 34 per cent to adopt	Next 34 per cent to adopt	Last 16 per cent to adopt
2. Attitudes and values	Scientific and venturesome	Progressive	More conservative and traditional	Skeptical of new ideas	Highly traditional beliefs; fear of debt
3. Abilities	High level of education; ability to deal with abstractions	Above average education	Slightly above average education	Slightly below average education	Low level of education; have difficulty dealing with abstractions and relationships
4. Group memberships	Leaders in local, state, and national organizations; travel widely	Leaders in organizations within the community	Many informal contacts within the community	Little travel out of community; little activity in formal organizations	Few memberships in formal organizations other than church; semiisolates
5. Social status	Highest social status, but their practices may not be accepted	High social status; looked to by neighbors as a leader	About average social status	About average social status	Lowest social status
6. Sources of information	Scientists; other innovators; research; books and magazines	Highest contact with local change agents; magazines	Few magazines; friends and coworkers	Friends and coworkers	Mainly friends and coworkers

154

In summary, the adoption of principles of a model for differentiated staffing is not accomplished successfully without deliberated examination of the needs and aspirations of the community moderated by the support factors for delivery, namely staff, facilities, and support.

STUDY OF IMPLEMENTATION

Traditional newspaper and broadcast media interviews of victims of nuclear bombing in World War II and, in more recent years, those accidentally exposed to nucelar radiation, often ask, "How do you feel?" when in actuality the true answer can be made decades later if not by succeeding generations. In the same way, the degree of success gained from implementing a differentiated staffing program might better be analyzed in a decade or so in the future. Admittedly, it represents an involved, sensitive, and troublesome process dealing primarily with physical, mental, and social habits and values. It has been and should remain as an individualized task with each step singular to the uniqueness of the local setting. It cannot be prepackaged from one community to another, nor can the success or failure of one experience necessarily influence the proceeding at another stage in any similar school system.

In initiating implementation, questions of unknown magnitude occur as normal expectancy. Campbell identifies the present status:

> Much of the discussion on differentiated staffing in the literature has centered on such questions as these. How many regular teachers should make up the team? What qualifications should they possess? Should teachers be ranked on some prestige scale of importance? How many non-professionals should be used? How many teaching machines, etc.? From our vantage point there are as yet few solid guidelines to follow. Certainly a teacher should not be performing tasks that a para-professional, a teaching machine or an older pupil teaching a younger pupil can perform just as well.[10]

One point of agreement tends to permeate all plans and programs—to maintain and identify at least one teacher with a child more than with all other teachers. This means of personal identification also exists in the background philosophies of all departmental types of school organizations, particularly in middle and junior high school plans.

Someone has philosophized that if one could "start from scratch," the process of implementing a differentiated staffing program would be ideal.

[10] *The Community School and Its Administration*, ed. by Clyde Campbell, Mott Foundation and Michigan State University, **10**, No. 7:3 (Mar. 1972).

From the simple process of making decisions on the physical dimensions of the room and, to a lesser extent, the recruiting of professional staff, this position could be defended. From the point of long-range success, however, the smooth, interlocking, integral interrelationship that distinguishes a successful working team must represent a polished life-style— sometimes only after personal and professional abrasions have corrected loose fits or rough edges. Age, talent, sex, religion, or clothing as identifiable agencies of success themselves do *not* stand as measures to place or substitute for a smooth working team. One of the authors visited a new elementary school with a reputation for a successful program with differentiated staff overtones. The school, its educational climate, and smooth operation were credited in part to small size (less than 300), its enlightened director, and the four professional teachers. The director and the board had deliberately recruited teachers of a definite quality for the first opening of school—all must have had elementary teaching experience in a rural school with the K–6 teaching experience that entailed. It was particularly apparent that all were women and at least in the late forties in age—but the spirit that they typified justified the success of the recruiting and that of the school. It is possible that a group of men in their early twenties could be equally successful. The point is that those serving *did* succeed in embodying the spirit of differentiated staffing and its resulting success.

One cannot dismiss the procedure of implementing the theory of differentiated staffing by only recommending the reader to compare his or her school to one of many models noted in a footnote. Necessarily, each school and district can move from one step to another in deciding, for example, that two teachers and two paraprofessionals can do as good a job, if not a better job, than four full-time professionals. In some instances, we could generalize that the salary savings gained should be used to support two instructional aids and perhaps a portion of a clerical aid's compensation. Such decisions, however, are realistic only in the specific situation. Hickey reserves overall advantages of the program.

> with proper investigation and planning in relation to a particular district's goals, resources, facilities and staff, it may offer that particular school a significant advancement in improving its structure if it is appropriately implemented.[11]

In implementing a differentiated staffing plan in the fifth levels (grades) of a school, we could assume that before the change the breakdown would be like that shown in Table 6–3.

[11] Howard Hickey, "Differentiated Staffing—Panacea or Passing Fancy?" *The Michigan School Board Journal*, 18, No. 11:30 (Jan. 1972).

TABLE 6–3

						Totals
Teacher	A	B	C	D	E	5 + teachers
Students	30	30	30	30	30	150 students
		specialists				variable
		student teachers				variable

A model for the system with differentiated responsibilities could be the one shown in Table 6–4.

Obvious is the attempt to have pupil needs served by a wide variety of assistance based upon possessed skills, interests, talents, hobbies, ambitions, and desire. This talent would range from the sixth level (grade) student who specializes in knowing how to keep fish in any aquarium healthy to a retired pediatrician interested in childhood diseases of minority children. The clerical aid is able and willing to work with accelerated students in typing "their" newspaper as well as aiding those retarded in cutting a two-color stencil for publicizing a room bake sale. The potentials and expectancies of a team communicating vertically as well as working laterally result in beauty that cannot be accurately described—or photographed.

Intrinsic is recognizing means (unorthodox as they may be) to overcome obstacles to learning. While visiting an experimental-program elementary school, one of the authors was dismayed to find only the teacher's desk in a room scheduled to service soon a group of thirty-five students

TABLE 6–4

				Totals
	½ coordinator			1
Instructor	A	B	C	3
Instructional Aid	A	B		2
	Clerical Aid			1
	student teachers			variable
	parent or community volunteers			variable
	college students and observer participants			variable
	tutors and volunteer specialist			variable

in a work session on cursive handwriting. In a few minutes the concern was replaced by amazement as the students appeared each carrying his own folding personal chair. Within a few minutes the chairs were set, writing arm in place, and the teacher-led lesson was in progress. This particular school had overcome the major problem of room utilization heretofore limited by the size and number of desks for each age/size group by eliminating room chairs and assigning each pupil his or her own folding chair, which the pupils carried from room to room, group to group. Admittedly a bit unusual, but in this particular school a relatively simple solution to a major concern had eliminated a problem of pupil accommodation by adding flexibility.

In short, implementation of differentiated staffing cannot be prescribed or adequately demonstrated by models. Each school, each group must develop implementations in the spirit of the rationale of selection and moderated by inherent school and personnel restraints—whether physical, mental, or social. It takes time, cooperation, and dedication— and adjustments must be continuous in realizing realistic goals.

INHERENT CONFLICTS

Although the number of schools actively involved in some phase of differentiated staffing is unknown, the total would be at this time relatively small percentagewise, although a continuation of federal and state funding could measurably alter the future number of participants. Those that are involved probably represent schools with measured alertness to changing patterns in education, with interest in experimentation, that are recipients of specific funding programs or are under financial pressures to seek alternate means of maintaining present school populations. It is probable that differentiated staffing does propose some problems that have handicapped or restricted its acceptance. Operating individually or in combination with other factors, some of the more pervasive problems can be identified as follows:

1. *Delegation of authority.* Administrators must be conditioned to the need to share decision making with professionals. Teachers must also develop competency and skill in accepting their role in making decisions. Interacting support from both must be maintained when decisions are made.
2. *Time for change.* Patience for detailed, long-range planning is often in short supply, especially when various phases of community participation must be included. If a "holding pattern" is

in effect on salaries, supplies, and so forth during a one-to-three-year planning segment, perseverance is needed.

3. *Fewer teacher positions.* With nonprofessional support an integral part of differentiated staffing, fewer teachers are needed to service a given number of students. Professional teachers and organizations view this action as substituting nonprofessional staff for those who are "better prepared" for the role. Organizations that enjoy collective bargaining contracts see the use of nonprofessionals as a challenge to their power.

4. *Financial overtones.* The use of salary savings to underwrite the nonprofessional is considered a first step by school systems in decreasing the future use of professionals and increasing the numbers of the nonprofessional staff. If school costs continue to escalate and teacher salaries also move upward, one break in the impass is to hire fewer teachers. Teacher preparation institutions are also concerned by school use of student teachers as full-time teacher substitutes.

5. *Coordination.* It is obviously a difficult responsibility to coordinate ten to fifteen people working with two hundred to three hundred pupils, especially if this assignment is but one-third of a coordinator's load. Too often, supervision loads increase as financial support decreases. Many present coordinators lack specific administrative background and experience to handle adequately overload assignments.

6. *Establishment of salary differentials.* Semblances of merit pay hover over compensating both professional and nonprofessional workers. Professionals maintain that merit pay can exist only when every teacher has a similar task and responsibility. Professional teacher negotiation teams have had limited experience with this challenge.

7. *Reduced professional contact with pupil.* By delegating segments of traditional teacher responsibility and the resulting times, the professional teacher has less contact with the pupil. Proponents of differentiated staffing maintain that the skill and intent of the contact does not necessarily suffer in sharing the responsibility—in some cases it can be to the gain of the child. A difficult situation to resolve objectively.

8. *Complexity.* If the ideal teaching situation *is* one instructor to one child, the vertical and horizontal interrelationship growing out of differentiated staffing models tends to consume increasingly time and monies from the teaching process. The administration of the coordinator would tend to require more support if other elements of the group increase in time, numbers, and

financial compensation. Tones of bureaucracy are evident from the teacher's point of view.

9. *Overconfidence in reorganization.* We have little evidence that restructuring patterns of school organization *in themselves* bring about sustained improvement. It is the enabling freedom to improve that is inherent in differentiated staffing. Without efforts to utilize the newly released opportunities, the movement or structural change of differentiated staffing is meaningless.

10. *Evaluation.* Few significant studies have been undertaken to justify either the embrace of a program of differentiated staffing or to maintain one already in operation. Isolated research probably could be cited to move in either direction. It would seem that some parts of the total component plan have better than average chances of being encompassed within many organizational structures, that is, community resource talent, volunteers, and paraprofessionals—but perhaps in less obvious positions of responsibility.

Summary

Even a quick overview of the concept of differentiated staffing would cause one to hesitate to take a strong stand on predicting its future acceptance development. Various models are in operation and out-district funding is encouraging other schools to sample its potential. Recent professional publications are including more discussion of its position in relation to the future of education, especially in the United States.

It is apparent that on professional grounds the major teacher organizations have mixed reservations about its effect upon the teacher's role in professional education. Teacher preparation institutions note that community colleges are offering professional courses for paraprofessionals. Social groups of the community have found a new role in participation in the schools, and the pressure of individualization of all instruction has caused additional stress upon the preparation (pre and intern) of elementary teachers. The cost of instruction shows little movement in stabilizing, and the diminished mobility of tenured teachers has increased salary expectations but hampered the employment of newly graduated teacher candidates.

Most of these observations would seem to enhance the spread of the differentiated staffing movement unless the situation of relative weight of each condition is examined. Cost of school operations, for example, is becoming somewhat less of a factor (although still a major one) as state and federal agencies readjust their support basis. Some past experimentation with differentiated staffing has been initiated with an eye to holding school costs to more reasonable levels. Teacher organizations contend that this will not result, but increased funding from outside-district agencies could encourage future experimenting.

Evaluation of initiated programs in differentiated staffing remains as an anticipated development with wide reading implications for the future. With growing encouragement for expanded systems of school and teacher accountability, state and national assessment programs, and lifelong educational expectations, significant advantages of differentiated staffing based upon recognized research techniques would produce positive, if not immediate, endorsement from many school communities. For the present, there will be continued experimentation, pilot development of newly structured models and probably some financial support for necessary effort to study and evaluate the projects already in operation. Regardless of the outcome of these later, the ideals of differentiated staffing will not leave the American scene of innovative education in the foreseeable future.

SUGGESTED ACTIVITIES

1. Review your own elementary and secondary school preparation. Can you recall four or five specific instances or classroom activities where you would have *benefited* from individual rather than group consideration by the teacher? Conversely, can you recall where the reverse situation was to your advantage? Be specific in your examples.
2. As one specializing in the teaching of elementary school children, do you feel competent to accept the responsibility for all activities associated with teaching a given grade in the elementary school? Where do you feel you have particular strength? Weaknesses?
3. Mr. Charles Jones, assistant superintendent of the Stoneville School System, is interviewing elementary teachers interested in being employed in a differentiated staffing program in their elementary school. Assuming you are interested in the position, list or identify six major questions you would pose to Superintendent Jones in gaining information about the position. Check your six questions with a friend's six. Are they similar? How do they differ?
4. You have asked to represent your student teaching group from the Atwater Differentiated Staffing Model to attend a National Education Association regional meeting next week. In anticipation of your appearance on a panel with four teachers with nondifferentiated staffing experience, identify four to six questions you would expect the experienced teachers to raise in the discussion. As a warm-up, identify three or four you hope they do *not* raise.

5. Consider teaching in the primary grades in contrast to a teaching experience in upper grades. Which level suggests a request for supplementary assistance? Why? Identify the rationale that would encourage differentiated staffing in one area and not another. Defend.

6. If your parents, relatives, or friends are patrons of an elementary school at present, assume you are opposed to initiating differentiated staffing next year in the school. Rank six reasons in rank order. Would you prefer to "sell" the opposing side to your family or friends? Why?

7. Assume you are visited by a teacher from a foreign country and are requested to explain to her/him the means of fitting a differentiated staffing model to a given school. How would you proceed to explain? Would it differ from an explanation afforded to a teacher from this country? Detail how it would differ.

SELECTED BIBLIOGRAPHY

Allen, Dwight W., and L. W. Kline. "Differentiated Teaching Staff." *National Business Education Quarterly*, 37 (May 1969).

Barbee, Don. "Administrative Implications of Differentiated Staffing." *The National Elementary Principal*, 11, No. 4 (Jan. 1972).

The Community School and Its Administration. Ed. by Clyde Campbell. Mott Foundation and Michigan State University, 10, No. 7 (Mar. 1972).

Curtis, Bernard, in conjunction with the Mott Foundation research group. "A Differentiated Staff Proposal for Averill School." Presented by Clyde Campbell to the Lansing (Mich.) School's Instructional Council (Spring 1970).

Dempsey, Richard A., and Rodney P. Smith. *Differentiated Staffing*. Englewood Cliffs, N.J.: Prentice-Hall, Inc., 1972.

English, Fenwick. "AFT/NEA Reaction to Staff Differentiation." *Phi Delta Kappan*, 36, No. 2 (Jan. 1972).

——— "The Differentiated Staff: Education's Technostructure." *Educational Technology*, 10, No. 2 (Feb. 1970).

Hansen, John, and Arthur Hearn. *The Middle School Program*. Chicago: Rand McNally & Co., 1971.

Hedges, William B. "Differentiated Teaching Responsibilities in the Elementary School." *National Elementary Principal*, 47 (Sept. 1967).

Hickey, Howard. "Differentiated Staffing—Panacea or Passing Fancy?" *The Michigan School Board Journal*, 18, No. 11 (Jan. 1972).

Hoffman, C. William. "Differentiated Staffing—Panacea or Passing Fancy?" *The Michigan School Board Journal*, 18, No. 11 (Jan. 1972).

Liberman, Myron. *The Future of Public Education*. Chicago: University of Chicago Press, 1960.

National Education Association, National Commission on Teacher Education and Professional Standards. "The Teacher and His Staff: Differentiated

Roles for School Personnel." Miami Beach, Fla.: NCTEPS, State Chairman and Consultants Conference, June 1968.

Reich, Charles A. *The Greening of America.* New York: Random House, Inc., 1970.

Reynolds, Malvina. "Little Boxes." Pete Seeger's album, *We Shall Overcome.* New York: CBS, 1963.

A *Selected Annotated Bibliography on Differentiated Staffing.* Compiled by Bernard McKenna. Washington, D.C.: National Commission on Teacher Education and Professional Standards, National Education Association and ERIC Clearing House, Oct. 1969.

Staropoli, Chas. J., and George W. Rumsey. "A Career-Ladder Preparation Model Designed to Implement Differentiated Staffing Patterns." *The Journal of Teacher Education,* **23**, No. 4 (Winter 1972).

Staumbis, George, and Alvin Howard. *Schools for the Middle Years.* New York: International Book Co., 1969.

Trump, J. Lloyd. *Images of the Future—a New Approach to the Secondary School.* Commission on the Experimental Study of the Utilization of the Staff in the Secondary School—Summary Report. Urbana, Ill.: 1959.

Chapter 7

Planning Learning Experiences

What are your plans for today? Do you plan to sleep in, to get up early, to skip breakfast, to finish an assignment for one of your classes, to go to the library, to go shopping, to watch a favorite television program, to make plane reservations for a vacation trip, or to go to a party tonight? As we go about our daily living, we have many objectives we want to accomplish within a period of time. Planning implies formulating methods, techniques, and procedures for efficiently and effectively attaining our objective or objectives.

As you read this chapter, the following cognitive objectives should be kept in mind:

1. The reader will be able to justify the necessity of planning.
2. The reader will be able to formulate a set of criteria to guide a teacher's planning.
3. The reader will be familiar with varied types of plans a teacher may be expected to make.
4. The reader will be cognizant of many factors involved in successful teacher-pupil planning.

NEED FOR PLANNING

Just as people need some kind of plan to give direction to their daily lives, teachers need plans to guide the many decisions involved in providing a child the best opportunities possible for learning. In fact, the most success-ful teachers the authors have known possessed the ability to plan carefully and imaginatively. Certainly, one of the keys to effective teaching is good planning.

A teacher needs to plan in order to (1) formulate and select what is most appropriate for children to learn (objectives), (2) consider a variety of materials and approaches and select those most likely to result in the hoped-for learnings (procedures), and (3) employ the best means of de-termining the extent to which the objectives have been attained (evalua-tion).

Understandably, detailed plans are more essential for the less experi-enced teacher than for an experienced teacher. Carefully developed plans by all teachers, however, provide security and confidence and result in less wasted time and effort, both on the part of the teachers and pupils. Plan-ning better provides for individual needs and interests within the group; thus it is likely to result in better continuity of learning.

Although the effect of planning upon teaching and learning cannot be established by research evidence, most educational leaders propose the necessity of planning. For instance, Hudgins says:

> planning for teaching is preferable to not planning. In the absence of planning, teaching can become confused, disorganized, and chaotic, resulting in negative consequences both for the learning of pupils and for their attitudes toward the teacher and school. The teacher who can con-sistently provide meaningful education experiences without giving careful prior consideration to his goals and the means of achieving them is rare, or, more likely nonexistent.[1]

GUIDELINES FOR PLANNING

Some teachers—sometimes referred to as traditional, inflexible, or auto-cratic—are characterized as those who announce, "This is what we are going to do, and this is how we will do it." Some teachers—sometimes referred to as modern, open, or democratic—are characterized as those who announce, "This is your classroom. You can do anything you wish. What would you like to do?" Both characterizations are probably unfair, and it would be difficult to find more than a few teachers who would fit either category. Most teachers would agree that planning is essential. The plans, however, would be held tentative and adaptable. Since the kinds and amounts of planning are debatable issues, each teacher will have to

[1] Bryce B. Hudgins, *The Instructional Process* (Chicago: Rand McNally, 1971), p. 63.

plan in terms of his personal needs and the needs of the learners with whom he works.

The following suggestions are offered as guidelines in planning opportunities to facilitate success in learning.

What Is to Be Learned

A well-thought-through set of attainable objectives—what the child will know or do as evidence of learning—should serve as the most important guideline in planning educational activities. Popham and Baker suggest that we depart from the more common practice of planning in terms of what teachers will expose the learner to and instead plan an instructional sequence in terms of what kind of entry and en route behaviors are expected of the learner before he successfully achieves the desired objectives.[2]

Appropriateness of Content

Many elementary teachers have been accused of being too content-orientated, and perhaps rightly so in some cases. Nevertheless, children do not learn in a vacuum. They learn by dealing meaningfully with concepts, topics, principles, ideas, concerns, relationships, expressed values, and so forth. Ultimately, the teacher is held responsible for the content of the curricular experiences of pupils under his direction. Generally, the teacher has a high degree of freedom in selecting and organizing the content he deems most appropriate for teaching-learning purposes in terms of the set of selected objectives. However, if the plans are to be realistic, he must take into consideration some delimiting factors. For example, all states have legislation that requires the teaching of certain subject areas or topics. Some states and school systems may require the use of single adoption or prescribed basal texts. Also the local community may have powerful pressure groups that insist on teaching or not teaching particular topics. In planning the content of the program, the teacher must be cognizant of the preceding and of other restrictions; however, his chief concern should be that of determining what scope and sequence of content will best achieve the objectives. Helpful sources of information on appropriateness of content, particularly in the early stages of teaching, are textbook teacher's manuals, curriculum guides, courses of study, resource units, experienced teachers, and the pupils.

Characteristics of Learners

Plans are more effective when they reflect the teacher's knowledge of child growth and development. Although it is difficult to plan adequately for a specific group of children until after working with them for a while,

[2] W. J. Popham and E. I. Baker, *Planning an Instructional Sequence* (Englewood Cliffs, N.J.: Prentice-Hall, 1970), pp. 45–61.

the planner should find it helpful to review his teacher preparation background in terms of children's general needs, interest, abilities, attitudes, and attention span at various levels. He can also examine children's past records and consult with the children's previous classroom teachers, special education teachers, and parents. The more information the teacher possesses about children, the better the guidelines for planning exciting and appropriate experiences.

Content Detail and Format

Enough detail should be included in the plan to insure a feeling of competence and confidence in working with children. A number of factors influence the degree of detail incorporated in a teacher's plan. Some of these factors are the teacher's experience, the topic under consideration, the level or maturity of the learners involved, the objective or objectives, the learning environment, and the use to be made of the plan. There is no recipe answer to how detailed teachers' plans should be. Some teachers prefer to jot down only major ideas in outline form, whereas others feel the necessity to write out their plans in detail. Regardless of the kinds and amount of information included in a plan, the individual teacher needs to use his ingenuity and creativity to develop a form or organizational pattern that is practical for effective use.

Psychology of Learning

Planning should reflect knowledge and application of principles of learning. Pupils are more likely to participate actively in activities that are comfortable and satisfy one or more needs. Since a wide range of human variabilities—intellectual, social, physical, and cultural characteristics; interest; attitude; natural drive; motivation—exist within a group of youngsters, plans should provide for learning at different rates and in a variety of styles.

Learning should be related to pupils' experiences. If what is to be learned is related to a pupil's experience, he is more likely to perceive learning as meaningful and relevant. The learner, therefore, is apt to approach the task with interest and vigor. Learning experiences need to be planned to help the child recognize that what he is to learn is related to what he has already been doing or to what he already knows. Plans should provide for a gradual transition of learning from the concrete to the abstract or from the simple to the complex. Bruner, in discussing decisions that affect planning for learning, says, "What is most important for teaching basic concepts is that the child be helped to pass progressively from concrete thinking to the utilization of more conceptually adequate modes of thought."[3] The much desired constant progression of growth has a better

[3] Jerome S. Bruner, *The Process of Education* (New York: Vintage, 1960), p. 38.

chance of occurring when the teacher plans learning experiences in terms of children's experiences.

A group of children represent a variety of maturity and interest levels. *Readiness,* therefore, must be a factor when planning meaningful learning experiences. A question often asked is, Are the children ready for this? Better questions to ask yourself in planning experiences for which the child is ready might be the following:

1. What is the child ready for now?
2. What does he know or what can he do that relates to what he will be expected to accomplish?
3. Will he be likely to attack the situation with interest?
4. Will he perceive the task as being important to do?
5. Is he likely to be highly threatened or to feel comfortable?
6. Can he best attain the objective working alone or in conjunction with other learners?
7. Does he possess the prerequisites needed to find an element of success?
8. What can be done to help the child begin this with interest and success?

In planning the conditions of learning that need to be made, Gagné suggests we start with the statement of expected terminal behavior and proceed to identify a set of subtopics or subordinate objectives. "Each subordinate *objective,* then, is derived by systematically applying to the *next higher objective* the question, what must the student already know how to do, in order to learn this performance."[4] Learning experiences should be planned in terms of both what the child already knows or can do and what he may need to know or do in the future.

A pupil is more likely to apply his learning and to retain what he learns longer when he experiences meaningful practice. Plans should provide for relatively short periods of practice spaced over a period of time.

Plans Should Be Tentative and Flexible

Careful planning to clarify goals, materials, and procedures can serve to make teacher's thinking rigid and less sensitive to pupils, but this need not be the result. The teacher should recognize that his plans only represent his best projection of what the impending teaching-learning situation may actually be. When viewed in this context, the teacher's intent is to use his plans as a guide when actually working with the learners. As stated by the authors in another book:

4 Robert M. Gagné, *The Conditions of Learning,* 2nd ed. (New York: Holt, 1970), p. 329.

The plan developed by the teacher is his best estimate of the most direct route to reach educational objectives and is made prior to embarking on the lesson. Just where one may encounter detours, or a new section of opened freeway which necessitate reevaluation and possible changes in plans, so it is in teaching. Things happen during a school day that are not foreseen—a convoy of the latest army artillery equipment passes by on the highway before the awed eyes of standing children; two red birds land on the window sill; John breaks his arm in a playground accident; Mary brings some thousand-year-old Mayan pottery chips which her parents gave her on their recent return from Guatemala; or a college student from Niagara visits the school. All or any of these unforeseen events can alter a teacher's plan. The teacher plans in advance, but he continually analyzes the current situation and alters his plans as he perceives new and more effective means of goal achievement.

The fact that a plan should be flexible so that it can be easily changed or altered as the occasion demands does not negate the need for serious and careful planning. Punctilious plans will make the teacher more sensitive to changing circumstances and allow more freedom to make needed modifications. In fact, the real basis of the argument for planning is not to limit the teacher but rather to free him for creative teaching. Although many events affecting learning cannot be predicted, the greater the number of possible occurrences, reactions, interferences, and alternatives that the teacher anticipates, the better chance he has of making the best decision at the best time—the teachable moment . . .

For either a beginning or an experienced teacher, the most carefully made plans cannot account for all the factors or conditions that influence learning. Properly developed, plans should assure all concerned that the known and predictable factors that may either aid or deter learning have been taken into account.

Careful planning is the teacher's best guarantee that unpredictable conditions will not become disruptive influences to the learning process.[5]

When planning is done on the basis of a good knowledge of child growth and development and of the processes through which behavioral change occurs, effective learning is more likely to occur.

Interaction

Planning should encourage interaction between and among pupils and teacher. One way of activating children's thinking and stimulating interaction is the use of well-thought-through questions. Unless some thought is given in planning to the most appropriate questions to ask, the predominant type of questions asked when actually working with children will be the traditional "closed" variety that simply require a pupil to repeat

[5] C. C. Collier, W. R. Houston, R. R. Schmatz, and W. J. Walsh, *Teaching in the Modern Elementary School* (New York: Macmillan, 1967), pp. 116–117.

the "facts." Too often responses to questions of this type are accepted as evidence that the child is a "good thinker." Granted that some questions eliciting specific factual information are desirable, they should be balanced with "open-ended" type questions planned to aid pupils in stating an opinion, perceiving relationships, sensing continuity, weighing information, making inferences, forming generalizations, drawing conclusions, and evaluating. In terms of the material studied or certain issues, the teacher could plan to ask open-ended questions such as the following: If you know this, then—? What do you think would happen if—? What do you think are the greatest needs of—? How could we best improve—? What would the affect be—?

When questions such as the preceding, at higher levels of intellectual functioning, are asked, immediate answers should not be expected. The teacher should plan to ask fewer questions than if he were asking closed-type questions and allow more time for thinking and reasoning. In discussing creative teaching, Smith claims that, "Well-planned questions develop convergent and divergent, critical and creative thinking processes among most of the children most of the time."[6]

Organizing Room and Materials

Planning is necessary to provide maximum flexibility in use of classroom and efficient storage and availability of learning materials. As Joyce Evans so aptly says, "Careful planning of room arrangement can provide children with a sense of stability, security, and order. In addition, careful planning can save the teacher time needlessly spent in moving furniture for various activities, hunting for lost equipment, and picking up at the end of the day."[7]

The classroom needs to be planned to accommodate varied learning activities in which children will be engaged. After the needs of the class are determined, furniture such as bookcases, portable bulletin boards, and screen dividers can be placed to set apart areas for noisy work, for semiquiet work, or for quiet study.

A great deal of educational material and equipment is needed in a classroom to meet the varied needs of youngsters. The handling and management of a wealth of materials so they are *readily available* to the learner when wanted or needed call for careful planning. As suggested in *Bits and Pieces*, "Whether new or used, selected or found, 'boughten' or junk, every material is a tool or a medium for problem solving or expression or communication. Storing materials so they suggest and invite their good in-

[6] James A. Smith, *Setting Conditions for Creative Teaching in the Elementary School* (Boston: Allyn, 1966), p. 105.

[7] Joyce S. Evans, "Classroom Planning for Young Special Children," *Teaching Exceptional Children*, 4:57 (Winter 1972).

corporation into busy production can make considerable difference in the way children use them and learn from them."[8]

Perhaps you have known, as we have, some teachers who have ordered or collected a lot of good learning materials that are seldom used because they are stored in miscellaneous fashion "out of sight" in drawers, cabinets, or closets. If your goal is to have a neat, orderly-looking classroom, you can accomplish your objective and still have materials obviously available by devising a plan for the classifying and orderly storing of materials in a visible array. Materials may be classified (and children can help) according to some criteria such as shape, size, color, type, or texture of material. Shelves, racks, pegboard with hangers, and containers of varying size and shape such as cigar boxes, shoe boxes, shirt boxes, coffee cans with plastic tops, and plastic dishpans can be utilized creatively to solve the storage problem. The containers should be labeled in lettering or with a picture of the objects or a sample object to facilitate locating the materials for use and replacing them when finished, ready for someone else to use.

Children generally react positively to a classroom carefully planned to encourage choices. Many teachers have found it advantageous to organize their classroom into learning centers—a sort of miniclassroom—where materials are readily available for selection and use by children in terms of a special interest or curricular area. In such a setting the class may seldom meet as a group; instead pupils are encouraged to choose and select from a variety of experiences and materials and to work independently or in small groups on study projects. As suggested by Joseph Featherstone, "An organizational change—the free day, for example, or simply rearranging classroom spaces—is unlikely to make much difference unless teachers are really prepared to act on the belief that in a rich environment young children can learn a great deal by themselves and that most often their own choices reflect their needs."[9]

A teacher may plan one or several learning centers in his room. Some may be for a short period and some for a longer time, for perhaps the school year, depending on pupil interest and need. The following are some examples of classroom learning centers:

1. Listening: The center may have a piece of carpeting, easy chairs, and pillows and radio, record player, or tape recorder equipped with headsets. Available for listening might be music, stories, poetry, or information prepared to build concepts or provide practice in concepts in one or more academic areas.

[8] *Bits and Pieces: Imaginative Uses for Children's Learning*, ed. by Sylvia Sunderlin (Washington D.C.: Association for Childhood Education International, 1967), p. 60.

[9] Joseph Featherstone, *Schools Where Children Learn* (New York: Liveright, 1971), p. 19.

2. Creative Writing: The area needs only a table, chairs, a supply of paper, pencils or pens, and perhaps a dictionary. Younger children may dictate their thoughts to the teacher or an older pupil within the school. Pupils may be encouraged to write on topics of their own choice, or a card file of ideas may be placed in the center from which children select one to write about.
3. Mathematics: Materials would include a variety of printed math material, manipulative materials, measuring devices and materials to measure, practice or drill materials, games and puzzles, problems to solve, and table or tables on which to work.

LONG-RANGE PLANNING

Learning is a unified, continuous, and sequential experience; therefore much thought needs to be given to long-range planning if children are to realize the best possible learning experience throughout the school year. Long-range plans provide an overall perspective for considering the innumerable possible learnings pupils might acquire during the course of a school year. Long-range plans are concerned with the yearly or semester programs of learning, providing a much needed guide for realistic short-range plans: unit, weekly, daily.

Long-range planning is needed to identify and formulate the broad objectives and to outline generally the major areas of study for the year. Planning for a relatively long period of time permits the teacher to think developmentally and to anticipate better what will be needed to attain the agreed-on objectives. Without long-range plans to serve as a guide, it is easy for the best-intentioned teacher, inexperienced or experienced, to discover to his dismay at the end of the year that some areas have been practically ignored whereas others may have been overly emphasized. As many experiences as possible should be previewed, alternatives considered, and priorities established. Before one launches into a program of instruction, tentative judgments should be made as to how the various curricular academic areas, topics or units of study, and materials of instruction can contribute to the broad long-range objectives. When a teacher does a considerable amount of long-range planning, the total program of learning experiences have a good chance of being synchronized into a logical relationship.

Textbook, curriculum guides, courses of study, and resource units can be a great help to the teacher in planning. A point we wish to emphasize is that you should use these materials; don't let them use you! For example, textbooks can aid you in planning the. program, but they should not be the program. Long-range planning provides the opportunity to preview available learning-teaching material—to determine what aspects would best contribute to the objectives, what could be deleted, what easily can be adapted, what would need to be supplemented, and what sequence would be most advantageous. One cannot hope to have children learn all the things that are desirable. Long-range planning will facilitate limiting instruction to the most significant topics at various levels and seeing that the selected topics are dealt with in the most efficacious manner possible.

A teacher needs to look at the total school year and try to anticipate what effect certain factors or events will have on the program, such as declared school holidays, scheduled events in the school, special days that are observed or celebrated in the community or nation, birthdays, seasons of the year, and parent-teacher conferences. Also, there may be field trips to schedule, resource people to contact, and, perhaps, instructional media materials to order. Through long-range planning, these and other factors having an impact on children's school experiences can be dealt with appropriately and advantageously. If you let them become immediate problems, they are likely to be handled hurriedly and unsatisfactorily.

Even though long-range plans are anticipatory and tentative in nature, they constitute an important phase of the total aspect of planning. In determining the most feasible instructional departure point and the place where he hopes to be at the end of the school year, the teacher has the opportunity to consider the scope, sequence, and balance of curricular experiences and also the availability and appropriateness of a variety of instructional resources from which relevant choices can be made. When done well, long-range planning offers assurance that children's time in school will be spent efficiently and effectively.

The Teaching-Learning Unit

For years teachers have been trying various methods of planning and teaching in a search for better ways of helping pupils tie together their learnings into a meaningful whole. Widely accepted as one of the most promising means of planning and organizing classroom experiences to facilitate unified learning has been the *teaching-learning unit*.

Since the early part of the twentieth century, curriculum writers, schools, and teachers have identified and described many different types of units: science units, social studies units, activity units, experience units, subject-matter units, process units, centers of interest units, discovery units, and personal-social needs units. These attempts to differentiate between so many kinds of units have probably served to confuse rather than to clarify the meaning and purpose of the unit concept to teachers. Most of the recently proposed definitions of a unit express a consistency of meaning. "A unit, or a unit of work, can be defined as a purposeful learning experience focused upon some socially significant understanding that will modify the behavior of the learner and enable him to adjust to a life situation more effectively."[10] Shuster and Ploghoft define a unit as ". . . a series of related learning experiences which are developed around the interests, needs, and problems of children, are socially significant, and produce purposeful activities resulting in a modified behavior of the learner."[11] Beauchamp describes a unit as a "means of organizing a series of studies or activities around some central theme or problem."[12] The common thread running through these definitions and the meaning of a unit as described by the authors of this book refer to the organization of learning around a significant theme, focal point, or problem area meaningful to youngsters with opportunities for individuals or groups of learners to work toward some consociate purpose over an extended period of time. The advantages of unit teaching have been listed as follows:

1. It provides for the interrelatedness of subject matter.
2. It satisfies the innate drives of children.
   (a) The drive to be active.
   (b) The drive to manipulate and construct.
   (c) The drive to satisfy curiosity.
   (d) The drive to create.
   (e) The drive to communicate.
   (f) The drive to dramatize.
   (g) The drive to satisfy ego-integrative needs.
3. It provides opportunity for the functional use of skills.
4. It provides for democratic group living.
5. It provides for individual differences.[13]

In planning units, the teacher must consider the nature of the central theme or problem and the maturity levels of the pupils. The length of time that can be devoted profitably to a unit varies; some successful units have been terminated after a few days and others have continued for a semester or the major part of the year. Generally though, depending upon the level of pupils in school, the time length range for a unit is two to six weeks. The daily time spent on a unit may occupy a small portion of the day, a major portion of the day, or the full day. If interest and work level begin to ebb significantly, this should be a signal to move to something that better meets the needs of the learners.

[10] Lavone A. Hanna, Gladys L. Potter, and Neva Hagaman, *Unit Teaching in the Elementary School* (New York: Holt, 1963), p. 117.

[11] Albert H. Shuster and Milton E. Ploghoft, *The Emerging Elementary Curriculum* (Columbus, Ohio: Merrill, 1970), p. 112.

[12] George A. Beauchamp, *Basic Dimensions of Elementary Method*, 2nd ed. (Boston, Allyn, 1965), p. 161.

[13] Lavone, Hanna, et al., op. cit., pp. 127–139.

In a unit, teaching-learning materials and activities are organized around a central theme disregarding traditional subject-matter lines. This does not mean that a unit will necessarily include every curricular area or that knowledge, skills, and attitudes associated with the various curricular areas will not be developed. In the planning of a unit, a variety of activities are outlined to encourage and help the pupil use information and skills from any subject-matter area that contribute to the attainment of the unit objectives or the solution of problems arising out of the unit. When there is indication that a pupil does not possess the knowledge or skills necessary to answer his questions or solve his problems, the teacher helps him develop the particular knowledge or skills needed. By focusing his attention and efforts on a problem that ignores subject-matter lines, and most real problems do, the learner is likely to be cognizant of the interrelatedness of the various fields of knowledge. The pupil, then, should perceive his learning as purposeful and integrative.

Planning the Unit

If a unit is to be successful, much planning is demanded of the teacher both prior to choosing the unit and during the course of the unit. Whether the unit is selected by the teacher or whether pupils are involved in the selection, guidelines or a set of criteria for selection should be planned to aid in choosing units most interesting and profitable to the pupils. Also in advance planning, the teacher needs to give considerable thought to objectives, surveying content; identify suitable learning activities; list and collect possible resources; and determine possible means and techniques for evaluation. Planning *for* a unit increases the chances of success in planning a unit *with* children, providing the teacher's preplanning is done with the full expectation that some or many of his ideas will be deleted, altered, or supplemented as he plans with the pupils.

Selecting the Unit

The actual selection of the unit should be cooperatively done by the teacher and the pupils. The teacher, however, must assume a major responsibility for being well prepared to provide needed data during the deliberations prior to final selection of the unit. The freedom and flexibility available to the teacher and pupils in selecting the unit are affected by various factors. It is the teacher's responsibility to be aware of and knowledgeable about the factors and the degree to which each needs to be considered. For example, he needs to be familiar with state regulations and also the policies and objectives of the school system and the particular school in which he is employed. Some schools have a predetermined set of criteria to guide the selection of units, some have an approved list of units from which units to be studied in the school or at a particular level are to be selected, some have a committee of teachers or teachers and pupils who screen and approve the selection of units, and some leave the decision entirely to the discretion of the individual classroom teacher. Some states may require that certain themes or units be taught at particular grade levels.

Before one discusses possible units of study with pupils, a careful examination should be made of available materials such as study or curriculum guides, scope and sequence charts, resource units, previous study units used in the school, and children's school records. Teachers, particularly beginning teachers, often find it advantageous to discuss with the supervisor, principal, or other teachers the appropriateness of possible units for a particular group of learners. Care must be exercised to avoid selecting a unit that is insignificant, repetitious, or inappropriate. Answers to a list of questions such as the following could serve as a good guide in choosing an appropriate and effective unit:

1. Is the unit appropriate in terms of the interests and ability of the group?
2. How does it fit the pupils' social and emotional maturity?
3. Will the unit promote the overall goals of the school?
4. How does it relate to the nature of the community?
5. Is the unit significant and comprehensive enough to justify its inclusion in the school program?
6. Does it relate to and extend children's past experiences?
7. Is it related to the real everyday life situations children face?
8. Can it be adequately developed and completed within the time?
9. Are adequate resources relating to the unit available?
10. Can provisions be made for the acquisition of important concepts, understandings, and skills?
11. Will it provide opportunities for developing group action skills and democratic behavior?
12. Is growth in problem solving likely to result?
13. Will it satisfy the natural drives of youngsters?
14. How will it accommodate the individual differences within the group?
15. Will it assist children to integrate knowledge, understandings, and skills gained from various sources?

Discussion with pupils of an appropriate title for the unit may be quite important to the success of the unit. The title should indicate major areas to be studied and something of the scope of the unit, but more importantly it should interest and excite pupils to pursue the unit.

When it is possible, selecting a unit in the spring for the next school year, or well in advance of the starting date for the unit, increases the opportunity to develop a most worthwhile unit. This early selection of the unit provides ample time to gain a better background of knowledge about the learners and the content of the unit and also to review, order, and collect materials.

Unit Objectives

After the unit has been selected, the next step to insuring success is the determination and formulation of clearly stated objectives the teacher desires his pupils to attain in their study of the unit. Some teachers find it helpful to write a brief overview describing the nature and scope, with some general statements, of hoped-for accomplishments. From this overview, specific objectives are written as behaviorally as possible. Various types of learning should result from studying the unit. Objectives, therefore, are generally listed separately for understandings, skills and habits, and appreciations and attitudes. After the teacher has decided on the objectives, he should plan with the pupils in assisting them to form objectives that are most meaningful. The resultant set of objectives should be the basis for planning learning activities and for evaluating the outcomes of the unit.

Initiating the Unit

The statement, "So goes the introduction, so goes the unit," emphasizes how critical the introductory phase is to pupils' subsequent work periods on the unit. The importance of careful planning of activities that are most likely to establish a pleasant and comfortable feeling on the part of pupils, arouse their curiosity, stimulate interest, connote the significance of studying the unit, and reveal relationships to what has preceded and to what is to follow cannot be overemphasized.

Successful teachers have used a variety of ways to get a unit off to an exciting start. Some initiatory ideas that have been used successfully include a stimulating classroom environment, a dramatic skit, a catchy bulletin board, a guest speaker, showing a motion picture, performing an experiment, a demonstration, reading or telling a story, discussing a local or national issue, taking a field trip, displaying or exhibiting a collection of related materials, and asking stimulating questions.

The Teaching-Learning Phase

A variety of problems to be attacked, learning procedures and activities, and a laboratory of resource materials must be planned and organized to keep the unit moving toward the attainment of expressed objectives. The teacher preplans suggested learning experiences directly related to the content and goals of the unit. Pupils are then encouraged and assisted in using any of these suggestions and also those of their own in whatever way seems best to the pupils and teacher for exploring interests, raising and answering questions, and solving problems related to the central theme. Meticulous preplanning of learning activities and resources should get pupils off to a good start in the unit. Continuous planning, however, must be done while the unit is in progress to meet the diversity of needs of individual learners, small groups and committees as they seek answers to questions, solutions to problems through extensive reading, data collecting and analysis, construction activities, experiments, research, and discussion sessions.

Meaningful and functional use of content or subject matter is built-in as an important aspect of unit activities. When they study in this manner, pupils learn many essential skills as well as, if not better than, by the more traditional textbook method. But owing to the nature of some subject areas, most teachers who use the unit approach also schedule specific periods during the unit to teach some basic skills, particularly in reading and mathematics.

Culminating and Evaluating the Unit

Provisions for culminating the unit on a high note and for evaluating the unit's effectiveness need to be responsibly planned. Evaluation techniques and procedures most likely have been used throughout the unit by the teacher and pupils for assessing progress toward goals, clarifying needs, and determining next steps. Well-planned culmination activities offer many additional opportunities for pupils and teacher to evaluate together what has been accomplished from studying the unit and to determine other possible units for study that might be related or lead naturally from the present unit.

Some teachers find it profitable to have pupils participate in culminating activities such as an original play or skit; a mural or time-line depicting unit activities; dramatizations; debates; exhibits of materials used in the unit; an assembly program; and making a tape, filmstrip, or mosaic. Whether or not there is a planned special occasion program in culminating the unit, opportunities should be provided for pupils to share experiences, accomplishments, and satisfactions summarize important learnings; formulate generalizations; and deepen understandings of the value of having studied the unit.

SHORT-RANGE PLANNING

The importance of doing long-range and unit planning, which has been discussed in the preceding pages, in no way lessens the necessity of thoughtful and thorough short-range weekly and daily planning. Within the general framework of long-range plans the teacher needs to do much weekly and daily planning to provide the best possible experiences to serve the more immediate needs of learners. In short-range planning the teacher is concerned with scheduling the daily program and planning lessons.

Scheduling the Daily Program

Only so much instructional time is available in a school day. This necessitates developing a budgeted time plan if a balanced program of experiences and activities is to be offered. This budgeted plan should not be considered as a rigid time schedule that must be adhered to religiously. Instead, it should be construed as a flexible and elastic framework within which alterations can be easily made to deal with unforeseen interruptions or to take advantage of opportunities that may suddenly arise.

Learning does not happen by the clock. Regardless of how carefully a teacher has scheduled the day's program, he should permit pupils, whenever possible, to pursue an activity for a longer time than scheduled or terminate an activity sooner than planned in terms of what is best for learners at the time. Research and experience indicate there is no best time of day to schedule a particular subject matter area or activity. The same sequence of experiences, then, need not be followed every day. Rather, the objectives to be attained and the interests and needs of the group should be major considerations when one is planning the sequence of the daily program.

Some state departments of education and school systems require or recommend that a certain amount of time be spent on particular curricular areas. Also in some schools a suggested daily schedule is still issued to teachers. In most schools some children will be regularly scheduled during the week for particular activities, such as physical education or music, or for special assistance in reading. Even when these conditions exist, most teachers can exercise a great deal of freedom to experiment in determining the best sequence and time blocks for program scheduling.

Few teachers continue to schedule the day into very short periods of time around narrow concepts or areas. Instead, teachers generally build the day's program around related areas scheduled in rather large blocks of time. The following examples illustrate flexible schedules of a daily program for fourth grade:

8:45– 9:00	Routine matters and planning
9:00–10:30	Mathematics
10:30–10:45	Recess
10:45–12:00	Language Arts
12:00– 1:00	Lunch hour

1:00– 1:45	Fine Arts
1:45– 2:30	Social Science
2:30– 3:15	Science
3:15– 3:30	Evaluation

8:45– 9:15	Routine matters and planning
9:15–10:30	Work period on unit activities
10:30–10:50	Physical education or free play
10:50–12:00	Individual and small group work on skills
12:00– 1:00	Lunch hour
1:00– 2:30	Work period on unit activities
2:30– 3:00	Free, creative, or club activities
3:00– 3:15	Evaluation

Lesson Planning

A widespread difference of opinion exists as to the degree of planning a teacher should do for a lesson and with respect to the format or type of plan. Most textbook writers, administrators, and teachers concede the need for planning prior to teaching a lesson. Naturally, for security and direction, the inexperienced or younger teacher needs to do considerably more planning and plan in more detail than an experienced teacher.

Lesson plans should grow out of long-range or unit plans and should be planned to accomplish specific objectives with a group of learners over a short period of time, usually only a day or a few days. When there is a good knowledge of the children with whom the teacher is working and of the particular situation, daily lessons can be planned realistically and purposefully to deal with a specific concept, topic, or skill. Since various lessons require different kinds of instruction and individual differences exist among teachers, there is no single best form or type of lesson plan. Each teacher should strive to develop a form or type of daily lesson planning that best serves his needs for a particular purpose at the given time. Regardless of the subject, grade or level, and type of lesson, a well-prepared lesson plan should contain information on the following:

1. The topic, concept, or skill with which the lesson is concerned.
2. The grade or level and the time limits expected to complete the lesson.
3. The objective or objectives of the lesson stated as behaviorally as possible.
4. The prerequisites the learner should have to deal with the lesson successfully.
5. Activities, materials, and procedures that are most promising for attaining the objective or objectives. What you will do, and what the pupils will do.

6. Assignments for reinforcement and practice.
7. Alternatives and provisions for meeting individual differences.
8. Means of evaluating the outcomes of the lesson.
9. Possible extensions in future lessons of ideas learned.

Perhaps each of the above nine ideas or similar ideas can serve as individual sections for the lesson plan format. Under each section ideas can be recorded in short phrases or in outline form. Long paragraphs in prose form generally are of little use as they require too much reading time to serve as an aid to the teacher while working with children in a classroom situation. If the plan format is kept simple, the teacher should be able to refer to it quickly for ideas as needed without interfering with or interrupting the teaching-learning situation.

TEACHER-PUPIL PLANNING

In a democracy such as ours, we argue long and loud that people should be involved in decisions that affect them; that for people to live and work together successfully, productively, and happily, certain skills such as cooperation, participation, discussion, thinking, planning, problem solving, and decision-making are necessary; that the development of skills requisite for democratic living is an important goal of public education; and that active involvement leads to better learning.

Because children live and work together in a school learning setting over a relatively long period of time, it seems desirable to have these children actively involved in planning, implementing, and evaluating classroom activities. If one agrees that what happens in the classroom and how it happens affects everyone in the room, then teacher-pupil planning becomes a significant factor in the teaching-learning process. Teacher-pupil planning means "planning educational activities with pupils so that the needs and desires they have and recognize are taken into consideration. It means that the teacher is constantly alert to see that the needs she knows exist for her students are also met. It means that teachers and pupils plan, work, evaluate together—and that in this process the skills necessary for democratic living are gradually developed."[14]

Productive learning is unlikely to occur if teacher objectives and pupil objectives are at cross-purposes. Teacher and pupils need to express their objectives, examine them, alleviate any conflicts, and cooperatively arrive at agreements in order that both the teacher and pupils may move toward

[14] Yvonne Waskin and Louise Parrish, *Teacher-Pupil Planning for Better Classroom Learning* (New York: Pitman, 1967), p. 5.

common purposes. When pupils have a meaningful part in planning, all members feel they are important to the group; and classroom activities and the attainment of objectives become group concerns—not just something the teacher wants pupils to do.

Even though the concept of teacher-pupil planning has been widely accepted for years as being important, in actual classroom practice the degree to which pupils are involved in planning varies from little to claiming all the decisions. Making teacher-pupil planning work effectively is not an easy task. In fact, teachers who have utilized the technique successfully report they must do more planning and assume greater leadership responsibilities than if they did all the planning themselves.

> Teacher-pupil planning does not mean the class can do anything they wish. Far from it! The teacher does not abdicate his responsibility for planning and coordinating learning activities. He shares this responsibility with the group of children under his educational guidance. Just how much responsibility the pupils can be given in the planning depends upon many factors: their mental maturity, physical development, background of experience, previous experience in this sort of planning, home and community background, interests, and willingness to work cooperatively. The teacher needs to obtain evidence on as many of these factors as possible in determining the readiness for and the extent to which pupils may successfully participate in the cooperative planning activity.[15]

Teachers can find teacher-pupil planning an enjoyable and profitable way of teaching when they have deep faith in the democratic process and confidence in the nature and ability of youngsters to implement the process. The teacher must also possess the ability to "set the stage" for success and be willing to accept the responsibilities that are his for making the process work. As stated by Waskin and Parrish, "Just as pupils learn through teacher-pupil planning that responsibility accompanies freedom, so must teachers realize that certain obligations are hers when she takes upon herself the task of planning with pupils."[16]

Some of the responsibilities a teacher must accept if teacher-pupil planning is going to flourish are (1) encouraging and promoting respect for self and others, cooperative attitudes, initiative, and acceptance of responsibility; (2) being honest with the pupils (If there are to be limits within which children are to plan, these should be made clear in the beginning; all involved should understand the ground rules for discussion and decision-making. Attempts should not be made to coerce or manipulate pupils to do what the teacher may have already planned for them to do.);

[15] C. C. Collier et al., op. cit., pp. 120–121.
[16] Yvonne Waskin and Louise Parrish, op. cit., p. 92.

(3) supplying ideas, information, and suggestions, when needed, to clarify issues and to keep things moving (The teacher needs to be well informed. He is the recognized leader and contributing member of the group. Pupils naturally look to him for *helping them* find answers to their questions and solutions to their problems.); (4) willingness to give and take as other group members do when the situation demands; having one's idea or suggestion bypassed in favor of someone else's considered to be better by the group; (5) becoming well informed about each member of the group; knowing about their strengths, weaknesses, likes, dislikes, background of experiences, drives, and motives; and (6) adjusting the kind and quantity of pupil participation in planning to areas that are appropriate and also to the maturity and experience level of the learners. Start with a particular topic or area of the school program that the pupils can handle successfully. As pupils gain insights and competence in the teacher-pupil planning process, increase their responsibility.

The school day offers many opportunities for involving pupils in planning. For example, teacher-pupil planning has been successfully used in planning the schedule of activities for the day, deciding on criteria for selecting a topic for study, rearranging the room, planning a field trip, selecting behavior standards, arranging a classroom party, selecting the plan of action preferred from a list of alternatives, arranging an assembly program, deciding what resources are needed in studying a particular topic, and providing for the culmination of a unit.

COOPERATIVE TEACHER PLANNING

Because of the many intricate problems involved in operating an interesting, appropriate, and effective program for all involved, cooperative planning by teachers in a school system or building is highly desirable. The pooled thinking of many teachers, for instance, is needed in (1) planning a set of overall objectives that have an excellent chance of being implemented, (2) developing and organizing a program of content and activities that provides breadth, depth, and continuity of learning experiences each year a child is in school, (3) beginning an innovative program in the school, (4) selecting a new basic textbook series, (5) planning in-service activities or programs, and (6) helping the individual teacher to see the total program in perspective.

More cooperative planning is done during a school year than perhaps most teachers realize. Sometimes teacher cooperative planning is done in formally called meetings or through an organized structure; at other times it occurs informally when two or more colleagues are together. Depending on the situation, problem, or need, cooperative planning may be done by the total staff in a faculty meeting, at grade level meetings, in committees, or by a group who "get together" in the lounge, at lunch, or before or after school.

SUMMARY

Failure to plan or poor planning usually results in a disorganized, chaotic, ineffective classroom program and dissatisfaction with teaching. A prime contributing factor to success and happiness is the teacher's ability to plan well. Three types of plans for which the teacher has responsibility have been discussed—long-range or yearly plans, short-range or unit plans, and daily or lesson plans. In planning, the teacher also has the responsibility of providing opportunities and finding ways to involve pupils actively and effectively in the process. Plans, when done creatively and purposefully, provide a sense of direction and serve as a guide to decision-making both for the teacher and pupils.

SUGGESTED ACTIVITIES

1. Eight "guidelines for planning" were discussed in this chapter. Which of these do you consider most important? Which least important? Justify.
2. Select a subject area taught in the elementary school, for instance, social studies or language arts, and for your grade level or teaching interest level, outline long-range plans—the major areas of study for the year.
3. Choose one of the concepts outlined for study in the second suggested activity, and state the hoped-for outcomes in behavioral terms.
4. Through the process of teacher-pupil planning, a unit for study has been selected to begin a month from now. What will you do relative to planning between now and then to make sure the unit is a success?
5. School has been in session for five months. You are very pleased with the exciting, democratic, humane atmosphere in the classroom and also with the pupils' attitude toward learning, their high motivation, and the success they are experiencing. One afternoon the principal calls you in to express his concern about the disorganized, noisy room he has observed. He also reports that teachers have asked that he talk with you about the poor teaching in your room. What approach will you take? Is your teaching-learning approach defensible? Why? How?

SELECTED BIBLIOGRAPHY

Bits and Pieces: Imaginative Uses for Children's Learning. Ed. by Sylvia
    Sunderlin. Washington, D.C.: Association for Childhood International,
    1967.
Bruner, Jerome S. *The Process of Education.* New York: Vintage Books, 1960.
Evans, Joyce S. "Classroom Planning for Young Special Children." *Teaching
    Exceptional Children,* 4 (Winter 1972), 56–61.
Featherstone, Joseph. *Schools Where Children Learn.* New York: Liveright,
    1971.
Gagné, Robert M. *The Conditions of Learning.* New York: Holt, Rinehart &
    Winston, Inc., 1965.
Hyman, R. T. "Individualization: The Hidden Agenda." *Education Digest,*
    (Oct. 1973), 48–51.
Leeper, Sarah Hammond et al. *Good Schools for Young Children.* New York:
    Macmillan Publishing Company, Inc., 1974. Chapter 10.
Palardy, J. Michael. *Teaching Today: Tasks and Challenges.* New York: Mac-
    millan Publishing Co., Inc., 1975.
Perrone, V., and L. Thompson. "Starting Point for Development." *Clearing
    House* (Feb. 1974) 361–65.
Popham, W. J., and E. I. Baker. *Planning an Instructional Sequence.* Engle-
    wood Cliffs, N.J.: Prentice-Hall, Inc., 1970.
Smith, James A. *Setting Conditions for Creative Teaching in the Elementary
    School.* Boston: Allyn & Bacon, Inc., 1966.

Chapter 8

Personalizing Instruction

Parents are frequently frustrated and sometimes angered by the refusal of their adolescent children to accept adult suggestions and advice in attacking problems or challenges. This common concern is eased somewhat in later years as the maturing son or daughter gradually realizes that personal and professional experiences of other people can be of advantage to them in problem solving—regardless of age or maturity. The field of education also has had problems of gathering and using information from *all* facets of society except that in many instances it has been the needs and experiences of *youth* that have been ignored or overlooked.

For some children the matching of need with instructional strategy comes belatedly—with others it is a matter of decision. From New Zealand, Sylvia Ashton-Warner perhaps oversimplifies the teaching situation:

> I see the mind of a five year old as a volcano with two vents: destructiveness and creativeness. And I see that to the extent that we widen the creative channel, we atrophy the destructive one.[1]

Few teachers still firmly envision a group of thirty fifth-graders as *one* "typical" fifth grade student multiplied by thirty seats or desks. Many kindergarten teachers now accept the situation that some beginning stu-

[1] Sylvia Ashton-Warner, *Teacher* (New York: Simon & Schuster, 1963), p. 33.

dents read successfully *before* coming to school whereas some upper grade students still lack desired reading skills. In short, people are different. So are children in the schools. One can assume that we have passed the stage that provides mechanical separation and instruction by the criteria of sex, size, weight, chronological age, or blood type.

We are also more aware today of more *types* of student need. Some of our elementary school teachers are attempting to meet the differing requirements of twenty to thirty children in reading but conveniently "lumping" equaly diverse student needs in mathematics into two categories—those who can understand the textbook themselves and "those others," who need help. In the community itself, stereotypes of differences of individuals are frequently drawn between those who do or do not ride school buses, do or do not take ballet lessons, do or do not tell dirty stories, do or do not support school millage increases—the list is endless. But regardless of our fit as teachers to categories of differing as individuals, we are united by the challenge of providing opportunities for any child in our somewhat bewildering assortment of responsibilities in the school and community. We cannot accept the assumption that children are more alike than they are different unless we also accept them as endless reproductions of a given grade model in two versions, male and female.

Understanding that both limitations and expectations are personal and are a realistic part of the individual role is a basic responsibility of the teacher and the school program. In the following discusion, we will explore some of the ways and means of fulfilling this professional and community expectation. As a result of this exploration, you should be able to

1. Describe the difference within children that necessitates the need to differentiate among them.
2. Describe and contrast the various ways of providing for individual differences.
3. Contrast the advantages and disadvantages of school organizational patterns for individualizing.
4. Describe and identify the rationale of varying deviating needs for personalized instruction.
5. Describe the steps of identifying teacher response to individual pupil need.

CHILDREN ARE DIFFERENT

Each pupil in an elementary classroom is a synthesis of unique characteristics that, in combination, result in his individuality. The manner in which these physical, social, emotional, and mental factors develop varies both within an individual child and among members of a peer group. When some children are in periods of rapid growth, others of the same chronological age may be growing at a very slow rate, while still others are actually regressing.

The elementary school teacher, therefore, needs to have an understanding of and deep appreciation for child development in order to adapt the curriculum goals to the children in the classroom. From birth to adulthood, boys and girls mature at a rate that is unique to themselves and yet follows some broad, general patterns. By recognizing that these patterns of child growth and maturation can be approached in the classroom by a wide variety of teaching strategies, teachers can implement learning activities that will be most beneficial to a given child or group at a given place and time.

Teachers as human beings are often impressed by the capability of a student and can quickly project the individual as an adult and as an exemplary professional, politician, or industrial leader. More difficult is the envisioning in a positive sense of an adult life for the slow learner, the behavioral misfit, the extrovert, or the silent back-row daydreamer. Examine the typically American senior high school yearbook and match the caption (supposedly humorus) with the student's list of accomplishments for the four-year period. Typically, those who seem to have achieved the least do not enjoy the "in" captions compared to their more successful classmates. If this observation bothers you, do you wonder if the less successful student was so because the teachers were unsuccessful in adequately adjusting patterns of learning for his individual needs? Is it possible that he was an outsider because we as adult professionals were a bit insensitive to his chosen pathway for developing true social or class relationships? In fact, is it possible that he is "out" while others are "in" because teacher efforts catered more to the needs of a group in the middle of the range of class differences rather than accommodating to the expectations of the two extreme end groups as well?

Individuals in a class have personal strengths and expectancies—and they also have limitations. Individualizing instruction implies recognition of these restrictions as well as accepting the more typical pupil identification with greater intellectual capacity. Legend has it, for example, that the famous black scientist, George Washington Carver, frequently repeated the story of his humble understanding with God:

> When I was young I said to God—God tell me the mystery of the Universe. But God answered—that knowledge is reserved for me alone. So I said,—God tell me the mystery of the peanut. Then God said— Well, George, that's more nearly your size—and he told me![2]

[2] Comment attributed to Dr. Carver by students of his midwestern classes.

Growth

Within an age span of one to five years typically found in a classroom, the teacher can identify considerable differences in physical characteristics of children other than sex. The most obvious differences are in height and weight. It is possible to obtain averages in height and weight for boys and girls at a given age, and many such studies have been made. Although this kind of information is useful in forming generalizations about an age group and in comparing its members, it also provides identification of other physical differences that might otherwise go undetected. Some children are fortunate enough to come from homes where parents have consulted physicians frequently about their children's physical development. However, when this medical attention does not occur, improper diet or other physiological imbalances can cause problems that are undetected during early childhood. The undernourished or obese child in today's schools can receive assistance through agencies, but too often it is the responsibility of the professional teacher to identify children who exhibit unique physical abnormalities and to provide direction and assistance for corrective measures.

Many physical differences between children not easily detected are important to understand for the teacher to encourage maximum learning. Differences in sight, hearing, speech, coordination, energy, temperament, and general appearance provide clues to need for professional assistance. As a child continues on his growth cycle, new deficiencies may appear that were not apparent six months or a year before. Because of the physical changes continually occurring in each individual, teachers must be constantly attuned to the physical characteristics of children in class. Fortunately numerous health, welfare, and civic agencies are available to cooperate with school efforts in safeguarding the physical health of children.

In spite of our best efforts, however, some physical limitations to learning still go undetected in our schools today. Progress has been made in identifying some children who are handicapped in learning, but specific means of identification of numerous handicaps still lacks the sophistication to enable detection of all physical problems that we believe affect learning.

Intellectual Development

The intellectual development of children has been exhaustively investigated during the past few years. Tests such as the *Stanford-Binet* and the *Wechsler Intelligence Scale* have been constructed to examine the mental processes of individuals, and the continued use of these and other tests has enabled psychologists to establish some general performance expectations of various age levels for children. The fact that differences do occur among individuals in use of verbal and nonverbal symbols is rather well established, but the cause of these differences and mental qualities affecting change in an individual continue to be debated at this time. Analysis of test results to date indicates that the growth of intelligence is continuous from infanthood through maturity.[3]

Moreover, current research is now being conducted in assessment of the intellectual development of children who grow up in a culture that differs from the cultural base of the testing sample. It has been found that "for children growing up under adverse circumstances, the I.Q. may be depressed by a significant amount and that intervention at certain points (and especially in the period from ages three to nine) can raise the I.Q. as much as ten to fifteen points."[4]

Cultural Differences

The classroom combines children who often come from vastly varying backgrounds. This is becoming increasingly true today because of the high rate of mobility found among parents and the demands of travel in gaining occupational advancement. As parents move to a new neighborhood, their children enter schools to work with other children who may come from homes differing measurably from theirs. The son of a coal miner from the rural South who moves to Los Angeles finds the values of the urban dweller quite unlike "back home." Patterns of speaking, means of validating oneself as a person, responses to teachers and school, all vary considerably among cultures within the United States. A new pupil in the suburban school may have moved from a school where the real "heroes" encouraged and won frequent fights. Anyone who would refuse to accept the challenge to fight would therefore be viewed as "weak" and treated accordingly. In seeking acceptance in a new school he would apply the techniques learned in his old neighborhood and become the originator of fights and other physical conflicts. The effect of his fighting in this environment would probably have the same effect upon him as *not fighting* would have had in his previous school situation. Therefore, until he learned the cultural pattern of the new area, he would probably remain largely rejected by his peers.

Of particular frustration to educators are the problems presented in providing for the "third culture" child who is most commonly located in schools operated for children of servicemen stationed in countries other than their own. The United States government, for example, operates an extensive system of schools overseas for military dependents. Located on

---

[3] Arden F. Frandsen, *How Children Learn* (New York: McGraw-Hill, 1957), pp. 62–63.

[4] Benjamin S. Bloom, Allison Davis, and Robert Hess, *Compensatory Education for Cultural Deprivation* (New York: Holt, 1965), p. 12.

military bases and staffed primarily by "stateside" teachers, these schools provide K–12 curricula similar to those enjoyed within the fifty states. The problem of the third culture child emerges from a multitude of circumstances, but a simplified example could be illustrative. Seaman 3rd Class Juan Smith, USN, is Chicano and has married the daughter of a Japanese merchant and is housed in a naval housing unit at a United States Navy nuclear submarine base in Japan. Their boy, José, attends an elementary school on the base. Since his father is often on assignment at sea for intervals lasting many months, José spends a great deal of his time in contact with his mother, her family, and relatives. He is already somewhat bilingual at age ten but more comfortable in conversation and in interest in his mother's language, Japanese. Yet in the American-style school instruction, discussions, reading materials, and announcements are in the English language. Socially, José feels more comfortable with those students who speak Japanese, but is frequently sought out by other Chicano children, whose parents are from the United States. His appreciation for Chicano culture and the Spanish language is less than for Japanese, but he is frequently rejected by the Japanese children who speak English in both school and homes. Black and white children also polarize toward groups and individuals experienced in American cultural and social grouping, in many instances excluding from each other those differing from minimum group norms. Like José, a black-Japanese girl will often suffer from exclusion by black, Japanese-American, and white students. The problem is duplicated in other nations and schools, with the culture and language changing with the location of the base. In nonmilitary schools similar problems can be observed, especially if strong national or ethnic ties are held in high esteem by a minority of the school patrons and if language, dance, and social "schools" are strongly supported to supplement the public school curricula.

Successful educational strategies to counter these differences in cultural mores are isolated, but continuous study is needed. A bilingual teacher, for example, is of positive assistance as are attempts to give particular attention to all individual melds of social and cultural interchange. Realization of each child's role in a room, school, or community is a minimum expectancy, and the need for the teacher to emphasize this responsibility or contribution is patently obvious in any culture sensitive to change.

Social Differences

Some children adapt to their peer group in the classroom environment in a comfortable manner that is satisfying to themselves, other children, and their teachers. Other children have considerable difficulty in making the necessary adjustments to group living in the classroom. The shy child finds it difficult to perform tasks that call attention to himself whereas the demanding child finds it difficult to remain on the sidelines while his classmates assume dominant roles. Teachers strive to identify social differences and assist individual children in developing a realistic self-image by analyzing the pupils' social interaction.

During the process of maturation, individuals change their behavioral pattern because of changes developing among their peers or within themselves. The shy boy may enjoy a period of rapid growth resulting in superior performance in athletics. Physical development and the resulting success in athletics may eliminate his earlier shyness and encourage him to develop leadership ability in the classroom.

Another child may be self-assured until he reaches a point of failure or frustration causing him to change his behavior toward others. Fear of being unwanted at home, for example, may cause undesirable behavior in school and further rejection by children and adults.

By use of sociometric devices, teacher observation, cumulative data, and outside resources, a history of social development can be developed for each child. This information can be of great assistance in enabling teachers to construct an environment that fosters sound social relationships for all children, especially when rapid change in individual attitude develops.

Children and Their Interests

The modern elementary school provides an atmosphere designed to capture the imagination and interest of children who will work and play together. Attractive classrooms stimulate children to reveal their current interest and to develop new ones. Children can be expected to have general interests at a given age, but interest patterns differ among members of any age group. Warner indicates, "Although children tend to follow the interests of other children of their age level, they also show interest patterns that are highly individual."[5] Knowledge of current interests of children can do much to assist teachers in motivating pupils and to enable them to be successful in school experiences.

If the teacher is able to capture interest in the classroom and direct this interest to new areas of learning, school becomes an enjoyable place to be. By listening to children's conversations, providing opportunities for creative writing, and planning activities with children, a teacher can develop an adequate interest inventory for his classroom. This inventory provides the basis for units of study that will insure pupil participation in planning and carrying out the unit to completion.

Cumulative records usually contain information that provides clues to pupil interests. In the process of examining these records and keeping them

---

[5] Ruby H. Warner, *Elementary School Teaching Practices* (Washington, D.C.: The Center for Applied Research in Education, Inc., 1962), p. 49.

current, a teacher is able to gain insight and understanding that should help him to keep the classroom an enjoyable place for children to work. Parent-teacher conferences enable teachers to tap a source of ideas for motivating pupils through interests that parents observe in pupils' home activities. Once pupil interests are identified, the classroom can become the center for expansion of interests. When pupils identify school as a place where their interests are fostered, avenues for all school-related learning are paved for future utilization.

Attitude Development

All pupils entering school for the first time do not begin at the same point in terms of chronological age and readiness to learn. In addition, children have varying perceptions about themselves and school. If a child has heard such statements from his parents as, "Wait until you get to school, the teacher will straighten you out!" he will probably have genuine reservations about attending school. If, on the other hand, school has been described as an enjoyable experience, he will likely be eager to begin his school career.

Of particular interest to the development of attitudes in the beginning school years are the opportunities provided by the organizational concept of the extended session or twelve-month school year. Although established patterns for this organization still vary widely nationwide, in general, the extended school offerings provide for a continuous school session during the calendar year with both students and faculty "vacationed" at regular intervals. One singular feature of this concept permits a child who is too young for admission to school in the fall to enter at the beginning of the winter or spring sessions. Thus a child is not denied admission for a twelve-month period, but instead becomes eligible for readmission at the beginning of each three or four month period. Resulting is a more homogeneous student body with differences in chronological ages being reduced and a continuum of student admissions throughout the year. The effect of these enlightened admissions is apparent in positive attitudes on the part of the child, the teacher, and the parent. Continual parental criticism has been leveled at schools for admitting one child who met the minimum chronological age by one day and denying another child entrance because his age fell one or two days short of the minimum cutoff date. Perhaps the educational lockstep of matching school opportunities to chronological age can be challenged at this crucial time of child growth and development by enlightened admissions.

During the time pupils are in school, they have additional opportunities to change old attitudes toward learning and toward other children, adults, and themselves. If pupil efforts in the classroom result in success and satisfaction, continued learning becomes possible, if not probable.

During the time children are attempting to learn to read, they are also developing a multitude of attitudes—toward reading, the teacher, other children, and themselves. If these attitudes are positive, it may be because of positive experiences that encourage even greater successes. If the attitudes developed are negative, it is likely that some success will be necessary before they can change. Success in learning in one area can encourage success in other fields because a pupil identifies himself as *someone who can learn.*

CHALLENGES OF INSTRUCTIONAL ORGANIZATION

It is not an easy task for any teacher to provide for all the many needs of individuals found in a classroom. To some degree all teachers recognize individual differences among their pupils, yet in many instances far too little is initiated in the classroom. When a teacher meets a new class of pupils in the fall, he soon becomes aware of the wide range of their previous learning. However, to *recognize* this range is only the first step; he must then make provisions for these differences in the *way* he teaches. When adjustments are made, they may be for the whole class rather than for an individual. One frequently hears comments made by teachers such as, "They are a slow group," "I have a sharp group this year." These gross generalizations tend to set the pace for learning that will be expected by the teacher. However, the range of ability and previous learning between two such groups may vary. For example, the bright students in a class designated as generally "slow" are at a decided disadvantage, as slow students would be who happen to be in a class that a teacher has earmarked as "sharp." Although it is normal to find differences in groups of children, teachers must remain aware of the needs and ambitions of all the individuals within the classroom setting.

Many teachers experience frustration in attempts to individualize instruction because of the vast number of variables that must be considered in working with a class of unique individuals.[6] This concern for individualized instruction generally does not arise originally from the pupils, but develops from the accumulated disappointments of teachers attempting to cope with the task of teaching each child in a fitting approach or strategy. Some teachers experience frustration in teaching based upon a desire to be consistently effective with all children at all times. The very uniqueness of the teaching-learning process makes this goal an unrealistic one, and those who measure success upon total class development will experience constant impediment to happiness. Rose has identified this anxiety as a

[6] Gale W. Rose, "Performance Evaluation and Growth in Teaching," *Phi Delta Kappan*, **45**, No. 1:48–53 (Oct. 1963).

normal reaction. Therefore, successful teaching must include provisions for adequate measures of success upon which a teacher may assess his effectiveness, and these must be based upon the individual progress of the learners.

Grouping

Teachers attempt to meet the multitude of individual differences in the classroom by employing one of several organizational plans for grouping pupils. As a means of identifying closer with a pupil's needs, many teachers divide their classrooms into two or more groups and work with one group at a time. Traditionally, this practice is extensively employed in primary-grade reading. Unfortunately, the same principle is not applied in many other areas of the curriculum where the individual needs of pupils are as great, if not greater, than in reading. If it is possible for a teacher to be more effective in teaching children to read in smaller groups, it should be equally possible in mathematics, social studies, language skills, and science.

Most elementary teachers find that planning for instruction when groups are used is a time-consuming task. With the challenges of developing three plans for reading groups, many teachers are not anxious to become involved in the same type of multilevel planning for the rest of the curriculum. This difficulty stems mainly from the manner in which planning and evaluation of the work are carried out. If the teacher assumes the responsibility for the planning and preparation of all materials, the practice of grouping is frequently limited, modified, or dropped. Therefore, if a teacher wants to use grouping as a means of providing better instruction for individuals, he will have to adjust his planning in a manner that prevents it from becoming too time-consuming. One way in which teachers are able to cope with the problem of time is to share the planning with pupils. When a teacher discusses objectives, procedures, materials, and evaluation with pupils, it is possible to involve them as active participants in planning. If the children know, for example, that the objective in the science unit involves a more complete understanding of the systems of the human body, they are able to supplement the classroom episodes with resources and materials from home, library, and community. On the other hand, if these objectives are not shared with students, the identification and preparation of materials for instruction becomes the sole responsibility of the teacher.

There does not seem to be any particular number of groups that are most effective for classroom use. Some teachers, therefore, plan all activities within one grouping plan. At the other extreme is the teacher who "individualizes" twenty-five to thirty pupils—thus providing for that many different teaching bases. This is a decision each teacher must make on the basis of the curriculum, students, and environmental setting. There are undoubtedly times when individual needs can be met by the teacher's working with the entire class as well as times when instruction becomes completely individualized. Regardless of the grouping procedures used, the teacher who is aware of the needs of individual students will use grouping only as a vehicle to reach goals. Grouping pupils by achievement, for example, reduces the range of teacher planning and preparation and permits the teacher to work specifically at a predetermined level. Selecting several pupils with similar learning difficulties and working with them as a group sharpens the focus of study. Ideally, grouping is done for these reasons, but it is possible to be just as regimented in working with a group as when working with the entire class. If instruction is of a highly regimented nature, it makes little difference whether a teacher is working with ten children or fifty. The most ideal teaching situation is one in which students are able to communicate witht the teacher on a personal basis and work together toward a commonly established goal.

The teacher's role changes to meet the needs of the children. The teacher's part in each of the organizations shown in Table 8–1 is as follows:

TABLE 8–1
Grouping Pupils to Provide for Individual Differences

1. The Class as a Whole	2. A Grouping for Committee to Plan
T c c c c c c c c c c c c c c c c c c c c c c c c c c c c c c c c	c c c c c c c c c c c c c c c c c c c c c T c c c c c c c c
3. A Grouping for Work	4. A Grouping for Reporting
c c c c c c c c c c c c c c c c c c c c c c c c c c c c T	c c c c c c c c c c c c c c c c c c c c c c c c c c c c c T
5. A Grouping for Spelling	6. Individual Work by Pupils
cc cc cc cc cc cc **cc** c c c c **cc** c c c c T cc c c c c	c c c c c c c c c c c c c c c c c c c c c c c c c T

1. Teacher develops a lesson.
2. Teacher guides committee activities.
3. Teacher helps one group.
4. Teacher and class hear a committee report.
5. Teacher pretests one group while other children study in pairs.
6. Teacher helps one child while others work independently.[7]

One of the most enterprising attempts to adapt teaching to the individual differences of learners has been the recent trend toward individualized instruction. Proponents of this innovation insist that it is based upon a true consideration of adapting instruction of media to individuals rather than attempting to meet individual needs through a form of in-class grouping. Undoubtedly, the most widespread use of individualized instruction has been in the area of reading at the elementary level. Should teachers find greater pupil achievement in reading when instruction is individualized, support would be indicated for individualizing instruction in other areas of the curriculum and beyond the elementary grades. At the present time most achievements in this area of individualized teaching have been made by a pioneering group of interested teachers. There is a great need for more teachers to become involved in using and evaluating this method of teaching. When efforts do become intensified and broadened, it will become possible to assess more fairly the accomplishment of individualized instruction.

Individualized instruction cannot be viewed as the panacea for all teaching problems, for if maximum growth is to occur, children need opportunity to relate to their peers as well as to the academic content. Somewhere between a totally individualized program and one of massed involvement, there is a balance that every teacher must discover for himself and his classroom. Whatever manner of organization within a classroom is employed, the identification and utilization of individual differences will remain paramount. The teacher who tends to be individual-oriented will be this way, whether teaching a whole class, a group, or an individual. Similarly, the teacher who tends to be regimented will tend to regiment his teaching. A recent study by Dankowski concluded that "individualizing teachers have the attitudes and professional initiative long considered to be indicative of superior teachers."[8] The teachers who reflect a favorable opinion of pupils, administrators, and other people tend to individualize instruction more than teachers who are less positive toward others. This information supports the view that positive attitude development must be fostered as well as skills in subject-matter areas if we expect teachers to individualize instruction. Individualizing teachers tend to have

[7] *The Elementary School Curriculum* (Albany: Bureau of Elementary Curriculum Development, New York State Education Department, 1954), p. 141.

[8] Charles E. Dankowski, *Teachers Who Individualize Instruction*, Commission Study 2 (New York: Columbia U. P., Teachers College, 1965).

more understanding of pupils and to direct their efforts to individual pupils rather than to academic subject matter alone. Their classrooms favor democratic procedures and are more conducive to productive learning.

Open Classrooms

A relatively new organizational structure for elementary school instruction is the open classroom. Its teachers propose to not only individualize instruction for students but also encourage them to proceed to the limits of their abilities, ambitions, and interests. Sometimes discussed in terms of individualized self-pacing instruction, open classroom instruction places a major emphasis upon teacher-pupil planning, individual strategy implementation, effective monitoring, and evaluation. As implied, this structure encourages children to find their own procedures for attacking problems and, in a sense, the development of environments that enhance individual growth and success. As a result, one of the observable patterns that develops with open classroom teaching is a free-activity type of classroom climate. Children seem to personify a wide variety of learning styles with physical accommodations ranging from a belly-down floor position to a secluded "library" nook, student-constructed from an empty cardboard refrigerator box. Neither these individualized learning centers nor the variation in conversation levels should necessarily typify open classroom instruction, but to many traditional school patrons these patterns of learning are described in terms ranging from chaos to unprofessional. Perhaps the development of many private "free" schools along similar patterns of organization has muddied the public's (and teacher's) vision.

Within a decade, a more objective analysis and measure of open school instruction should be available. Meanwhile, we should be aware that frequent conclusions are drawn about this mode of instruction based upon singular features such as student activity and classroom environment rather than measurable results such as performance and competencies realized by varying individuals. In its early years of development, open classroom teaching already has experienced extremes of professional polarity from participants and observers. Urban school systems are openly experimenting with their "version" of open classroom instruction, but admittedly keeping close contact within the system to sense community and professional reactions. It is probable that assessment of the program in the 1980s or 1990s will be of more value than the shallow conclusion now being made to justify positions both pro and con.

Contract Teaching

Spawned in a brief period of educational development by state and federal grants to individual school systems, contract teaching (or performance contract teaching) burst into national prominence in the 1960s as a new way of realizing success in approaching the educational problems of urban youth. Although other economic school areas were funded by governmental agencies, the major thrust was to improve development of individual pupil and school performance levels within urban school centers where children of minority and low socioeconomic school neighborhoods enjoyed scant improvement when compared to state and national norms.

In essence, private corporation-supported task groups contracted with school boards to assume major elements of classroom instruction to produce a guaranteed pupil growth in achievement within a given period of time for a prescribed sum of money based upon a cost-per-pupil minimum. If the minimum rise in achievement was not realized, a reduced cost per pupil came into play, with some contracts suggesting that only minimal operating costs would be expected if results were not satisfactory.

With governmental funds encouraging the innovation, financially pressed schools signed contracts with private contractors for given areas of concentration—mathematics and reading being common to many agreements. The private contractors were responsible for teacher recruitment and in-service training. Schools provided facilities and determined the standardized instruments used to measure the hoped-for achievement changes. Specialized equipment, improvement of facilities, pupil selection, and specifics of teaching materials were generally decided by contract negotiations.

Incentives for pupil encouragement received considerable publicity because they involved gifts, special privileges, and released time for recreation. Teacher organizations were infrequent participants in the performance contract negotiations and for this reason and others tended to view performance contracting as a challenge to their profession. Areas under contract favored skill development and other processes where achievement measures could be utilized. Children selected were generally in those classifications of achievement that were at the bottom of minimum growth lists if not below minimum school and parent expectations.

As of the mid-1970s, relatively little governmental funding remains to encourage performance contracting, and the cumulative verdict as to the impact of this innovation by private industry is not clear. Some reports are in conflict whereas others are based upon participating groups that do not lend themselves to valid projection. For example, where achievement was enjoyed, the impact of ideal pupil-teacher instruction, specialized environment (computers, air conditioning, stereo music, and so forth), and flexible scheduling could possibly have produced similar results if noncontract students were able to share the same facilities. On the other hand, in overall effort, some private contracting agencies were able to produce specific skill growth at modest cost where the conventional system had not been successful. Ideally, performance contracting should be given a reasonable trial in a variety of school situations, assigned to a range of student abilities, and responsible for total curriculum, not mere skills. Such an effort would be most helpful in enabling teachers to grasp the opportunities as well as limitations of performance contracting. Until those results are available, it would be decidedly unfair to generalize upon the specifics of success or failure for private industries' venture into public and private education.

The size of a class does appear to have an effect upon the way a teacher works with children. Pugh[9] found that there are more small-group individual activities in small classes than in large ones. Instruction in large classes tends to be directed primarily to the total group, although a considerable amount of time in small classes is also of the same nature. Therefore, teachers who are inclined to individualize instruction would have best opportunity to do so if class size were not overly large. (For details on differentiated staffing, see Chapter 6.)

Deviation Within the Classroom

Every child in a classroom could in some manner be classified as a deviate, for each child is unique unto himself. Because of this uniqueness, all who work with children must remain aware of the individual and refrain from generalizing, for in every classroom there will be one or more pupils who differ from the norm in some manner. This may be because a pupil has a mental age several years older than other pupils in the classroom or has a unique socioeconomic background. There are children who are deviates because of unique physical, social, or emotional differences; therefore, the challenge presented by the deviate is one of the most challenging for the teacher.

Regardless of the manner in which a teacher organizes a classroom, special provision must be made for the deviate; and when the teacher is fortunate enough to have only one or two in the classroom, the task is relatively easy. However, when a larger number of deviates are present, it may be that administrative consultation or assistance is necessary. The teacher, therefore, has a responsibility to discuss individuals in his classroom who deviate from norms in major proportions with the building principal. For example, when a kindergarten teacher discovers that a child in the classroom is able to read fluently, this situation should be made known to the principal; for although it is not usual to find pupils who have learned to read by age five, the child is indeed a deviate in need of special attention and consideration beyond conventional classroom processing.

The teacher is always the key to assisting the deviate in accepting himself as a worthwhile individual as well as assisting other children in their peer relations with the deviate. A teacher needs, first of all, to provide for individual needs of a child in a manner that will enhance his self-image. One of the dangers to effective learning by one who deviates from the

---

[9] James P. Pugh, Jr., *Performance of Teacher and Pupils in Small Classes*, Commission Study No. 1 (New York: Columbia U. P. Teachers College, 1965).

norm is the tendency to perceive talent as a handicap rather than an asset and therefore as a gap that is present between himself and other pupils. The teacher who ignores the reading ability of the child in kindergarten or who does not assist him in the development of this asset can contribute to negative learning on the part of the pupil.

Children differ physically as well as mentally or socially. A child who is abnormally tall in a classroom may begin to think of himself as entirely different from other children; and when this does not occur, a tall child may draw attention to his height in an attempt to determine if his self-perception of being different is valid. Therefore, a teacher should work with the class to develop an understanding of differences in physical growth to enable them to accept the individual who is abnormally tall or short. The same deviate behavior is often found among many children who come from culturally different homes. These deviates act out behavior patterns to test teachers and other pupils as well as to determine if their self-image is valid. It is not always easy for a teacher to work with a deviate child in a positive and constructive manner if the child has formed a poor self-image that is well developed. To unlearn this reinforced image is a difficult task for the learner; however, it is vital to the mental health of children to come to an understanding of themselves and their peers with whom they must relate throughout their lives. A teacher must remain alert to the needs of all children lest their unique assets turn into liabilities; but when this does occur, the liability may become paramount in their lives to the extent that other learning cannot occur in a normal manner. If a child feels different from other children in the classroom because of certain unique characteristics, this feeling will dominate his thinking in any new learning situation. Consider, for example, the case of an exceptionally tall child. The teacher may have as an objective helping her children improve their appreciation of music by taking the class to a concert, but upon entering the theater the tall child may think of nothing but his own height. He may hear little music because he is acutely aware of conversations of other people, attempting to find justification through their criticisms for his self-perception—that he is a giant. When a situation such as this occurs, learning time is lost by the student; and unless efforts are made toward adjustment, learning will continue to suffer. The key to development of the deviate is the classroom teacher, who recognizes the child who deviates from the norm and then works with him in a manner that will recognize and coordinate his contribution to developing personal and group competencies.

The Exceptional or Deviating Child and Special Education

Most school districts provide specialized instruction and facilities for children who deviate from the expectations of a typical school program in individual needs. These departures from the norm could range from communication disorders to sensory handicaps. Included in a given school could be youngsters with mental deviations, behavior disorders, or orthopedic or related health impaired restrictions.

It is difficult to estimate the number of children who are entitled to specialized attention in the classroom—some figures include ten per cent to fifteen per cent of the school population, for example, as being at the extremes of either mentally retarded or intellectually gifted. Special education programs have made commendable progress in recent years in providing needed assistance to deserving children either in assisting teachers already in the classroom with specialized programs and materials or through the recruitment and training of teachers especially qualified to work with children in need of specialized assistance. Yet the success of the specialized programs (and the resulting state and federal financial endorsements) have at best reached approximately one third of the two and one half million children in need of these services.

Formal education has seemingly accepted the need for providing specialized preparation for certain student groups. Plato was an early supporter of special education for the intellectually gifted, and referral of speech-handicapped children has existed in the profession for centuries. Teachers continue to support ideas that involve referral of students to specialized teachers and/or rooms, but in doing so also continue to endorse the idea that children with specialized needs should be separated in part or completely from other "normal" children. Admittedly, we no longer imprison or cage epileptic children, but many teachers still do not welcome these pupils to their classrooms. We have overcome the practice of channeling children with partial sighted handicaps to restricted training programs for future piano tuners, but fail in openly providing needed opportunities for them in the elementary and middle school classrooms.

Our tardiness in utilizing special education programs within our classroom is a major reason why such a small number of exceptional and deviating children are being serviced in schools today. In fact, it is relatively impossible to house and finance the numbers of these deserving students under the system of separate room and teacher assignment. Therefore, of recent years there has been a significant move away from special education rooms toward resource room organization, thereby encouraging the retention of deviating or exceptional children within conventional classroom parameters and utilizing special education teachers and facilities as resource features to aid both the child and the room teacher. Frequently, a child with a sensory handicap will spend scheduled time with a special education resource teacher, but increasingly move parallel with similar time periods for work with teachers of music, art, and physical education. In short, the needs of deviating children are becoming the responsibility of the classroom teacher working closely with the program entities and materials supplied by special education teachers. In turn, school organization programs are reflecting the flexibility demanded by the teachers. The nongraded organizational pattern, for example, supplies the vertical and lateral mobility of, say, a third level boy who has unusual talents in areas more traditionally encountered by sixth grade pupils. He can now work with children chronologically his superior, but retains group identity with his classmates who are mentally inferior. Heretofore, he was locked in by school programs to compete successfully in physical education with boys and girls his physical equals, but denied the challenge to succeed with his intellectual equals at the upper grade level. In like manner, only now are state and federal agencies supporting physically handicapped facilities so that a girl restricted to a wheel chair has the individual mobility to move between and within buildings of home, school, and employment.

Demands for more participation of exceptional and deviating children within the classroom will continue to require teacher insight and responsibility for developing new methods and procedures for accommodating a widening range of pupil response to instructional stimuli. Fortunately, the challenge is within the expectation of teachers and the reaction of children to this need has been and will continue to be most supportive.

PROGRAM MATERIALS

The continuing development of program materials for instruction provides teachers with a wealth of prepared teaching aids for individualized instruction. It seems likely that many of the programmed materials will be suited to both bright and slow students and thereby relieve these individuals from standardized tasks that frequently discourage rather than motivate when assigned or confronted in current texts and workbooks. Many individuals can develop some skills and knowledge by use of teaching machines or programmed textbooks. For the self-motivated student in an area such as mathematics, a programmed text may enable him to become emancipated from the milieu of the generalized mathematics text. If these newly developed tools for instruction are utilized in a judicious manner, it becomes possible for teachers to better adapt their teaching to the needs of individuals.

Many of the textbooks and workbooks universally available in classrooms today can be utilized as materials for individual instruction. To a degree this is what is accomplished when a teacher divides a class into three reading groups, each group reading from a different level textbook. This realization of differing skills, needs, and readiness can be enjoyed in mathematics, social studies, science, or any area of the curriculum. However, to employ a number of textbooks does not guarantee in itself an improved, individualized program. The teacher must establish suitable goals and adapt materials to the interests and abilities of pupils. Obviously, a teacher must fully understand the nature of the learning process, for if a pupil is accelerated in arithmetic and is assigned a programmed text that enables him to proceed at his own pace, his entire daily schedule may need to be revamped. A pupil involved in individualized programming should not be also held responsible for detailed work of the rest of the class in arithmetic, nor should time spent on this subject be so out of proportion to the rest of the curriculum that the student feels burdened or overworked.

A few years ago, a metropolitan school system initiated a specialized program for "deserving" children. These selected students were invited to participate in a systemwide special program for accelerating their individual abilities by exposing them to enrichment materials, teacher assistance, and programmed materials of a wide variety and depth. Almost as an after-thought, the program announcement anticipated a question from eligible students and their parents by revealing that because of space requirements and the involvement of teachers, all program activities would necessarily be contained in a time period beginning *after* school extending into the evening hours. Pupil participants, the announcement continued, would proceed to the assigned program centers directly *after* their regular school day was completed.

As one might anticipate, the program died very quickly, for in addition to other factors its major tenet was based upon asking a child to participate in the program not as a totally selected, differentiated individual, but rather as one who assumes specialized opportunities *after* completing a routine day in the classroom. Perhaps there were Cinderellas in this school system who would benefit by changing their identities after school hours, but the failure of the program probably identified a common concern that specialized materials and opportunities for pupil advancement should be an integral part of the total curriculum and school day so as to motivate the individual, not as an add-on to discourage this participation.

One of the concerns of every teacher is the varying rate at which children complete an assignment. As long as a teacher attempts to regiment a class with a common beginning and ending point, there will be a ragged finish among members of the class. If the teacher chooses to ask the early finishers to "wait patiently," she defeats much of the value of the lesson. On the other hand, it is not fair to the slower pupils to be distracted by those of the class who have completed their work quickly. Ideally, a teacher should build a resource of worthwhile learning situations into which the early finishers may delve, for many of the problems that teachers encounter during the day stem directly from a lack of suitable materials for instruction to challenge the wide range of individual needs and interests. Every teacher should experiment with ways of adapting current materials to individualized instruction, for the development and utilization of programmed materials should grow from classroom needs and explorations. Only through the development of this type of communication will programming materials to enhance learning come into common usage for the benefit of the individuals in the elementary classroom.

Peterson[10] identifies three broad types of individual instruction now being used in elementary schools. One is the assigned contract plan in which through the guidance of the teacher, pupils progress through a series of assignments at their own rate. A curricular area is divided into units of work and designed for rather easy transition from one lesson to the next for the duration of the unit. The contract plans permit pupils to move at a pace that is comfortable for them and removes upper and lower limits for individual daily performance. It is also possible for students to correct their own work in many contract plans, so that learning is enhanced through self evaluation procedures. Solutions to meaningful problems can be provided for students at the end of each lesson or at the end of the unit, and corrections made under the guidance of the teacher.

The second type of programmed instruction encompasses the multitude of self-instruction devices often referred to as teaching machines. In general, these programs tend to be more expensive to obtain and use, but many have been introduced into elementary schools each year. The quality of commercial programs is improving and some seem to be equal to, if not better than, those contract-type plans developed by individual teachers.

The third type is unique to the field of reading and is organized in a manner by which individual records are kept on each child throughout the year. The pace and timing of instruction is established for each pupil, and no attempt is made to regulate reading progress or interest of students as a class. The current research available is still too sketchy to permit generalizations to be made about the relative merits of the individualized reading programs. However, teachers who have experimented with this plan continue to be enthusiastic about the possibilities available through its expanded usage.

USE AND DEVELOPMENT OF CUMULATIVE DATA

A wealth of personal and professional data accompanies every child from kindergarten throughout his school career in the form of cumulative school records. Information about a pupil's previous school experience can help a teacher develop a more complete understanding of the child. However, knowledge about previous experience, learning, and accomplishment is of

[10] Dorothy S. Peterson, *The Elementary School Teacher* (New York: Appleton, 1964), p. 398.

little value unless the teacher uses this knowledge in a manner that benefits the pupils. If the cumulative records indicate that a boy has a reading vocabulary two years above the norm for his grade, it becomes the task of the teacher to find the best means of utilizing this information. Although the cumulative records are but one source of information, they enable a teacher to have a headstart in knowing the individual needs of his pupils. The pertinent data that each teacher adds to these records can do much to aid the future learning of all pupils.

Every teacher should compile additional data on all children for use during the year. A manila folder for each child, started at the beginning of the year, can provide a storage center for data throughout the year. Papers, notes, tests, and anecdotal records can be useful in parent conferences and provide a wealth of information in assessing the progress and needs of individual children. Teacher-made tests, sociometric results, pupil comments, and bits of weekly information about each child are the backbone of recorded information upon which decisions on pupil needs are based. Too often pupil behavior that indicates a learning need goes undetected by all conventional methods of teaching in the classroom. So it becomes the responsibility of every teacher to record such behavior so that utilization of expressed pupil needs will provide needed direction for the teaching-learning process.

One of the considerations all beginning teachers must make is the degree to which they will be able to adjust their teaching techniques to individual needs. It is not uncommon for teachers to move to provide for individual differences, but to ignore the responsibility of recognizing their implication for teaching. Every beginning teacher needs time—student teaching, internship, or perhaps an additional year or two of experience— before he arrives at a point where optimum use of knowledge about the needs of individual children can both be gleaned and used in instruction. Armed with this knowledge, the beginning teacher plunges too rapidly into trying to provide for observed individual differences. He may find that because of focusing upon minor rather than major needs, his entire classroom climate is affected.

When a teacher does make provision for individual assistance to a pupil, the entire class benefits. For example, if a teacher gives an assignment and all of the class except one pupil understands the procedures, the class can still begin, with the one child receiving additional assistance. Because the teacher has realized that the class was composed of children of many different abilities, he anticipates the possibility that all of the pupils will not understand the directions. Rather than take additional time from the entire class when only one pupil has questions, the teacher will find it more profitable to provide singular attention to the individual without detracting from the entire lesson.

When a teacher adjusts the lesson to accommodate the pupils in the room who represent a wide difference of ability in a learning situation, there will generally be individuals who need special attention if they are to meet a general requirement for the class. Teachers find it a good practice to circulate among children who are working at their seats and provide additional assistance in spelling, writing, or computation. When the teacher assists pupils in this manner, it does not call undue attention to the child who is having difficulty, yet provides the teacher an opportunity to provide assistance on a one-to-one basis.

Quite often it is possible for a teacher to divide an assignment into smaller parts, so that when pupils complete the part of the assignment, they are able to bring their papers to the teacher for examination and comments. With such a practice pupils know in advance that they can complete their work in class. Thereby are promoted sound study habits for completing an assignment. In addition, all pupils have an opportunity to have their papers examined individually by the teacher. Thus individual assistance is provided to anyone having difficulty. The individual's rate of accomplishing any task will provide a time-spread, so that as the fastest pupils complete the first parts of the assignment, they will be able to have their papers corrected while their classmates are still working on the assignment. Unless some adjustment such as this is made by the teacher, children who encounter difficulty in completing their assignments soon will give up. An alternative would be to ask slower-working pupils to finish their assignments at home or during other periods. There is the disadvantage, however, of depriving these children of free time or time that should be devoted to other learning. As adults we do not all elect to do the same kind of work, but we do elect work at which we can feel some success. Children do not have this alternative in the typical classroom situation; so it becomes the responsibility of the teacher to provide for these limitations placed upon children by the classroom environment.

An increasing number of classrooms are being organized on varying versions of contracted learning—not of the type or magnitude discussed earlier in performance contracting, but on a pupil-centered scale. Typically, this strategy encourages individual members to decide what portion of a given topic they choose to study—often choosing from a list of options prepared by the class and the teacher. In writing up their "contract," the students define reasonable parameters and agree to a time schedule of sequential attack, generally culminating in a written report or perhaps successfully achieving above a minimum point on some evaluative instrument.

This self-pacing approach to learning places maximum attention upon pupil ability, ambition, and realistic appraisal of efforts expended. Teachers are in a position to fit the individual to differences inherent within the attack or to the understandings sought from individual and cooperative class efforts. Wide ranges of pupil ability and interest can be challenged on an individual basis, and evaluation can range from specific segments of an individual contract to the total development of a classroom. Necessarily, the teacher must have access to a variety of materials to be able to implement this approach, and even an abundance of materials for pupil use will be inadequate unless effective teacher planning is present in its utilization. Many original programs for pupil contracting have experienced difficulty, if not failure, when school and teacher planning fell short of minimum pupil expectancy.

PLANNING

The planning session is an excellent opportunity for teachers to uncover new information about individual children in the classroom. When a teacher uses the ideas of pupils in planning, it also becomes easier to provide for individual differences in the work-study session that follows. If pupils have an opportunity to express their ideas about the program, they will suggest and use concepts suited to their level of experience and maturity. In addition, pupils have ideas that frequently extend beyond the initial thoughts of the teacher; and, once pupils are involved, many of their talents will be discovered. The planning session for any unit of work should be one in which students have an opportunity to set goals and define individual tasks. Everyone likes to do those things he can do well; so pupils tend to identify themselves with tasks suited to their known abilities. When planning of this kind is done, there is an opportunity for the creative and imaginative child to suggest ideas that will provide an outlet for his special talents. Cooperative planning gives pupils an opportunity to both share their own thoughts and recognize the worth of other students' ideas. The entire working atmosphere of a classroom is greatly enhanced when pupils are able to take part in an open discussion during the planning stages, and the teacher has an opportunity to learn more about individual strengths and characteristics of all the children in the classroom.

Whenever a lesson is begun, teacher plans must include provisions for the individual who will need special help. Teachers who recognize that there will be individual differences in performance compensate for these differences in a variety of ways. In evaluating pupils' work, one must do more than recognize the differences in performance. For example, when a fourth-grade teacher is reviewing the multiplication facts with the class, he will find out that some students are able to write the answers to the one hundred combinations in less than four minutes, whereas some require five minutes, and some more than six minutes. This recognition does not really benefit the student if it is limited to mere identification of the differences in rate of computation. To praise students who complete the combinations in less than four minutes and criticize those who do not complete the combinations in six minutes does not really enhance learning. It does reward the fastest pupil and punish the slowest pupil; however, it helps neither student operate at a higher level of proficiency. In a task such as learning the multiplication combinations, there are some children who have poor work habits that interfere with the rate at which they compute answers. A true accounting for individual differences would be one in which the teacher identified why some particular pupils took longer than four minutes to complete the combinations. When this was determined, he could then assist pupils in learning a more expedient process for handling the one hundred combinations. It may be that one child is slow because there are four or five combinations that have not been mastered; and therefore, whenever he encounters these combinations, he must stop and solve the problem with repeated addition, counting, or some other inefficient procedure for multiplication. If this pupil continues to practice the combinations in an attempt to increase his speed, he will undoubtedly continue to solve these combinations using the inefficient method. The teacher needs, therefore, not merely to recognize that children will vary in their rate of work, but constantly strive to determine why pupils are unable to work at a suitable level. Once this identification of need has been made, it becomes possible for the pupil and the teacher to work toward an improved learning situation. It is now that the teacher can provide for the individual difference in a fruitful manner.

EVALUATION

The great variance found in pupil's work at any school level makes it exceedingly important that a teacher select and use appropriate evaluation devices. The vast differences in the learning rate of individuals vary more than a letter grade as an end result. Unless papers have constructive comments suited to improving the deficiencies noted by the teacher and written for the benefit of the student who initiated the paper, little can be gained. When a pupil has a paper returned to him, he invariably glances at it to see if there are such specific notations. Many pupils do not go beyond this, and a teacher cannot assume that a pupil will profit from his errors without specific guidelines, motivation, and encouragement.

A superior method would be one in which a teacher would review work with individual children. When this is done, it is possible for the pupil to raise questions and come to a more complete understanding of evaluative comments by the teacher. Many teachers find that a procedure such as this saves time. If a teacher constantly needs to correct the same errors on a pupil's work and the correction of these errors does not lead to improvement, time should be taken to explain these mistakes on an individual basis. A good example of this can be found in such subjects as language arts, where pupils habitually make the same mistakes and teachers routinely discover and correct these errors, with little change in the individual performance of the student. One might reasonably question the large percentage of teacher time spent in correcting papers in isolation, because of the little carry-over that is extended when students receive these corrected papers. An evaluation conference between teacher and pupil, much the same as a parent-teacher conference, would do far more to assist learning than the independent marking and returning of papers that predominate in many classrooms today.

Most elementary schools in the United States make use of standardized tests at some time during the school year. The test itself cannot take into account the wide range of differences among pupils in a typical classroom. Some children, especially the less mature, may find the test exceedingly threatening or perhaps overwhelming. It may be that, with a suitable knowledge of individuals in the classroom, the teacher will single out an individual or two for a separate testing period. In other instances, the teacher may work with groups of children rather than the entire class in giving directions and administering the test. Regardless of how the situation is handled, the teacher remains the key in adapting any curricular media to the needs of individual pupils.

Test results provide teachers with an additional means of diagnosing pupils' achievement and needs. This analysis of test results provides a means for improving the instructional program. When this is done, the teacher "puts the grease where the squeak is" rather than planning instruction on the basis of the textbook alone.

SUMMARY

Many ways have been developed to determine physical, social, emotional, and academic differences in pupils. Many of the devices for identification of these differences are marketed and easily adapted to school use by classroom teachers. With a broad base of testing and resource personnel, teachers today have available to them more information about individual children they teach than has ever been possible in the past. A continued need exists for the identification of needs of all pupils to adapt methods and techniques suited to improved learning for children with special needs. The classroom teacher is in the unique position of being able to implement ways of providing meaningful instruction for children. This goal, with recognition of differences that still exist, needs to remain paramount in the eyes of every elementary teacher, so that the advantage in identifying differences does not become an end in itself. It is not until the knowledge of differences between individuals is utilized in improved learning that the recognition of differences can be of real value.

SUGGESTED ACTIVITIES

1. You have just completed your first day of school. On the desk in front of you are the cumulative folders of twenty-nine pupils. An examination of these folders indicates that pupils have an I.Q. range of from 144 to 76. The median I.Q. in your class is 94. You discover that you do not have I.Q. scores for three students. In addition, you find that most of the children come from lower socioeconomic homes. Nine children live in a home with no father. Eleven families indicate that they are receiving A.D.C. (aid to dependent children). All children walk to and from school, and there is no lunch program at school. The cumulative folders indicate that some children are far below grade level in reading, arithmetic, and language skills. The class average is two full years below the norm for the grade. Your impression of the children today was positive, and they seemed happy to be in school. Before leaving this afternoon, some children told you they were glad to have a young teacher this year. In what ways will the instruction need to be individualized?
   (a) How would you use the data you have in order to plan for next week?
   (b) What additional information would you like to have about children in your classroom and how would you go about getting it?
2. Examine an elementary classroom carefully in terms of the physical size, equipment, and facilities. What provisions are there for differences in the physical differences of children? Mental?
3. Select two or three physical qualities of the classroom that limit use to certain children. Identify what action you could initiate that would enable greater utilization by children. For example, the chalkboard's lowest point is one meter (39 inches) above the floor of your second grade room.
4. Mary Lou and her twin sister, Marilyn, have recently transferred into your room. Their cumulative records show that they have been together in the same room with the same teacher each year. Their records also show that Mary Lou is aggressive whereas Marilyn is shy; Mary Lou is one to one and one half years behind level in reading whereas Marilyn is approximately the same number of units above level; Mary Lou appreciates the company of boys, yet the girls favor the companionship of Marilyn. Both are healthy, respectful of others, and seemingly of average intelligence. Choose two organizational patterns of instruction,

and contrast the advantages and disadvantages of each plan for the twins.

5. The special education "room" has been discontinued, and all instruction of these children will be conducted in the "regular" classrooms. As one of the newer teachers, you have been given the choice of accepting or rejecting five of the children into your present classroom of twenty students. State your decision; justify the rationale you employed in arriving at your choice. Identify any specific reservations involved in the decision.

6. Two full-time teacher aids are available to the teacher in your school who can best use their assistance in moving from the present class organization to an "open" classroom setting. Assuming you are interested in this opportunity, identify how you could justify these adults in individualizing instruction. Be specific.

7. Some of your pupils who come from homes where socioeconomic conditions are restrictive are enjoying school-sponsored free breakfasts as well as participating in the noon hot lunch program with other pupils. Your homeroom parents have prepared a petition to the school board to provide hot breakfasts for *all* pupils so as to assure all school children equal opportunities. They are asking you to sign the petition. What is your reaction? Justify your response.

8. Jeff is a tall, nine-year-old boy weighing some 115 pounds, who is a ward of the court. He has a background of broken homes, orphanages, juvenile homes, and social welfare centers. He is clean-cut but rebellious: experienced, worldly but socially sheltered; reasonably intelligent, but innocent of normal school room manners—his cumulative record is understandably massive. The principal appreciates your past record of providing successfully for a wide range of pupil deviations and differences. He now is seeking admission for Jeff in your class of eight-year-old students. On what basis could you justify accepting Jeff? Rejecting him? Identify five to six factors that would be major considerations in your choice.

SELECTED BIBLIOGRAPHY

Ashton-Warner, Sylvia. *Teacher*. New York: Simon & Schuster, Inc., 1963.

Bloom, Benjamin S., Allison Davis, and Robert Hess. *Compensatory Education for Cultural Deprivation*. New York: Holt, Rinehart & Winston, Inc., 1965.

"Competency/Performance-Based Teacher Education." (Special Issue) *Phi Delta Kappan*, 15, No. 5 (Jan. 1974).

Conners, Keith C. "What Parents Need to Know About Stimulant Drugs and Special Education." *Journal of Learning Disabilities*, 6 (Mar. 1973).

Cutts, Norma, and Nicholas Mosely. *Providing for Individual Differences in*

the Elementary School. Englewood Cliffs, N.J.: Prentice-Hall, Inc., 1960.
Dankowski, Charles E. Teachers Who Individualize Instruction. Commission
    Study No. 2. New York: Institute of Administrative Research, Columbia
    U.P., Teachers College, 1965.
Frost, Joe L., and G. T. Rowland. Curricula for the Seventies. Boston:
    Houghton Mifflin Company, 1969.
Handbook on Learning Disabilities. Ed. by Robt. Weber. Englewood Cliffs,
    N.J.: Prentice-Hall, Inc., 1974.
Hass, Glenn Wiles, Kimball Cooper, Joyce and Don Michalak. Readings in
    Elementary Teaching. Boston: Allyn & Bacon, Inc., 1971.
Haywood, Chas. Social-Cultural Aspects of Mental Retardation. New York:
    Appleton-Century-Crofts, 1970.
Johnson, Doris J., and Helmer Myklebust. Learning Disabilities, Educational
    Principles and Practices. New York: Grune & Stratton, Inc., 1967.
Jones, L. Problems and Issues in the Education of Exceptional Children.
    Boston: Houghton Mifflin Company, 1971.
Kirk, Samuel A. Educating Exceptional Children, 2nd ed. New York. Houghton
    Mifflin Company, 1972.
Kirk, Samuel. The Education of Exceptional Children, Forty-ninth Yearbook
    of the National Society for the Study of Education. (Part II) Chicago:
    University of Chicago Press, 1950.
Levine, Daniel (issue editor). "The Reform of Urban Education." Phi Delta
    Kappan, 52, No. 6 (Feb. 1971).
Perceiving, Behaving, Becoming, 1962 Yearbook. Washington, D.C.: Associa-
    tion for Supervision and Curriculum Development.
Petersen, Dorothy S. The Elementary School Teacher. New York: Appleton-
    Century-Crofts, 1964.
Pugh, James P. The Performance of Teacher and Pupils in Small Classes.
    Commission Study No. 1. New York: Institute of Administrative Re-
    search, Teachers College, Columbia University, 1965.
Romine, Stephen. "Disadvantaged Students Need Compensatory Educational
    Opportunity." School and University Review, 2, No. 2 (Spring 1972).
Rose, Gale W. "Performance Evaluation and Growth in Teaching." Phi Delta
    Kappan, 45, No. 1 (Oct. 1963).
Silberman, Charles. The Open Classroom Reader. New York: Vintage Books,
    Inc., 1973.
"Special Education Trends and Issues and Innovative Programs." Phi Delta
    Kappan, 55, No. 8 (Apr. 1974)
U.S. Office of Education. Better Education for the Handicapped. Annual
    Report. Washington, D.C.: Government Printing Office, 1970.
Warner, Ruby H. Elementary School Teaching Practices. Washington, D.C.:
    The Center for Applied Research in Education, Inc., 1962.
Wilson, L. Craig. The Open Access Curriculum. Boston: Allyn & Bacon, Inc.,
    1971.
Wright, Beatrice. Physical Disability: A Psychological Approach. New York:
    Harper and Row, Publishers, 1960.

Chapter 9

Environment for Learning

Every living thing, if it is to continue to grow and flourish, requires an environment suited to the living element's particular needs. We take great pains to provide the proper environment, through careful cultivation and nourishment, for our favorite flower or fruit tree if we wish it to produce in terms of its potential. If we desire our children to use their potentialities profitably, both for themselves and society, we must provide an environment that will help learners develop their interests, attitudes, talents, abilities, and skills.

At a time in our history when the world is changing at an ever-increasing pace, it becomes imperative that we take a serious look at what we are doing or not doing to provide the kind of environment that helps people to develop a desire and the ability to learn throughout their life span. Generally, it is agreed that a person learns within the spectrum of his total societal environment. The American public, however, has designated the school, and the school has accepted the responsibility for providing a "set of conditions" in which learning can best occur. This is a very difficult task, considering that the children in our schools are a captive audience of widely varying abilities and interests. Nevertheless, it is generally agreed that a prime responsibility of the teacher is to establish and maintain an environment conducive to learning. Even though we accept the idea that a teacher cannot make a person learn, we do believe he can create an environment that stimulates and encourages learning.

According to the American College Dictionary, *environment* means "the aggregate of surrounding things, conditions, or influences." Everything a child experiences within the school program affects what he learns and how he learns it. Still, more than any other factor, it is the teacher who works day to day in an intimate school relationship with pupils who sets the stage for learning. It is he who ultimately is held accountable as to whether the school environment is conducive or detrimental to learning.

Leading educators for years have spoken and written about beliefs, factors, and criteria deemed to be important in promoting learning. Teachers, almost without exception seem to be sincerely interested in helping every youngster learn all he can. This desire on the part of educators in general has resulted in much experimentation and change, but too often the efforts have been concerned mainly with improving curricular content or teaching methodology. We have no quarrel with these being important factors in an appropriate and effective educational program. But methods of teaching and curricular content may be of little avail unless the environment in which they are applied fosters many kinds of learning. A teacher doesn't teach—he creates an environment for learning. What, then can a teacher do to create conditions that best assist children to learn?

The following cognitive objectives are suggested to guide your reading of this chapter:

1. The reader will be able to recognize the interrelationships of various conditions that affect kids in a learning situation.
2. The reader will be able to list several activities that would encourage a learner to express his real interests, concerns, and feelings.
3. The reader will be able to describe Leland Haine's four stages through which a person goes when seeking self-concept.
4. The reader will be able to discuss factors that contribute to a desirable physical environment for learning.

CONDITIONS CONDUCIVE TO LEARNING

Our desire is that teachers create a learning environment that provides efficacious conditions for helping children develop their potential for living effectively with themselves and their fellow man in a complex world setting. In discussing educators' responsibilities to the young learner, Jack Frymier talks about a system for helping people develop:

> Helping people develop is intended to mean fostering, facilitating, encouraging, expediting, cultivating, and assisting other people to move in directions which make sense to them and which are productive, posi-

tive, hopeful ways in which to go. A system for *helping people develop* should be characterized by operations which expand choice rather than restrict it, maximize information rather than diminish it, enhance the value of the individual rather than demean it, and foster growth and life rather than decay. Intimidation, demands, discouragement would not be found. Cooperation, facilitation, encouragement, discussion, exploration, and valuing would be everywhere . . . Teachers would respond to students instead of expecting students to respond to them.[1]

Providing a learning setting that encompasses aspects of which Jack Frymier speaks requires consideration of the interrelationships of various conditions that affect kids in a learning situation. Some environmental conditions that significantly affect learning will now be discussed.

Motivation

One of the perplexing problems that teachers often express is how to motivate a group of youngsters or how to motivate Johnny when he seemingly is not interested in learning. This concern for motivating children to learn in school seems to be at odds with what we know about a child's basic motivational drive to grow, to develop—to become. People who observe elementary age children in and out of school situations generally find them curious and interested in learning. Perhaps in many cases the school environment is a barrier to learning because it is so different from learning situations in which children have found success outside of school.

Another reason why some youth do not learn in school is that our expectations and curricular offerings do not provide for individual uniqueness. We do nothing but set up blocks to learning when we expect the child to respond to concepts that are meaningless or even inconceivable to him. How are people motivated to learn? One strong position is that the chief motivational factors reside within the individual learner. Another viewpoint is that an individual is chiefly motivated to learn because someone (teacher) does something to the learner through the school program. As suggested by A. Gerthon Morgan,[2] director of the Institute for Child Study, University of Maryland, if we look at motivation as a transaction process between the learner and what is to be learned, we need to consider both the motivational factors within the learner and the environment that will facilitate the development of the particular individual.

Learners are more likely to be motivated where the environment is flexible and responsive to a wide variety of backgrounds, interests, talents, development rates, readiness for learning, and response to stimuli.

[1] From a speech presented to the Michigan Association for Supervision and Curriculum Development (Oct. 27–29, 1971).

[2] A. Gerthon Morgan, "Motivation in Elementary Education," *Motivation* (E/K/N/E) (Washington, D.C.: National Education Association, 1968), pp. 14–20.

The environment within which the child lives and works can more significantly influence learning than carefully devised plans or devices to provoke a person to learn. This viewpoint is supported by Bernard Spodek:[3] "Young children need little incitement to learn when the modes of learning provided to them are consistent with their own wishes for exploration and their own needs for movement, and where the activities that are designed for them by the teacher are tailored to their needs, their behavior patterns, and their development levels." Spodek goes on to say that teachers ". . . could benefit more by looking for new and exciting ways of conducting classes and introducing knowledge than by divising cute ways of moving or exciting children to function in dull, inappropriate classroom activities." This implies that teachers start each school day with the attitude that every child is an active, seeking individual capable of learning and willing to get involved. Whether out of school or in school, children learn more easily and most often through activities. A seemingly reasonable approach, then, for a teacher to determine how children learn best would be to present them with a variety of materials and observe the children as they approach and work their way through various activities. Knowledge gained through these observations together with knowledge of various subject areas can provide the teacher a defensible basis in planning classroom activities that relate to the natural interests, drives, and learning modes of children. Rather than continually trying to motivate a child to get involved in an activity in which he is not interested, successful teachers suggest altering or changing the activity. Perhaps the most powerful motivational force for learning is not some contrived "gimmick" or external incentive, but children experiencing success while participating in challenging, interesting, appealing activities.

Resource Materials

The chances of children are better if the environment has a plethora of varied resource materials, including objects, people, animals, and things from nature. Children are naturally curious. Of course, all children are not curious about the same things nor to the same degree. Materials that interest one child may not particularly interest another; therefore, if we are to provide opportunities for all children to explore and extend their curiosity, a variety of learning materials is a requisite.

Man is a multisensory animal. If he is to develop fully his potential, his learning environment should consist of readily available multisensory materials. Yes, materials that the child feels free to observe, feel, smell, taste, listen to, manipulate, read, or talk to for as long a period as he wishes

[3] Bernard Spodek, "Motivation in Early Education," *Motivation* (E/K/N/E) (Washington, D.C.: National Education Association, 1968), pp. 12–13.

or for as short a time as he feels necessary—or to come back to for exploration and interaction from a different angle or in greater depth. Many available or easily constructed multisensory materials can be utilized, such as cans of junk, "feelie" boxes, smell boxes, sound boxes or tapes or records, puzzles, typewriters, film clips, filmstrips, pieces of wood of various sizes and shapes, and mystery bags or boxes.

The child's learning environment is not confined to the four walls of the classroom or to the school building. The wise selection and use of environmental learning resource materials can help the learner relate and integrate his in-school living and his out-of-school living experiences. This means sometimes resources from the outside, both material and human, will be brought into the school setting. Sometimes learners will be taken to societal resources such as a nearby stream, wildlife preserve, governmental agency, health center, business, or industry.

Filling a learning environment with resources may or may not prove to be of much value. It is more what the teacher permits and encourages learners to do with the materials that influences learning. The tenor of the environment needs to be such that, as indicated by Leland Jacobs, the learner and the resource become committed to a confrontation—encounter transaction engagement resulting in the resource becoming either a "nothing" or a "something." According to Jacobs, when the resource becomes a "something," "it becomes a meaningful expression of one's self . . . In other words, a resource is a lived meaning when these resources, whether they are objects or persons or environment, have become a thing that a person might think about or a new way a person might think about it."[4]

An environment rich with resources that excite children and assure their curiosity offers opportunities for learners to wonder, to explore, to raise questions, to find answers to questions, to form generalizations, to create.

Alternatives and Options

An individual is inclined to exert more effort to achieve an objective that is of real concern to him, is more interested in some things than others, and learns some things more rapidly than others. As long as a teacher expects all children to do the same thing, in the same way, in the same time, about all he can hope for is prosaic responses.

If we want excited, responsive, actively involved learners, the environment needs to offer alternatives from which the learner can option both what he wants to do and approaches for achieving what he wishes to ac-

---

[4] Leland B. Jacobs, "Illuminating the Lives of Children: More Effective Use of Resources in the Elementary School," *Keeping Up With Elementary Education*, American Association of Elementary-Kindergarten-Nursery Educators (Washington, D.C.: NEA, Spring 1971), p. 7.

complish. How can a person learn to make wise decisions unless he has opportunities to make choices from alternatives and then evaluate the results of his decision against other possible choices?

Many teachers and prospective teachers have become excited about British open classrooms and indicate they want open education. If you are planning to develop an open classroom environment, Roland Barth suggests you seriously examine your reactions to several assumptions about conditions of learning to which successful open educators both in England and in America agree and adhere. Among these assumptions are, "Children have both the competence and the right to make significant decisions concerning their own learning" and "Children will be likely to learn if they are given considerable choice in the selection of the materials they wish to work with and in the choice of questions they wish to pursue with respect to those materials."[5]

No learner wants to be told precisely what he is to learn, how he is to learn it, and how well he is to learn it. As Ronald Gross says, "Teaching and learning should start and stay with the student's real concerns, rather than with the artificial disciplines, bureaucratic requirements, or adult's rigid ideas about what children need to learn."[6]

Reports from Britain indicate that children seem to be interested in and to enjoy what they are doing in school more than American children enjoy their school experiences. The excitement and enjoyment on the part of British pupils appears to be related to the learning environment in which learners have available to them a number of significant options consistent with their interests, abilities, and maturity levels.[7]

Depending more on resources and materials than on teachers' vested interests, the child may pose his own problem or choose an activity from a list of alternatives. Having selected a problem, he may choose to pursue its solution alone, with a partner, or as a part of a group. As needs dictate, he may consult with the teacher, peers, and resource people; use available materials; and work any place in the room, in the school, on the school premises, and in the community.

The teacher's role in this kind of learning environment is different, but every bit as significant as in the traditional classroom setting. As the learner seeks solutions to problems the learner has identified as important to him, the teacher truly assists the child in his quest by arranging optimum learning conditions, by helping the child formulate questions, by making

[5] Roland S. Barth, "So You Want to Change to an Open Classroom," *Phi Delta Kappan,* **53**:98 (Oct. 1971).

[6] Ronald Gross, "From Innovations to Alternatives: A Decade of Change in Education," *Phi Delta Kappan,* **53**:23 (Sept. 1971).

[7] Roland S. Barth, "When Children Enjoy School—Some Lessons From Britain," *That All Children May Learn We Must Learn.* (Washington, D.C.: Association for Childhood Education International, 1971), pp. 64–69.

accessible needed resources, and by encouraging and assisting the child to gain the knowledge and develop the skills needed to bring his project to fruition.

Opening the learning environment so the child has alternatives and options means teachers must be willing and learn how to support and help learners, ". . . as energetically with their own choices as we once helped them do the things we told them to do."[8]

Feelings and Learning

Feelings and emotions determine to a large extent how an individual will react in a particular situation or to an encounter. How a person feels influences his attitude toward himself, other people, and what he is asked or wishes to do. Have you not heard people of almost any age make such statements as "I feel great today," "I feel rotten today," "I don't feel like working," "I feel happy," "I feel sad and blue," "I feel like hitting someone," "I don't feel very creative today," "I feel relieved," "I feel like being quiet," "I feel uncomfortable," "I feel in a good mood," "I feel like reading," "I feel like playing," "I feel like a failure," "I feel proud of myself."

If the learning climate is to be effective for individual pupils, it must accommodate a variety of feelings. Teachers who perceive learners as individuals recognize that "Children bring to the classroom a variety and intensity of emotions, ranging from feelings of fear, anxiety and failure to self-confidence, self-reliance, and success; from feelings of rejection and insecurity to belongingness and security; from attitudes of prejudice and intolerance to acceptance and respect for differences."[9] How do you feel about working in an intimate learning relationship with a group of children whose attitudes, feelings, and emotion vary to the extent mentioned earlier? Moustakas believes teacher's attitudes are conveyed to children and suggests, "In his own relations with individual children the teacher must learn to respect unique perceptions and to live authentically with the child on the basis of those perceptions."[10] Teachers need to be sensitive to children's feelings and alter the learning environment accordingly.

The more information a teacher has about the family, needs, interests, feelings, attitudes, and hobbies of pupils, the greater the likelihood that the classroom intellectual, social, and emotional climate will be sensitive to human variables. A frequently used means of gaining valuable information about the children in your classroom is to ask them to complete a questionnaire or inventory the first week of school. For example, a questionnaire or inventory similar to the following may be used.

[8] John P. DeCecco, "Tired Feelings, New Life-Styles, and The Daily Liberation of The Schools," *Phi Delta Kappan*, 53:171 (Nov. 1971).

[9] Clark Moustakas, *The Authentic Teacher. Sensitivity and Awareness in the Classroom*. (Cambridge, Mass.: Howard A. Doyle, 1966).

[10] Ibid., p. 41.

I have _____ brothers.
They are _____ years old.
I have _____ sisters.
They are _____ old.
My father's occupation is _____ .
My mother's occupation is _____ .
The thing I like to do most at home is
_____ .
The sport I like to play best is _____
_____ .
The food I like best is _____ .
The book I like best is _____ .
My best friend is _____ .
My favorite trip was _____ .
The thing I like to do most is _____
_____ .
The thing I like to do least is _____
_____ .
My favorite hobby is _____ .
The TV program I like best is _____
_____ .
I like the TV program because _____
_____ .
The subject I like most in school is
_____ .

The subject I like least in school is
_____ .
I like to play with my friends at _____
_____ because _____ .
I have a pet _____ .
I do not have a pet because _____ .
The place I like to visit is _____ .
What I like most about teachers is ___
_____ .
What I like least about teachers is ___
_____ .
I feel most comfortable and happy
when _____ .
I feel most upset and afraid when ___
_____ .
I like the age I am because _____ .
I would like to be older because _____
_____ .
I would like to be younger because __
_____ .
If I could have three wishes, I wish I
1. _____ .
2. _____ .
3. _____ .

Some teachers attempt to learn about pupil's feelings by formulating a list of statements and asking each pupil to react to the statements by checking √ yes if the statement describes how the pupil usually feels or by checking √ no if the statement does not describe how the learner usually feels. Before reacting to the statements, the pupils should understand there are no right or wrong answers. The list might include statements such as the following:

	Yes	No
1. I get along well with others.	_____	_____
2. I get upset easily.	_____	_____
3. I am dependable.	_____	_____
4. I like to be alone most of the time.	_____	_____
5. My parents understand me most of the time.	_____	_____
6. I'm generally successful in what I do.	_____	_____
7. I get discouraged easily.	_____	_____
8. I'm rarely unhappy.	_____	_____
9. It is difficult for me to express myself.	_____	_____
10. I feel good about myself.	_____	_____

The school environment should help the child cope with his feelings as they relate to his physical and interpersonal world. Yet pressures, both outside and inside the school, are leading many youth to mask their feelings or even to deny that they have feelings. Lois Murphy, writing in *Feelings and Learning,* says, "To a large extent the child's feelings about himself are shaped by his feeling of trust that the environment will provide what he needs and be good to him . . ."[11]

A child needs to grow, work, play, and learn in a school setting where teachers accept him for what he is as an individual human being with feelings. Boys and girls need opportunities and encouragement to express their feelings freely and honestly. Teachers can help the child express his feelings in productive ways by talking with him, listening to him, or through appropriate activities in the various curricular areas. As suggested by the director and staff of Hillcrest Children's Center, "Music, movement, art, creative dramatics and writing afford opportunities in which children may reveal their happiness, joy, success, fear, anger, acceptance, rejection, love and hate."[12] We must resist the temptation to tell pupils what to do. Much of the teacher's time may be spent more productively in promoting meaningful learning by encouraging and assisting the learner to articulate his *real* interest, concerns, and feelings. The learner may do this by thinking and writing about self and others, by composing a poem or song, by painting a picture or drawing a cartoon that illustrates how the world appears to him; or the child may express how he feels about a personal matter or social conflict or dilemma, through role playing or creative dramatics.

Acceptance

Children want to feel accepted, liked, respected, and trusted. Many elementary age children have already experienced enough disapproval and rejection to make the world in general appear to be hostile. If the learner is suspicious of people, he will not open up in the classroom until he feels confident that the environment is really an open and honest one and that he will not be doublecrossed by his teacher or peers. Kaplan claims, "A child who feels that nobody cares for him may well avoid trying to succeed, returning instead to an earlier comfortable and more infantile way of responding to the environment . . .[13]

The way a teacher behaves and how he says something as well as what

[11] Association for Childhood Education International, *Feelings and Learning* (Washington, D.C.: ASCD, 1965), p. 27.

[12] Nicholas Long et al. "Helping Children Cope With Feelings," *Childhood Education,* 45:373 (Mar. 1969).

[13] Bert L. Kaplan, "Anxiety: A Classroom Closeup," *Elementary School Journal,* 71:75 (Nov. 1971).

he says either encourage or discourage children to be themselves. In discussing the learning setting for young children, Harms says, "The way people treat him is as real a part of his environment as the materials on the shelves or the space provided for block building."[14]

In a study conducted by Davidson and Lang, a checklist of trait names was administered to 89 girls and 114 boys in grades four, five, and six for the purpose of determining the relationship of children's perception of their teachers' feelings toward them to self-perception, academic achievement, and classroom behavior. The study revealed a positive and significant correlation between children's perception of teachers' feeling toward them and self-perception. It was also concluded that the more favorable the child perceived teacher feelings toward him, the better his academic achievement and classroom behavior.[15]

Just as learning materials and physical surroundings are important factors in the teaching-learning environment, so are the affective conditions of mutual acceptance, trust, and sharing of feelings. Can you accept a child for what "he is" rather than what you would "like him to be"? A child wants his teacher and peers to care about him as a person. If the child is to continue trying to learn in the school setting, he needs to feel that what he says and does is accepted as being important. If a person is to feel free to deal with new ideas and explore a variety of approaches and procedures, errors, mistakes, and blunders should be expected and accepted as a normal part of learning.

Young people, growing up in a world of confusion and conflict of values, experience acute difficulties arriving at decisions relative to what and how to think, believe, and behave. Some maintain that "The children and youth of today are confronted by many more choices than in previous generations. They are surrounded by a bewildering array of alternatives. Modern society has made them less provincial and more sophisticated, but the complexity of these times has made the act of choosing infinitely more difficult."[16]

Most adults, including teachers, have been interested in helping children and youth develop "desirable" values. Youth, however, generally resist the approaches most often used by adults, either moralizing-inculcation or laissez-faire. Certainly, young people do not want or need adults making all their everyday life decisions, but, at the same time, they do want and need adult understanding, help, and guidance. Many adults, teachers in

<hr/>

[14] Thelma Harms, "Evaluating Settings for Learning," *Young Children.* 25:304 (May 1970).

[15] Helen H. Davidson and Gerhard Lang, "Children's Perceptions of Their Teachers' Feeling Toward Them Related to Self-Perception, School Achievement and Behavior," *Journal of Experimental Education*, 29:107–118 (Dec. 1960).

[16] Sidney Simon, Leland Howe, and Howard Kirschenbaum, *Values Clarification* (New York: Hart Publishing Co., 1972), p. 15.

particular, are finding the values-clarification approach an interesting and effective means of helping youth think through values issues and construct their own value system.

Where values-clarification is a part of the child's school experiences, various approaches are used. In some schools values-clarification is treated as any other curricular area, and the teacher allocates time for it each day or each week. In other cases, the teacher incorporates values-clarification with concepts and skill development in one or more subject-matter areas. Many ideas and strategies have been developed and are available for classroom use. For a list of materials and strategies write to the Adirondack Mountain Humanistic Education Center, Upper Jay, New York 12987.

Self-concept

Much has been written and spoken about the importance of teachers helping children develop a healthy and positive self-concept. Many have proclaimed that a person's behavior—what he does—is primarily determined by how he sees himself and the situation he is in. Combs claims a person's self-concept "is his personal reality and the vantage point from which all else is observed and comprehended."[17] According to Combs, "hundreds of research studies document the fact that what a person believes about himself affects how well he learns."[18] Self-concept, the picture a person has of what he is like, begins to form at birth and is ever developing in terms of the experiences he has throughout life. The self-concept is not something a person puts on and takes off as he pleases. Whether we like it or not, it is always with us serving as a screening device by which an individual determines for himself those experiences that are relevant and those that are irrelevant. Everything that a person senses—hears, sees, touches, smells, feels—affects his self-concept and hence influences how effectively he is able to cope with particular circumstances in his environment.

Self-concept seemingly is learned primarily from experiences with significant others. Someone has said we are what we think we are, what others think we are, and what we think others think we are. How a person feels about himself, other people, and the world around him is perhaps the strongest determinant of his behavior as he interacts with his environment. Much has been spoken and written about the need for teachers to help pupils develop a healthy positive self-concept, to believe in themselves, to develop a sense of respect for self and others, to become competent, self-directed individuals. Teachers need to have self-esteem and a good self-image and to be open if they are to help pupils develop these qualities. A

[17] Arthur W. Combs, Donald L. Avila, and William W. Purkey, *Helping Relationships* (Boston: Allyn, 1971), p. 42.
[18] Ibid., p. 151.

teacher who understands and accepts self is usually understanding and accepting of others. A variety of materials are available for helping both teachers and pupils to become more humanistic and more sensitive in understanding self and others. Examples of these materials include The Scholastic Kindle Kits—Who Am I? and also How Do I Learn?, *Scholastic*, 50 West 44 Street, New York, New York 10036; Mary Greer and Bonnie Rubenstein, *Will The Real Teacher Please Stand Up?* (Pacific Palisades, Calif.: Goodyear Publishing Company, 1972); Stanley Coopersmith, *Antecedents of Self-esteem* (San Francisco: W. H. Freeman and Co., 1967); William Glasser, *Reality Therapy* (New York: Harper, 1965).

Leland W. Howe describes four cyclical but nonsequential natural growth stages that people from childhood to death go through again and again seeking self-definition. These four stages are (1) fantasizing—an adventure that permits a person to explore in the protective realm of his mind who he is, who he would like to be, what he would like to do, what he believes, and what he values; (2) gaming—through the relatively low risk technique of "Let's pretend" the person tries on his fantasy to check the potential consequences with the knowledge that he can call a halt to the game at any time; (3) encounter—trying it out in the real world but on a limited and controlled basis; (4) actualizing—playing for keeps as committing oneself to go all the way. If we are really educating to make a difference, the learning environment of our schools must provide pupils:

> with opportunities and encouragement to fantasize, to verbalize their fantasies, to write and talk about them, and to explore them in depth . . . to go beyond fantasy; to risk and actualize in games, through encounters, and for keeps . . . to extend themselves into new ways of doing, seeing, being, behaving, and becoming . . . to see how they did by evaluating the consequences of their behavior.[19]

A person's self-concept positively or negatively develops from the experiences he has and the knowledge gained from those experiences. Walcott Beatty classifies experiences of learning about self into four areas and believes a person seeks experiences that enhance the feelings in each area. In relating these areas to learning, he states:

> Feelings of worth develop from the experience of being loved by others and included in their activities. Feelings of being able to cope arise as a child is successful in . . . response to the demands of the world. . . . Feelings of being able to express one's self develop as a child is able to verbalize and act out the good and bad feelings he experiences. . . . Feel-

[19] Leland W. Howe, "Educating to Make a Difference," *Phi Delta Kappan*, 52: 549 (May 1971).

ings of autonomy grow as an individual . . . finds that his own behavior and decisions enable him to gain satisfaction in the world and, in a sense, to control his own destiny.[20]

An open, relaxed, humanistic environment appears to contribute to a positive self-concept. A study of 939 pupils, grades three to six and ages eight to 12, comparing the self-esteem of pupils in two school settings found that ". . . pupils in an innovative and humanistically oriented elementary school evidenced more favorable self-esteem than pupils in a comparable but traditionally oriented elementary school."[21]

If the school environment is to facilitate the development of a positive self-image, the learner needs to be able to explore things in diverse ways, truly express his feelings, make mistakes, and experience success, knowing that the teacher is sensitive to his particular needs and that the interpersonal relationships are such that he is thought of as a worthwhile and important member of the group.

A study of eighth grade students to determine the effect of teachers rated high in sensitivity or low in sensitivity concluded that "lack of teacher sensitivity to students who are shy and insecure or to those who have poor opinions about school and themselves has a marked negative effect on their self-esteem and consequent learning attitudes."[22] Everything a teacher does or fails to do, in some way affects the learner's self-concept. The most significant school experiences people generally remember are those associated with the *way* teachers worked with them in the learning situation—the personal relationships, the interest, the understanding and encouragement shown. Many of you, undoubtedly, can remember vividly instances when a teacher's behavior influenced learning—for better or for worse.

Challenge and Threat

Many factors influence learning, and one set of conditions may be more conducive to a particular kind of learning than to another. Generally, however, learning is more likely to occur in an environment that is challenging yet peaceful and enjoyable. Children are more likely to have a zest for learning when they live and work in an environment that is stimulating and challenging but interlaced with happiness, encouragement, and satisfaction.

Children build confidence and develop ability to cope with situations

[20] Walcott H. Beatty, "The Feelings of Learning," *Childhood Education*, 45:364–365 (Mar. 1969).

[21] W. W. Purky, William Groves, and Mary Zellner, "Self-Perceptions of Pupils in an Experimental Elementary School," *Elementary School Journal*, 71:170 (Dec. 1970).

[22] Dwight Webb, "Teacher Sensitivity: Affective Impact on Students," *Journal of Teacher Education*, 22, No. 4:458 (Winter 1971).

when challenges and expectations are reasonable. It is not enough that the teacher deems the challenge or problem as reasonable. Unless the child feels he has a good chance to succeed, he will perceive the situation as threatening. One of the most important roles of the teacher is to create a learning environment that challenges pupils without threatening them. People are motivated to participate actively in situations and activities that are challenging, enjoyable, and satisfying. They tend to shy away from or avoid things that are nonchallenging, unpleasant, and dissatisfying. The learner needs an open, accepting environment that encourages daring, venturing, exploring, examining, trying out new ideas without the fear of being "raked over the coals" for making an honest blunder or a harmless mistake.

Some children in our schools live from day to day in frustration and the fear of failure because of the unreasonableness and unattainability of the tasks. A person will generally exert efforts to overcome difficulties and unfavorable conditions if he perceives the objective to be worthwhile and reasonable. Teachers' efforts to motivate the child through the use of reproach, sarcasm, and threats only tend to harm the learner emotionally and psychologically. In this respect, Garrison says:

> Neither child nor adult who is under tension from anxiety, fear of failure, self-reproach, jealousy, hate, or any of the stronger emotions, even excessive love with its distorting side affects, can be expected to behave efficiently, to maintain an attentive attitude toward new material, to concentrate for long periods of time, or to perceive with objectivitty, thus with accuracy.[23]

A learning environment characterized by boredom, lethargy, tension, anxiety, fear, or frustration has a detrimental affect on the mental health of both teacher and pupil. Too many school youngsters live in the extremity of either boredom or frustration. The demands of the learning situation should not be so trivial and easy that the child sees no need to make any effort. On the other hand, the child who exerts effort toward the tasks should realize some successes each day. The teacher's role in this is not an easy one. Nevertheless, he must accept the responsibility of creating an environment "in which a person feels (a) that it is safe, (b) reassured that he can, (c) encouraged to make an attempt, and (d) satisfied to do so."[24]

Physical Environment

When working conditions are pleasant, pupils are more likely to learn and want to continue to learn. In order to make sure the school's total

[23] K. C. Garrison, A. J. Kingston, and H. W. Bernard, *The Psychology of Childhood* (London: Staples Press, 1968), p. 202.

[24] Combs, op. cit., p. 120.

physical environment—the site, playground, and building—facilitates learning, the teacher needs to survey and study the physical setting so that all its possibilities are utilized to the best advantage.

Within recent years many new physical plants have been planned and constructed in an attempt to provide adequate facilities for educating our youth. In an effort to make the school plant more functional in terms of educational programs, classroom teachers, administrators, and architects have cooperatively developed many of our newer facilities.

Most of our newer facilities tend to present a desirable physical setting for learning. However, the physical setting does not have to be new to make it an attractive, inviting, comfortable, pleasant, and esthetically appealing environment in which to play, work, and learn. As the trend seems to be toward more involvement in planning new facilities and the alteration of existing ones, it is important that teachers become acquainted with principles of design and the characteristics of current building materials if the resultant physical environment is to be most conducive to achieving the school's educational objectives.

Although much progress has been made in recent years, innovative and creative teachers can still make most physical environments more educationally supportive. A few new shrubs strategically planted on the grounds, the redeployment of some playground equipment, the rearrangement of the classroom furniture, a large packing crate to form a room within a room, a new picture in the room, a few growing plants, a mobile, an aquarium, a few throw rugs, or an easy rocking chair may make the school setting a more pleasant, stimulating, and enjoyable place to learn.

In planning and utilizing the physical environment, a teacher must keep in mind that different settings are needed for different types of learning and that a particular aspect of the physical setting will affect children differently. For instance, some people are more sensitive to color stimulation than others; some may choose a quiet place to work alone whereas others prefer to interact with a group or to work where there is background noise; some may work comfortably and effectively near a window, but others find this location very distracting; some may learn best on the school grounds or in the community; others may find the library a more effective learning setting.

In discussing the educational and psychological impact of the physical environment, Anderson states:

> In countless ways the school environment provides experiences which inform and influence the child. Objects in that environment have color, dimension, texture, and function. They are seen, heard, touched, smelled, and manipulated. They are either pleasant or unpleasant, relevant or irrelevant, useful or useless, monotonous or varied, stimulating or un-

stimulating, ordinary or extraordinary. In sum, at any given moment, they play either a positive or negative role in the morale and the learning set of individuals who inhabit the environment.[25]

A teacher has some responsibility for the school's total physical environment, but he has the major responsibility for creating a classroom environment that contributes to learning. If we could accept the view that the classroom is a place where children learn rather than a place where teachers teach, children would be much more involved in trying to make the room as pleasant, attractive, exciting, and interesting as possible. At least the pupils should have a voice in how the room can be arranged to meet their learning needs best.

The teacher is responsible for making sure the classroom is properly lighted, heated, and ventilated. A room that is extremely cold, hot, stale, or stuffy is known to have an adverse effect on learning. A temperature level of 72° Fahrenheit, humidity levels between 40 and 60 per cent, and brightness contrasts not exceeding a rate of ten to one are generally considered optimal for concentration and comfort.

The most recent trend in planning school plants is toward "open buildings," where most of the interior separating walls are eliminated. For teachers, this wall-less environment is both welcomed and feared. Certainly, the relatively large unpartitioned area offers a wide variety of space uses. Some still unresolved problems are the desired quality and quantity of temporary divider materials to provide privacy to children and activities when needed and also the number and location of conference rooms, work rooms, and storage areas. Along with the "open school building" there is a growing interest in "open education," wherein many learning activities are pursued in the physical environment outside the classroom and outside the school building. This movement requires us to consider seriously the question, How can we utilize to the best advantage the total environment in which the child lives for educational purposes? The child lives and learns within his total environment; thus teachers must begin to consider more seriously what kinds of learning can occur best within the classroom and what kinds of learning occur just as effectively, if not more effectively, outside the classroom. The question we must explore much more diligently than we have in the past is, How can we correlate or mesh the various aspects of the child's environment to support and extend his opportunities for learning? A major goal should be to enhance the wide range of learning opportunities for helping the learner understand, appreciate, cope with, and use widely the environment that surrounds him.

[25] Robert H. Anderson, "The School as an Organic Teaching Aid," *The Curriculum Retrospect and Prospect*, NSSE, Seventieth Yearbook, Part I (1971), p. 281.

Interaction-Involvement

For years we have had research evidence that shows a person learns more effectively when he is intimately and actively involved. The learning environment tends either to encourage or discourage the learner to become involved. When there is free and easy interaction between teacher and pupil, and between pupil and pupil, the learner is likely to become involved. In other words, if we want involvement, we need to provide for effective interaction.

The idea of interaction as an important aspect of the teaching-learning process has received emphasis in recent years. One type of interaction is classroom talk or verbal interaction between teacher and pupils, pupils and teacher, and between pupils. The recognized importance of verbal behavior in the classroom has led to a number of systems designed to analyze classrom talk. Among the more popular of these, has been the Verbal Interaction Category System (VICS). VICS provides a technique for classifying the verbal interaction that occurs in a classroom into a twelve-category observation scale. Table 9–1 shows the VICS categories ". . . grouped

TABLE 9–1
The Verbal Interaction Category System (VICS.)

Teacher-Initiated Talk	1. Gives information or Opinion: presents content or own ideas, explains, orients, asks rhetorical questions. May be short statements or extended lecture.
	2. Gives Direction: tells pupils to take some specific action; gives orders; commands.
	3. Asks Narrow Question: asks drill questions, questions requiring one or two-word replies or yes-or-no answers; questions to which the specific nature of the response can be predicted.
	4. Asks Broad Question: asks relatively open-ended questions which call for unpredictable responses; questions which are thought-provoking. Apt to elicit a longer response than 3.
Teacher Response	5. Accepts: (5a) Ideas: reflects, clarifies, encourages or praises ideas of pupils. Summarizes, or comments without rejection.
	(5b) Behavior: responds in ways which commend or encourage pupil behavior.
	(5c) Feeling: responds in ways which reflect or encourage expression of pupil feeling.

TABLE 9–1
The Verbal Interaction Category System (VICS.) (*cont.*)

	6. Rejects: (6a) Ideas: criticizes, ignores or discourages pupil ideas.
	(6b) Behavior: discourages or criticizes pupil behavior. Designed to stop undesirable behavior. May be stated in question form, but differentiated from category 3 or 4, and from category 2. Gives Direction, by tone of voice and effect on pupils.
	(6c) Feeling: ignores, discourages or rejects pupil expression of feeling.
Pupil Response	7. Responds (7a) Predictably: relatively short replies, usually, which follow category 3. May also follow category 2, i.e. "David, you may read next."
	(7b) Unpredictably: replies which usually follow category 4.
	8. Responds to Another Pupil: replies occurring in conversation between pupils.
Pupil-Initiated Talk	9. Initiates Talk to Teacher: statements which pupils direct to teacher without solicitation from teacher.
	10. Initiates Talk to Another Pupil: statements which pupils direct to another pupil which are not solicited.
Other	11. Silence: pauses or short periods of silence during a time of classroom conversation.
	Z. Confusion: considerable noise which disrupts planned activities. This category may accompany other categories or may totally preclude the use of other categories.

according to whether they involve teacher talk or pupil talk, and according to whether the talk is initiatory or responsive."[26]

If we use the category system presented in Table 9–1, all verbal interaction that occurs during a classroom situation can be observed (by a trained observer, perhaps another teacher, or the conversations can be recorded) and classified on a three-second interval basis by assigning an

[26] Edmund Amidon and Elizabeth Hunter, *Improving Teaching* (New York: Holt, 1967), pp. 10–11.

appropriate number from the VICS categories to each statement. The following example from Amidon and Hunter illustrates how the sequence of category numbers are determined, then transferred as a sequence of ordered pairs into cells of a seventeen-row by seventeen column (17 × 17) scoring interaction matrix. See also Figure 9–1.

Teacher	Open your books to page six.	2
Pupil	Which book should we be looking at?	9
Teacher	If you had paid attention, you would know.	6b
Teacher	Now, on page six there is a diagram which shows the relationship between population density and types of occupation. I think this is an excellent diagram for our purposes.	1
		1
Teacher	Does anyone have some ideas about why these two factors might be related?	4
		4

When the recorder finishes his tallying, he will pair the numbers in the following fashion.

$$\begin{array}{l} 2 \text{) 1st pair} \\ \text{2nd pair (} 9 \\ 6b \text{) 3rd pair} \\ \text{4th pair (} 1 \\ 1 \text{) 5th pair} \\ \text{6th pair (} 1 \\ 4 \text{) } n\text{th pair} \\ 4 \end{array}$$

The first pair is 2–9, the second pair is 9–6b, the third pair is 6b–1, and so on. The particular cell in which the tabulation of the pair of numbers is made is determined by using the first number in the pair to indicate the *row*, and second number in the pair to indicate the *column*. Thus, 2–9 would be shown by a tabulation in the cell formed by row 2 and column 9. The second pair, 9–6b, would be shown in the cell formed by row 9 and column 6b. The third pair, 6b–1, is entered in the cell formed by row 6b and column 1. Notice that each pair of numbers overlaps with the previous pair; and each number, except the first and the last, is used twice.

Once the tallies are entered on the matrix, then the interaction pattern in the classroom can be interpreted by studying that matrix.[27]

In this type of analysis not only is the number of occurrences of a particular type of verbal behavior obtained, but also the number of times a particular behavior is followed by a certain other behavior. The Verbal Interaction Category System can be used by teachers and teachers-to-be in recording, studying, and analyzing verbal behaviors during various teaching activities. Examination of teaching in this way should help teachers (1) to become more sensitive to the importance of verbal interaction, (2) to develop a broader repertoire of verbal behaviors, and (3) to select kinds

[27] Op. cit., pp. 215–217. This reference includes Fig. 9–1.

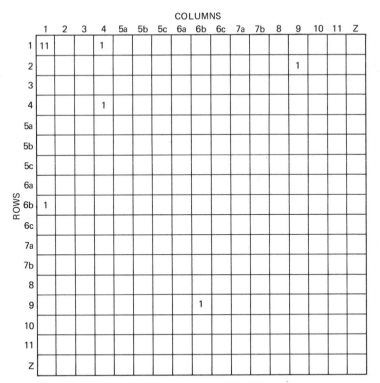

FIGURE 9–1.

of verbal behaviors most appropriate for the learning situation. For a detailed discussion of the Verbal Interaction Category System and its use, read Edmund Amidon and Elizabeth Hunter, *IMPROVING TEACHING, The Analysis of Classroom Verbal Interaction.*

A pupil will want and attempt to become a part of the action when he feels that (1) he knows he can express his honest feelings without worrying about how he will be received by his teacher or peers, (2) he can ask any question he wishes, (3) he does not always have to wait for the teacher's specific directions but can pursue activities and alternate paths of his own choosing, (4) the teacher will assist him when he needs it to accomplish the task he has chosen, and (5) he will receive recognition from his teacher and peers for pursuing and completing a task to the best of his ability.

Many children spend too much of their time in a quiet, dull, mundane classroom atmosphere, sitting quietly reading or performing other assigned tasks. In these cases, the learner is actually involved very little through interaction with his environment. Where there truly is interaction, one generally finds noise created by the excitement of trying out hunches, discovering, and learning. As stated by Browman:

The buzzing room of children's talk and movement is a learning sign. A sign that ideas are taking form, questions being asked, thoughts being shared, objects being created, discussions being planned, children learning from children, and children learning from the teacher.[28]

One of teachers' expressed goals is to help learners become independent thinkers, yet children may spend much of their classroom time listening to the teacher state a problem situation and immediately give the answer, or tell or show pupils what they ought to know (as defined by the teacher). Even when children are asked questions, too often only factual answers are expected or accepted. We have emphasized critical thinking and problem-solving for years, "yet research spanning more than a half-century indicates that teachers' questions have emphasized facts."[29]

Questions that elicit specific, concrete answers are needed, but these should be balanced with open-ended questions that promote diverse thinking—the expression and exploration of many viewpoints. If interaction and involvement are to relate learning to the affective domain as well as to the higher cognitive levels of application and if analysis and synthesis are considered a desirable objective, then teachers need to ask types of questions now not generally employed. Educational psychology tells us that learning is highly personal and unique and occurs in school when a pupil is involved as an active participant in the process.

SUMMARY

Everything through which the child comes in contact in the school environment—living things and inanimate objects—affects the child's learning for better or for worse. The teacher must exert every means possible to make this environment warm, friendly, inviting, pleasant, intriguing, challenging, and supportive.

Children should feel free to explore and test their ideas, knowing that their questions and expressions will be respected because each individual's uniqueness is accepted and prized.

The environment should provide a richness of materials and experiences, so that each learner has many options in the process of deciding what is to be done and how to do it.

A teacher cannot make a person learn. But he can create and maintain a favorable learning environment that promotes self-confidence, independence, initiative, positive self-concept, concern for others, open-mindedness, curiosity, and creativeness.

[28] Betty L. Browman, "Too Much Shushing—Let Children Talk," *Childhood Education*, 46:132 (Dec. 1969).

[29] Meridith D. Gall, "The Use of Questions in Teaching," *Review of Educational Research*, 40:712 (Dec. 1970).

1. List what you consider to be some detrimental factors to learning. How would you plan a learning environment to alleviate these factors?
2. You are the teacher in a classroom of twenty-five youngsters of widely varying abilities and interests. In this situation what do you propose as a "set of conditions" that would be most conducive to learning?
3. Describe what you see as the role of children in establishing a good learning climate?
4. You have been encouraged to resist the temptation to tell pupils what to do. Outline a procedure you would use to get the learner to articulate his *real* interests, concerns, and feelings.
5. List four or five principles you consider to be crucial in helping pupils develop a healthy, positive self-concept. Choose one of these principles, and describe how you would implement it.
6. Try some of the following to discover more about yourself and others:
    (a) Lie down on a piece of paper and have someone draw your outline. Inside the outline write, draw, or color what you feel describes you. Let others add what they see within you.
    (b) You want to be a different person than you are. List reasons why you cannot change. Are any of the reasons you listed sound? List the characteristics you now possess that you want to keep. Might you be a better person than you thought?
    (c) Try carrying on a three-minute conversation with a partner without using any questions.
    (d) Choose some small object. For two or three minutes explore the object in every way you can think of; then try telling someone else all you can about the object.
    (e) Close your eyes. Listen as intently as you can for a few minutes to what is going on inside you as well as to what is happening around you. Try describing as many of the details of the experience as possible.
    (f) Walk around the room you are in three times trying to discover something about the room you did not know before. How do you feel about the things you discovered?

SELECTED BIBLIOGRAPHY

Anderson, Robert H. "The School as an Organic Teaching Aid." *The Curriculum Retrospect and Prospect.* National Society for the Study of Education, Seventieth Yearbook, Part I, 271–306.
Bany, Mary A., and Lois V. Johnson. *Educational Social Psychology.* New York: Macmillan Publishing Co., Inc., 1975.

Barth, Roland S. "So You Want to Change to an Open Classroom." *Phi Delta Kappan*, 53 (Oct. 1971), 97–99.

Beatty, Walcott H. "The Feelings of Learning." *Childhood Education*, 45 (Mar. 1969), 364–65.

Combs, Arthur W., Donald L. Avila, and William W. Purkey. *Helping Relationships*. Boston: Allyn & Bacon, Inc., 1971.

DeCecco, John P. "Tired Feelings, New Life-Styles, and the Daily Liberation of the Schools." *Phi Delta Kappan*, 53 (Nov. 1971), 168–171.

Gall, Meridith D. "The Use of Questions in Teaching." *Review of Educational Research* (Dec. 1970).

Harms, Thelma. "Evaluating Settings for Learning." *Young Children*, 25 (May 1970) 304–306.

Howard, E. R. "School Climate Improvement." *Education Digest* (Apr. 1974), 10–13.

Howe, Leland W. "Educating To Make A Difference." *Phi Delta Kappan*, 52 (May 1971), 547–549.

Kaplan, Bert L. "Anxiety: A Classroom Closeup." *Elementary School Journal* (Nov. 1971), 70–77.

Purkey, W. W., William Graves, and Mary Lollner. "Self-Perceptions of Pupils in an Experimental Elementary School," *Elementary School Journal*, 71 (Dec. 1970), 166–171.

Simon, Sidney, Leland Howe, and Howard Kerschenbaum. *Values Clarification*. New York: Hart Publishing Co., 1972.

Chapter 10

Discipline

Management of a classroom is the responsibility of every teacher. Regardless of a teacher's background in subject matter or desire to teach, accountability in maintaining an orderly classroom is of prime concern to parents and administrators. Classroom management probably is the area of greatest anxiety for all teachers and causes many individuals to leave the field of teaching. Why is this one element of teaching the cause of such great concern? Many reasons could be given; and although there is seldom one answer, in the eyes of many, good discipline is equated with good teaching.

STUDENT FEEDBACK

Direct feedback from students, in the form of problems for the teacher and behavior that is a detriment to positive learning experiences for other children, is provided the teacher who does not grasp the fundamentals of individuals and group control. The teacher who has trouble in classroom management knows that she is having trouble. In addition, this information is readily observable to others in the building and therefore increases anxiety for the teacher and often causes existing problems to multiply. In an attempt to prevent overt misbehavior on the part of children, the teacher will often concentrate on behavioral problems at the expense of sound learning experiences, and the net result is inevitable—increased problems in discipline.

Today's children are not always responsive to management techniques of the past. As Alam says in describing an experience of college instructors in the Lansing, Michigan, Public Schools, "Many of these children simply will not respond to threat, which left us teachers helpless."[1]

The teacher who depends upon reflections of her past as a learner in school will often find that the source of data is lacking in providing answers to today's problems in discipline. Rapidly changing events of today should provide us with the direction for the future if they tell us nothing more than that we must continue to be flexible and expect the children of tomorrow to respond and to react differently to teacher authority than is the case at present or was true yesterday.

The following objectives should guide your reading and study of this chapter:

1. Each reader will be able to identify teaching behaviors that are used to
   (a) Establish sound classroom behavior.
   (b) Maintain sound classroom behavior.
   (c) Restore sound classroom behavior.
2. Each reader will be able to assess pupil behavior as it occurs in the classroom and select a suitable teacher response for that behavior.
3. Each reader will have an identifiable knowledge basis for making classroom decisions relative to pupil control.
4. Each reader will develop procedures to involve pupils in the decision-making process relative to discipline without delegating complete classroom responsibilities.

WHAT IS GOOD DISCIPLINE?

Although an absolute answer to this question is impossible, it is possible to describe a setting that provides appropriate guidelines for most classrooms. When pupils are engaged in worthwhile learning activities and are pursuing objectives that do not place the learning of others in jeopardy, a teacher could be said to have good discipline. The nature of the learning activity, the physical environment, the number and nature of the students involved, the goals of the teacher, and the goals of the learners all enter into the assessment of a situation. However, regardless of the complexness

---

[1] Dale Alam, "School Is Now and We're Late," *Educational Leadership* 4:87 (Oct. 1970).

of the task, all teachers have the responsibility to assist pupils in learning to handle difficult personal and interpersonal situations.

Use of Influence Techniques

Teacher behavior in handling pupil discipline problems can be classified into three forms of influence techniques: (1) establishing sound classroom procedures, (2) maintaining procedures that have been established, and (3) restoring classroom order when the level of activity exceeds normal working conditions.

Establishing Classroom Discipline

The experienced teacher draws upon a multitude of specifics to establish good working conditions in the classroom. Prior to the beginning of a lesson, time is devoted to necessary details in order that each child will know what is to be accomplished. The procedures of the lesson will be discussed, and pupils will have opportunities to express their ideas and views and also receive necessary clarification from each other as well as from the teacher. In this way, the task of establishing a learning situation that will flow smoothly is knit together prior to the beginning of the task. When all pupils know what a teacher expects from them and are in general accord with the task at hand, discipline problems are at a minimum. The combination of planning, motivation, and directing by the teacher serves to establish the desired classroom tempo. However, many of these behaviors on the part of the experienced teacher are subtle and not easily observed by the novice. Indeed, the reaction of the novice oftentimes will be that the establishment of this type of order in the classroom is rather easy; that is, until it is tried with a group of children.

Maintaining Classroom Discipline

In most cases it is not enough merely to establish a good working condition in the classroom, but the teacher must work to maintain the situation. This is accomplished by one or more of the following: moving about the room, praising a student for his results or continued effort, making a general statement to the class such as, "We still have ten minutes so continue your work," and so forth. Upon noticing that one or more individuals are finished or have become tired of working, the teacher proceeds to assist them in finding a new direction or working in a manner that does not disturb the remainder of the class. Again, this type of activity on the part of the teacher may often go unnoticed by the novice. The specific statement that is made to one student may often be intended as an influence factor on the entire classroom. If a teacher desires students to sit up straight at their desks, often all she needs to announce is, "I really like the way Billy is sitting up straight and tall while working this morning." The effect will be an immediate change in posture for most members of the class to a stance that is similar to that of Bill's.

Restoring Classroom Discipline

Some say that a teacher never has real confidence in her ability to manage classroom instruction until she has experienced "losing" a class and getting them back. This may mean that the children detach themselves from the learning task at hand and become involved in some type of horse play that everyone, including the children, knows is out of step with group work behavior. It is at times such as these, and they do occur, that the teacher must act to restore the classroom order. For the beginning teacher, this may be a moment of great anxiety and also an area of learning void. It is very difficult to be prescriptive in this area except to say that a teacher acts calmly and rationally and in a businesslike manner to get the situation back under control quickly and safely. There are times when the teacher should interfere with the behavior of children to restore a situation. Examples of these times are as follows:

1. When there are physically dangerous acts occurring (fighting, playing with a dangerous object, throwing objects).
2. When someone requires psychological protection (use of racial names, scapegoating, and so forth).
3. When the level of excitement reaches too high a peak (if a game is getting out of control, tempers are flaring).
4. When property needs protection (either property of an individual or community property such as school equipment).
5. When an ongoing class activity needs protecting. (One or two children should not be permitted to upset an entire classroom.)
6. When a negative contagion begins to develop: if a teacher is aware that tension is mounting in a classroom, the teacher should act to prevent a spread of this behavior to other students. (One student is not paying attention and is building a paper airplane, partially to amuse his peers.)
7. When a value area or school policy needs highlighting (explaining rules that are established for mutual assistance, why everyone can't be first in line, running in the hallway).
8. When a conflict with the outside world is to be avoided (when pupils are engaged in activities such as field trips or study in the community beyond the walls of the school building).

Subtleties of Good Classroom Management

The integration of good teaching technique and frequency of discipline problems are so interwoven that the untrained observer is often unaware of just what is going on in a given classroom. One teacher can teach one class for an hour and have excellent results with a minimum of conflict between teacher and pupils. The same class can then be taught by another teacher with many problems, and the class assumes an entirely new posture toward the teacher and learning. Unfortunately, the subtle aspects of good teaching and good discipline that go hand in hand also escape the average student in a classroom. However, the negative elements seldom escape and are imprinted in the minds of very young children. Usually, for this reason, when one asks a college student about discipline tactics that occurred while he was in school, the examples are usually those that would be included in the restoring area. Items such as being sent to the office, writing sentences, being slapped, hair pulling, being sent to the hall, teacher screaming, slamming books, and so forth, are remembered by many from their elementary school experiences.

After a goal or an interweaving of many goals has been identified, a decision is made to actualize its attainment. A particular decision is based on three considerations:

1. Perceived relevant conditions.
2. Perceived theories of physical, sociological, and psychological relationships.
3. Perceived alternate procedures.

Perceived Relevant Conditions

One of the factors that influences a decision is the extent to which relevant conditions of a situation are perceived. There are, of course, "real relevant conditions" that exist but are screened by each person's senses. Some are accepted and others rejected as being immaterial, untrue, inconsequential. The mind is not a *tabula rasa*, as Francis Bacon considered it, that is, a blank wax tablet on which the world writes experiences. The mind is active; indeed, it is *highly selective* about what perceptions are received. Not only does the mind control which of the myriad perceptions will be considered, but it also *directs* the appropriate sense organs to obtain additional data deemed important. The driver of an automobile directs his eyes to the road ahead, to incidents near the road that might influence his actions, to the rear view mirror. He does not simply wait and hope his senses will bring needed information; rather, he actively directs their attention. Past experience with similar situations have suggested data-gathering processes. The more extensive the active previous experience, the more likely is a person to identify cues that are significant.

The positive, instructional tactics as mentioned in establishing and maintaining good classroom discipline have gone unnoticed by the majority of student teachers. Perhaps this is the reason that when student teachers are under stress, from minor disruptions in pupil behavior, they revert to acting toward children the way they remember their former teachers behaving.

The Teacher as a Decision-Maker

The pervasive role of the teacher is as a decision-maker. Let us examine this role as it relates to making decisions as the teacher guides pupil behavior.

Decisions in this realm are goal-directed. The teacher has in mind certain long-range and intermediate goals as he organizes the class, structures certain activities into the school day, plans with children for necessary housekeeping tasks, and regulates behavioral patterns. Many of these goals (optimum use of class time, effective completion of the concepts in the curriculum guide) are explicitly considered. Many others (maintaining order in the classroom when the principal is present, looking organized) are implicitly considered by the beginning teacher. These implicit goals, although not formally stated, are important when classroom staging occurs and contribute just as significantly to the strategies employed in guiding pupil behavior.

So it is with the teacher in the classroom. Identification of important cues is dependent upon previous active experience in similar situations. Carefully watching pupils' expression and change of expression, posture, or movement and noting physical aspects of the classroom such as stuffiness, drafts, lighting, and so forth, are developed as the teacher studies and identifies relevant clues to a good, deteriorating, improving, or bad classroom climate. Perhaps beginning teachers fear the area of discipline, for they recognize their inability to read the relevant "road signs," which are so often poorly marked.

Perceived Theories of Physical, Sociological, and Psychological Relationships

Physical relationships are believed to exist in certain predictable ways. Man has continually sought to identify the nature of these relationships. At one time, the world was thought to be flat, surrounded by water and covered by a gigantic dome, with peep holes (stars) and trap doors that opened when it rained. Over the centuries, this conception has changed as we have gained more extensive knowledge about our physical world. Sir Isaac Newton contributed to increased knowledge by identifying some predictable physical relationships; Albert Einstein modified them; and most likely someone some day will further refine our notions of the earth, solar system, space, and time. Man's knowledge of physical relationships has continued to grow and expand through the years. He is always *in the process of learning more*; never will he learn all. At this time, man does not have a complete understanding of the interrelationships that exist among physical elements, but he has some general notions that appear to be correct and upon which he makes decisions.

There are also some general understandings about the nature of man himself as a psychological, sociological being. This area, however, is even more complex to comprehend and has been the focus of study for a much shorter time than has been the study of the physical world. Our understanding of these psychological and sociological relationships is not nearly so developed as that of the physical sciences. However, concerted study during the past six decades has begun to pay off in certain "hunches" or theories of human behavior. During the next few years we can anticipate even more dynamic discoveries about the nature of man. To date, a number of isolated research endeavors have been conducted that may give direction to the teacher who is guiding the behavior of pupils. These studies form the basis for the bulk of this chapter and are identified for further reference by the reader interested in greater detail.

PERCEIVED ALTERNATE PATHS

The third aspect that affects decisions is the breadth of understanding of alternate procedures that could be pursued. The person who considers seven potential courses of action is, theoretically at least, more likely to make a better decision than the person who considers only one.

Alternatives are limited by *exterior boundaries*. A teacher teaches certain things because they are part of the school curriculum, uses certain textbooks and materials that are furnished, and teaches certain pupils assigned to his classroom. These are limitations to his decision-making power over which he has little or no control.

But alternatives are also limited by *interior boundaries*. The teacher's own perception of the situation and his evaluation of relevant conditions impose boundaries limiting the possible courses of action. These interior boundaries are *real*, even though they may or may not be *valid*. We often hear teachers remark, "We can't do that; our principal would not permit it." And just as often, the principal notes that he wishes his teachers would do that very thing! Limitations resulting from "second-guessing" a superior, limitations of personal knowledge, limitations resulting from deep-seated values—these interior boundaries exclude consideration of certain data or alternatives as completely as those imposed from outside the person.

Amalgam

Consideration of the forces operating in decision-making focuses on the need to make decisions regarding pupil behavior based on evidence rather than mere whim. Too many decisions are made in haste and regretted at leisure. Emotions run high as two or more individuals interact. In guiding pupil behavior, one must give consideration to: (1) relevant conditions of the situation, (2) hunches or theories of human behavior, and (3) consideration of a wide range of alternate paths.

That Term—Discipline

The word *discipline* has been used in so many ways that it is difficult to have any intelligent discussion of the problems related to it without first considering just what it is that is being discussed. In common language, discipline may indicate a condition existing within a classroom—"Mr. Simmons has good discipline." It may mean a form of punishment or a method of achieving control over a group. It may infer an area of study— "science is a discipline." The *Dictionary of Education* lists six definitions of the general term and follows with eleven definitions of specific types of discipline.

Cronbach has provided a good working description of educational discipline, which dovetails into an overall effective program for directing pupil behavior.

> Classroom discipline is a condition where pupils are using their time in educationally desirable ways. The teacher who cannot establish this condition cannot teach. Good discipline does not require every student in his place, every pupil silent save one, everyone focused on the speaker. In such a classroom the listeners may be learning nothing. Discipline has not failed when six eager children burst out with an idea at once, so long as they are willing to listen to each other. It is good for a class to break up into groups doing different things, all humming with business and work-related conversation. The test of discipline is whether or not the behavior of the group permits everyone to work effectively.[2]

From birth the child has been directed as to how he is expected to act. Adults have notions of how the child ought to act, and they spend considerable time in directing him toward those expectations. Most of these expectations eventually are formulated into customs or mores that children abide by almost automatically. So it is in school. When the child first entered kindergarten or first grade, he was *taught* to act in certain

[2] Lee J. Cronbach, *Educational Psychology* (New York: Harcourt, 1963), p. 534.

prescribed ways. Teachers constantly influence or attempt to influence children. An encouraging word, a smile, specific directions for going to the cafeteria, a quiet motion with the hand, a conference with a pupil—in these and many other ways a teacher directs and teaches pupils acceptable behavioral patterns.

In teaching the multiplication facts, the teacher does not present them once and expect pupils to have full understanding and mastery. The facts are introduced, discussed, worked with, reinforced; and after much experience they are learned. A good classroom environment is not developed by presenting a set of established rules and procedures once, but through extended and reinforced experience. *Principles of good teaching are as important here as in Social Studies or Language Arts.* Developing positive pupil behavior is accomplished via effective teaching.

Concepts of how good discipline is established have evolved over the years. In colonial times, for example, classroom control was maintained through quite severe and rigid controls. The following illustrates the expected behavior and how it was enforced in one state during the colonial period:

> For boys and girls playing together, four lashes; for failing to bow at the entrance of strangers, three lashes; for blotting copy book, two lashes; for scuffling, four lashes; for calling each other names, three lashes.[3]

This was appropriate treatment when there was little or no recognition of natural forces—physical, psychological, and sociological—operating. In school, for example, children had to be quiet. No knowledge of the need for activity in learning or for catharsis as a constant factor in development was evident. Power was vested in strength, and parents and parent-designates (such as teachers) were to be obeyed without question. There was no question, as might be raised today in a sociology class, of *legitimate power.* In this superior-inferior relationship, the child had to submit. Little or no attention was paid to how he felt or to his wishes, likes, or dreams.

Over the years there has been a shift in emphasis from imposition of the will of a stronger person to a situation where *discipline is the natural result of the act per se.* Within this stance, caution should be exercised. In becoming sensitive to the needs of children, a few teachers, parents, and administrators tend to overindulge, overprotect, forgive, and excuse the child. Such action or lack of action prevents the child from learning the natural outcomes of his actions.

[3] William E. Drake, *The American School in Transition* (Englewood Cliffs, N.J.: Prentice-Hall, 1955), p. 229.

UNDERSTANDING PEOPLE IS IMPORTANT

Know Thyself

An important component in developing an adequate classroom climate is knowing one's strengths and weaknesses. Yet this is one of the most difficult tasks an individual faces. The mental attitude of the teacher is probably the most important single factor in the development of a classroom that is conducive to learning. According to Clarizio, "research on anxiety reveals that, when intense, it can have debilitating effects on both intellectual and personal functioning." The efforts of excess in anxiety can be observed both in children and in teachers' behavior.[4]

Children sense phoniness or uncertainty in teachers. They may sense, for example, that underlying the informal, democratic behavior of a beginning teacher is a reluctance and fear to assert himself. Good classroom control evolves when the teacher knows his own strengths, utilizes them as he moves toward his objectives, and constantly evaluates progress. Further, teachers must be themselves. A teacher cannot "play the role" of a teacher. Neither can he simply mimic others whom he has observed.

Children respect teachers for what they *are*, as well as for what they *know*. The same qualities generally admired in a leader—clear-cut purpose, sense of humor, incisive decisions, and quiet assurance—are essential in the classroom. Would a fifth grader be more likely to torment a vacillating, easy-to-please teacher or a quietly assured one? Would he be more likely to play practical jokes on a rigidly humorless teacher or on one who can laugh and then return to classwork? Adequate lesson planning is important, but is not sufficient. No amount of cognitive knowledge will supplant the personality factor, nor will personality suffice without knowledge.

One's attitude toward children is important. Appropriate questions to ask include, "Do I really like children? All children? Do I like the dull child? The dirty child?" If the answer is "Yes," the children will know without telling them; if the answer is "No," they will soon find out.

Know the Children

To guide children, we must first know them—their interests, dreams, desires. Effective teachers consciously work to learn as much as possible about their pupils. Robert Bush summarizes the results of a study of teacher-pupil interrelationships: "In general, the teachers who know most about their pupils and are aware of and sympathize with their individual needs and interests have effective relationships with a larger number than do the teachers whose major concern is knowledge of subject matter."[5]

---

[4] Harvey F. Clarizio, *Toward Positive Classroom Discipline* (New York: Wiley, 1971), p. 129.

[5] Robert E. Bush, *The Teacher-Pupil Relationship* (Englewood Cliffs, N.J.: Prentice-Hall, 1954), p. 169.

The effective teacher understands child growth and development patterns. He senses the "flow of growth" from early childhood to adulthood. Furthermore, he studies more intensely the particular characteristics of the age groups he is teaching. He systematically studies the literature and compares research findings with his observations and knowledge with actual classroom behavior.

The teacher utilizes cumulative record cards, individual conferences, and other data-gathering means to gain depth knowledge of each individual he is teaching—probing each one's academic performance, health, home, aspirations, desires, interests, friends, and so forth. This is not an easy task, especially in classrooms where the load is heavy. In many schools, however, services are available to aid the teacher, such as visiting teachers, counselors, remedial reading teachers, subject-matter supervisors, teacher aids, and so forth.

The Open Classroom

Today we are hearing more and more about the open classroom, wherein responsibility for discipline is shared by all students and the teacher. For many persons who might desire to employ the open classroom concept, actual practice in this area is a formidable challenge. Kohl[6] lists three problem areas that interfere with standard accepted school practice in most instances. These are (1) noise, for an open classroom is not a silent place, although it can be modulated but not eliminated; (2) dirt, as student activities in multidimensional learning produce more clutter than is seen in most traditional classrooms; and (3) the fact that students are threats, especially in spreading the word among other students that "things are happening" in the classroom.

The removal of standard authoritative barriers in one classroom cannot help but affect other teachers and pupils in a building.

The shared concept of discipline in the open classroom extends far beyond the boundaries of sharing that are found in the average classroom. Student involvement in self-selection in learning content and media results in less confrontation between teacher and pupils. However, this design requires learning of new roles for students as well as teacher and the task of learning to be responsible for oneself in the social context of classroom and school.

Not only does the teacher learn about the general characteristics of children and the background of individuals being taught, but he studies the group and its subgroups. In fact, the teacher is a *group worker*. Unless he understands the dynamics of the group and uses these to his advantage, guiding behavior is difficult if not impossible. Techniques such as socio-

[6] Herbert R. Kohl, *The Open Classroom* (New York: Vintage Press, 1969), pp. 77–86.

grams, interactions analysis, and direct observation of free play and open-class time aid the teacher in sensing the tenor of the class, its subgroups, and the constantly shifting role of pupils within the group.

SOME GUIDELINES IN EFFECTIVE PUPIL DIRECTION

Pupils Respond to Teachers Who Like Them

A positive attitude in the classroom is contagious. Children respond more consistently and with greater enthusiasm to encouragement than if the approach is negative. All too often the approach in school is negative. It seems so much easier to discuss aspects that are wrong, to discourage, to criticize. Thus we begin by pointing out mistakes. Dreikurs emphasizes that this approach seldom is for the pupil's benefit, but is to strengthen the teacher's ego. He further notes that teachers who do not know how to influence the child are inclined to blame the child for their own ineffectiveness.[7]

In a research study of teacher-pupil interaction, Amidon and Flanders found that "the average teacher tends to use twice as much criticism as praise. The amount of criticism used is typically 3 to 4 per cent as compared to less than 2 per cent praise and encouragement. *There is a positive relationship between teachers who use a very limited amount of criticism (1 per cent or less) and high pupil achievement with superior attitudes.*"[8]

Emotional contacts where the teacher consistently accepts pupils and expresses warm feelings toward them influence pupil's self-concept. Lehmusvuori interviewed pupils of two groups of teachers—those who were considerate of pupil feelings, and those who were not so concerned. Each pupil performed a simple intellectual task, then stated the score he expected to make on the next task. Prior to stating this expected score, he was alternately told he had done well or that he had done poorly on the previous task. Pupils taught by nonacceptant teachers changed their aspirational level on every task. Pupils of more acceptant teachers tended to set their goals on the basis of experience and paid less attention to the evaluation of the authority figure.[9] Evidently, the latter type of teacher had helped pupils develop the habit of independent self-evaluation more effectively than the former.

Interest in the child cannot be expressed in words alone; it must be

[7] Rudolf Dreikurs, *Psychology in the Classroom* (New York: Harper, 1957), p. 42.

[8] E. J. Amidon and Ned A. Flanders, *The Role of the Teacher in the Classroom* (Minneapolis: Paul S. Amidon and Associates, Inc., 1963), p. 48.

[9] Heimo Lehmusvuori, "The Effect of Teachers' Authoritarian and Democratic Attitudes on the Children's Level of Aspiration After Success and Failure," *Research Reports,* Department of Psychology, Jyvaskyla Institute of Pedagogics, No. 13 (1958), pp. 7–20.

demonstrated. Real interest is shown through a few personal remarks expressing concern and familiarity with children's interests, needs, and activities. Individual guidance is often difficult to find time for in the hustle and bustle of a busy school day; but the thoughtful teacher assures the pupil that he is interested in the pupil's new shoes, in his father's picture of a horse, his reasons for being tardy, and his reasons for failing to finish four lines of his homework. A child needs to know that the teacher cares and that he is important as an *individual* as well as a pupil.

The very children who may *need the teacher most* are quite likely to be the ones he *wants the least*. These children may be the dirty child, the academically slow child, the noisy child, or the class bully. They may have been raised in a culture quite different from that of the usually middle-class teacher. Their goals, ideals, and activities may be difficult to comprehend. But it is exceedingly important to understand and to show warmth toward them. All too often school is a source of irritation rather than support to these children. Cronbach concludes that children from reasonably well-to-do homes, especially those who are college bound, are generally given more emotional support and teacher approval. They capture class offices and predominate in extracurricular activities, except athletics.[10] As teachers, we must remember that every item in a culture is *value impregnated*. Cleanliness is certainly a *fact*, but it is also a *value*. No item is value-neutral. In working with children from other cultures or with other value-patterns, we must constantly evaluate our own stance.

A word of caution is in order: we must express genuine, positive, warm feelings toward our pupils. Many beginning teachers have the idea that it is their job to keep the children "happy." They feel they are being "mean" to a child when they correct him, and "nice" to him when they allow him to run wild. Nothing could be further from the truth. Teachers are not in a popularity contest. Ironically, the teacher who does not directly seek the affection of pupils is more likely to have it showered on him.

Proper Environment Is Important

Industry has found that changing the physical environment of office or plant can improve production and increase morale. This is also true in the classroom. Rooms that are poorly ventilated, poorly lighted, stuffy, overcrowded, or unattractively decorated tend to be containers for poor pupil behavior. Even old outmoded buildings can be made reasonably attractive with appealing pictures, displays of children's work, interesting and informative bulletin boards, and materials such as books, magazines, maps, and so forth, displayed in such a way that children know they are for *their* use. Many classrooms are deadening, not only because of dullness, but

[10] Cronbach, op. cit., p. 647.

also because of a lack of stimuli. There is little in the classroom to cause children to want to learn, to pique their interest.

The task of beautifying and keeping a room or school attractive is not one that the teacher alone assumes. This is an excellent base for cooperative teacher-pupil action.

Classwork Is Interesting and Appropriate

Pupils are always motivated toward something. The question is, What? Their energies may be expanded in all directions, their work may lack long-term vision, they frequently lose sight of their goals, but they do not lack a will to work, and they enjoy increasing their competence. "Healthy children are coiled springs ready to make something whirl. This may sound like an exaggeration to the teacher who prods and tugs at an indifferent class. Yet these same 'indifferent' pupils are spending countless hours planning dances or inventing skits for a carnival. The problem in motivation is not to awaken an inert audience, but to direct the energy of an alert group into constructive channels and keep it there."[11] Fritz Redl, who has studied the problem of classroom management and discipline over a number of years, supports this view. "Every normal child will kick if you bore him or tire him more than is legally permissible. Only idiots don't care. Normal children will become indifferent and wander off in fantasy, or become obstreperous, or play with each other, or kick each other—in other words, create a behavior problem."[12]

Instructional practices have either a positive or a negative effect on pupils. In classrooms where instruction is directed only to the average group, discipline is likely to be a major concern. Challenging every pupil in social studies when all are studying the same material is not possible. The brighter children are bored and the slower children are lost. The brighter ones will go unchallenged and bedevil the teacher and their classmates. The slower ones will feel inferior and search for trouble. Instruction within a classroom must be geared to several levels of ability and to a multiplicity of interests and needs.

Studies in child growth and development indicate that learning is more effective when the pace of learning is varied. A teacher who works to make his classes effective will use a change of voice, a change of tactics, a change of emphasis, a change of pace. These enable the teacher to keep the attention of the class and at the same time allow the pupils to enjoy the different approaches. The effective teacher learns to sense when he is losing the class's attention. Any change of pace, any little surprise may help to alleviate the situation.

The effective teacher constantly checks the "atmospheric pressure" in

[11] Ibid., p. 498.
[12] Fritz Redl, "Discipline in the Classroom," *Child Study*, 21 (1944), p. 105.

his classroom. When the students are about to explode with glee or something exciting has happened, he enters in, is part of the fun and enjoyment, but after an appropriate time turns the attention of the class back to the topic at hand. The light touch, instead of the pompous look, is generally more effective.

Lesson planning must be flexible, and so must the teacher! He must be ready for almost anything! One of the joys of teaching is the unanticipated happenings and challenges that occur, one after another, throughout the day. It is also one of the frustrations. Effective teachers not only live with the unexpected, they also thrive on it.

Continuous evaluation of lesson plans and procedure is important. Some questions asked by the teacher of himself might include the following:

1. Am I making the subject content interesting, vital?
2. Is the lesson worthwhile, realistic, clear to pupils?
3. Are the activities meaningful, proportionally important to the time spent on them?
4. Have I planned sufficiently?
5. Have I made good use of available materials and resources?
6. Have I approached each day with zest and enthusiasm?
7. Have I provided for individual needs and aptitudes?
8. Do I encourage pupils or squelch their initiative?

For, in reality, it is the ability of the teacher to put into practice effective plans rather than the planning that is important. As with proving pudding, it's the eating that's important.

Activities Are Well Organized

That there is a need for a well-organized classroom is evident in the conclusion of a research study of discipline in the classroom by Sidney Celler. He found that the use of attractive teaching aids, enthusiastic teaching, and the use of mechanical routine for certain background classroom procedures are associated with effective discipline.[13] Organization in the class tends to establish a climate conducive to learning. Routines are established for handling such matters as money collection, going to lunch, taking attendance, lavatory excuses, changing rooms for music, art, and so forth.

Organization implies development of standards for conduct of pupils. It implies that these are explicitly stated and known by all concerned, and hopefully, that all pupils involved will have participated in

[13] Sidney L. Celler, "Practices Associated with Effective Discipline" (Ph.D. diss., Johns Hopkins University, 1949).

the standards developed. Children work best when they have goals to direct them and when they know what is expected of them. Rigidly imposed rules are questionable—they constitute a challenge to some pupils, do not take into account individual differences and difference of behavior in different activities. Reducing pupil behavior to a few specific rules is difficult. Some classrooms have so many rules for pupil conduct that no active pupil can hope to avoid criticism.[14]

Planning by the group produces important changes in social relations within the class and thus enhances classroom climate. Cliques fade away as the group begins to work actively together. At the end of the work, friendship choices are likely to be spread thoroughly among the group.[15] What is not so obvious is that friendliness grows more rapidly in a group working toward a common goal.[16]

Pupil Disruptive Behaviors

Usually, when teachers or student teachers are talking about discipline problems, they are referring to disruptive behaviors that occur in the classroom. As has been pointed out, the frequency and seriousness of these problems are directly related to the nature of the learning activity. If a teacher has plans well charted for pupil learning and if there are interruptions, it is likely that confrontation between teacher and pupil will occur.

In a recent study by Driscoll,[17] it was found that the most frequently occurring pupil disruptive behavior consisted of acts that could be classified as being a nuisance and as harmless. These included items such as whispering in class, failing to follow directions, making noise in the hall, talking out while the class was working, daydreaming in class, reading or writing while the teacher was talking, chewing gum in class and clicking pens. A survey of 667 elementary and secondary student teachers in the state of Michigan indicated quite clearly that although these nuisance behaviors occurred frequently in the experience of student teachers, they were likewise considered as harmless.

A second classification of pupil disruptive behaviors were also surveyed in this same study. The serious forms of pupil disruptive behavior

[14] E. G. Williamson, "Preventive Aspects of Disciplinary Counseling," *Educational and Psychological Measurement*, 16:68–81 (1956).

[15] K. J. Rehage, "A Comparison of Pupil-Teacher Planning and Teacher-Directed Procedures in Eighth Grade Social Studies Classes," *Journal of Educational Research*, 45:111–115 (1951).

[16] Leonard Berkowitz et al., "Effects of Performance Evaluation on Group Integration and Motivation," *Human Relations*, 10:195–208 (1957).

[17] Robert L. Driscoll, "A Survey of Pupil Disruptive Behaviors As Viewed by Student Teachers" (Ph.D. diss., Michigan State University, 1970).

included possessing guns, being under the influence of narcotics while in school, turning in false alarms and bomb threats, stealing materials from school, stealing from another student, stealing from the teacher, starting fires, possessing brass knuckles and/or Molotov cocktails, and possession of narcotics. It was this area that caused greatest anxiety and concern for student teachers, and yet these behaviors seldom occurred. However, the fact that they do occur at times is sufficient for their inclusion in items for consideration in teacher preparation courses.

Teacher-Pupil Interaction

Verbal and nonverbal interaction occurs in the classroom between the teacher and an individual child, between teacher and the class or subgroups of the class, between individual children, and between an individual child and the class or its subgroups. The kind of interaction permitted and encouraged affects the tenor of classroom climate. In many classes the children are insulated from one another by a restrictive teacher. He may forget that the purpose of school is not to isolate pupils, but to use group dynamics in a positive way. After all, if the power of the group were for naught, children could be educated via television or self-instructional devices individually in their own homes. An apparent characteristic of man is that when he is emotionally excited, he seeks out someone with whom to talk. Cliques, coffee breaks, teen-age phone calls are evidence of this. Classroom management does not mean a well-drilled group of children responding to orders, but rather a well-directed class where the child is allowed to move, talk, work, play, study, and think in his own way as long as he does not interfere with the well-being of others.

A pupil should not always have to be interacting, doing something. There should be an opportunity to think, to consider quietly the day's activities, to explore new vistas, and to plan for the future. A teacher recently related the following experiences. "I remember last year when the principal was in my room observing. Tommy was wandering from one area of interest to another in the room. To the principal it appeared he was doing nothing, so he walked up to Tommy and asked him what he was doing. Tommy's reply was, 'I'm just thinking for a while; isn't that all right?' And all right it was so far as I was concerned."

Flanders has studied the verbal behavioral patterns within the classroom and concludes that sheer amount of teacher-talk affects pupil attitudes. When he divided classrooms according to pupil attitude, there was a greater percentage of teacher-talk in the "below-average in attitude class" than in the "above-average in attitude classes." In both types of classes someone was talking two thirds of the time, but in the above-average classes, only 40 per cent of this time was teacher-talk, while in the "below-average in attitude classes," from 66 to 75 per cent of the talk was teacher-talk.[18]

Amidon and Flanders note the following:

> The key to developing more effective verbal behavior is opportunity to experiment with and practice desired communication skills. Among the most important of these skills are: (1) ability to accept, clarify, and use ideas, (2) ability to accept and clarify emotional expression, (3) ability to relate emotional expression to ideas, (4) ability to state objectively a point of view, (5) ability to reflect accurately the ideas of others, (6) ability to summarize ideas presented in group discussion, (7) ability to communicate encouragement, (8) ability to question others without causing defensive behavior, and (9) ability to use criticism with least possible harm to the status of the recipient.[19]

In directing discussion, novice teachers at times have difficulty asking questions which educe pupil critical analysis, comment, and amplification. Perhaps a partial classification of types of questions and the responses elicited would serve to aid in having better discussions in all areas, and particularly as they relate to pupil behavior, as shown in Table 10–1.

In the first two kinds of questions, only a single, definite, specific answer is appropriate. After it has been given, no other need be made. The third kind of question, related to a directed discovery technique where certain

TABLE 10–1

Teacher Question	Response
1. Should one talk when others are speaking? Was John Adams second president of the U.S.?	Yes or No
2. At what time does school begin? In what year did Columbus discover America?	8:45 1492
3. What arithmetic pattern do you find in the following pairs of number sentences? $3+4=\square$ $4+3=\square$ $7+2=\square$ $2+7=\square$ $15+6=\square$ $6+15=\square$	Commutative Property
4. What could be done if there were no teachers? What might have happened if the South had won the War between the States?	Varied responses

[18] Ned A. Flanders, "Analyzing Teacher Behavior," *Educational Leadership*, 19: 173–175 (Dec. 1961).

[19] Amidon and Flanders, op. cit., p. 3.

stimuli are so structured as to elicit the desired result, a generalization is needed. Such a generalization can be discussed and tested with other examples. The last type of question requires imagination, insight; it permits the full range of pupil creative endeavor. This type of question can be employed to improve existing classroom situations, to fantasize about what might have been without the deterrent of being either right or wrong. In the end, these open-minded questions permit summarizing and solidifying important ideas, drawing tentative hypotheses, and testing them in practice. This type of question is difficult to compose, but is important in developing class interaction and verbalization.

Standards Developed Cooperatively

Using discussion techniques noted previously, teachers develop standards of behavior cooperatively with pupils. When children understand the need for certain standards and have a part in establishing them, they are more likely to abide by the standards. This does not infer that the teacher relinquishes his position and responsibility as a leader in the class, but that he shares this responsibility with the class. Pupils expect the teacher to direct and to maintain standards, but they also expect him to treat them pleasantly and to listen to their suggestions.[20]

The teacher shares a dual role. Some rules and regulations are made for a larger group than his classroom, for example, the school, school district, city, or state. Many times the teacher has had no voice in making the rule, but he does have a responsibility to his pupils to help them understand the rationale behind the directive. He has a second responsibility to his pupils. If the new ruling is not a good or a fair one, he has the obligation to communicate this to the proper authorities, He is not expected to be, nor should he be, a human sponge soaking up indiscriminately all moisture provided; he must be a thinking rational human being, capable of evaluating.

Consistency Is a Watchword

Consistency of action, rules, and behavioral expectations is important in maintaining a good classroom climate. Nothing distresses a child or adult more than never knowing where he "stands." Nothing undermines pupil security more than a teacher with widely variable moods—anything goes today; nothing is right tomorrow. By consistency we do not mean rigidity. There are, of course, extenuating circumstances in which decisions must be altered. The analysis of as many relevant conditions as possible prior to making a decision is significant to the decision-making model developed earlier in this chapter. The teacher is more effective when dealing

[20] Louis Milde Smith, "Pupil Expectations of Teacher Leadership Behavior," Final Report, Cooperate Research Project No. 750 (St. Louis, 1960).

with principles rather than with many finely graded rules and their punishments. Studies show that consistent behavior is more important than severity, strict control, or overpermissiveness.[21]

POSITIVE APPROACH TO CLASSROOM DISCIPLINE

However hard the teacher may try, discipline problems are bound to occur in the classroom. In the previous section discussion has focused primarily upon guidelines for working with individuals and the total class in developing and guiding pupil behavior. In this section, attention will be concerned with breaches of expected conduct. These outbursts are *results* of previous actions—actions that might have taken the form of pupil-pupil or pupil-teacher or pupil-curriculum interaction. The child lashes out at whatever is bothering him (and, at times, he does not know exactly what it is that is of concern and lashes out at anything and everything). He may become aggressive in his actions, and the teacher immediately recognizes that there is a problem. Or he may withdraw and develop negative or apathetic behavior. He may avoid participating in class activities, become self-deprecating, and cringe at other-person contacts. Both avenues of retaliation are of concern to the teacher; unfortunately, the latter is more difficult to diagnose, but perhaps more harmful to the future development of the child.

D'Evelyn states that about ten per cent of children "show behavior deviant enough to cause real concern to the teacher."[22] Others have estimated this number to be greater or less. No hard and fast line exists between normal and abnormal children, between children with problems and children without problems. Problem children differ from normal children more in degree than in kind.

Boys particularly conflict with teacher and school expectations. During the intermediate grades, when their developmental growth emphasizes interaction with peers, peer acceptance, and approval, boys are likely to be noisy, rough, and demonstrative. Meyer and Thompson in a study of sex differences in teacher approval and disapproval found that sixth grade teachers scold boys four times as often as girls. Boys received, on the average, equal amounts of approval and disapproval, whereas girls received about twice as much favorable as unfavorable comment. They conclude that the constant threat of punishment for normal role behavior produces conflict in boys and contributes to a dislike for school.[23]

[21] Goodwin Watson, "Fresh Evidence on an Old Problem," *Child Study*, 21:99–101 (1944).

[22] Katherine E. d'Evelyn, *Meeting Children's Emotional Needs* (Englewood Cliffs, N.J.: Prentice-Hall, 1957), pp. 39–40.

[23] W. T. Meyer and G. G. Thompson, "Sex Differences in the Distribution of Teacher Approval and Disapproval Among Sixth Grade Children," *Journal of Educational Psychology*, 41:97–109 (1950).

Deviation in behavior that is reinforced tends to breed further deviation. Children who *cause* difficulty in school are likely to be those who have *had* difficulty in school. So often we are prone to view this behavioral pattern as the cause of a child's problem ("I would not have to punish him so often if he would only be good") rather than the result of multiple other factors. Mullen studied pupils aged nine to sixteen who had caused classroom discipline problems or who had been truants. Table 10–2 sum-

TABLE 10–2
Relation of Classroom Discipline and Pupil Background Factors

Background Factors	Per Cent	
	TRUANTS	CLASSROOM DISCIPLINE PROBLEMS
Repeated one or more grades	64	60
Interrupted attendance	34	21
Reading disability	27	25
Defective teeth	49	41
Defective vision	30	28
Broken home	53	31
Poor work habits	14	53

marizes data from his study and indicates that an impressive number had suffered from remediable physical and educational handicaps.[24] The implications of this study are far-reaching in the development of an educational program and its auxiliary diagnostic and remedial services.

Misconduct by a child is rarely committed with criminal intent. It is more often the result of a combination of circumstances and conditions that must be analyzed, understood, and taken into account as the teacher works with specific situations. Pupil factors influencing behavior include home and family background, peer relations, pupil interests, needs, and goals. The teacher should be sure he is working on conditions and not symptoms.

Some cases are so difficult and complicated that the best course of action is to refer them to the school counselor or principal. This action by a teacher should not be construed as a confession of failure, but as an acknowledgment that help is needed in analyzing the situation and taking remedial steps. Many people may become involved in such action—the

[24] F. A. Mullen, "Truancy and Classroom Disorder as Symptoms of Personality Problems," *Journal of Educational Psychology*, 41:97–109 (1950).

school nurse, psychologist, principal, pupil, parents. A "team" approach is instituted. This is somewhat like the diagnostic council in a large hospital that is composed of specialists from several fields of medicine who discuss symptoms and analyze from their separate vantage points. In a coordinated effort they, like the school, attempt to diagnose a patient's difficult problem.

Goals Are Important

In working with children who are having behavioral problems, goals are important. Guidance is needed to give the child some behavioral goals to work toward rather than away from. Just as it is more important for Americans to be for democracy instead of just *against* communism, we need to develop the attitude that we are working for good behavior rather than just against bad behavior. Negativism only results in more negativism —and the results are extremely unreliable.

Recently in a discussion of school discipline, a teacher illustrated the need for emphasizing the affirmative when asking questions. His point was that one never asks a question for which he hopes to elicit the response "Yes," but which might be answered "No." One never gives a choice to the responder between something or nothing. For example, if one asks someone for a $5.00 loan, he is likely to get a negative answer. But if the question is, "Would you rather loan me $10.00 or $5.00?" there is a better chance he will get the $5.00.

Simply telling a child what his goals are is a mistake, even though the teacher may be correct in his assumption. Questions related to his goals, what he wants, not what he is, are appropriate. Attempt to elicit why he misbehaves. In such a discussion one talks *with the child* not at him. In initial discussions with a child, see if he can tell:

1. What happened.
2. How he made his mistakes.
3. How he might avoid making the same mistake again.

To assume that he does not want to do better is a mistake. Believing in the child is important to a successful conference leading to better behavior.

Accent the Positive

Most teachers recognize that in the practical life of school, some punishment is necessary. Teachers also need to recognize that most punishment is negative and that social behavior is seldom changed through its use. It only temporarily stops the child; it is a deterrent, but it does not change basic attitudes.

Accenting the positive can change pupils. Each time a child acts in a manner that shows effort to do the desirable, acknowledge this in a positive way. The teacher praises with a pat on the back, a nod, a smile, or a word of encouragement.

When Punishment Is Necessary

If the objective is simply to improve conduct while children are under the direct observation of the teacher, consistent punishment may be appropriate. If the goal, however, is to develop self-discipline without teacher pressure, punishment will not necessarily be effective. In studying various control patterns in kindergarten, Lounin and Gump concluded that pupils were more likely to respond as the teacher wanted when he indicated positively what he wanted. Furthermore, harshness in handling a misbehavior disturbed the whole class, not just the pupil being punished.[25] According to Zipf, punishment arouses resistance to the teacher and a dislike for the activity, and the effect continues even after the threat has been removed.[26] Pupils conform to the punitive teacher because they must. Although they may not yield to temptation as often as pupils of nonpunitive teachers, neither are they as likely to develop rational self-control.[27]

When punishment is necessary, attempts should be made to keep personalities out. Rather, the teacher seeks to help the child understand that punishment is necessary because the pupil did not conform to the accepted rules of the class. Hopefully, the pupil will understand that the punishment is a natural consequence of the behavior act itself.

When the punishment is directly related to the act, it is more effective. For example, if the child did not complete an assignment within the allotted time, he can finish it later while missing a desired activity. If he does not roll out the pie crust, he cannot place it in the pie plate; if he does not get the paint jar, he cannot mix the paints. As often as possible, let the punishment be related to the offense.

Punishment is usually more effective when not excessively used. Extreme or excessive punishment is damaging to the child, to the pupil-teacher relationship, and to the rapport of the class. The more often it is used, the less effective it becomes.

The novice is prone to be preoccupied with the various types of punishment rather than working with pupils to alleviate the underlying conditions. Some teachers and even schools seem to rely almost completely on punishment to give direction in pupil conduct, whereas almost all make

[25] Jacob S. Lounin and P. V. Gump, "The Comparative Influence of Punitive and Non-punitive Teachers upon Children's Concepts of School Misconduct," *Journal of Educational Psychology*, 52:144–149 (1961).

[26] Sheila Zipf, "Resistance and Conformity Under Reward and Punishment," *Journal of Abnormal and Social Psychology*, 61:102–109 (1960).

[27] Cronbach, op. cit., p. 494.

some use of it. Punishment is easy, but directing children *through punish-ment* is difficult.

Ultimate Objective Is Self-discipline

The ultimate goal of all discipline is to develop self-discipline in each child, a process whereby he progresses from a state of complete dependency to one of independence as an adult. It is a process whereby he learns to interact with his fellow man in acceptable social ways. It is a process whereby he develops control over his emotions and his actions, becoming their master, not their slave. It is a process in which he develops confidence in himself, his decisions, and his actions. A criterion of good classroom discipline is not how quiet the children are or how rapidly they respond to teacher commands, but the extent to which pupils are developing toward self-discipline.

SUMMARY

One of the often unwanted yet necessary responsibilities of a classroom teacher is establishing, maintaining, and, if required, restoring a form or forms of discipline that contribute to positive learning experiences of all children in the class.

Relationships of selected physical, sociological, and psychological factors to human behavior have been discussed. The need to understand pupils and to work with them in developing a set of behavior goals in a cooperative manner has been stressed. Several guidelines to pupil direction have been presented for your consideration as you strive to help each child under your supervision progress toward the objective of self-discipline.

SUGGESTED ACTIVITIES

1. The love of teaching is filled with a number of rules for good discipline. Discuss the following sayings. Are they valid? Why do you think so? Do they have any support in psychological or sociological research?
   (a) Praise in public, censure in private.
   (b) Permit children to "save face" when they are in a spot.
   (c) Don't punish the group for the misbehavior of an individual.
   (d) Never use schoolwork as punishment.
   (e) Using idle threats as a disciplinary weapon is worse than no weapon at all.
   (f) Punish at the time the act is committed, not later.
2. On page 26, in *The Role of the Teacher in the Classroom* Amidon and

Flanders describe nine important communication skills. Give illustrations of each of these skills and how each might be used in the classroom.

3. Interview a sample adult population, asking them (a) to compare the discipline of schools today with that of schools when they were pupils, (b) to discuss the extent to which they think schools are aiding boys and girls develop self-discipline, and (c) to suggest procedures they feel would improve pupil discipline in today's elementary schools. Summarize your findings for class discussion and presentation.

4. Prepare a report on discipline, describing techniques that you feel would be helpful in maintaining a good classroom climate.

5. Janet is a girl who has constantly been in trouble at school. From her actions in your sixth grade class, you judge that she has some real potential for becoming a useful citizen, you have established good rapport with her, and she seems to have been straightening out remarkably in your class as far as you can tell. Elsewhere, she seems to continue to get into trouble. However, after one such scrape, the principal decides the time has come to draw the line and has informed the faculty that the next time Janet engages in any inappropriate action, she is to be suspended from school for one week. When you enter the washroom the next day, you discover Janet writing obscene words on the wall. She pretends not to have been doing this, but both of you know that she is guilty. What action would you take; what criteria would guide you in your action, or what additional information would you need?

6. Observe several different teachers for a period of one hour each and record the statements that teachers use to provide students with feedback about their behavior. Upon completion of the observations, classify each statement as being one of (a) establishing, (b) maintaining, or (c) restoring classroom behavior.

7. Arrange a classroom discussion about a problem that is evident to all concerned, and attempt to solve the problem by consensuses of the group. Be certain that the individual rights of all are not violated by any decision that is reached.

SELECTED BIBLIOGRAPHY

Alan, Dale. "School Is Now and We're Late." *Educational Leadership.* **4** (October, 1970), 87.

Amidon, E. J., and Flanders, Ned A. *The Role of the Teacher in the Classroom.* Minneapolis: Paul S. Amidon and Associates, 1963.

Berkowitz, Leonard *et al.* "Effects of Performance Evaluation on Group Integration and Motivation." *Human Relations,* **10** (1957), 195–208.

Bush, Robert E. *The Teacher-Pupil Relationship.* Englewood Cliffs, N.J.: Prentice-Hall, 1954.

Celler, Sidney L. "Practices Associated with Effective Discipline." Ph.D. Dissertation. Johns Hopkins University, 1949.

Clarizio, Harvey F. *Toward Positive Classroom Discipline.* New York: Wiley, 1971.

Cronbach, Lee J. *Educational Psychology.* New York: Harcourt, 1963.

d'Evelyn, Katherine E. *Meeting Children's Emotional Needs.* Englewood Cliffs, N.J.: Prentice-Hall, 1957.

Drake, William E. *The American School in Transition.* Englewood Cliffs, N.J.: Prentice-Hall, 1955.

Dreikurs, Rudolf. *Psychology in the Classroom.* New York: Harper and Row, 1957.

Driscoll, Robert L. "A Survey of Pupil Disruptive Behaviors As Viewed by Student Teachers." Ph.D. Dissertation. Michigan State University, 1970.

Flanders, Ned A. "Analyzing Teacher Behavior." *Educational Leadership.* **19** (December, 1961), 173–175.

Kohl, Herbert R. *The Open Classroom.* New York: Vintage Press, 1969.

Lehmusvuori, Heimo. "The Effect of Teachers' Authoritarian and Democratic Attitudes on the Children's Level of Aspiration After Success and Failure." *Research Reports.* Department of Psychology, Jyvaskyla Institute of Pedagogics. Number 13 (1958), 7–20.

Lounin, Jacob S., and Gump, P. V. "The Comparative Influence of Punitive and Non-punitive Teachers Upon Children's Concepts of School Misconduct." *Journal of Educational Psychology,* **52** (1961), 144–149.

Meyer, W. T., and Thompson, G. G. "Sex Differences in the Distribution of Teacher Approval and Disapproval Among Sixth Grade Children." *Journal of Educational Psychology,* **41** (1950), 97–109.

Mullen, F. A. "Truancy and Classroom Disorder as Symptoms of Personality Problems." *Journal of Educational Psychology,* **41** (1950), 97–109.

Redl, Fritz. "Discipline in the Classroom." *Child Study,* **21** (1944), 105.

Rehage, K. J. "A Comparison of Pupil-Teacher Planning and Teacher-Directed Procedures in Eighth Grade Social Studies Classes." *Journal of Educational Research,* **45** (1951), 111–115.

Smith, Louis K. "Pupil Expectations of Teacher Leadership Behavior." Final Report, Cooperative Research Project No. 750. St. Louis, 1960.

Watson, Goodwin. "Fresh Evidence on an Old Problem," *Child Study,* **21** (1944), 99–101.

Williamson, E. G. "Preventive Aspects of Disciplinary Counseling." *Educational and Psychological Measurement,* **16** (1956), 68–81.

Zipf, Sheila. "Resistance and Conformity Under Reward and Punishment." *Journal of Abnormal and Social Psychology,* **51** (1960), 102–109.

Chapter 11

Using Instructional Materials

The teacher makes several basic decisions concerning instructions. First, he specifies broad goals and specific instructional objectives. The origin, analysis, and writing of objectives was treated in Chapter 3. After objectives are identified, instructional strategies and resources are specified that facilitate pupil achievement. At one time, the lecture was the major tool of the teacher, but today's teacher can select from among a wide variety of instructional resources one that may be most effective for a particular objective and most efficient when one is considering the need for a variety of instructional modes. Furthermore, the teacher can individualize instruction through media where not everyone is forced to participate in the same activity at the same time. Skillful use of instructional materials can enhance classroom instruction. In this chapter, you will explore media, their characteristics, and their uses. More specifically, the cognitive objectives of the chapter are the following:

1. The reader will be able to specify the process and criteria for selecting instructional materials.
2. The reader will be able to describe the operation of a learning resources center.
3. The reader will be able to analyze the characteristics and uses of specified instructional resources.

TEACHING IS COMMUNICATION

Marshall McLuhan's often quoted remark, "The medium is the message," characterized the importance of instructional resources in effectively teaching children. They not only support instruction through communication; they are instructive because they are communication media.

The more effective the communication process, the more effective learning is likely to be. For centuries the only tool of communication was verbalization. The wisdom of man was transmitted tediously by word of mouth from one generation to the next. Written communication did not become a significant tool of education until the invention of the printing press; but as printed materials became cheap and plentiful, they became the *chief teaching tool* in the classroom. The twentieth century has brought still other media of communication suitable for classroom use—still pictures, motion pictures, sound tapes, self-instructional devices, television. As each new medium was added to the tools of communication, the teacher's chances of teaching more effectively were increased. He had the *potential* for more effective communication of ideas—*if* he employed a wide variety of media rather than limiting his selection to one or to a few and if his choices were made on the unique strengths of each medium.

The easiest course of action in planning a lesson or series of lessons is to take the course of least resistance. One could look around, consider what was successful yesterday, and repeat the same technique tomorrow. Such a procedure would lead to nothing but dull, monotonous, apathetic lessons. The diet of methodology and of communication must be varied for most effective results. The effective teacher guards against excessive parsimony, which might lead to boredom, and overabundance of media, which could confuse learners with meaningless choices.

Wilbur Schramm points out that at least four elements are required for communication: (1) a source, (2) a message, (3) a channel, and (4) a destination.[1] Brown et al. further note, "The message may be designed for, and received by, one person or many. The message may be conveyed by expressions, gestures, spoken, or written symbols, or by drawn or photographed pictures. Communication theorists call the source an encoder, the message a signal or sign, and the destination a decoder."[2]

Instructional materials are designed to enhance learning by providing *channels* of communication. A variety of instructional approaches and materials aids effective communication and effective learning. Children are encouraged to experiment and to demonstrate. They picture, draw, and

[1] *The Process and Effects of Mass Communication*. Revised Ed. ed. by Wilbur Schramm and Donald Roberts (Urbana, Ill.: The University of Illinois Press, 1974), p. 1.

[2] James W. Brown, R. B. Lewis, and F. F. Harcleroad, *A-V Instruction: Materials and Methods*, 2nd ed. (New York: McGraw-Hill, 1964), p. 9.

paint. They read, write, debate, discuss, and listen. They dramatize and role-play. They construct and exhibit. They visualize, create mentally, and invent. They do these things in all subject areas, in and out of school.

> The normal learner, insofar as the functions of his perceptor mechanisms are concerned, gains understanding in terms of multiple impressions recorded through eye, ear, touch, etc. These functions do not occur in isolation but rather through a blended pattern from any or all of the perceptor mechanisms that are stimulated by external occurrences. Effective perception is thus a blending of sensations . . .[3]

A constellation of educational media is needed to provide effective communication with children possessing an ever-widening experience pattern.

LEARNING RESOURCES CENTER

Many instructional resources are located in individual classrooms or in open instructional areas. They may have been purchased by the school district or brought from home by children or the teacher. Those resources, which are seldom used, are often stored in a learning resources center of the school or in a central location for the school district. Generally, the cost and extent of use determine the placement of materials. For example, a filmstrip that is seldom used may be placed in the school-district-level center; but if a demand were to develop, multiple copies might be purchased for each school. The pull between ease of accessibility and variety of materials is always present as educators strive to utilize most effectively the funds available.

The school-district center is generally a coordinating unit for the various building centers. Its size and the scope of its responsibilities vary considerably according to the size of the district. Most contain a reservoir of 16-mm. and 8-mm. films, filmstrips, and records; equipment models, and charts; collections of curriculum materials (curriculum guides, out-of-print textbooks, aggregations of materials on particular units of study, and so forth); and the professional library. Repair of equipment and the ordering of books and other instructional materials are usually part of the responsibility of the center.

The learning resources center is the hub of individual school activities and a veritable beehive of activity. It is a resource *to which* teachers can take their whole class or small groups or individual pupils or *from which* they can secure materials, books, and equipment for use in the classroom.

[3] Walter A. Wittich and Charles F. Schuller, *Audio-Visual Materials: Their Nature and Use* (New York: Harper, 1962), p. 30.

The learning resources center is an outgrowth of and an expansion of the school-library concept. In the library, sources are primarily books or journals; in the learning resources center, these are supplemented by records; charts; television; motion pictures; and individual posts for listening to tape recorders, viewing filmstrips, or working with self-instructional devices. The learning resources center encompasses the full range of potential learning materials. The extensive use of such a facility is illustrated by a two-hour visit to a school to observe a center in action. The incidents are real, drawn from an observation that was unannounced, uncontrived, and typical.

Plumbrook School

The Research Center of Plumbrook School in Utica, Michigan, is a large area (about fifty feet by fifty feet) opening directly onto ten fourth-, fifth-, and sixth-grade classrooms that surround it. The floor level of the center is two feet lower than the surrounding corridors and classrooms and is almost entirely carpeted. As there are no doors in the research center or in the classrooms, one is immediately impressed with the size and openness. Partial sound and visual barriers are formed by display cases, bookshelves, and bulletin boards.

At first glance the center seems sparsely furnished. On one side are movable library bookshelves and odd-shaped sectional tables. In the center of the room is an island with tiled floor, a sink, and several aquariums, terrariums, models; there is also an electrically lighted microscope. Displays of children's work and evidence of a stimulating environment abounds. Displayed in various parts of the center were (1) a model of the Golden Gate Bridge, (2) some tin-can art, (3) a model of the earth, (4) an electric-light display, (5) some children's pictures of various modes of transportation, (6) an adobe hut model, (7) a model of the Taj Mahal, (8) some plastic models of prehistoric animals, (9) a display of musical instruments, (10) a description and display of sand casting, (11) a shell collection, (12) a model-car collection, (13) some birdhouses, (14) some rocks (labeled), and (15) a display of industrial bearings. Hanging from the ceiling was a mobile made of toothpicks by a pupil.

A bioscope, movie projector, television receiver, overhead projector, controlled reader, opaque projector, filmstrip projector, tape recorder, filmstrip hand previewer, records, tapes, and filmstrips are among the equipment and aids available in the center.

Pupils from two sixth-grade classes were sitting on the floor in one portion of the room watching a film on conservation. A few of their classmates had remained in their rooms working on individual projects. In another part of the center three fifth-graders were sitting at library tables, searching through reference materials for information on Greece. Two fourth-grade pupils were rummaging through a pile of books on a table marked "Recently Received Books." After the film ended, a short discussion ensued, and the sixth-graders went back to their classes; the vacated space next was occupied by a fifth-grade class watching a Spanish lesson on television.

A third-grade class came to the center for its regular research-center orientation period. They sat in the library book corner and were instructed by the resource teacher who directs the center. Two sixth-grade girls came in and began putting library cards in newly received books and stamping them with the school name. In an adjoining work room, some second-graders were making a papier-mâché model of a dinosaur when some sixth-graders entered and began working in another part of the room on a model featuring a coliseum and gladiators.

The third- and fifth-grade classes both left the center at about the same time, and for a few minutes it seemed void, but then another third-grade class entered. Their teacher showed a filmstrip to about half the class while the rest explored the library shelves and checked out books. Three sixth-graders with special reading problems were being tutored by the resource teacher, using a controlled reader. Two fourth-graders were engaged in a chess game in one corner of the center, both sitting on the floor.

All during this time many children had been procuring and returning audiovisual equipment and materials—a third-grader returned a filmstrip, two boys rolled a projector down to their room, and two others borrowed a chart on the muscular system.

Movement was free and open. During the two-hour observation, individual children were continually coming to and leaving the center to work on projects, seek assistance, and check out books. Interestingly enough, with all of the activity, there was little noise. The carpeting and acoustical treatment of the center are such that noise in one part is not transmitted to another.

Among the many pupil-made charts on varied subjects, one stood out. It is shown below.

GUESS WHAT HAPPENED TO ME IN THE CENTER

One day I was doing research on Norway and I decided to look through some of the old textbooks to see what I could find. My search proved to be very profitable because I found quite a bit about Norway—but, besides that, I found a dime! My teacher said that there was no way of telling who the dime belonged to and that I could keep it.

So keep searching, fellow students. You never can tell what you might find.

Selecting Instructional Materials

Individuals appear to differ in their preferences as to the senses primarily used in dealing with the outside world. Some appear to learn best through visual cues, some prefer auditory cues, and others prefer the tactile sense. Research evidence of this is more abundant with students who have learning disabilities than with average students; however, it is likely that normal children display the same characteristic sensory preferences.

Piaget postulated that young children (in the concrete operations stage) will tend to achieve more readily when they can manipulate, feel, and see actual objects. Older children may learn just as well by verbal descriptions. Pictures may be more useful for younger children and poor readers. Poor readers tend to learn more effectively through hearing than through reading. Children who are self-directed do better than those less internally oriented in self-directed study, programmed instruction, and contract teaching. Although research continues, highly generalizable or functional relationships between different media and individual learning styles have not been established.[4]

The key to selection and use is determined by the objectives sought, what the teacher wants students to demonstrate—new cognitive behaviors, affective behaviors, and psychomotor behaviors.

The selection process also includes an evaluation of the value of a specific method or approach in a given situation and of the quality of the specific materials to be utilized. Are the materials of good technical quality (photographic clarity and composition, artistic balance and color, and so forth)? Are they accurate? Are they appropriate for the age level and interests of the audience? Are they available when needed?

Physical arrangements for the use of media are important to optimum use. Opaque projectors and movie projectors require darkened rooms, and television may need an outside antenna. In some schools special rooms are provided for this equipment; in other schools room-darkening shades are provided in the classrooms. Pupil movement is sometimes a consideration when moving a class to a special room. Within the room, equipment and materials are arranged for optimum learner attention and use of projection time. In darkened rooms, the heat and poor ventilation caused by closed windows can add yet other dimensions for consideration by the teacher.

Media have specific characteristics that determine how they can be used. Sequence cannot be changed with a filmstrip, but with slides it can be. Recordings, tapes, and radio programs require the teacher to decide

[4] L. J. Briggs, P. L. Campeau, R. M. Gagné and M. A. May, *Instructional Media: A Procedure for the Design of Multimedia Instruction, A Critical Review of Research, and Suggestions for Future Research*, Monograph No. 2 (Palo Alto, Calif.: American Institutes for Research, 1967).

what pupils will look at while they listen. Pictorial prints may be too small for group use. Motion pictures and television have their own pace, unity, and fact density. The teacher is limited in his influence on students during the presentation. He can specify those things they are to search for during the film and recap the film, using questions or descriptions following it. Portable television provides instant replays of teaching episodes, plays, games, talk about pupils, or other activities where self assessment may be involved.

One basic key to the effectiveness of instructional materials and teaching strategies is the extent of active participation by the learners. Readiness for such participation is developed by directing attention to key ideas, to the purpose of the ensuing lesson, to major concepts or sequences to look for or issues to consider. Directions, guide sheets, or questions by the teacher prior to and during the use of media aid in directing attention to key ideas. Active interaction as an integral part of the ongoing lesson is possible and useful for most media, although a few, such as motion pictures, rely primarily on introductory and follow-up activities.

Evaluation is an integral part of any lesson; it provides a basis for changes while the lesson is in progress as well as the basis for future plans. Actually, *evaluation is teaching*. When instructional materials are used, evaluation of their worth is an important part of their use. For example, how effective was a particular technique or media in the situation? How might its use have been improved?

INSTRUCTIONAL MATERIALS AND EQUIPMENT

Each type of media, each instructional aid, each of the materials that teachers use have their own sets of unique characteristics that contribute to their effectiveness. These are described in the following paragraphs.

Real Things

Classrooms include an abundance of real things to stimulate pupil learning. Included may be such diverse things as an ancient Indian arrowhead, stamp collections, growing plants, butterflies, fish, a bird's nest, or a ship's wheel. Such displays make possible an accuracy of impression unmatched by other types of instructional materials. Children may view, touch, smell, and taste real things, which provide multisensory contact.

Real objects are often limited in their usability in the classroom. Some are too large to bring to the classroom (for example, a steamship); others are too small (an atom). Some are too delicate (porcelain figurines). Some are too enclosed to reveal important parts (engine). Some are too removed from their natural environment to be meaningful (desert sand).

Some are too dangerous (gasoline). However, the stimulus of the object itself is so strong that teachers use every opportunity to bring such things from the pupil's out-of-school environment into the classroom.

Learning is not limited to the four walls of the classroom or to the school grounds. The study of the community and use of community resources provide meaningful experiences. Every community abounds in many learning possibilities. They include natural and man-made resources to visit (rivers, fields, mountains, courts, air terminal, museum) and human resources to invite to school (people with special skills, interests, occupations, backgrounds).

Field-trip possibilities are readily available. They may include a walk in the neighborhood or an extensive out-of-town trip to a factory. Field trips can be significant, even though many pupils have previously been to that particular location, *if* the purpose of the trip is clearly focused and the preplanning is complete.

A first-grade teacher took her class on a field trip in the woods across from their school. It was in the fall, and the leaves of the maples, oaks, and other trees were in glorious color. Before the trip was taken, its purpose was carefully discussed, activities to be completed while on the trip were outlined, and an organizational plan was drawn up. Pupils suggested the "buddy" system to insure that no one would be lost. One activity included was to collect specimens of the leaves of various trees. Another activity was to focus attention on the shape of trees, the difference in shapes of the evergreens and other trees, the color of the various leaves, and the color and texture of the bark of trees. While on the trip, the teacher pointed out and discussed with pupils these features of the woods. When the class returned to the room, they continued to discuss their excursion, eventually writing a story about it. They spatter-painted their leaves to accentuate their shape. They drew pictures of the forest, using the multicolored leaves as guides to coloring the trees and their memories to remember to shade tree bark from light brown to nearly black. Although these pupils may have been in the forest many times, never had their attention been focused on these details.

In the planning and actualizing of field trips, the following procedures may be of value:

1. Determine the purpose, and state it in terms of desired pupil behavior.
2. Decide on the most effective procedures for bringing about the realization of goals. Weigh the potential effectiveness and benefits of a field trip against the problems and weaknesses of the trip. Criteria for selecting a field trip are delineated by Brown, Lewis, and Harcleroad as questions to be answered before planning further:

- Does the trip fit naturally into the work students are doing in the classroom?
- Can it be completed in the allotted time?
- Does it have enough value to justify taking considerable class and teacher time?
- Will it provide important observational experience which is unobtainable in other ways?
- Is the trip suitable to the grade level, and one which will arouse the students' interest?
- Is it a representative location with general application?[5]

3. Determine a potential site or route for the field trip.
4. Discuss the proposed trip with the principal and make necessary preliminary arrangements for transportation, time schedule, and so on.
5. Plan the trip carefully and cooperatively with the pupils. Determine the purposes of the trip, list questions to be answered by the trip, and establish routines so that management is not a problem. Plan for transportation. In some cases, parents provide transportation; usually, the school bus is used. Discuss the trip with an appropriate official of the place to be visited. Specific plans as to time of arrival, length of tour, questions of pupils, things to avoid, and mode of transportation should be discussed. If possible, an advance tour is taken by the teacher as a "dry run." If special clothing is required, this information is relayed to the pupils.
6. Send out parent-permission forms. This step is required by almost all school districts as a matter of school-community communication for school activities.
7. Study background information. Discuss the nature and content of the forthcoming trip. What do pupils already know? What misconceptions do they have? Such discussion may aid in focusing on certain aspects of the trip not previously considered. Read about the area; study it; build a sound background knowledge. Time so spent pays dividends in increased perception during the trip.
8. On the trip organize the class so that all the pupils can experience significant phenomena, not just the few aggressive pupils who push to the front while the remainder of the class are relegated to the background where they are unable to see or hear. Some demonstrations may have to be repeated. Sometimes the class is divided into tour-learning clusters of four or five pupils and a parent. Intermediate grade pupils often find note-taking an effective procedure for documenting the trip.

[5] Brown, Lewis, and Harcleroad, op. cit., p. 398.

9. Follow-up activities are designed to clinch the concepts learned on the field trip. Class discussions and further study contribute to an ongoing exploration rather than a single trip that might be just entertaining. Appropriate thank-you notes by the courtesy committee or by individual class members to those people involved are important. Evaluation of the activity in terms of objectives and of pupil actions culminates the field trip and sets the stage for further study.

Models

Size and convenience of firsthand observation are often serious problems in using real things with pupils. In such cases, models, either larger than or smaller than the real thing, may provide a solution. Such models permit a class to visit an iceberg or an Indian village or gain perspective of the mountainous terrain of Colorado. Neither does the size of the atom lend itself to direct observation and comparison. Models of the earth, steam engine, chemical elements, or the ear aid children in learning about the nature of the real objects. Accurate reproductions of many things are currently available commercially. Teachers and their classes build models for special needs. Some models are accurate reproductions of the original, some use color to emphasize certain parts, and some simplify the model for ease in detecting important parts, whereas others may have a portion cut away for ease of observation of internal parts—some moving, others to be taken apart and reassembled.

Many models can be made in the classroom; however, caution should be exercised in making them. Many times the model is distorted to such an extent that pupils are led to incorrect concepts. Models of the solar system have been made in some elementary classes in which the sun and each of the planets were approximately the same size and where the distance between planets was the same. Models of Indian villages and salt relief maps with inaccurate details can be worse than no models at all! Research by pupils about the scale, size, and color of the real things prior to making the models is important to insure their accuracy and correctness.

Projected Still Pictures

Greater and more diverse use of still projections in the classroom is being made. Some newer schools are building overhead and filmstrip projectors into the cabinets, and others furnish several projectors for each school, so that they are readily available. This is indicative of the value attached to this medium of communication by educators. When it is used effectively, the total class is able to view objects or slides that might otherwise be difficult for pupils in the back of the room to see. Each type of projected material, however, offers unique advantages. In the following paragraphs these characteristics will be explored.

FILMSTRIP.   A wide variety and number of filmstrips are available. Some are accompanied by sound records or tapes, some include captions, and many have teaching guides accompanying them. They may be shown at a fixed or varied rate to meet the maturity level of the class and the objectives of the lesson. Any frame can be shown as long as is necessary, or it can be eliminated. The sequence of frames is fixed, which at times is a disadvantage, but often aids in systematically developing ideas. The timing is flexible; the sequence is inflexible.

Previewing filmstrips before showing them to the class is a "must." Because of the large number currently being produced by many sources, some have poor quality or are not directed to the age level of a particular class. Furthermore, such a procedure is essential to most profitable use in the classroom. In the previewing, the teacher can decide how to present the filmstrip to the class, what parts to use, and which ones to omit. The most effective introduction can thus be planned, with key questions formulated and new pupil terminology anticipated. No filmstrip is exactly what a teacher wants, but it can readily be adapted to meet his needs.

A tachistoscope is a modification of the filmstrip projector; it flashes words or number groups on a screen at controlled speeds. Developed during World War II to teach rapid airplane identification, the tachistoscope is currently used to increase pupil perception rate and to accelerate individual reading rates.

MICROPROJECTOR.   The microprojector projects microscopic details onto a screen so that the total class can view them. It permits pupils to see details the instructor wants stressed, and the total group views simultaneously details that only one child could see using a microscope. Wood fibers, block smears, insect legs, and bacteria come alive when enlarged with the microprojector. Prepared slides are commercially available or can easily be prepared by class members.

OVERHEAD PROJECTOR.   One of the most versatile instructional aids recently marketed is the overhead projector. Operated from the front of the room, the teacher can write or project transparencies while facing the class. Thus, visual cues from class members are more easily noted by the teacher than if he is occupied by working on a chalkboard with his back turned to the class.

Sheets or rolls of clear film (acetate) may be written on with grease pencils or colored felt pens. The film is easily cleaned or erased when no longer needed. Diagrams or assignments may be written in advance, facilitating lesson presentation. Prepared transparencies of single ideas or the multiple overlay of sequential material are currently being marketed by a number of commercial firms. The teacher himself can readily reproduce almost anything in black and white, using a photocopy technique. More and more schools are including both the photocopy machine and overhead projectors as standard equipment.

OPAQUE PROJECTORS.　　The opaque projector, using the principle of reflected light, can project almost anything in its natural color. It is limited by the size of the objects or pictures to be projected, which cannot generally be over ten inches square, and the screen image, which is not as brilliant as that of direct-light projectors. Sample uses of the opaque projector include placing single copies of books in the projector to be read by the total class, exhibiting individual pupil's work, and enlarging portions of maps. Through the use of the opaque projector, an unlimited amount of nontransparent illustrative material is available for projection and enlargement at little or no cost.

Motion Pictures

Alone or in combination with other instructional materials, the motion picture is one of the teacher's most powerful teaching tools—able to arouse pupil interest, to re-create the past, to show the petals of a flower open in seconds, and to condense complex information from many varied sources.

Numerous research studies have been conducted during the past forty years in which films were compared with other media, varying instructional procedures were followed, and differing production techniques were tested. A brief summary of them follows:

1. Films are effective when movement is a necessary part of the understanding.
2. Increased learning results when the film is introduced, and the purpose and importance of it are explained.
3. Note-taking during the film interferes with attention and thus learning.
4. Learning from a film can be increased by repeated showing, particularly when complex situations are involved.
5. Special vocabulary used in the film should be discussed prior to showing.
6. When used extensively, films lose their appeal and are not so effective.
7. Films with built-in viewer participation increase learning more than

films without such a feature. Activities planned by the teacher for the class during or after a film and related to it are likely to increase comprehension.

Sixteen-mm. films are more expensive than most other instructional materials. The selection of those that are to be purchased is therefore quite important. Such questions as the following are raised regarding the purchase of a film: Will this film be used extensively enough to warrant purchase rather than rental? Does the film contain authoritative information? Is the production of high quality?

Film rentals supplement the local film library. State universities, state departments of education, and commercial houses have large selections available to schools and other educational agencies at a nominal rental fee. Each publishes and distributes to schools a catalog describing films—their length, producer, grade-level audience, whether they are in color or black and white, and brief description.

Films sponsored by various business and government associations are offered free to schools as a public relations service. Many are highly professional and avoid direct advertisement of their product; however, because they are commercial, they must be previewed and evaluated in terms of educational objectives, potential contribution to the curriculum, and propaganda effect.

Most films are accompanied by teaching guides, although materials centers differ in procedures for handling them—some automatically enclose the guide when sending the film, others retain the guide in their files unless it is specifically requested.

General guides to using instructional material previously noted apply equally well to the use of motion pictures. The projector, screen, and speaker should be set up in advance so that valuable class time is not lost with mechanical details. In some schools, upper-elementary pupils are trained for this task and operate projectors for the staff, but this does not negate the teacher's responsibility for knowing how to operate the equipment.

Showing the film without stopping is only one way of using motion pictures. The film can be run in segments, stopping periodically for review and discussion; projected without sound; reshown with different objectives and aspects to emphasize; or shown only for a short episode. Or a combination of these and other techniques may be used.

The use of 8-mm. films offers new and less expensive educational possibilities. Short (thirty-second to four-minute) single-concept film clips are now available. Each is packaged in a cartridge, ready for insertion into a special projector without threading or rewinding. Because of their ease of use and convenience, such clips can be used by individual pupils or as an integral part of an ongoing lesson. Sound pictures using 8-mm. film offer possibilities for developing pupil creativity, interest, and competence. A seventh-grade science class recently filmed a rocket flight to the moon, using mock-ups of the rocket ship and moon surface for life-sized shots and a model of the rocket with earth, space, and moon diorama for long distance views. Tremendous background reading and research concerning the surface of the moon, rockets, and production techniques preceded the actual filming. In this case, the film was primarily a motivational technique to stimulate pupil depth study into an area of science.

Teachers have used this inexpensive tool to enhance classroom learning. Shots of a Mexican marketplace taken during a summer vacation by a teacher or parent add an important dimension to the class. The 8-mm. movie can be effective in communicating ideas about faraway places; it is also important for showing nearby but inaccessible places or things (for example, a dangerous factory). Equipped with auxiliary camera accessories, teachers have recorded time-lapse exposures of a growing plant in the classroom over several weeks to highlight the general growth pattern of the plant.

Nonprojected Pictures and Materials

An abundant supply of still pictures, graphs, clippings, and other materials designed to enhance learning is readily available. Magazines are packed with them; foreign embassies and commercial firms will send posters and printed materials about their country or products upon request. Files of such materials are started by many teachers while still in college and prove exceedingly useful in illustrating concepts.

Such materials are used to motivate pupils in the study of science units, to stimulate creative writing, to focus on pertinent current events, to develop concepts of unseen places and things, or to develop perceptual skills as pupils speculate about the background or nature of a picture.[6] Certainly, "a picture is worth a thousand words!" Bartlett describes several levels of response by pupils to drawings or photographs: (1) naming objects, (2) grasping import, (3) observing detail, (4) relating the picture to experience, (5) drawing inferences, (6) adding imaginative elements, and (7) engaging in further activities suggested by the picture.[7]

Research has indicated some guides to effective use of pictures. French studies the preferences of elementary pupils and teachers for simple or complex illustrations. First-grade children consistently selected simple illus-

---

[6] For an enjoyable paperback describing this technique and containing interesting photography, see Hart D. Leavitt and David A. Sone, *Stop, Look, and Write!* (New York: Bantam, 1964).

[7] Mary M. Bartlett, "Early States of Picture Reading," *Teaching With Pictures* (Grand Rapids, Mich.: Informative Classroom Pictures Publishers, 1943), p. 10.

trations whereas their teachers tended to prefer more complex drawings.[8] Although colored pictures attract more attention than black and white,[9] Rudisill concluded that color is more effective when the picture is realistic.[10] Children prefer pictures that contain action, tell a story, are related to previous experiences, and are larger in size.[11]

In addition to picture-selection criteria suggested by the previously described research, teachers consider the following:

1. Is the picture appropriate to the age level of the pupils in this class?
2. Will the picture contribute to an understanding of the concept being developed?
3. Is the picture interesting enough to catch the eye of its intended audience?
4. Is the information conveyed accurate?
5. Is the picture well produced (good balance, clear-cut central forms); is the photographic technique effective?

Dioramas are three-dimensional scenes representing real-life impressions. They are built in cardboard boxes with an entire side cut out or a peep hole cut out for viewing the scene. Clay or plastic figures are used in the scenes, along with plaster-of-Paris or papier-mâché models, mirrors for water, and painted background scenery. They are of much value in picturing scenes of faraway places or of long ago, particularly in the planning and staging sequences.

"Movies" of changing scenes composed of several flat drawings on rolls of paper are another way of exhibiting classroom or pupil work. The scenes are rolled onto one roller, then unrolled past a viewing window in a box onto a second roller.

Display surfaces in the classroom have been noticeably increased in recent years. Several areas have characteristics that make them an important part of the classroom. Chalkboards are best used for spontaneous work in the class. Before using the chalkboard in a room for the first time, the teacher should preview its use by writing on all parts of it, then surveying it from every area of the room. Glare, caused by an imbalance of light in the class, may cause certain parts of the chalkboard to fade out when viewed from certain parts of the classroom. The teacher should determine how his script appears from these various vantage points. Is it

[8] John French, "Children's Preferences for Pictures of Varied Complexity of Pictorial Matter," *Elementary School Journal*, 52:90–95 (Oct. 1952).

[9] Edmund Faison, *Audio-Visual Communication Review*, 2:80 (Winter 1954).

[10] Mabel Rudisill, "Children's Preferences for Color vs. Other Qualities in Illustrations," *Elementary School Journal*, 52:444 (Apr. 1952).

[11] William H. Allen, "Audio-Visual Communication," *Encyclopedia of Educational Research*, 3rd ed., ed. by Chester W. Harris (New York: Macmillan, 1960), p. 121.

large enough? Legible? Written too low? Only from such a deliberate class-room survey can one evaluate the potential trouble spots of chalkboard use.

Bulletin boards are excellent for displaying clippings, pictures, pupils' work, graphs. For most effective use they should be eye-catching, with a center of interest, captions for various aspects, and aesthetic balance and unity.

Flannel boards and magnetic boards are useful in building up overlays and can display some objects and flat materials more easily than bulletin boards. They have the weakness, however, of requiring special backing materials (felt, sandpaper, or magnets).

Peg boards can support three-dimensional objects with bentwire hangers or pegs.

Books and Printed Materials

An important part of the instructional materials in a school is printed. Most children have textbooks on various subjects. Journal and magazine subscriptions are part of many school budgets, and contributions from pupils often enhance available resources. Library books, encyclopedias, atlases, dictionaries, and other reference materials are significant to pupil development.

Perhaps at this point a word of caution about textbooks is in order. In some classrooms the textbook determines the content and sequence of lessons. It is the sole determiner of what will be taught, when it will be taught, and how. Certainly such an approach is a gross violation of principles of good teaching and of the use for which the text was originally written. In the first place, no single text is, or can be, suited to the interests and abilities of all pupils in a class. A textbook is usually three to five years in preparation and is used for five to six years before being replaced. Thus, materials are not always current. Most textbooks do not provide several varying points of view for pupils to evaluate and compare; thus they are limited. On the other hand, textbooks have many advantages. They are inexpensive, can very effectively be used to teach new skills, and provide a common basis for discussion.

In selecting library books, teachers employ several sources for reviews, evaluation, and listing of "basic collections." One such source is the *Children's Catalogue*[12] and its annual supplements. Books are listed in it by Dewey decimal classification, by subject, by author, and by grade; thus several different vantage points may be considered in selecting books. A second source is *A Basic Book Collection for Elementary Grades*,[13] produced jointly by several interested professional organizations.

[12] Marian L. McConnell and Dorothy H. West, *Children's Catalogue* (New York: H. W. Wilson).

[13] American Library Association, *Basic Book Collection for Elementary Grades* (Chicago: American Library Association).

Audio Techniques

There are few subjects in the curriculum that do not lend themselves to auditory teaching procedures. A sixth-grade class listens to a news broadcast over the radio; a second-grade class listens to "Masters in Music" on their phonograph; a fourth-grader, using earphones and a tape recorder, practices the multiplication facts by listening and reacting to recorded facts and questions; a small group of children with speech problems listen and replicate recorded sounds; a fifth-grader individually paces himself in a foreign-language laboratory; a third-grade class listens to Winston Churchill's "blood, sweat, and tears" speech; a first-grade group records their first oral reading. Obviously, auditory devices are widely used in schools today. The values of the radio, language lab, tape recorder, and phonograph are apparent when one considers this wide range of activities.

Television

In numerous research studies that compare the effectiveness of television with face-to-face methods, television has been judged to be at least as effective.[14] Encouragement for the use of this medium has been accelerated through huge grants from the Ford Foundation and the U.S. Office of Education. Today educational television is a reality for almost all metropolitan areas in the United States, with additional schools using closed-circuit television facilities. National Educational Television (NET) provides nationwide linkage among television stations; individual states have networks.

Some programs are regular features of educational television stations, with sequential teaching tasks. The classroom teacher is provided a course outline, denoting the content of each program and suggestions for use in his classroom. Other programs are of special interest, with no continuity or unity. Current events programs presented over commercial channels offer yet another possibility for enriching the classroom experience. Pupils can hear the President's "State of the Union" message, see a satellite orbiting the earth, view current events happening around the world, hear the philharmonic orchestra, or see Shakespeare's *Hamlet*.

The classroom teacher's role for such programs can be summarized as follows:

1. Care for the physical climate in the classroom—temperature, lighting, and so on.
2. Position television receivers for optimum use by the class, taking note of special seating arrangements for those pupils with sight problems.

[14] William H. Allen, "Audio-Visual Communication," *Encyclopedia of Education Research* (New York: Macmillan, 1960), p. 118.

3. Eliminate distractions.
4. Introduce the program and make sure pupils are ready to watch it from the beginning.
5. Employ appropriate follow-through, using questions, evaluation, and so forth.
6. Provide for individual differences among pupils.

Many worthwhile television programs are shown after school is dismissed. The teacher encourages his pupils to watch certain regular and special programs. In so doing, he also is obligated to follow them up with appropriate activities.

In addition to those programs broadcast to the classroom, television offers tremendous possibilities for analyzing certain kinds of procedures. A television camera can be used in the classroom for image magnification, so that pupils see things not possible in regular demonstrations. Recent development of inexpensive television cameras, receivers, and portable video tape recorders now make it possible to record almost anything for replay at a later time. Pupils can see themselves writing or performing at play practices or shooting goals in basketball. Such instantaneous replay offers tremendous and currently untested possibilities for aiding pupils in self-improvement. After use, the video tape is easily erased for future use.

Autoinstructional Materials

During the past few years increasing attention has been paid to autoinstructional materials. The possibility of individualizing the rate of learning coupled with more flexible classroom organizational procedures has many potentialities.

Although the devices have gone far beyond his original conception, Sidney Pressey is generally credited with being the father of "teaching machines."[15] An autoinstructional device is one that presents to the learner a single question or bit of information at a time. A method for pupils to make an overt response to the frame is provided, and a procedure is developed to indicate to him whether or not the response is correct or not. Thus, the pupil can progress at his own rate through the program; and as he encounters each of the small bits in each frame, he is instantly appraised of the accuracy of his response.

In selecting the most appropriate program, Gotkin stresses the need for answering four questions: (1) is the content appropriate? (2) is the content well programmed? (3) what have students learned from trial uses

---

[15] For a description of his work, see Sidney L. Pressey, "A Simple Device Which Gives Tests and Scores—and Teachers," *School and Society*, 23:373–376 (Mar. 20, 1926).

of the program? and (4) what are the characteristics of the student population or populations involved in such trial runs?[16]

Teaching machines currently available may be classified broadly as either "linear" programs or "branching" programs. The linear program has been advocated and developed by B. F. Skinner. In this program students complete all items in the program in the same order. Each new learning task is a very small progression from the previous task, with correct response cues built into the procedure. In such a program the correct response is almost always elicited; Skinner believes that it is the repeated reinforcement of correct responses that is significant to the learning task.

Norman Crowder is the pioneer of the "branching" program. In each frame the pupil selects an answer from among several. He is then referred to another part of the program; and if his answer is correct, he proceeds to the next frame in the program plan. If his response is wrong, he is given further instruction before being directed to the next frame in the main sequence of the program. Thus, some pupils complete "side loops" to strengthen their understanding before continuing through the program.

Computer-assisted Instruction

Computer-assisted instruction employs programmed instructional texts combined with the versatility and speed of a computer. In some programs students communicate using a typewriter attached to a computer terminal. Each pupil identifies himself and the lesson he is studying. The computer then types out a problem, instructions, or directions. The pupil responds, and, depending on the correctness of his answers, the computer either congratulates him and types out another problem, or it asks him to try again. This process continues until the lesson is completed. Other CAI terminals use cathode ray tubes, which permit greater speed and more pages of printed or graphical data to be presented to the learner. Some have built in sophisticated branching sequences of instruction. At this point in its development, CAI is an expensive, rigid, but potentially important media for instructing children.

Educational Games and Simulations

Educational games and simulations built upon models of the world permit pupils to practice decision-making and to see quickly the consequences of their decisions. They provide a simulated environment, set of conditions, strategies, and consequences of those actions. Players abide by the rules of the game, are motivated to attempt the potential best actions,

[16] Lasser Gotkin, "Choosing a Program: How to Start," *Programmed Instruction*, 1:4, 6 (Oct. 1961).

and receive almost immediate feedback on their actions. Games produced include "Life Career," "Disaster," "Consumer," "Democracy," "Life," "Peace," "Stock Market," and many others.

SUMMARY

Instructional materials are a vital part of the instructional program of the modern elementary school; indeed, in our increasingly technological age, they will no doubt assume ever greater sophistication and usefulness in the program. Devices and materials are often better suited to one particular kind of learning task than to another, or to pupils of one specific age or background. No device is suitable for everything; it is the teacher's responsibility to choose the most appropriate one.

A word of caution is in order. With many new and exciting instructional materials being marketed today, it is important that each be evaluated according to its usefulness in enriching learning rather than its technological sophistication or "newness." Furthermore, it is more important to be selective than to employ a large variety of aids. As teachers, we must bear in mind the objectives sought in today's schools—and instructional materials are means to those ends; they are not the ends themselves.

SUGGESTED ACTIVITIES

A. Diversity in using learning materials and activities is an important part of teaching. Listed below are a number of learning materials and activities. Refer to this list, and extend it, so that activities you design may reflect the widest range of alternatives possible.
1. Audio tapes
2. Books
3. Computer-assisted instruction
4. Charts
5. Film strips
6. Games
7. Kinescopes
8. Kits
9. Microfilm
10. Models
11. Movies (8-mm., 16-mm.)
12. Musical instruments
13. Newspapers
14. Periodicals

15. Program instruction materials
16. Slides
17. Specimens
18. Transparencies
19. Video tapes
20. Workbooks
21. Simulations
22. Demonstrations
23. Drama
24. Field trips
25. Film productions
26. Interviews
27. Laboratory experiments
28. Painting
29. Conferences
30. Role-playing
31. Sports
32. Surveys
33. Videotaped productions
34. Diorama
35. Bulletin boards
36. Felt boards
37. Realia
38. Manipulative materials

B. Mary Bartlett, op cit., p. 10 suggests seven levels of response to pictures (see page 278). Discuss these levels—are they distinct? Is there a sequence of levels of importance or depth? Is there a developmental sequence implied in the listing; that is, would the person group number one, then two, three, and so forth?

C. The statement has been made that almost 90 per cent of our experiences are visual. Is there any basis in fact for this statement? Is there any basis for the popular notion that some persons learn most visually whereas others learn most from their sense of hearing?

D. Think back over your school experiences. What do you think were the commonest mistakes made by your instructors in using instructional materials? How could these have been improved?

E. Plan a field trip to a local place of interest. Personally visit the place and describe significant details. What preplanning is necessary? What concepts and activities should be planned before going on the trip? What outcomes would you hope for from the trip? How would you plan the tactical aspects for the trip? How could it be evaluated?

F. At a PTA program, you, as a beginning teacher, have been asked to discuss and demonstrate modern instructional materials. In the question and answer period, a parent attacks the use of instruction aids. "They are expensive," he says, "and are just gadgets. Because pupils just look at them, they encourage children to be passive. They cause children to want to be entertained and to think of school as a show rather than a place to learn." What reply would you make to his criticisms?

G. Identify an objective or set of objectives that are appropriate for and meet the needs of pupils in a classroom. Be sure they are written in such a way that they meet the criteria for objectives stated in Chapter 3. Then specify instructional strategies and instructional materials that would facilitate pupil achievement. Justify your choices. In a second phase of this activity, use the instructional resources in a minilesson or microteaching session; then assess the effectiveness of the lesson, paying particular attention to materials.

SELECTED BIBLIOGRAPHY

Bettelheim, Bruno. "Play and Education." *School Review*, 81 (Nov. 1972), 1–13.

Boocock, Sarene S., and E. O. Schild. *Simulation Games in Learning*. Beverly Hills, Calif.: Sage Publications, 1968.

Dale, Edgar. *Audiovisual Methods in Teaching*. 3rd ed. New York: Holt, Rinehart & Winston, Inc., 1969.

Erickson, Carlton W., and David H. Curl. *Fundamentals of Teaching with Audiovisual Technology*. 2nd ed. New York: Macmillan Publishing Co., Inc., 1972.

Hayes, Alfred S. *Language Laboratory Facilities: Technical Guide for the Selection, Purchase, Use, and Maintenance*. Washington, D.C.: U.S. Office of Education, 1963.

Kapfer, Philip G., and Glen F. Ovard. *Preparing and Using Individualized Learning Packages for Ungraded, Continuous Progress Education*. Englewood Cliffs, N.J.: Educational Technology Pub., 1971.

Twyford, Loren C. "Educational Communications Media." *Encyclopedia of Educational Research*. Ed. by R. L. Ebel. New York: Macmillan Publishing Co., Inc., 1970.

Chapter 12

Assessment of Learning

The process of teaching is an integrated one, in which the instructor sets objectives, provides activities designed to facilitate pupil achievement of objectives, and gathers evidence on the effectiveness of such instruction. Evaluation and measurement are integral to all phases. Examine the sequential record in Table 12–1, which illustrates this process.

In each stage, the teacher collects data and continually makes decisions about *relevance* and *effectiveness*. The extent to which these decisions are based on evidence will determine, to a major degree, the effectiveness of the learning experiences.

Basic to decision-making are evaluation and measurement techniques. Previous chapters have considered establishing goals and writing objectives, designing learning activities, and developing an integrated program based on student needs and background and on societal patterns. This chapter focuses on the underlying constructs of evaluation and measurement. More important, it includes ideas and clues for practicing teachers to use with children. Objectives for this chapter follow; and after studying this chapter, you should be able to

1. Describe the distinction between measurement and evaluation.
2. Distinguish among levels of measurement.
3. Define reliability, validity, and objectivity in operational terms.

TABLE 12–1

Goal Setting (Broad goals for a unit are determined.)	Are these goals important for these pupils?
Diagnosis	What do pupils already know? What can each one now do? What areas need particular instructional attention?
Specific Objectives	Do objectives contribute to goals? Are they realistic and appropriate for each pupil? Are they worthwhile?
Planning Instruction	Are activities logically related to objectives? Will they likely lead to pupil achievement of objectives? Do they provide for individual differences?
Learning Activities	During learning activities, are pupils sufficiently interested and active? What evidence of pupil misperception is evident? Should activities or objectives be modified based on feedback from pupils?
Evaluation	With respect to objectives, how effective are learning activities?

4. Describe at least four data collection procedures.
5. Construct a test item that measures a given objective.
6. Discuss the use of standardized tests.

EVALUATION AND MEASUREMENT

Often the distinction between evaluation and measurement is confused, with the two terms used interchangeably. Measurement usually refers to one dimension or aspect of a situation, whereas evaluation is concerned with a number of measurements in a broader perspective. Evaluation is more inclusive than measurement. Furthermore, measurement generally reflects only the quantitative aspects of an attribute, whereas evaluation includes both the quantitative and qualitative aspects. Evaluation is value-laden, not value-sterile, as it relates to something valued.

Perhaps two illustrations will clarify the distinction between evaluation and measurement. The size of a fifth-grade classroom can be measured, and its dimensions stated as thirty feet by forty feet, with a nine-foot ceiling. But in the evaluation of the size of the room, many other considerations are involved. How many pupils are scheduled for the room? What activities are planned? What equipment is in the room, and how is it arranged? What underlying educational philosophy permeates the use of the room? These considerations involve value judgments. Furthermore, several different measurements are woven into this evaluation. One is able to *measure* the size of the room, but one evaluates the usefulness of that size.

A second-grade child scored below average on the standardized mathematics test. This is a measure of his mathematics achievement. This score is *evaluated* by considering the nature and objectives of the test. (Does it measure the curriculum pursued by this child? Does the test perhaps measure understandings deemed important five years ago, but no longer significant in the rapidly changing field of mathematics? Are the measured objectives similar to those held for this child?) Furthermore, the score is evaluated in terms of expectations for him, special circumstances present when he took the test, and so forth. The test score provided a measure of pupil understanding that was evaluated by using other criteria.

Evaluation

Evaluation is a process which anyone carries on when he considers how well he is accomplishing what he set out to accomplish. In thinking about evaluation, two key ideas need to be kept clear: the concept of a goal, giving direction to the behavior being evaluated, and the concept of some norm, standard, or value being applied to the behavior to determine its adequacy. . . .

The root word in evaluation is value. In most cases, we as teachers or the children as learners are evaluating when we are judging the value of our activities to achieve our goals. This value judgment is of two parts; first, one judges whether what he is doing has something to do with his goal, be it arithmetic, history, or teaching (this is called validity), and second, one judges whether what he is doing in arithmetic, history, or teaching is adequate in relation to some known or imagined standard.[1]

The first aspect of vital consideration in evaluation is the establishment of real, specific objectives that can be evaluated. Classroom goals must often be stated in terms of expected pupil behavior, so that evaluation is possible. This aspect of the school program is one of the most abused. Poorly conceived and poorly stated objectives cannot be evaluated. Even specifically stated objectives must be measured and evaluated with appropriate instruments. In either case, results presently are based almost completely on chance factors. Bloom underlines the importance of specifically stated objectives if quality control of instruction is to be assured.

[1] Virgil E. Herrick, in *Strategies of Curriculum Development*, ed. by James B. Macdonald, D. W. Anderson, and F. B. May (Columbus, Ohio: Merrill, 1965) pp. 114–115.

The criterion for determining the quality of a school and its educational functions would be the extent to which it achieves the objectives it has set for itself. . . . Our experiences suggest that unless the school has translated the objectives into specific and operational definitions, little is likely to be done about the objectives. They remain pious hopes and platitudes.[2]

Both teaching procedures and evaluation procedures are directly related to objectives. Objectives determine *what* is to be included in the curriculum, what excluded, what emphasized, and even *how* this will be done. Evaluation aids in determining the extent to which objectives are being attained.

It should be emphasized, however, that evaluation is not something that occurs after the lesson is taught. Evaluation is intertwined throughout the lesson, ascertaining pupil understanding, attitudes, readiness for further work, level of performance, and so on. Evaluation provides a basis for teaching. In fact, *evaluation is teaching.* It is such an integral part of the teaching sequence that it cannot be psychologically structured out. Teachers constantly sample pupils' achievements and attitudes, both informally and formally, during a lesson. This constant feedback provides the basis for lesson development.

So far discussion has centered on one aspect of the evaluative process —the relation of goals to evaluation. Determining criteria for success is the second aspect, and in many ways it is as difficult, particularly for beginning teachers, as setting objectives. Progress is assessed in terms of some standard, which varies from individual to individual and situation to situation. The same observed behavior in two different children might be evaluated differently, depending on the standard of adequacy applied.

The simplest standard to be applied is whether or not a task has been completed. Was an arithmetic problem right or wrong? Was the book read or not? Was the paper turned in or not? The evaluative process in relation to the standard is simply to observe a process and ascertain whether a given behavior is present or absent.

A second standard commonly employed is a population norm. A set of behaviors are compared with the central tendency for a population similar to the one being evaluated. Achievement in spelling is measured and compared with the achievement of other children of similar age and educational background. Using these data, one can speculate that this individual or group of children are as proficient as, less proficient than, or more proficient than, a comparable group. Test norms and standardized scores are based on this concept.

A third standard derivative is the comparison of an individual's be-

---

[2] Benjamin S. Bloom, "Quality Control in Education," *Tomorrow's Teaching* (Oklahoma City: Frontiers of Science, 1961), p. 54.

havior with his expected capacity to perform in that area. His present and past performances are considered; he is, in effect, his own standard.

A fourth standard employed is that of socially or educationally desirable behavior. Behavior patterns that enhance social or educational goals are used as reference points in judging the adequacy of given behavior.

Measurement

"In its broadest sense, measurement is the assignment of numerals to objects or events according to rules."[3] Measurement is not so simple as we often consider it. In the measuring of attributes of linearity (a stick is five inches long), the measurement is closely aligned to an observable physical characteristic. It is often said that one measures objects or events; however, in reality, it is the *properties* or *characteristics* of these objects or events that are measured; that is, one does not measure the stick; one measures the *length* of the stick. But even this is not entirely accurate. One actually measures *indicants* of this property. In the measuring of length or sex or color, it is relatively simple to observe the property directly; however, many educational measures are more elusive, more difficult to observe or measure directly. In the measuring of pupil intelligence or anxiety, it is necessary to *infer* degrees of these properties from observation of *indicants* of them. If a pupil marks a test in a certain way, it is inferred that he is intelligent. If a child readily completes an assigned task, it is assumed that he is cooperative. If his hands are clinched into a white-knuckled fist during a certain task, it is possible to infer that he is anxious, although in other circumstances he might simply be angry or ready to cry.

Some types of measurement are more simple than others; they are more *direct*. Measuring the length of the stick or the amount of carpeting required for a floor are illustrations of direct measurements. The measuring instrument is of the same nature as the attribute to be measured and is directly applied to it. Measuring temperature is an illustration of *indirect measurement*. Temperature is not measured directly, but is indicated by the expansion or contraction of mercury in a sealed tube. The mercury reacts to changes in temperature, and an arbitrarily assigned scale is used to assign numbers to changes in volume of the mercury. A watch, as an indicator of the passage of time, is another indirect measuring instrument. The watch does not measure time directly; it is not the same attribute as time. Through mechanical means it consistently indicates a regular pattern with which we have associated time. Most educational measurements are indirect and thus more difficult to deal with than direct measures. Achievement, intelligence, hostility, or creativity are all measured through the observation of something that we *infer* is related to these characteristics.

[3] S. Stevens, "Mathematics, Measurement, and Psychophysics," in *Handbook of Experimental Psychology*, ed. by S. Stevens (New York: Wiley, 1951), p. 1.

LEVELS OF MEASUREMENT.   There are four general levels of measurement
—nominal, ordinal, interval, and ratio. The lowest level is *nominal mea-*
surement. Groups of sets are simply named; they are labeled. Although the
labels may be numerals or alphabetic symbols, no quantitative meaning is
inferred. Illustrations of nominal scale classifications are *white, male, Ger-*
man, and so on. All members of a set are assigned the same numeral or
symbol, and no two different sets are assigned the same symbol. Furthermore, the assignment is unambiguous—there is no question to which set
any given object will be assigned, given a particular set of rules for assignment.

Ordinal measurement infers that the objects can be ranked or ordered
on the measured property. That is, if we have three objects, *a, b,* and *c,*
and *a* is less than *b* on a particular scale and *b* is less than *c,* then *a* is less
than *c.* Ordinal measures indicate only rank order. Any numbers assigned
indicate neither that they are absolute quantities nor that the intervals
between numbers are equal. Furthermore, there is no absolute zero point,
no indication that an individual has none of an attribute.

Interval scales not only possess the characteristics of nominal and
ordinal scales, but also include equal intervals between numbers. Equal intervals on the scale indicate equal intervals in the property being measured.
If the numbers 11, 8, 4, and 1 were assigned to four objects on an interval
scale, we could infer that the differences between the first two objects
$(11 - 8 = 3)$ is equal to the difference between the last two $(4 - 1 = 3)$.
We could not, however, assume that the second object, rated 8, has twice
as much of the attribute as has the third object, which was rated 4. With
this scale we can add and subtract *intervals,* but not *quantities.*

Ratio *measurement* has all attributes of the other scales, and in addition it has an absolute zero with empirical meaning. With an indication
for zero, the numbers on the scale indicate the actual amounts of the
property being measured. It is possible to utilize all arithmetic operations
and to operate on the quantities themselves. Thus, one can with this scale
indicate that 8 is twice as great as 4. In most educational measurement,
scales are limited to nominal and ordinal scales. Questionnaires asking for
yes-no responses, place of birth, sex, and so forth, are basically nominal.
Achievement and intelligence tests are basically ordinal. It is possible to
infer that, on this attribute, one person has more than another; but not to
indicate an equal interval between numerals on the scale. It cannot be inferred that the difference in I.Q. between 124 and 128 is the same as between 93 and 97. The intervals on the scale are the same, but the intervals
between *real* I.Q.'s may not be. These numerals simply indicate the rank-
order positions of the four persons on this scale. Neither can it be assumed
that an I.Q. of 140 is twice as great as 70.

Even though most educational measuring scales are, strictly speaking, *ordinal*, they are often treated as *interval* scales. Probably many do approximate interval scales fairly well. The teacher employing and interpreting the results of tests must be alert to the limitations of testing procedures and to the possibility of gross inequality between scale intervals, and interpret them in this light. There are few absolutes in education testing, only indications.

Selecting and Employing Measuring Instruments

In measuring educational attainment, teachers often employ standardized instruments or make tests themselves for a specific purpose. Various ramifications of this facet of evaluation will be explored in this section. In considering the worth of tests, three terms are considered—reliability, validity, and objectivity.

Reliability

Tests are devised to sample behavior. If the sampling procedures are inadequate or inappropriate, the results are not indicative of the true characteristic. Another sample would result in different scores.

All measurement is an approximation of the *real* attribute. When a teacher indicates that a desk is thirty inches long, he infers that it is thirty inches to the nearest inch—its true length is somewhere between 29½ inches and 30½ inches, according to our scale. If the ruler *always* measures that desk or any other linear distance consistently, one assumes that it is *reliable*. But if the scale were laid out on a rubber band, varying numbers would be associated with the length of the desk on subsequent measurements, and the reliability of the instrument would be low. The results would be inconsistent.

Educational measurements vary from occasion to occasion. Some are more stable and reliable than others. Their measure of an attribute is more consistently the same; they are more dependable. Reliability of a measurement is an indication of consistency, stability, dependability. If a set of objects is measured several times with the same instrument, will we get similar results? Reliability is the relative absence of errors of measurement in a measuring instrument.

Kerlinger suggests four ways one can improve reliability.[4] First, write each item in the instrument with clear and straightforward purpose. An ambiguous item decreases reliability because different individuals can interpret it differently. Second, add more items of equal quality. This increases the size and range of the sample and decreases the chances for random

---

[4] Fred N. Kerlinger, *Foundations of Behavioral Research* (New York: Holt, 1964), pp. 442–43.

errors caused by sample size. Third, clear and standard instructions tend to reduce errors of measurement. And, fourth, administration of instruments under standard, well-controlled, and similar conditions increases the chances for reliability. These suggestions are appropriate not only for making tests but also in using standardized tests as the teacher recognizes the work of the test developer and the necessity for strict compliance with administration and scoring instructions if resulting norms are to be useful.

Reliability of published tests are often described as "reliability coefficients" derived from several formula and basic theoretical constructs. Perfect reliability is 1.00. A reliability of .94 is more consistent than .87, for example. Some tests are more reliable than others, and varying norms have been employed in the interpretation of their usefulness.[5]

Validity

When direct measuring instruments are employed (ruler to measure length), it is not difficult to determine that we are measuring what we think we are measuring. But with much educational measurement, quite indirect means of measurement are employed. At times the means are so indirect that the validity of the measurement is questionable.

Reliability is concerned with *how a characteristic is measured*; validity is concerned with *what is measured*. It is epitomized by asking, Are we measuring what we think we are measuring? Tests purported to measure broad generalizations may include items eliciting only knowledge of factual data. They may measure knowledge of facts quite well, but are not valid for the purpose for which they were designed. It behooves the teacher to consider the items in a test and to evaluate their validity for his use. In order to do this, an explicit statement of objectives is required in terms of desired outcomes in pupil behavior.

Objectivity

Most people have biases, including teachers and test makers so it is important to rid the test of as many biases as possible. This means that items are clearly and unambiguously stated, that they are appropriate for the age level being tested, that directions for taking the test are clearly stated, and that directions for scoring the test are unambiguous. Ease of administration and scoring, the necessity for special skills and competencies to administer the test, and availability of population norms are other factors to consider.

All educational instruments must be critically examined for their reliability, validity, and objectivity. Despite the difficulties inherent in achieving reliable, valid, and objective measurements, great progress in

[5] For a more comprehensive discussion of methods of determining reliability, see Georgia Sachs Adams, *Measurement and Evaluation in Education, Psychology and Guidance* (New York: Holt, 1964), pp. 68–102.

testing as an aspect of evaluation has been made in this century, and will continue to be made in the future.

TEACHER-DESIGNED INSTRUMENTS

The most prevalent testing and evaluation in the elementary classroom is by informal instruments or observations developed by the teacher. Although they are important, he does not rely completely on commercial and standardized devices since they are not directed specifically to the particular objectives sought in his classroom; they are not directed to his *particular* children. They do not consider differences in content or approach of this specific curriculum, nor can they measure many of the significant aspects of a school program. Standardized tests are designed to test fairly widely accepted objectives and are employed in the elementary school to compare pupils with a large population, but they are not specific enough for many evaluative situations that crop up in the classroom. Both formal and informal tests are necessary. To collect additional data on pupil progress, teachers employ a wide selection of informal techniques. Some of these are explored in the following paragraphs.

Conferences and Interviews

Conferences and interviews with individual pupils or small groups are important evaluative devices. Such conferences can be long and well structured or short, informal moments as the teacher bends over a child's desk. In such interviews, the child is given undivided attention. The teacher becomes a good *listener*; he learns little while talking.

Conferences are often evaluative and also instructive. "Miss Stevens, I can't do my English," is often the spark for a short diagnostic conference. In such a case, the teacher probes first for pupil understanding, attempting to find trouble areas. These, in turn, form the basis for instruction. When problem areas are general, groups within the class or the total class may be instructed.

Conferences provide opportunities for pupils to share with the teacher their hidden dreams, desires, fears. These may appear unreal or unimportant, and the time at which they are raised may be inopportune. But they are important to the child, and listening to him and counseling him are not only helpful to the child, but rewarding to the teacher. Cut him short a few times, and he will not be likely to return. Through conferences the teacher learns about what is inside the child, not just his surface features.

Observations

Observations are another important evaluative tool. Through classroom observations the teacher sees the social-emotional development of his children; he notes leadership, belligerence, conflict. He is able to observe children in the *process* of completing learning tasks, not just measure *products* of learning. This is an important part of teaching; an example may underline its importance. Alan is learning manuscript writing. His letters look neat and accurate, but observing him in the *process* of making them indicates (1) his posture at the desk is atrocious; (2) the paper is not properly placed and aligned, and thus his hand and arm movement are stilted—he is drawing his letters; (3) his pencil is being tightly gripped very near the tip; and (4) some letters are being made incorrectly. (He begins at the bottom in making the letters *c*, *s*, and *z*.) None of these characteristics that hinder his progress in handwriting and that will become more difficult to correct as he progresses are obvious in examining the *product* of his handwriting exercise. While pupils are working, most teachers walk about, observing them in process.

Records

Cumulative records are maintained by probably every school district in the United States. When a child is first enrolled in a school, his record is initiated with certain actuarial data (name, address, birthdate, and so forth). Each year the record is extended to include academic progress, results of standardized testing programs, and brief comments from his teacher. These cards or folders are valuable in initially becoming acquainted with children assigned to a classroom in a special problem area. Some teachers have been heard to say, "I never look at cumulative record cards before I meet my children." This attitude denies the value of records and an evidence-based, decision-making progress.

Several sociometric techniques are appropriate in assessing the social strata and makeup of a group of children. Questions such as, "Who would you choose to be on a social studies committee with you?" "Who is your best friend?" "Who would you select to lead our room in games?" elicit significant responses. These are often graphed into "sociographs" or "sociograms," which pictorially describe one dimension of social interrelationships as a specific point in time.

Performance tests are utilized to provide samples of manual dexterity skills. Crafts skills, handwriting, and manipulation of mechanical components can best be tested through actual performance with the teacher as a process observer or produce observer.

In the middle and upper grades, *autobiographies* indicate past occurrences that are significant to the child. He writes about those things that have happened to him that he feels are important. Careful and critical reading of them offer insights and information of value to the teacher.

Anecdotal records are short, concise statements about pupil activity and are usually taken over a period of time. Because events that happened several weeks ago are colored by succeeding events, reports written at the time are more valid than one's memory. Each anecdote is given perspective by a description of the time and setting of the event. Each anecdote is a normative account of a situation. The writer should carefully discriminate between a record of what happened and his own personal feelings about what happened. After many anecdotes have been recorded, the record may be read and evaluated. Events that seemed insignificant at the time take on new perspective when considered in a broader context.

Informal and Teacher-made Tests

Constructing tests to measure pupil attitude and achievement is one of the important yet least emphasized roles of the teacher. For the results of these tests form the basis for decisions that go far beyond their initial value—grades for report cards, pupil comparison with others, self-concept, and perception of self-worth. In this section, the various types of tests will be explored whereas the next section delineates procedures for relating measuring instruments of all types of objectives.

Some general suggestions for writing test items are summarized in the following statements, with a discussion of specific types of tests following:[6]

1. Test only the more important factors, avoiding the inconsequential or trivial.
2. Keep the reading difficulty level of the test low in relation to that of the class.
3. Eliminate ambiguous questions and directions.
4. State whose authority or opinion a question is based on, if it is based on opinion or authority.
5. Try to avoid using expressions with different meanings for different pupils.
6. Avoid questions that provide cues to the correct response for other questions.

Essay questions test the pupil's ability to organize his understanding concerning a problem and to communicate this in writing. The teacher can determine the problems to which a pupil is sensitive. How does he formulate his response? What range of intellectual resources does he muster? The essay type of question is particularly appropriate when the teacher does not wish to structure a pupil's response; when he wants the pupil to compare two ideas, events, people, or objects; when he wants the pupil to make a decision and explain why; or when he wants the pupil to write a summary.

Ambiguous essay questions that have no clear task are easy to prepare;

[6] W. Robert Houston, F. B. Blackington, and H. C. Southworth, *Professional Growth Through Student Teaching* (Columbus, Ohio: Merrill, 1965), p. 251.

but stating essay questions in such a way that content is sampled adequately, questions can be answered with some depth, and the result can be evaluated and compared with other pupils' answers is a difficult task. In preparing essay questions, it is usually more effective to include several questions that require shorter responses than a single more pervasive question. Prior to reading and scoring responses, the teacher should determine the criteria to be applied, weighing each criterion and indicator. To what extent will grammar and sentence structure be considered? Creativity of approach or ideas? Persuasiveness of arguments? Grasp of underlying concepts?

A *short answer* question is another form of a recall question, in which the answer is not provided the pupil. An incomplete sentence includes a blank in place of a significant idea. All too often this type is misused by abstracting a statement directly from the textbook (virtually causing the pupil to memorize the text) or is employed only to recall facts, not ideas. It has some advantages over essay questions in that scoring is more valid and a wider sample of content can be taken.

Two principles are considered in designing and marking short answer questions. First, the shorter the response required of the pupil, the more reliably the answer can be scored. And second, a scoring guide is prepared in advance that has specified alternate acceptable answers.

True-false questions consist of statements to be judged correct or not. A wide range of content can be sampled with this type of question, but the limitation of only two possible responses encourages mechanical guessing. This type is probably the most misused and poorly written objective-type question; this is true because of the *ambiguity* and *confusion* in the phrasing of the items. Each item must be true or false without qualification. Long and involved statements are to be avoided, as are interlocking statements and the use of specific determiners, such as no, always, never, only. Because they so often require only recall, true-false questions tap only low-level cognitive processes by pupils.

One variation sometimes combined with essay is to make a statement with which the pupil agrees or disagrees and then is asked to support his belief in a short paragraph.

The *multiple-choice* item is by far the most popular one in current use. An incomplete statement, or "stem," is followed by several alternate responses, one of which is significantly more appropriate than the others. Recall of factual data as well as generalizations can be tested with the item. Suggestions for writing such items would (1) include in the stem any words that would otherwise be repeated in each response; (2) avoid negatively stated items when possible; (3) make incorrect responses plausible and grammatically correct completions of the stem; and (4) have responses apply to answering the stem, not completing a sentence.

Measurement Related to Objectives

Chapter 3 explored various educational objectives. One illustrative objective was, "Can tell time by the hour, half hour, and minute intervals." With such a behaviorally orientated objective, it is readily possible to determine the extent to which a pupil or group of pupils function in relation to it. Pupil understanding can be measured by having pupils tell the time shown on prepared clock faces. Conversely, pupils can be asked to illustrate various specified times on a clock face. The evaluation program would be comprised of the full range of possibilities included in the objective, such as times set at the even hour, half hour, and minute. Measuring could be done by pencil-and-paper tests or through the use of real clocks or simulated clock faces. The *method of measurement* is a logical derivative of the stated objective. After the extent of pupil understanding of this objective has been determined, an evaluation of this measurement is in order. Based on this evaluation, further teaching procedures may or may not be in order.

Selecting appropriate measuring instruments requires consideration of the strengths and weaknesses of various data collection procedures, which have just been considered. After deciding on the data collecting procedures, appropriate testing items must be either selected or written.

Okey and Ciesla[7] suggest two rules for developing test items. First, *develop at least one test item for each objective.* The tendency is to write test items for only the most difficult objectives or to attempt to test several objectives with one item. Such a practice precludes pinpointing precisely where a pupil is having difficulty. When it is feasible, more than one test item should be written for each objective. Second, *use test items that* fit the objectives. "For example, an objective might be to 'prepare a wet-mount slide of an Elodea leaf.' Now if the test item for this objective asks the student to 'describe how a wet-mount slide is prepared,' something is wrong. The test item does not measure the behavior described in the objective."[8] Some assessment procedures are not appropriate for this objective; true-false or multiple-choice questions, for example, would not assess whether the pupil could "prepare a wet-mount slide." One must carefully consider the objective, and particularly the verb form, in considering the test item.

Howard J. Sullivan has suggested a continuum of action words used in objectives. Examine each set of verbs and consider the testing situation that is most appropriate:

[7] James R. Okey and Jerome L. Ciesla, *Teaching for Mastery* (Bloomington, Ind.: National Center for the Development of Training Materials in Teacher Education, Indiana University, 1972).

[8] Ibid., pp. 3–2.

1. Identify (equivalent terms and phrases—choose, compare, discriminate between or among, distinguish between or among, indicate, mark, match, select).
2. Name (equivalent terms and phrases—analyze, characterize, define, diagram, discuss, explain, replicate, report, represent, reproduce, tell how, tell what happens when).
3. Construct (equivalent terms and phrases—build, draw, formulate, make, prepare, synthesize).
4. Order (equivalent terms and phrases—arrange in a pattern, arrange in order, catalogue, categorize, classify, list in order, outline, write, relate, sequence).
5. Demonstrate (equivalent terms and phrases—perform an experiment, perform the steps, role-play, show the procedure, participate, show your work, simulate).[9]

Some of the terms just mentioned lead to convergent processes whereas others lead to divergent thinking. For example, the action word *identify* can result in convergent behavior in a testing situation ("identify or map the location of Moscow"). The same term can also be used for divergent thinking. (Identify as many ways as you can the means of measuring the length of our classroom.) In either case, the evaluation should be consistent with the action verb and with the intent of the objective. For some objectives, paper and pencil tests are adequate. For others, performance is required, with either observation of performance or written description of it as the mode of analysis. It is important, however, that teachers prepare or select *appropriate* test items and procedures for each objective.

STANDARDIZED TESTS

A balanced evaluation program includes not only personalized, particularized, teacher-made instruments, but also standardized tests that permit comparison with a wide sample of the population. Most school districts have established a comprehensive testing program whereby students are periodically tested with standardized instruments. Results for each individual child are recorded in his cumulative record folder and schoolwide scores are summarized; thus each can be compared with some norm or average for a general population. Unfortunately, some school people have misinterpreted the usefulness of such norms, interpreting them as a *standard* of achievement rather than as simply a description of the average attainment of a group. Rivlin emphasized the point and elaborated on it in the following statement:

[9] Philip G. Kapfer and Glen F. Ovard. *Preparing and Using Individualized Learning Packages for Ungraded, Continuous Progress Education* (Englewood Cliffs, N.J.: Educational Technology Publications, 1971), pp. 85–87.

The table of norms does not set the goal for any class, since it reflects nothing more than the average attainment of large groups of students, bright and dull, eager and apathetic, well-taught and incompetently taught, in well-equipped schools and in impoverished schools, etc. The National norms indicate what average (i.e., mediocre) students achieve when they attend average (i.e., mediocre) schools and are taught by average (i.e., mediocre) teachers. No teacher who is dissatisfied with mediocrity can accept norms as indicating the goals towards which he and his class must strive. On the other hand, under less favorable conditions, use of the norms as standards may set goals far beyond anything which these boys and girls can hope to achieve.[10]

Standardized tests are generally more refined than teacher-made tests, embodying careful writing, tryout, and rewriting of the test items. These are tested for reliability, validity, and objectivity. Instructions are written for administration of the test; a sample representative population is tested and norms are developed for the instrument.

Achievement tests are designed to test understanding in various content areas—science, social studies, mathematics, and in such areas as problem-solving or listening skills. Past experience and depth of understanding weigh heavily in performance on these tests. Some achievement tests sample general understanding; others are keyed to a specific published-text series, and still others are diagnostic in character—that is, they provide more than a total score; they suggest areas for reteaching. They are usually administered to groups of pupils and are designed for pupils at one grade level or a range of two or three grades (grades 1–3 or 4–6). The Sequential Tests of Education Progress (STEP), the Stanford Achievement Series, and the Iowa Basic Skills Tests are illustrations of achievement test series.

Results of intelligence tests are usually recorded as an intelligence quotient (I.Q.). This quotient is obtained by dividing mental age, as determined by the test, by chronological age, and multiplying by 100. Thus if mental age is 10 and chronological age is 10, the I.Q. is described as 100, average for his age. If, on the other hand, the mental age had been 12, the resulting I.Q. is 120.

Most schools administer group intelligence tests to pupils, sometimes administered by trained specialists, but usually by classroom teachers. Examples of such tests are the Otis Quick-Scoring Mental Ability Tests and the California Test of Mental Maturity. Because of the extensiveness of verbal aspects in such tests, results must be interpreted rather broadly for an individual child. Scores are seldom more than indications of ability. These tests are indirect measures of intelligence. They are indicants of this attribute. (Or is intelligence more than one attribute?) Individual intelligence tests are more reliable than group tests. They are administered by an

[10] Harry N. Rivlin, "The Teacher's Role in Achievement Testing," *Test Service Notebook*, No. 9 (New York: Harcourt, 1949), p. 2.

examiner to one pupil and therefore are time-consuming and expensive. Problems of a manipulative or nonverbal nature are utilized more extensively than with group tests. The more commonly used individual tests are the Stanford-Binet Scale and the Wechsler Intelligence Scale for Children. Both of these devices must be administered by trained specialists.

Projective techniques are even more indirect measures than the tests noted above. A person reacts to a stimulus (a blob of ink, a vague fuzzy picture), and his response is interpreted as indicating significant personality trends. Questions may be asked about likes, preferences, or desires. Clusters of responses tend to be associated with personality traits such as hostility, anxiety, regressive tendencies, and so forth. The Children's Apperceptive Technique (CAT) is one projective device employed in many schools.

Most standardized tests are called norms-referenced because their interpretation compares scores of pupils in a particular group with those in a more comprehensive population. These scores are often recorded in standard scores, percentiles, grade-level equivalence, or stanines.

Whereas *norm-referenced tests* compare the score of an individual with those of a normal group, *criterion-referenced* tests measure how well each pupil has attained stipulated objectives. Such objectives will have been written to include a behavior to be demonstrated, a standard of performance, and conditions under which the behavior is to be demonstrated. Criterion-referenced tests are used to determine whether or not the standard or criteria have been met. Most teacher-made instruments are of this type as well as many commercial tests related to particular curricula. They are particularly useful in diagnostic procedures.

Selecting an appropriate testing instrument from the many hundreds available is important. In some school districts a diagnostician or psychologist on the staff can provide guidance. Editions of *Mental Measurements Yearbook*, issues of the *Review of Educational Research* on "Education and Psychological Testing," bulletins of test publishers, and texts on measurement and evaluation are also of value in helping make valid judgments about appropriate tests.

Summary

Vital to educational decision-making of all sorts is evaluation. Without monitoring of goals and objectives and of activities designed to achieve them, little improvement in pupils or in the program would be possible. It is the catalyst in the education process and is also one of the more difficult and easily slighted of the teacher's roles.

An adequate evaluation program includes many closely spaced teacher-designed tests and informal assessments supported by a purposeful, organized standardized testing program.

1. Examine several achievement tests. How are they constructed? What directions are given for administration? What differences do you find among them?
2. What major classifications are found in Buros's *Mental Measurements Yearbook*? Your committee of teachers has been asked to select an achievement test battery in reading for the first grade. Using the yearbook, select one from reading the reviews and justify your selection.
3. In this chapter it is stated that "evaluation is teaching." Elaborate upon this statement.
4. From a curriculum guide, elementary school textbook, or other appropriate source, select three objectives and design appropriate testing instruments for them. Be sure at least one objective requires performance and at least one is a cognitive objective.
5. You have been asked to diagnose the mathematical achievement of a second-grade child. How would you begin? Upon what basis would you make items?
6. Evaluation of the effectiveness of a lesson is an important part of teaching. As a beginning teacher you have just completed teaching a concept of measurement. Select one of the measurement concepts listed in Chapter 2 as the concept developed. How would you evaluate the extent of pupil understanding of that concept? Be specific in your response; actually outline the procedure.

SELECTED BIBLIOGRAPHY

Armstrong, Robert J., et al. *The Development and Evaluation of Behavioral Objectives.* Worthington, Ohio: Charles A. Jones Pub. Co., 1970.
De Cecco, J. P. "How to Construct and Use Your Tests." *The Psychology of Learning and Instruction.* Englewood Cliffs, N.J.: Prentice-Hall, Inc., 1968.
———— "How to Interpret Standardized Test Scores," *The Psychology of Learning and Instruction.* Englewood Cliffs, N.J.: Prentice-Hall, Inc., 1968.
Educational Testing Service. *Tests and Measurements Kit.* Princeton, N.J.: Office of Information Service, Educational Testing Service.
Evaluation as Feedback and Guide. Ed. by Fred T. Wilhelms. Washington, D.C.· Association for Supervision and Curriculum Development, NEA, 1967
Gronlund, Norman E. *Measurement and Evaluation in Teaching.* 3rd ed. New York: Macmillan Publishing Co., Inc., 1976.
Johnson, Stuart R., and Rita B. Johnson. "Measuring Attainment of Objectives." *Developing Individualized Instructional Material.* Palo Alto, Calif.: Westinghouse Learning Press, 1970.

Klein, Stephen. "Evaluating Tests in Terms of the Information They Provide." *Evaluation Comment* 2, No. 2 (June 1970).

Popham, W. James, and Eva I. Baker. "The Evaluation of Instruction." *Systematic Instruction.* Englewood Cliffs, N.J.: Prentice-Hall, Inc., 1970.

TenBrink, Terry D. *Evaluation: A Practical Guide for Teachers.* New York: McGraw-Hill Book Company, 1974.

Townsend, Edward A., and Paul Burke. *Using Statistics in Classroom Instruction.* New York: Macmillan Publishing Co., Inc., 1975.

Tyler, Ralph W. *Educational Evaluation: New Roles, New Ideas.* Sixty-eighth Yearbook of the National Society for the Study of Education. Chicago: NSSE, 1969.

Chapter 13

Improving the Reporting of Pupil Progress

Practices of reporting pupil progress are in a state of continued change. A part of this change is the increased involvement of parents in all aspects of school activities and affairs. Parental involvement is the key phrase in programs that are funded by the federal government. Parents are becoming more involved in selection of teachers with screening committees that review applicants concurrent with school board personnel. In addition, school personnel instructional programs being considered for adoption are being previewed by parent groups. As parents serve as aids in the classroom and as volunteers in schools, they are becoming better informed about the aspects of school curricular design. This ever-increasing involvement of parents in all aspects of the school operation is having a decided impact upon reporting procedures.

Parents need to be brought into the formulation of a reporting system. They need to have an opportunity to understand the system and have direct input into changes that are being considered by the school. Some school districts have used extensive questionnaires to determine parental concerns.[1]

The more involved that parents become in the total operation of the school, the greater will be their input to the reporting procedures. At

[1] Marcella H. Nerbovig and Herbert J. Klausmeier, *Teaching in the Elementary School*, 4th ed. (New York: Harper, 1974), pp. 135–137.

times in the past, the lack of involvement and understanding on the part of parents has caused considerable confusion in changed reporting practices. Seemingly, as the rate of change continues to accelerate in schools, the need for involved parents in school affairs would dictate constantly upgraded reporting practices.

The objectives that follow should guide your study of this chapter:

1. The reader will be able to identify strengths and weaknesses of each of the following procedures of reporting pupil progress:
   (a) Report cards.
   (b) Narrative statements.
   (c) Parent-teacher conferences.
2. The reader will be able to select an appropriate procedure for reporting pupil progress for any reporting situation that might occur.
3. The reader will be able to communicate with pupils and parents in matters relating to an individual student's progress.

REPORT CARDS

The term *report card* has become firmly imprinted in the minds of American parents. It is the bench mark by which most parents measure the progress of their children in school. Most school systems in the United States have developed a report card in some manner unique to that system. In many instances, report cards will differ between buildings within the same school district. However, in spite of this uniqueness, report cards are similar enough to enable most parents to accept and understand them.

The basic purpose of reporting systems is to transmit to parents the school's appraisal of their children's development in school. Many attempts have been made to insure accurate and precise communication. Each plan has been limited in its usefulness in one way or another. At one time, schools generally employed a highly refined numerical scale. The grading on the reporting scale (0–100) was too fine for the evaluative devices that were available. It was somewhat like the man who described the length of a road in fractions of an inch, even though his measuring stick was calibrated only in feet.

Some schools adopted letter grades, such as A, B, C, D, and F, to provide a broader classification of student's work. This method of grading is still quite common today. However, some schools have found that letter grades do not adequately convey meanings intended by teachers and have adopted still other approaches. Among common procedures adopted is that of assigning a grade of either "satisfactory" or "unsatisfactory" in each of the curricular areas. Still others make use of plus or minus signs, or abbreviations such as *E* for excellent, *S* for satisfactory, and *U* or *N* for unsatisfactory. In general, these attempts to clarify grades for teachers, pupils, and parents have only served to confuse everyone. Broad classifications often have proved unsatisfactory to parents because too little information was transmitted. Parents do not feel well enough informed about their child's progress to know if he is doing satisfactory work in all areas of the curriculum. This confusion has prompted some schools to revert back to the use of letter grades, or in some instances to numerical ratings.

In other instances, an additional attempt has been made to clarify grades by utilization of a dual method of reporting pupil progress. Under this procedure, a child receives two grades in each subject. One grade signifies the student's attitude, aptitude, and progress. The second grade indicates the pupil's achievement in comparison with other children in the same grade. A pupil might receive grades of *A* and *D* in reading on one report. If he were from a limited environmental background and yet making significant improvement in reading, a grade of *A* for the first mark is certainly justified. However, in spite of the pupil's efforts, he might still be far below the achievement norm in the classroom and thus receive the second grade of *D*. Dual marking procedures are not always understood by elementary school pupils, for if one of the two marks received in any area is an *A*, a child tends to be pleased and satisfied. Children frequently total the *A*'s on their report cards, combining both marks, and compare these totals with each other. One child will say, "I have fourteen *A*'s and six *B*'s," and another may respond, "I got sixteen *A*'s and four *B*'s." A rather common reaction from parents is a weighting of the two marks. The deep-rooted tradition of grades leads to an overconcern for the grade that indicates rank in class and less concern about the grade indicating pupil effort.

Much of the confusion and concern about reporting practices stems from the assignment of an impossible task to report cards. The report card is not a vehicle capable of conveying much of the meaning intended by the reporter. A mark of *B* in reading is both a reward and a punishment to the recipient, and it serves to report very little. To the person who receives a *B*, the message is that he has done better than the majority (reward) but not as well as the best (punishment). An underlying message says, "I expect you to do better." However, the grade of *B* does not make explicit just how he can do better. The actual reporting is slight, for the *B* does not tell the student why he received a *B* rather than an *A* or a *C*.

To illustrate further this point, let us look at two fifth-grade pupils— each received a letter grade of *B* in arithmetic. One pupil was graded *B* because he was able to solve word problems very well but made errors in computation. The second pupil was graded *B* because he was very accurate in computational skills but had difficulty in solving word problems. The grade of *B* fails to communicate adequately actual achievement to either the child or the parent.

Because of the desire of teachers to do a better job of communicating meanings to parents, supplemental reporting procedures have been adopted. A survey of urban school districts reported by the National Education Association in 1961[2] revealed a definite trend toward use of supplements to report cards in schools. It also indicated that the traditional "report card" continues to be used by an overwhelming majority of elementary schools.

In spite of its many limitations, the report card serves as a vital link between home and school. It has become so firmly intrenched in the educational scene that its absence is missed and lamented by parents. In addition to the report card, supplemental means are utilized to improve communication between parents, teachers, and students.

Narrative Statements

Some report cards provide a limited space for teacher comments in addition to a place for the grades. These comments may be considered a form of narrative reporting, but they usually are very sketchy and nonexplanatory. Although such remarks are of some value in the interpretation of grades, they do not adequately substitute for a narrative statement.

The most satisfactory narrative reports are those that permit the teacher to report in detail those areas where a pupil shows strengths or weaknesses. Although a letter long enough to do justice to various curricular areas is time-consuming to write, it can be valuable to the pupil, the parent, and the school.

A paragraph explaining the circumstances and results of a pupil's achievement in reading can rather precisely inform parents just how well their child is progressing. By sharing this letter with the pupil, the teacher is able to support the child in his efforts to improve, to point out specific causes of trouble, and to suggest avenues of assistance.

The narrative report possesses an important public relations potential. A parent who is well informed about his child's progress will often tend to support his schools. The narrative report permits the teacher to share efforts being made to assist the pupil. The teacher is given an opportunity to explain the accomplishments and problems of each child. This ingredient is lacking when a letter grade is the sole reporting medium.

Some dangers exist in using the narrative method of reporting. Unless a teacher is careful in construction of the letter, the explanation can prove

[2] "Reporting to Parents," *NEA Research Bulletin*, 39:74 (Feb. 1961).

more difficult to understand than a letter grade. When a teacher makes use of terms common in teaching circles, he may fail to communicate the intended meaning to a parent. Herein lies one of the greatest limitations of the narrative statement. The communiqué is a one-way street, and there is always the danger of misunderstandings. Unless the parents respond by either sending a note back to school or asking a question about the report, the teacher cannot be certain that the letter accomplished its objective.

A parent's reaction to narrative statements is generally positive and sometimes tends to be overwhelming. On occasion, one of the writers was talking with a neighbor in his hometown. The neighbor, who was a lathe operator in a local factory, pulled from his pocket a well-worn letter. This letter, written in longhand, was a narrative report from a third-grade teacher about the progress of his nine-year-old daughter. With a combination of pride and respect, this man related how he felt about his daughter's accomplishments and his daughter's teacher. The letter was straightforward and simply worded, with the message about progress in reading, writing, and arithmetic well expressed. "This is the kind of teacher who should get a blank check each month rather than the $300 granted by the Board of Education to all teachers," he remarked. "Do you realize how long it would have taken her to write a letter like this for every child in the classroom!"

How long does it take to write a letter of this kind? The average letter can be composed in less than thirty minutes. It is difficult to imagine the degree to which home-school relations could be improved if every elementary school teacher took time to write one or two letters a year for each child in her classroom.

When a child is used as a messenger in delivery of a narrative statement or a report card, there is a potential hazard. Fear of unknown contents will do little except build anxieties in the mind of the pupil. Therefore, it is well for the teacher to review the report with the child before placing it in an envelope. This sharing between teacher and pupil also tends to strengthen classroom rapport for future working relationships.

Whenever any narrative report is made, a teacher needs to be considerate of the feelings of parents as well as convey the message that is intended. It is just as easy to write a tactful statement as a blunt one. For example, a teacher could write, "John does not get along with other children. He picks fights and is always hitting boys and girls. Other children don't like him," or he could say, "John continues to have difficulty in learning to associate and work with his peers in the classroom."

Some critics of the narrative report indicate that grades are more easily determined and far less time-consuming. Others indicate it is difficult to know enough about individual children to write reports of this nature.

A typical letter sent by a teacher might be the following:

Dear Mr. and Mrs. Smith,

Your son Jim is "all boy" and a real joy to have in my fifth grade. Jim is a leader in our classroom and is frequently elected to leadership roles such as committee chairman, project leader, and team captain by his classmates. As a leader he is considerate of the feelings of other children, and I am sure that other children respect him for this.

Jim is continuing to do well in reading. He is in the top reading group, and his comprehension and vocabulary continue to be above average for the fifth grade. Because of his good work habits and reading ability, Jim does well in other areas that require reading and imagination. He does very good work in social studies, science, and language skills. We are currently writing a book of tall tales, and Jim has contributed several stories, which I will send home with him when the book is completed. He is quite creative and his stories are very good.

The two areas where Jim still has some need for improvement are his handwriting and arithmetic. Jim has many interests, and these cause him to hurry through his work, which results in poor letter formation and handwriting that is not his best work. Jim and I have talked about this several times, and when I remind him frequently enough, he does make a special effort.

Although Jim is doing very well with our new work in fractions, he still does not check his work as carefully as he might and therefore is prone to make careless errors. Jim understands the concepts we are working with in arithmetic, and when he is concerned and careful, he can do well.

Jim's interest in athletics continues, and he is well coordinated for a boy who is growing as fast as he is at this time. He is a very happy boy and certainly enjoys living to the fullest extent. Jim is always courteous to adults. His interests and enthusiasm makes him a pleasure to the other children and myself.

Sincerely,

PARENT-TEACHER CONFERENCES

The earliest type of parent-teacher conferences were those formal meetings between school officials and parents who were called in the process of suspending a student from school. A meeting between a teacher and a parent was almost sure to compound the woes of any inept scholar.

Parent-teacher conferences have progressed a long way since that time. Conferences are commonplace today, with many schools providing released time for teachers to schedule conferences during school hours with all parents. The purpose of these conferences is to inform and discuss rather than chastise students. Conferences provide a means whereby a teacher can interpret to parents expectations of the school and classroom. It is a time when teachers can interpret test results and inform parents of just what a C in reading might mean on a report card. This two-way communication does much to assist parents in understanding both the objectives of the school and their child's progress. In this way it is possible for the parents to become familiar with the goals of the school and ways in which parents can complement teacher's efforts. Teachers also may use this conference time to assist parents in planning for the education of their children.

Parents sometimes fear conferences with teachers because of negative feelings about themselves or memories of prior relations with school. Because of this, teachers need to approach each conference in a manner that will put parents at ease. Plans for opening each conference need to be in terms of the pupil, the parent, and the objectives of the meeting. Above all, the teacher must have his objective for the conference clearly in mind. It does little good to be completely negative in a conference. It would be disastrous to the ego of a parent to hear a long list of problems without any knowledge of achievements and without suggested solutions to problems. For this reason, the teacher must clearly understand the specific point or points he wishes to make during the conference. These points can be made in such a manner that the parent is not forced to become defensive; the areas of need should be looked upon with mutual concern rather than as shortcomings of the pupil or parent. The parent must be given the feeling that the objective of the conference is to inform him of how the school is working to assist the child and how the home can also assist.

It is well to keep in mind that the criticisms a teacher may make about a child may be the first such direct remarks of this nature to be heard by a parent. Before a child attends school, relatives and friends tend to comment only on his positive characteristics. It may be a real jolt to a parent to discover that Sally is not perfect, even though this information is sandwiched between positive comments.

Often a child is more cooperative and easier for a teacher to work with after the parent conference. The reason for this is not always understood. Actually, a child generally looks forward to the time his parents will come to school for conferences with the teacher. This extra effort on the part of his parents and his teachers makes him feel important and pleased to think that they are going to talk about him.

Some teachers dread conference time. If the teacher prepares for the conference and then is tactful and considerate of the feelings of the parent, no conflict should result. This is not to say that conference time is easy for either parent or teacher, for both are under stress. The parent arrives with a feeling of anxiety, hopeful of hearing good things about his child and apprehensive about being told of shortcomings that would result in criticism of himself as a parent. The teacher might be hopeful that all is ideal, but knows that this is not always the case. Wanting to be objective and truthful and yet not destructive, he is anxious for fear of offending the parent or in turn being criticized for not having provided sufficient opportunity for the child to learn. The very least that results is a day of hard work for the teacher, but a great deal of satisfaction with his efforts. It is common to hear teachers comment on how much better they know a child after parent conferences than they did before that time. It is also common for parents to relate that the conference went better than they had expected and that they were satisfied with the progress of their child.

Parent-teacher conferences can provide teachers with a wealth of information about children that other reporting practices fail to capture. A first-grade child suddenly begins to have trouble getting along with other children. For no apparent reason he cries during the day. His earlier interest in reading seems to have suddenly abated and he spends his time daydreaming and playing. In addition, he is frequently and sporadically absent from school, although his previous attendance record had been very good. At the same time his father and mother have just concluded a matrimonial struggle that has resulted in the father's moving out of the home. The mother is left with three small children, only one of them in school. The legal involvement in separation and divorce procedures necessitate the mother's being gone from home for periods of time when she had previously been at home. The mother is so involved with problems at home and with adjusting to the new expectations of family, neighbors, and children that the school is not informed of the domestic difficulties that exist.

Through a conference with the mother, information about the home situation may be obtained. Together, parent and teacher can work on procedures that will result in greater security for the child and enhance his learning. Without this type of communication, a teacher may misinterpret the behavior of the child and react in a negative manner that confuses him. He may interpret his father's leaving as rejection, and then because of fear of losing his mother, he may daydream at school. This will get him into academic trouble and teacher's reaction may lead him to interpret further rejection of him by the teacher. Under conditions such as this it is unlikely that any progress will be made in learning to read. For such reasons the learning tasks require maximum communication between home and school.

Many parents welcome having teachers assist them in providing educational opportunities for their children. Parents often use the conference time to find out about books to purchase for their children or to learn how to assist their children in making use of the public library. The parent of a bright child can be informed of his child's potential in order that he can begin to plan for a higher education while the pupil is still in elementary school. Often parents do not consider a college education as a possibility for their child early enough to plan for the financial pinch that will occur when the time comes to enroll in college. This is especially true when few, if any, members of the family have attended college. Counsel from a teacher may make the difference in deciding whether or not a child will have the opportunity to attend college.

There is a special need for teachers to assist parents of children from lower socioeconomic areas in school-related matters. Frequently, these children come from large families and need assistance in developing good relations among siblings at home. Every child should have a place where he can read and study without being bothered by younger or older brothers and sisters. The rights of individuals within the home need to be respected if we are to expect a pupil to consider the rights of other children in the classroom. During conferences parents can receive suggestions on ways to help their children develop responsibilities at home that will further aid their learning in school. When the teacher works with administrators, community school directors, and parents in this manner, the maximum improvement of learning for children becomes possible.

Often there are advantages to be gained by having three-way conferences between teacher, parent, and pupil, especially in the upper elementary grades. A conference such as this can assist a pupil in understanding the mutual concern that teacher and parents have for his academic and social welfare. It also becomes possible during a conference to find joint solutions to problems that are identified or to fulfilling needs that exist. If a pupil has a particular talent, such as music, a commitment by a parent could involve an initial investment of several hundred dollars for an instrument. When the pupil understands his economic obligation and his talent that both parents and teacher recognize and wish to foster, he will be aware of the role he will be expected to fulfill. At times a child may identify problems that confront him as a pupil in complying with requests of his family and school. The three-way conference makes possible an immediate proposal to enable the pupil to work toward successful solution to these problems. Joint solutions to needs and problems that are worked out between parents, teacher, and pupil result in fewer misunderstandings and therefore have a greater likelihood of follow-through than is true in the two-way conference.

TEACHER-PUPIL CONFERENCES

Many teachers schedule individual conferences with pupils during the school year. Often these conferences are scheduled prior to other reporting periods or parent conferences. The pupil is provided an opportunity to discuss progress, concerns, and teacher expectation during the conference.

When opportunities for this kind of conference are provided for pupils, the communication between teacher and pupil becomes much more open. Certainly, it is a far cry from the anxiety-ridden practice of the past when report cards or messages were sealed documents to be transmitted by the pupil to parents without explanation of the content. Utilization of the teacher-pupil conference is a valuable tool for teachers to understand better the individuality of pupils in a class. Each pupil has an opportunity to express beliefs, desires, and concerns to the teacher. It is also a procedure to provide feedback to both teacher and pupil about the learning situation in the classroom.

INCIDENTAL REPORTING

Far too little reporting of a positive incidental nature is done by elementary school teachers. If a teacher has a problem with a child that persists over a period of time, the parents' assistance is frequently enlisted. This may be in the form of a phone call or a note. Although this type of communication between teacher and parents is frequently beneficial, it generally requires a traumatic experience. This need not be so. When a child is moved to a higher reading group, a note of commendation should be sent to the parents. When a child makes a unique contribution in any area, a note or phone call of recognition should follow. When a child performs a noteworthy accomplishment, the parent should be informed of the achievement. Reporting of this kind requires only a few moments of a teacher's time and can provide a means to improved rapport and learning in the classroom. Parents appreciate hearing good news from school. Positive reports elicit greater accomplishment and potentially more praise. This cyclic effect can lead to nothing but further improvement. When parents hear of progress, they feel more positive toward the role of the school and are then willing to assist schools to do an even better job. Parents will reward their children with praise for accomplishment and thus improve the self-image of the child. The child will react by increased efforts to do even better school work. We all enjoy doing things at which we are successful. Good dancers enjoy dancing and therefore tend to become better dancers. If a person dislikes dancing, he does not dance and therefore will not improve as a dancer and likes it even less. The same is true of a child who is successful in school. If he is successful and is rewarded, he will strive for additional successes. If school is a negative experience, he will attempt to shun all school-related experiences in favor of a more rewarding conquest.

Some children share their school experiences with parents in a manner that provides an open communication between the classroom and the home. However, not all children will tell about happenings at school.

When a child has a piece of his art work selected for display in the all-city art festival, parents should be informed by the teacher. A distinction such as this should not be left to the chance that either the child will tell his parents or that they will discover his work when attending the festival or they will read about it later in the newspaper.

There are some dangers inherent in the informal reporting of incidents. A teacher who makes it a point to call a number of parents each week to complain about the progress of children can do a great disservice to the child, the school, and the parents. When incidental reporting is negative, it loses its supportive impact upon the learning of the pupil. The school becomes the source of irritating phone calls about needs of pupils that parents may assume to be the responsibility of the school. The teacher becomes a figure to be feared by both the pupil and the parents. When a phone call from the teacher means trouble, few parents look forward to calls from school.

Some teachers often informally report progress to their pupils. Recently, one of the authors observed a student teacher in a fourth-grade classroom. A girl brought a short story to the teacher at the conclusion of a language arts lesson. Looking at the paper, the student teacher remarked, "That certainly is a neat paper," and after a pause continued, "but then, your papers are always neat and well done, aren't they?" The young girl beamed from ear to ear, and you can be sure that the next paper was at least as neat as the previous one. With praise such as this communicated by a teacher to a pupil, it becomes possible for a teacher to encourage outstanding achievements from children.

Reporting of this nature is not scheduled by a school district. It is not explicit in expectations of a teacher's responsibilities. However, it is up to each individual teacher to do as he sees fit. In the hands of a sincere, skilled teacher, it can provide the means to improved pupil-teacher relationship as well as improved teacher-community relationship. If all teachers are alert to the improvements made by children in their daily work and follow honest accomplishments with commendation, much can be gained. Reporting of this form is greatly needed in our schools and will accomplish more than can be imagined when it is employed.

COMMUNITY-SCHOOL REPORTING

Parents are concerned about the quality of instruction in their schools. They frequently are well informed about the quantitative aspects—total number of pupils at each grade level, classroom size, and classroom needs. Of equal importance is information about the quality of local educational programs. Some schools report this information through PTA meetings, but many working parents find it impossible to attend these sessions. A large segment of the population does not have school-age children and is not reached through school-centered activities. Teachers can work with administrators in providing data to the community through mass media. Newspaper articles about school events and changes in curriculum can keep adults in the community informed of progress. Whenever exciting or exceptional activities occur at school, the news photographer welcomes the opportunity to be invited in sharing the event with adults through pictures in the local paper.

Whenever radio or television programs include children participating in activities, there is interest on the part of adults in the community. Many events in elementary schools can easily be programmed and made available for public edification. Teaching in isolation from other adults is becoming a thing of the past. The increased level of education of parents in America today demands improved communication between home and school. Innovations such as nongrading, multigrading, and team teaching enable teachers to perceive their role in a new perspective.

Ease of communication through television, video tapes, and radio open an expanded network for all adults to understand better the schools within their community. Utilization of opportunities for dissemination of information about the quality of education will not achieve maximum enhancement without a deliberate effort on the part of members of the teaching profession. An expanded role in providing information about all phases of education to the community could do much to establish a sound basis for future change and improvement in educational programs.

A TRANSITION IN REPORTING

Over the years there has been an evolving pattern of school-home reporting. There was a time when the education of a child received in school was viewed as being apart from the education outside of school. However, through a better understanding of learning, less distinction is made between learning sources. The interdependence of home, community, and school learning has been recognized and is just beginning to be capitalized upon. Just as the bond between home and school has become strengthened, so also has a better understanding of the role of teachers developed. Parents no longer view teachers as people with all the correct answers. As the general educational level of the population has risen, a more realistic and understanding view of the teacher has evolved. This has made it easier for parents and teachers to communicate about academic progress, much to the benefit of children.

However, this changing role of the teacher has increased the necessity for teachers to assist parents in helping their children learn. An important and, in many instances, new function of teachers is to assist parents to provide a suitable attitude toward school and learning.

In instances where a child needs aid, the school can be of assistance in providing counseling for parents. Good rapport between home and school can be established by encouraging parents to ask their children about school daily. In addition, teachers can and should encourage children to discuss school events with their parents. A review of the day's program and highlighting events before dismissal can do much toward achievement of this goal.

With sound rapport teachers can further assist parents in formation of a structural environment for children to work and play within. All children need a quiet time, a study time, and a play time in their schedules. Some children need to be protected from their siblings, so that younger or older children do not take advantage of them. Teachers can assist parents in development of responsibility through care of personal belongings and the establishment of some routines. In busy homes, where more than one television set is becoming commonplace, some children soon master the technique of "blocking out" all noise. This habit may be of use in play at home, but, when carried over to the school, may result in a serious learning handicap.

The professional teacher of today has a responsibility to children both in school and at home. He can be of great assistance to children in his classroom by work with parents. The role of the teacher in assisting parents in the educational process is just beginning to develop its latent potential. Through continued efforts, great strides in pupil achievement may be made. The reporting process provides the key to unlocking this latent potential in learning for many students.

SUMMARY

With the increasing demand by parents and the general public for accountability comes an increasing responsibility for educators to improve their reporting practices of pupil progress. The primary purpose of reporting pupil progress is to establish and maintain effective communication between school, home, and community. Some of the strengths and weaknesses of various existing reporting techniques, that is, report cards, narrative statements, parent-teacher conferences, and teacher-pupil conferences, have been explored in this chapter. The constantly changing picture of reporting practices indicates that most schools are experimenting to find a satisfactory procedure or combination of procedures. Those most concerned —pupils, teachers, parents, and representative citizens of the community— should be involved in developing reporting procedures and techniques.

This seems to be the present trend. Hopefully, this trend will lead to reporting practices that maximize the learning opportunities of children.

SUGGESTED ACTIVITIES

1. Write a letter to a parent indicating that a student is not performing up to capacity and that his work is frequently incomplete. Do not offend the student or parent, but be frank in your concern.
2. Arrange to sit in on a conference between another teacher and parent and observe the process of communication between them.
3. Arrange a conference with a student and discuss his progress with him. Be sure to listen to the student's self-assessment of his progress and his concern about the learning activities.
4. You have been Henry's teacher for the past five months. His school records indicate an above average intelligence, good health, and a seemingly good home situation. Henry is now in his fourth year of school. Each year he has experienced considerable difficulty with most phases of school work. His parents have always shown interest and have been cooperative. They are now much concerned about their son's lack of progress and have called, requesting an appointment with you next Thursday. They claim the last two report cards have told them little or nothing about their son's school experiences.

    What are some of the topics you think should be discussed? What preparation would you make for the conference to help insure that positive communication occurs?

SELECTED BIBLIOGRAPHY

Ediger, M. "Reporting Pupil Progress; Alternative To Grading." *Educational Leadership*, **32**:253–56 (Jan. 1975).
Feddersen, J. Jr. "Establishing an Effective Parent-Teacher Communication System." *Childhood Education*, **49**:75–79 (Nov. 1972).
Giannangelo, D. M., and K. Y. Lee. "At Last: Meaningful Report Cards; Computer Assisted Reporting to Parents," *Phi Delta Kappan*, **55**:630–31 (May 1974).
Kahl D. H. "Talking About The Child's Program," *Today's Education*, **62**:34–35 (Feb. 1973).
Nerbovig, Marcella H., and Herbert J. Klausmeier. *Teaching in the Elementary School*. 4th ed. New York: Harper and Row, 1974.
"Reporting to Parents," *NEA Research Bulletin No. 39*, Feb. 1961.
Walling, D. S. "Designing a Report Card That Communicates," *Educational Leadership*, **32**:258–60 (Jan. 1975).
Wiseman, S. "Educational Obsticle Race; Factors That Hinder Pupil Progress," *Educational Research*, **15**:87–93 (Feb. 1973).

Chapter 14

Your Professional Role as a Teacher

Teaching has never been an easy task. In the erratic growth patterns of civilization, teachers have been commonly distinguished by the contribution of their efforts to particular successes of a nation or culture, but the distinction between personal and professional role is frequently fuzzy. We revere, if not envy, the impact of Plato or Socrates as teacher-philosophers, but are less familiar with the day-by-day trials that faced them as educational leaders and innovators of method. In the earlier days of Mediterranean trading, we uneasily accept the revelation that the more successful teachers and practitioners of mirror manufacturing, for example, were respected and well paid and occupied posts of unusual responsibility in the communities—and were forbidden to leave the city or country under threat of death. Their knowledge was so prized and their techniques and methods so skilled that they constituted a national monopoly. When they were apprehended in attempts to leave their schools or sites of employment to share knowledge with other cultures, they were summarily maimed or executed. Our problems with censorship of printed materials today bears some of the same overtones, but, fortunately, associated teachers and authors do not face death or disfigurement in their involvement.

Once knowledge could be exported and spread throughout the world through written communication, many national and political organizations developed around teachers as personal tutors for families or small social groups. Most frequently, these teachers were foreign to the culture and were indentured captives of national conquests. The Roman Empire rested for many centuries on this tutorial system of "second culture" instruction (especially in the middle and upper class socioeconomic families) until the strength and ideas of the indentured teachers helped topple the political organization. In colonial America, the "better" education for children again came from family tutors (frequently foreign educated) or private schools. Simplified, it meant the more affluent children had the opportunity for superior educational opportunities.

As schools rather than individual family education began to educate the majority of eligible school children, the need for full-time teachers emerged, although the professionals as we know them today did not appear quickly. As late as the fifties of this century, elementary education instruction was certified to teachers with educational backgrounds running from eighth-grade graduates to those completing a normal training program of a two-year duration. Teachers were encouraged to follow textbook suggestions faithfully to reap classroom success.

> It is the intention of the authors to include sufficient discussion and directions to teachers so that this book may be taught with the highest possible degree of efficiency.[1]

To meet this expectation, specific points of method for teaching grades fourth through eighth were highlighted:

1. The teacher must test her pupils on each lesson before they begin to study.
2. Each pupil should study only the words which he misspelled on this test.
3. Each pupil must be taught an economical method of studying.
4. Each pupil must see clearly what progress he is making.
5. The teacher must follow the distribution of the controlled reviews.
6. The teacher must strive constantly to develop sound purposes and interests.[2]

The rigidity of method identified with early teachers in many instances resulted in part from the attempts of textbook authors and experienced teachers to provide an all-inclusive, step-by-step teaching model for the often ill-prepared teaching novice. Once confidence and success were realized in the classroom, however, the opportunities to innovate and depart

---

[1] Ernest Horn and Ernest Ashbaugh. *The Horn-Ashbaugh Fundamentals of Spelling* (Philadelphia: Lippincott, 1928), p. iii.

[2] Ibid., p. xii.

from an established format awaited the yet-to-be-realized independence of the organized teaching profession.

Prior to the World War II period of 1918–20, a high percentage of the teachers of elementary school were part-time teachers, normal training program graduates (8–14 grade completion plus summer term extension work) and college graduates of academic disciplines who were temporarily certified on a year-by-year basis. But as population growth continued and local community expectancies for education increased, individual states began raising teacher certification minimums so that a comparable image of a professional teacher could be recognized. For the first time in educational history, an elementary teacher was recognized as one who was specifically prepared for teaching in the schools with minimum specified competencies for development of children in skills, understanding, habits, and community expectancies. Specific compensation scales became common in most states by the late 1950s and frequently were tied to teaching experience and levels or steps of professional preparation. Belated recognition of *differences* in teacher preparation and experience was now evidenced in salary scales and eventually in teacher tenure.

But the increased competencies of professional teachers of the elementary school were quickly met by increased responsibilities, changes in the teaching environment, and widened community expectancies. Improved teacher competencies and strategies cannot aid the instructional process if the original parameters of teacher role are excessively expanded. Professional teacher organizations took a stronger role in representing the classroom teachers in their attempts to exert some desired control over the countless variables that make teaching the complex skill that it is. Paralleling these moves by professional organizations at the local, state, and national levels was the success of labor and trade unions in gaining recognition for members' concerns in areas of compensation, working conditions, medical assistance, and retirement benefits. With the increasing costs of teacher preparation, certification, and professional involvement activities, teacher groups moved quickly to collective bargaining in efforts to improve their professional stature and to be assured that factors that influenced the teaching environment itself were within their responsibility and negotiable. In short, teaching was more than a common skill of any citizen—more than an art expression—more than a role for a part-time specialist in academic discipline—certainly not a position for an underling or an underprepared graduate of a summer term normal training session. The professional teacher had arrived—and at a time that society has some of its greatest needs, expectancies, and problems. If success breeds upon societal controversy, the elementary teacher of the last quarter of the twentieth century will have no equal. It *is* possible to accept the possibility that the development of the professional teacher for the elementary school over centuries of civilization is now reaching a point of unparalleled advancement and is in a most enviable position to initiate major improvements in the society that it serves. But is that more philosophical than pragmatic? Can we succeed in the classroom and fail in society? What issues are developing as major challenges to professionalism?

Without valid insight or prediction or confidence for the future of specific concerns of professional teachers of the elementary school, it would seem advantageous to identify and examine some of the issues confronting the classroom teacher. As a result of this study, we should be able to

1. Identify and describe the major tenets of professionalism in the teaching profession.
2. Recognize and sequence the evolving factors of teaching that have led to teaching professionalization.
3. Describe and compare the major challenges to the professionalization of teaching.
4. Categorize and identify the developments in teacher certification and contracting.
5. Identify and compare the reaction of the teaching profession to changing societal expectations.

PROFESSIONAL IDENTITY

In the early years of commercial television, the portrayal of a teacher by the actress Eve Arden was acclaimed. Miss Brooks, as enacted by Arden, personified the American school teacher in the eyes, if not the heart, of TV viewers. Her sex, race, clothing, hairstyling and extracurricular activities seemed to match with the image of the teacher held by the viewing public. Reruns of the original series after an interval of ten to fifteen years still find a receptive consumer market.

But to many teachers, Miss Brooks projected an image that was extinct stereotyping. They objected to her "old-maid teacher" hairstyle, her fear of the administration, and the contrast between her life-style and that of a realistic school community. Successive television series have responded to the range of opinion with teachers and schools covering educational enterprises from ghetto to private sectors, multiracial teachers, freewheeling students, and issues embracing moral, spiritual, and social overtones.

Today it is difficult to establish the identity of a "typical" professional teacher in the beginning years of service. We have some demographic clues to cite that the beginner is a woman, young, a four-year college graduate, who has successfully completed student teaching, is a member of a professional teachers organization, and will teach in a self-contained classroom in an elementary school. Even these characteristics are changing with the other elements of society, but of particular importance is the self-image that the individual teacher would like to embrace. Following are educational portraits of two elementary teachers, Martha and Ann. They are cast in different periods of educational history and were originally designed to contrast the role of the teacher in the community.

Since their creation, however, a number of teachers and parents have "polished" the versions portrayed by adding personal details that they have experienced or have encountered in conversations with other teachers. As Ann and Martha were discussed and developed, therefore, they became more than contrasting examples of teachers living in differing times of educational history . . . they are now composite examples of two teachers with differing responsibilities, expectations, and life-styles. To many teachers now, Ann and Martha are *not* identities separated by five or six decades of history. Rather, both *can* and *do exist* today, and neither Martha nor Ann can be cast as a model of a professional elementary teacher.

The situation is intriguing from the viewpoint that teachers are not what many professional organizations, universities, state certification boards and school patrons feel that they are or should be. To those who believe that there should be more Marthas, the lack of a bachelor's degree is insignificant. Professionals are relevant, they claim, and success in the classroom should not be tied to the number of courses completed or to the color of a teaching certificate. Supporters of Ann counter that the future of our society rests with the education of urban youth rather than the rural or suburban schools—they cannot envision a Martha existing in an inner-city school.

Fortunately, no all-encompassing portrait of a professional teacher can be painted. No one image can include the increasingly wide variation of individuals that, collectively, are teaching in our schools. But the aspirations of their personal commitment to teaching tends to cluster within a philosophical encirclement of professionalism . . . an agreement of purpose and dedication. Beyond that point, the pragmatic means of approach and accomplishment differs widely.

Examine the portraits of Martha and Ann for professional agreement and differences. Note that they are influenced by many pressures both intrinsic and extrinsic. Does either have a sure "professional" image as you envision her? Could you work with either or both of them in an elementary school?

Two Professional Teachers

MARTHA.   Martha was hired as an elementary teacher in 1910 by the community to accomplish certain specific things with and for children of the community. Society had identified areas of responsibility for her involvement with children and expected minimum performances, to say the least. Children in school were to be taught in a manner of tradition, and Martha's role was primarily (and in many instances completely) to follow established procedures to realize expected results. In a sense, her total expectancy in the community was to enact the role of instructional leadership in the manner that society had previously established.

Respect and community acceptance for "the teacher" was traditional, and her compensation, although small, was again representative of how the school patrons evaluated her in a service capacity. Her position like that of the minister and the librarian was on a year-by-year arrangement so that philosophical conflict could be readily concluded at contract-signing time or, if necessary, instant dismissal could be ordered by the school board if open differences of opinion threatened traditional practices.

Martha was expected to mirror an image of teaching. She attended church, purchased necessities of life from local stores, lived in the community, and was not expected to appear prominently in local society or newspaper features. She, like community children, was to be seen but not heard in community matters. There were exceptions, of course, as communities and individuals do differ. Some of Martha's friends sang in local church choirs or directed them. Rural school teachers were expected to present seasonal school plays, open houses, and musical recitals, but often were "boarded" in school board members homes in an effort to develop closer community ties.

Martha was a high school graduate (a bit unusual for her age group) and attended for a full twelve months an extended normal training course for teachers offered by the county normal school district. She attended summer "short courses" for the last few summers and enrolled in an extension course offered by mail from the State Teachers College. She had hopes of eventually accumulating sufficient normal-training credits and Teachers College courses to qualify for the state examinations with a life teaching certificate resulting from a favorable score.

Martha felt that she had a position of respect in the community and probably spent most of her adult life teaching in the local schools. Her wants were simple, her role had few financial requirements, and marriage, if it developed, provided an honorable reason for retirement to the career of housewife and mother.

ANN.   As a four-year, provisionally certified elementary teacher of the class of 1975, Ann enjoyed her first year of teaching in a recently renovated elementary school. She was one of the teachers in the 5–B team-teaching group working in a semi-nongraded curricular arrangement that took full advantage of the school renovation, which provided wall-less teaching spaces, easy-clean carpets, improved resource facilities—and a congenial group of fellow teachers. She was recruited by the acting principal because she was obviously willing to teach in a nontraditional manner as a part of a funded experiment in upgrading elementary education in financially distressed school districts.

She was raised in suburbia, but now teaches in the inner city. She feels secure in the school, working with children, but is cautious while out of the building and in commuting to her apartment some fifteen miles away. She is well paid because the teacher association is a strong unit and is militant on salary levels. The team class load is relatively heavy, but next year's negotiation team is planning a citywide strike if the school board is not receptive on this issue.

The 5–B team is a freewheeling group in attitude toward teaching. Ann uses the planning periods for the team staff efficiently, but admittedly does little work on issues and activities that are heavily dependent upon student participation and decision-making. When her team boys decided to bake pizza as a project for a unit on nutrition, Ann agreed that the result was a disaster, but felt that the boys learned a lesson on the need for cooperative planning and work.

She is still surprised by the difficulties the team has encountered in contacting and meeting with many of the parents. A considerable number do not respond to notes sent with students, and those who do appear on appointments seem to know little about the team's educational efforts. Ann has participated in some rather heated neighborhood bloc meetings held to help pass the new millage for school improvement (it was voted down) and senses some resentment toward the school and its teachers' approach to remedial skills latency, which the newspapers have played up as contributing to the school's poor scores on the statewide standardized testing program.

Ann is not ready for marriage—perhaps in the future sometime. Meanwhile, she wants to travel and to taste the adventure of living and, hopefully, teaching in different cultures. She is already working on her master's degree and plans to spend a summer at the university in digging into some research on the handicapped child. Thoughts of working in some research capacity in elementary education intrigue her, especially in the use of computer terminals for elementary pupils in their own classrooms. With a permanent certificate and her master's degree in five years, she is eligible for paid graduate study leave, but has not made definite educational plans as yet. Perhaps another look at the field of special education, or administration—or a year of study in Australia!

RESPONSIBILITY TO THE AIMS OF THE PROFESSION

Leading citizens and philosophers continually pay homage to teachers. Aristotle, for example, compared them favorably with parents themselves. He felt that those who educate children well are more to be honored than even their parents; through his philosophical eyes, parents only give children life—teachers, the art of living well. Yet since the Age of Reason, teachers have differed in attempting to forward man's knowledge of how to adjust to a changing environment. The "learned" professions of theology, medicine, and law too often are used to illustrate or exemplify the *action* of a group rather than the *function*. It has been suggested that teachers will never move beyond being an accumulative body of individuals engaged in a common effort, that is, educating or positively influencing the behavior of others. At present, a number of interesting opportunities for decision-making, if not professional awareness, are developing—brought about in part by the challenge of organized labor to the rather permissive organizational structure of educators. Basic points of difference exist primarily in the aims or goals of the group and the responsibilities associated with the expectations of the profession.

For all educators, the conclusive and all-prevailing purpose of education is summed up by John Goodlad:

> The right to learn is the goal we seek for the twenty-first century. We want for our children a range of learning opportunities as broad as the unknown range of their talents. We want a learning environment that nurtures those talents. We want our children to know themselves and, secure in that knowledge, to open themselves to others. We want them to have freedom, and the order, justice, and peace that the preservation of their freedom demands.[3]

The Teacher and Communication

Teachers traditionally are independent. Attempts to work cooperatively at the national level have not been very successful. As late as 1963, less than one half of the public school teachers were associated with a national organization.[4] As a result, the aims and ambitions of the teacher at the national level are not clearly defined and are heavily dependent upon volunteer information and scattered representation from many interests and areas. The National Education Association, the largest teacher organization, claiming some 1,000,000 members, attempts to present and protect the development of teacher unity, although recent challenges from organizations such as the American Federation of Teachers in the large city areas cannot be overlooked.[5]

Nationally, then, the aims and activities of the profession are neces-

---

[3] John Goodlad, "The Future of Learning: Into the 21st Century," *The Bulletin* (American Association of Colleges for Teacher Education), 24, No. 1:1 (Mar. 1971).

[4] 1964–65 NEA statistics show a range of 98 per cent of teachers enrolled in the state of Washington to 9 per cent in Louisiana. *NEA Reporter*, 4, No. 6 (June, 18, 1965).

[5] The reader is urged to check with local school and educational sources for the identity and address of professional organizations active in the improvement of education.

sarily limited by membership support and the subsequent relationship of limited funds. Existing organizations provide consultant, research, and accumulative information to the government, but as yet do not vote as a major influence or pressure group, unlike such giants of society as labor, manufacturing, agriculture, and defense. Paradoxically, the federal Department of Health, Education, and Welfare has grown rapidly to an interlocking involvement of national government in education with more employees than any other governmental department. The profession is now confronted with large funded government commitments to education, but with the voice and aspiration of the individual teacher somewhat muted by an apparent lack of concern for representative and influential spokesmen speaking for the field.

At the state and local level, the picture is somewhat brighter. The physical proximity and improved intracommunication have given the teacher a more effective means of voicing and coordinating diverse movement in a complex enterprise. Membership in state organizations commonly exceeds 75 per cent of eligible teachers, with school and district enrollment frequently reaching 100 per cent. Of interest to organizational groups is the dual enrollment apparently encouraged by two or more competing organizations seeking to represent a group of teachers as a bargaining agent. This points to the desire of individual teachers to be members of the "winning side" or, by another analysis, is indicative of the traditional fence-sitting of the profession when decisions involving individuals are forced.

In the present development, the aims of the profession are more easily exchanged and modified at the local and state level than nationally. It also follows that the individual dedication to and redefinition of current change are limited in practice to the lower echelons of the profession, even though philosophical and funded experimental programs enjoy national discussion.

What influences the dedication of the individual teacher to maintain the best aims of the profession? George Barr of the University of Wisconsin felt that the parallel question was, What makes or identifies a good teacher? Unfortunately for our examination, neither Barr nor anyone else has as yet pinpointed specific, inclusive earmarks of success to aid in arriving at a consistent and accurate answer.[6] Certain behavioral or interrelated incentives are operational in the process by which the teacher actively moves to implement personal and professional goals. Personal ego, competition with others, supervision, pressures, and so forth, are extrinsic in nature.

It is a primary assumption that teachers have a responsibility to their pupils to improve themselves continually. The attainment of an academic

[6] For qualities of acknowledged leaders, see D. C. Davis, *Patterns of Primary Education* (New York: Harper, 1963), Chapter 1.

degree does not terminate the teacher's educational pursuits, but represents instead a step or stage in a continuous process of education, growth, and development. It has been proposed that classroom teachers who are themselves involved in formal class work (generally at the graduate level) are more successful in their day-by-day elementary classroom teaching. In the area of mathematics, for example, a study concluded that teacher growth in understanding of the concepts gained in an in-service program was directly related to pupil growth in the same concepts.[7] It is not unreasonable to assume a similar relationship in other academic areas. Other influences have received less specific study, but are worthy of mention because of the cumulative, "snowballing" effect.

Mental Curiosity

Many teachers feel that their first few years of teaching were most productive in realizing the goals of the profession. Generally inexperienced and eager to succeed, beginning teachers seek active means of pursuing teaching success. Yet the professional innocence of a beginning teacher is closely akin to the enviable mental curiosity that constantly challenges an experienced teacher and permeates a "good" teacher's classroom. The ability to seek continually a *better* way of realizing a given goal differentiates a so-so teacher from the successful professional—a characteristic, incidentally, that is observable at all levels, in all schools.

Reflective Thought

Often characterized as basic to a good philosopher, the ability to look forward or backward, to consider and weigh an action, is in direct comparison to the impulsive approach. Teachers must consistently reexamine their progress and procedures. This *self-analysis* is a major key to flexibility in realizing goals or changing the approach to an objective. This trait encourages long-range planning, if not continuous study, of curricula design. Of course there are extremes. There is some truth to the charge that fear of losing one's job has kept American education at least fifty years behind its probable potential.

Recognized Responsibility

A person who intrinsically recognizes a duty or role will seek to fulfill that position, adjusting to the various obstacles and problems that complicate its successful completion. Administrators often seek this type of teacher in terms of maturity, professional honesty, dependability, and so forth. Regardless of title, the dedication of a teacher to a task cannot be

---

[7] W. R. Houston and M. V. DeVault, "Mathematic's In-service Education: Teacher Growth Increases Pupil Growth," *The Arithmetic Teacher* 54, No. 5:243 (May 1963).

effectively influenced by outside pressures alone. In a current study of teacher effectiveness, one of the authors was struck by the many high ratings of teacher effectiveness in the elementary school that were directly accountable to teaching responsibility—again as a characteristic of personal communication or belief. Often forgotten is the documented evidence that teacher responsibility and effort can overshadow what seem to be overwhelming obstacles. A prominent example was the restoration to normal childhood of a social isolate who was rescued educationally and physically from a silent world of darkness by devoted teachers and responsible citizens. The girl was able to assume conventional life in a period of two years while still less than nine years of age, but not without the faith of teacher conviction.[8]

Currently Knowledgeable

An always important characteristic, being currently knowledgeable, is basically a gross classification of a teacher's awareness of interrelationships within the current scene. Such a person has the wisdom or interpersonal relationships to fuse or tie together the isolated, if not divergent, developments of the environment. The ability to see relationship does not necessarily include the acute knowledge of all interlocking contributions. As is the case with the proverbial sorting of potatoes, it is of particular importance to recognize that potatoes are of various sizes, not to record the exact size of each potato. Too often the classroom teacher fails to realize the relationship between a social and an economic or a religious and a cultural development. This sensitivity cannot always be measured but is enjoyed and treasured when located. For example, an intermediate-grade teacher noted the forthcoming conference of a medical missionary group. Using class members in the project, she was able to invite classroom guests from the conference as well as to video or tape-record a series of interviews that gave oral descriptions of eye witness contacts with diseases of the world, few if any of which existed in the local school community.

Tied to this undertaking was the social and religious status of the group, portions of which were at that time enduring death and privation in a political-racial conflict on another continent. Few teachers have the insight to foresee the extent of such interrelationships, but many are capable of capitalizing upon them when they do occur or are identified.

Unknown Factors

Achieving the aims of a working profession as well as contributing effectively to them involves rational interpretation of recent developments as well as anticipating problems in the future. Some cynics have pointed

---

[8] M. R. Charles, *A Preface to Education* (New York: Macmillan, 1965), pp. 30–31.

to the school hot-lunch program as one influence that, in terms of intestinal disorders, must necessarily wait for evaluation until present students mature into retirement age. Teachers and nutritional authorities feel relatively safe in physical expectations for tomorrow's adults who have experienced this school innovation to the betterment of society. Nevertheless, the status of teachers, physically and mentally, is worthy of more than a passing consideration.

Early critics of elementary schools felt that the influence of celibate men and women overshadowed the more realistic, warm influence of mother or fatherhood. With school development and expansion, the number of unmarried men and women teaching in elementary schools bcomes progressively smaller; present estimates indicate less than one third of our teachers are unmarried. With this change in marital status and the growing number of men entering the field, the stability of the group is expected to increase. Already the turnover of the typical school staff from year to year is decreasing. Understandably, the cohesiveness and militancy have increased, a major factor noted in the bargaining developments between teachers and the school board. Veteran administrators identify a gradual change to schooltime teacher meetings (not after school hours), larger school staff (gradual move to departmentalization in upper grades), sparse evening school events (parental and moonlighting responsibilities), and increasing competition for recognized *good* teachers.

Coupled with these developments is the increased participation of communities in adult education, increased selectivity of prospective teacher candidates, and the demand for special services and consultant time in the schools, to mention only a few.

Far from moving in an accustomed path, the need for teacher attention to areas of the profession is painted in a conflicting scene of technological and social change.[9] The adaptation to the sociological revolution will be a true test for the profession and will be eventually measured by the product itself—the student—and *not* only by teacher's salary, school facilities, or the length of the working day.

Need for Current, Broadly Educated Teacher-Citizens

Establishment of personal needs for an elementary school teacher increasingly places a premium upon contemporary knowledge in a wide area of interests, often in contrast to an extreme depth of comprehension in a narrow field of concentration. One does not necessarily preclude growth in one at the expense of another, yet only recently have teacher-preparation

---

[9] For a layman's insight into this school problem, see Terry Ferrer, *Classroom Revolution* (Pamphlet, New York *Herald Tribune*, 1963), 15 pp.

programs themselves recognized the differentiation. Most recent changes in the curricula of teacher preparation tend to emphasize a *selective* program of studies rather than the earlier practice of offering contrasting programs stressing depth of experience versus a survey or broad-field approach.

This movement in teacher preparation is cited to illustrate a discernible lack of understanding on the part of some teacher observers in failing to recognize the *significance* of the change. There is a decided contrast between the needs of the teacher in interpreting contemporary society and a combination of course titles or credits required to complete a program or degree. For example, a major university recently revamped a successful elementary teacher-preparation program. One result of the careful study pointed to a need for more teacher preparation in the areas of science and mathematics. Required courses in these areas were reviewed and realigned. New courses were created, new facilities developed, and experimental sections inaugurated before the revised program was approved as a part of the total university program. On the basis of observation, feedback from elementary schools, and evaluation by campus agencies, the "new" program was more successful in meeting the needs of an emerging school society. Yet in *interpreting* the new program, an experienced administrator noted that a significant change "was the doubling of hours in science and mathematics needed for graduation." It is possible, if not probable, that the needs of the teacher had more than doubled in this particular area. A contrast between academic requirements of past and present presumes little change in knowledge, course presentation, application, or in the student himself. The futility of comparing course titles and credit hours is obviously tied to the inability of many educators to sense the need for seeking contemporary awareness of teaching competencies in and out of the classroom. To date, this has been a process of infrequent and casual self-evaluation.

The ability to upgrade or adjust to the changing demands of society is dramatized by the plight of workers in industry attempting to adjust to the changes dictated by automation. Laborers are frequently employed on the basis of their tested ability to be *reeducated*. This places a new demand upon a type of education that can instill the need for continuous study of changes in technology as well as the realistic recognition that change itself must be accepted. This competence is often conspicuous by its absence in modern industry, if not in education.

Recently, a group of teachers toured an automobile manufacturing plant that specialized in motor assembly. A new automated electronic machine was the center of attention. Using sophisticated controls and computer tapes, one man was able to operate the machine and to accomplish what formerly required the work of some twenty men. The operator was one of the twenty men originally involved in the assembly. More important, he was the *only* man of the twenty who was capable of being *reeducated* to operate the new electronic system. These experiences help to explain why industry is quickly becoming concerned with the individual's ability to adjust to new dimensions of science and technology, as well as the time consumed or speed of retraining. Teachers and preparation programs are attracting similar examination and review.

Changing demands of society upon education can sometimes be detected in advance.[10] The success of a technological innovation can quickly change or remain a current position. The family automobile, commercial television, and communication satellites are obvious examples of technology that change societal habits and the accompanying personal reactions that bring about changes in classroom teaching. The introduction of the farm tractor in the 1920s was a catalyst in the movement of population from a rural agricultural life to that of mass employment in the cities. Interest in world travel for the middle class has more recently placed an emphasis upon, if not an overenrollment in, foreign language courses at all school levels. Few, if any, developments point to a *lessening* of intercultural exchange between peoples of the world. The questions, interests, and problems posed by such trends will be reflected in the elementary classroom as well as in social and governmental structure. The alert and successful teacher is one who not only adjusts to changing demands, but frequently *anticipates* change in the pupil and community expectations.

FACTORS OF ELIGIBILITY, TEACHER CONTRACTS, AND CERTIFICATION

Parents and noneducators are awed by the "goldfish bowl" atmosphere of elementary schools. They see the teacher surrounded by an ever-changing environment of responsibility, routine, rules, administrators, and a multitude of problems associated with a roomful of children. If this observation is a valid one (and this might be open to question), one could expect that teachers would constantly practice self-evaluation as a means of maintaining progress, if not success. For the most part, the professionalism of teachers is recognized. In the *minority* are those individuals who fall short of maintaining minimal teaching expectations. Some, in particular, resist the efforts of the majority to aid them in improving their personal and professional contribution to the classroom.

As in most professions, the desire to police or maintain minimum standards has met with controversy. Those who feel the need for purging indifferent teachers are frequently direct in their observations, if not blunt. Curtin believes that there is "a small group of people whose conduct can-

[10] See Dorothy Petersen and Velma Hayden, *Teaching and Learning in the Elementary School* (New York: Appleton, 1961), pp. 504–507.

not be described as professional and who, therefore, must be helped if they are amenable to help. If they are not, they should be helped out of the profession."[11] Experienced but conveniently anonymous administrators suggest that a small minority of poor teachers continually retard the growth of the majority. In any observation of the profession, however, the responsibility for maintaining a form of protection for the child in the classroom must come from outside of the profession if the teachers themselves cannot agree or move to assure this standard themselves. The lack of strong internal support of this principle to date has been a major reason for criticism and for external controls, many of which have worked against self-determination or improvement on the part of the individual teacher.

Eligibility

By law, the minimum qualification for teaching in the school is defined. In practice, the interpretation of the statutes has encouraged a hodgepodge of conflicting and substandard position-holders who can by an extremely liberal interpretation of the term be temporarily classified as "teachers." Most school systems and communities desire the very best quality leader in the classroom. When confronted with problems of teacher supply, budget, working conditions, and medieval requirements, some schools settle for less—sometimes, far less.

With the exception of a few remaining states, the possession of a bachelor's degree is a stated minimum for a beginning teacher. Some states still accept less than the four-year degree, and "grandfather" clauses exempt older, experienced teachers from this minimum if they continue to teach and attend summer school. If it is not a trend, it is at least interesting to note that other states are moving to a five-year degree or is equivalent for beginning teachers. In the face of a continuing shortage of teachers, this increase in preparation seems to be succeeding in securing teachers, often because of the accompanying increase in average salaries. In lieu of a better standard, it is commonly assumed that a degree or degrees is a standard of quality and that a minimum expectancy *is* associated with this achievement. This assumption is fortunately qualified by other requirements, which are generally associated with accrediting bodies or agencies. These groups attempt to approve or certify that a given individual, having met given minimums of preparation, is entitled or approved to teach under varying periods of time and continuing preparation.

Before we examine the field of certification, it would be only fair to recognize that the extremes in employment practices are often the point of examples rather than the more common practices. In one community, for example, newspaper accounts highlighted the role of a custodian who was

[11] James Curtin, *Supervision in Today's Elementary Schools* (New York: Macmillan, 1964), p. 82.

"teaching" an intermediate-grade class in the community school. In truth, the custodian had been employed as a temporary substitute for two school days during an outbreak of influenza that had incapacitated a number of teachers and substitutes. The flow of publicity did not enhance the position of the school, nor did the reluctance or oversight of the reporter in adding in the original account that the custodian was a father of six children and a retired governmental employee who had to his credit twelve years of teaching children in overseas schools. Again, the connotation of the word *teacher* is varied and constantly charged with misunderstanding.

Certification

Colleges and universities engaged in the preparation of teachers work closely with state and regional associations in preparing teachers who possess qualifications that meet at least the minimum expectancy of the accrediting group. It would be futile for a teacher-preparation institution to graduate continuously teacher candidates who could not be legally approved to teach in the classrooms of the area or state. Note too the absurdity of an accrediting agency that arbitrarily sets minimum expectancies for approved teachers that are far above the financial or curricula levels of the schools of teacher preparation. Thus, a system of voluntary checks and balances is in effect between these and other areas involved in the final admission of a teacher to a classroom.

During the early years of the period following World War II, many state and regional accrediting agencies temporarily relaxed existing minimum requirements or refrained from increasing minimum teacher qualities because of the serious shortage of teachers. In some of these states a significant number of elementary teacher candidates withdrew from a four-year program at the end of the sophomore year to teach in elementary classrooms. This practice permitted elementary schools to operate—schools that would have been closed without the influx of "temporary" teachers. In time, with more teachers available, the issuance of the "temporary" teaching certificates was restricted, and today this emergency measure has been sharply curtailed.

The reconstruction of teacher-preparation programs often precedes changes in certification practices. As institutions of higher education and certifying agencies of state and regional levels increase their attention on cooperative study and discussion, the degree of difference between various areas of the nation tends to decrease. This progress has not been without controversy.

Some organizations, such as the National Council for the Accrediting of Schools for Teacher Education, have moved to set minimum standards for institutions preparing teachers by approving institutions that maintain the organization's standards and, in a sense, by suggesting that other non-qualifying schools move to a more acceptable position before reexamination or approval is attempted. As could be predicted, this attempt to improve the teaching product met opposition from some institutions, particularly those that were not originally given organizational approval. Justified or not, such attempts tend to focus upon common approval of tangible minimums for teaching. At present, for example, some thirty states have reduced regional or state differences of practice to permit original certification of teachers in any of the states if the candidate has successfully met the minimum expectations of an "accredited" institution. The progress has been slow and will continue to encounter both philosophical and cultural problems in attempting to realize a large, if not national, interlocking group of cooperative accrediting practices that would not be subjected to petty or discriminatory requirements exacted by individual schools or states.

As a part of an enlightened movement to reduce the differences retarding improvement of teacher preparation and employment, other less conspicuous events are developing. Without attempting to examine each in specific detail, some obvious conclusions can be drawn.

First, continuous certification is replacing fixed, permanent minimums. The "life" or "graduation-to-retirement" approval for teachers without additional course refreshment is being replaced by flexible requirements that encourage frequent teacher participation in graduate work, enrichment experiences, and so forth.

Secondly, there is a changing balance in school positions held by women. Contrary to stereotyping, positions in public schools held by women are frequently misunderstood. Although approximately 80 per cent of the elementary school teaching positions are held by women, less than 25 per cent of women occupy a principal's role. Beginning in 1963, federal legislation has attempted to guarantee equality of opportunity for women in education, but it would seem that significant progress in balancing the opportunities for both sexes will be a long-term effort.

> The truth is that, in the field of education, women confront biases in employment that reduce their opportunities for advancement, rewards, and leadership.[12]

Thirdly, closer agreement is being developed between all agencies of certification on the minimums expected of a mobile teacher supply. Gradually, the ability of a teacher to teach children is transcending the artificial barriers once set up and guarded by individual states and regions. In the transition the requirements for minimum preparation are also increasing, resulting in a total development of a well-educated, competent teacher capable and encouraged to teach throughout the nation as personal interest, service, and challenge dictate.

[12] Lindley Stiles and P. M. Nystrand, "The Politics of Sex in Education," *The Educational Forum*, 38, No. 4:435 (May 1974).

Fourthly, pressure is mounting for the profession to certify or license its own members in conjunction with, or separate from, the traditional agencies engaged in such recommendation. As identified earlier, the growing competition between teacher organizational groups is adding features embracing typical "professional" regulatory activities as well as features commonly associated with organized labor. It is probable that teachers eventually will enjoy, expect, or accept the better features of both movements in adjusting to the new role of service and enlightened responsibility.

Lastly, we come to pilot programs and study of increasing the regional certification of teachers. By tradition, state certification beyond the bachelor's degree is based upon successful teaching experience and a given number of graduate hours of credit earned from a certified college or university. There are attempts underway to base certification beyond the bachelor's degree upon successful teaching experience and the completion of a given number of in-service units of work prescribed and offered by regional teaching centers either within or between states. The direction of regional certification is away from the degree programs of higher education to a more pragmatic "learn it this morning—use it this afternoon" approach. In some regional centers, the majority of the board of directors by statute must be classroom teachers. The intent of shifting certification requirements from organized programs of higher education to nonacademic "in-house" options is difficult to summarize accurately but ranges from teacher efforts to "worry about kids rather than grades" to school systems that prefer that benefits from teacher improvement should be focused on *their* school textbooks, problems, and community expectations. The concern of teacher organization to influence, if not determine, the process of certification is obviously a factor in regional centers for certification. The full implication of this rather recent development should become more apparent in the next few years.

Maintaining Continuous Personal Growth

Elementary education in the past decade has been identified as that process that requires a successful teacher to worry and work twenty-four hours a day to be able to maintain the acceleration of the slowest student in the group. With due allowance for a bit of assumed liberty, the statement remains symbolic of the need for individual teacher mastery (or survival) in a rapidly changing technological society. Jerome Bruner and others have challenged the teacher and the graded system.[13] Gone is the security of the graded vocabulary list and the pegging of narrow concepts to arbitrary levels of "average" development—the earthworm is no longer an exclusive

[13] For information on the nongraded, see John Goodlad and Robert Anderson, *Ungraded Primary School* (New York: Harcourt, 1963).

"fourth-grade worm" and Leif Ericson now challenges Columbus as the discoverer of the American continent. The familiar classroom globe is repeatedly rendered obsolete within days, if not hours, of its original purchase. Societal change, speed records, and international disputes now intermingle with elementary offerings in foreign languages, computer usage, or the sweep of the magic eye of educational television. Suffice to say, the elementary teacher has the pleasure and the responsibility of maintaining touch and understanding with a changing society—plus the excitement of being a part of the change.

Admittedly, keeping up with developments in the private world of elementary children is sometimes awe-inspiring. Recognizing the sales potential and influence of youngsters, commercial products aim heavily at elementary children. On commercial television, Saturday is "children's day" —or at least a major portion of it. Recently, one of the authors tape-recorded the theme song portions of animated cartoons and adventure drama aimed at children. The playback was altered to omit the title of the program or the names of the cartoon characters. Of the children tested subsequently, *all* identified the themes with the correct programs. Of the elementary teacher candidates selected to respond to the same tape, few matched the music with the program; and those who identified more than two or three of the twelve possibilities were very definitely in the minority. It is probable that no major conclusions can be drawn from this rather simple examination of society except that the listening and activity world of youngsters consistently extends beyond the comprehension level of most adults—and a fair percentage of elementary classroom teachers, harassed parents excluded.

Concern for the quality of educational television is a point of discussion, especially when educational research in development produces continuous high consumer response, that is, Nielsen ratings. *Sesame Street* was probably one of the best-known television programs for preschool children viewed in the home, and its high viewer audience was envied by commercial television productions. What was singular to its success was an extensive educational research staff that identified areas of potential child learning (letters, numbers, body parts) before the program was developed and, in the role of good teaching, established a need for the child to learn.

> We didn't want to be teaching them what they already knew only, but to stretch them out into new areas. We tested (also) to see how long they could attend. Children are attending all day long but they are not attending any one thing for a very long time. Children don't come to their lessons with intrinsic motivation in the same sense as adults do. That was a fundamental goal of *Sesame Street*—to build the motivation into the materials, since it hadn't been built into the children.[14]

[14] Mafalda Marroco, "Edward Palmer Steers Sesame Street's Research," *Bulletin: American Association for the Advancement of Science*, 10, No. 1:8 (Apr. 1974).

Professional teachers "produce" daily programs in their classrooms to admittedly smaller audience groups, but the base of the learning epoch is and has been pointed to increase child learning through intrinsic motivation. Perhaps the profession should consider local editions of consumer ratings with emphasis upon the child rather than the community.

Individually, the profession itself demands teacher attention and contribution. Teachers are expected to assume a more active role in the community. Almost extinct are the black marks of earlier days of teaching. Seldom do teachers today encounter teacherages (school dormitories for single teachers), educational blue laws (spending three weekends of every month in the community itself), moral dictates (forbidden was public speaking, drinking, dancing, or "auto riding"), religious restraints (primary teachers were to sing in the Gospel Church choir), or kickbacks (a per cent of salary paid in script, redeemable only at the Crystal Café or the Midtown General Store). But with these needed adjustments remains the constant problem of teachers giving themselves to the needs of a school community as a taxpayer, a voter, and a citizen. Teachers who accept this means of maintaining a needed touch with rapidly evolving social, economic, and cultural developments are increasingly supplementing their growth and development by a militant, professional reading program. Petersen reported that close to 10 per cent of a group of 400 schools had no collection of books or periodicals for teachers.[15] There is a move to maintain professional contact through individual subscription or membership. Fortunately, a desirable cross section can be secured for a modest annual investment.[16]

Professional dues are now assuming a greater share of the teacher's dollar to support professional lobbying in government, political contribution, and intergroup recruitment of membership. More recently, to assure a base for personal security and growth, contributions to "strike or sanction" funds have projected the future of the individual teacher into an area where desirable performance becomes a guaranteed minimum, not a vague, often undershot expectation. It is too early and the developments are too fragile to be examined as to the reflection of individual teacher gain. Without doubt, however, teachers must maintain close personal touch with such educational growth patterns so as to be able to view actions from a stable personal and professional outlook.

---

[15] Dorothy Petersen, *The Elementary School Teacher* (New York: Appleton, 1964), p. 522. See also Margaret McKim, Carl Hansen, and William Carter, *Learning to Teach in the Elementary School* (New York: Macmillan, 1959), p. 538.

[16] Petersen, op. cit., p. 524.

A LOOK AHEAD

There is always room in the field of elementary and middle school teaching for a *good* teacher—we have heard this statement in the past, it is being voiced now, and no doubt it will be repeated in the future. There is substantial support for statements such as this if, as we indicated in earlier discussion, we can identify in some agreeable fashion the meaning of good teaching. With a stabilizing birth rate and an abundance of teachers available, teacher mobility is decreasing, and the profession is increasingly aware that there is substantial disagreement on the specifics of a good teacher. Many teacher education institutions are attempting to recruit, select, and prepare a more qualified teacher for the schools. Specialized programs of preparation are developing teacher competencies where heretofore school and community expectations have not been fulfilled, that is, special education, urban centers, preschool, and so forth. Understandably, many teacher applicants now possess extensive graduate credits in applying for their initial teaching position. School boards, however, are faced with professionally negotiated teacher contracts that, with the static movement of teachers out of the system, tend to retain the more experienced, more highly paid teachers. The results are expectable, if not upsetting. A good beginning teacher to many school systems is the cheapest one available. With some urban school systems now offering a beginning teacher at least $10,000, the cheapest teacher is not a financial insult, but rather an employment compromise that favors employment of a good *inexperienced* teacher rather than a good *experienced* professional.

As a professional group, teachers tend to accept this restriction on the employment of teachers as a temporary measure that should eventually diminish as factors of supply and demand become operative. Some reaction to this development has surfaced, however, including restriction on the number of prospective teachers admitted to teacher preparation institutions, more in-service preparation for experienced teachers, and initial legislative moves to enact an educational version of organized labor's "30 years and out," which would provide earlier retirement possibilities for experienced teachers and the subsequent replacement opportunities for the beginning professional teacher. In states where retirement funds are a governmental responsibility, the early retirement option portends to be one possibility for retaining the spirit and success of good teaching for both beginning and experienced professional teachers.

It is obvious that change is here to stay unless other sources of supply or an extremely competitive salary schedule can induce major security for the professional teacher. The change itself is not as important as the individual teacher's use or accommodation to the change. In the final analysis, the attitude of a teacher to *desire* self-improvement and to *pursue* this need is the key to present and future educational progress. Whether the teacher is self-directed or merely reacting to an external pressure, personal growth, awareness, and adjustment are the common denominators for elementary school success in accepting the responsibility for our evolving education. There seems to be no other viable alternative—for the teacher, the school, or the community.

SUGGESTED ACTIVITIES

1. Charlene Jasson has eleven years of teaching experience, a master's degree, and a mortgaged condominium. She commutes by car from her suburban address to her school assignment in the inner city. The school system has announced that it will terminate all teaching contracts next year for those teachers who do not live within the school district. Charlene's teachers' organization appealed the school board decision, but lost its case. Now, she is confronted with resigning, moving into the district, or, with the backing of the organization, joining other teachers in seeking a higher court reversal of the residency rule. What would you suggest professionally? Personally? Identify the basis of your position.

2. Mary and Lois are applying for the same teaching position opening in the Mosley Elementary School for the next academic year. Mary has two years of teaching experience, but fears the board will favor the application of Lois, who has just graduated and can be signed at a lower level on the salary schedule. Mary is tempted to offer her services at the same salary level as Lois, asking the board to "forget" her teaching experience. What would you expect to be the board's reaction to Mary's offer? Would you anticipate the position of the teachers' professional organization? What would be *your* reaction?

3. At what position or point in a person's teaching experience should the decision to leave or remain in the profession occur? On what basis could the decision be delayed? Advanced?

4. Some school systems are considering the use of standardized tests to help determine the need for individual teachers to return to the campus for additional graduate education. Consider a list of major advantages of such a practice. Prepare a similar list of disadvantages. Justify your responses.

5. You and your family have supported and voted for Republican party candidates since great-grandfather's days. Now, as a first year teacher, your professional teachers' organization is actively supporting a longtime Democratic party leader for school board membership in the board election next month. He has publicly stated he intends to upgrade the entire teacher salary schedule if elected, and with a Democratic majority

the board will probably become more politically involved in county and state politics. Will you accept chairmanship of the teachers' organizations committee to elect this aspiring board member? Identify your professional obligations as well as reservations. How do these match your personal desires? How do you think you will react to the invitation?

6. Consider the possibility that the school week will be extended to six days and the school year to eleven months. Identify the impact of these changes upon the responsibilities of the elementary teacher in terms of personal growth and development.

7. The Martha Washington School for Girls (private) has received a joint state/federal financial grant for an educational experiment, but has been notified that some men must be on the school staff to meet antisexism legislation requirements for all school grant recipients. As the only male teacher graduating senior not placed as yet by the university placement office, you have been invited to accept a position there next year at a fair salary. You recognize that if you accept, you will be a token male and that the tenure of the position could be tied to the continuation of the state/federal grant. Unofficially, some nearby neighborhood school teachers' organizations have encouraged you to accept the position "to break the sex line" and to further the cause of professional organizations. What factors of professionalism are involved? Personal? Societal overtones?

8. How do school systems compensate those teachers who consciously seek to improve their teaching background and philosophy? What improvements could be initiated?

9. Lorry has been reprimanded and docked a week's salary for refusing to abide by the minimal dress code for teachers established by the board and accepted by the negotiating team of the teachers' professional organization. She has filed a grievance appeal, and you are one of the local level judges hearing the appeal. After much testimony and accompanying legal documents, the issue boils down to Lorry's refusal to wear a bra while teaching. She maintains that the board and the professional organization (of which she is a member) cannot dictate her personal choice of undergarments. She cites her positive professional cumulative file, teaching awards, and graduate university record. After the hearing, the other two judges split in their opinion leaving the deciding vote and resulting decision to you. How will you vote? Why?

SELECTED BIBLIOGRAPHY

Braum, Robert J. *Teachers and Power.* New York: Simon & Schuster, Inc., 1972.

Campbell, Roald Fawcett, Novice Cunningham, Luvern McPhee, Roderick and Ralph Nystrand. *The Organization and Control of American Schools.* 2nd ed. Columbus, Ohio: Chas. E. Merrill Publishers, 1970.

Charles, M. R. *A Preface to Education.* New York: Macmillan Publishing Co., Inc., 1965.

Daigon, Arthur, and Richard Dempsey. *School—Pass at Your Own Risk.* Englewood Cliffs, N.J.: Prentice-Hall, Inc., 1974.

Davis, D. C. *Patterns of Primary Education.* New York: Harper and Row, Publishers, 1963.

Ferrer, Terry. *Classroom Revolution.* New York *Herald Tribune* (reprint pamphlet), 1963.

Goodlad, John. "The Future of Learning: Into the 21st Century." *The Bulletin.* American Association of Colleges for Teacher Education, **24**, No. 1 (Mar. 1971).

———— and Robert Anderson. *The Non-Graded Elementary School.* New York: Harcourt, Brace Jovanovich, Inc., 1963.

Gorman, Alfred. *Teachers and Learners.* Boston: Allyn & Bacon, Inc., 1974.

Greenlee, Jerri, and Elaine Morre. *Ideas for Learning Centers.* Belmont, Calif.: Fearon Publishing, 1974.

Hentzberg, Alvin, and Edward Stone. *Schools Are For Children.* New York: Schocken Books, Inc., 1972.

Horn, Ernest, and Ernest Ashbaugh. *The Horn-Ashbaugh Fundamentals of Spelling.* Philadelphia: J. B. Lippincott Co., 1928.

Houston, W. R., and M. V. DeVault. "Mathematics In-service Education; Teacher Growth Increases Pupil Growth." *The Arithmetic Teacher,* **54**, No. 5 (May 1963).

Lorton, Mary B. *Workjobs.* Reading, Mass.: Addison-Wesley Publishing Co., Inc., 1972.

Marroco, Mafalda. "Edward Palmer Steers Sesame Street's Research." *Bulletin: American Association for the Advancement of Science.* **10**, No. 1 (Apr. 1974).

McKim, Marg., Carl Hansen, and William Carter. *Learning to Teach in the Elementary School.* New York: Macmillan Publishing Co., Inc., 1959.

Petersen, Dorothy, and Velma Hayden. *Teaching and Learning in the Elementary School.* New York: Appleton-Century-Crofts, 1961.

Stanford, Gene, and Albert Roark. *Human Interaction in Education.* Boston: Allyn & Bacon, Inc., 1974.

Stephens, Lillian S. *The Teacher's Guide to Open Education.* New York: Holt, Rinehart & Winston, Inc., 1974.

Stiles, Lindley, and P. M. Nystrand. "The Politics of Sex in Education." *The Educational Forum.* **38**, No. 4 (May 1974).

Wiles, Kimball, and John Lovell. *Supervision for Better Schools.* 4th ed. Englewood Cliffs, N.J.: Prentice-Hall, Inc., 1975.

Index